Fodor's EXPLORING
AUSTRALIA

FODOR'S TRAVEL PUBLICATIONS, INC.

NEW YORK • TORONTO • LONDON • SYDNEY • AUCKLAND

WWW.FODORS.COM

Copyright © 2000 by The Automobile Association.
Maps copyright © 2000 by The Automobile Association.

Published in the United States by Fodor's Travel
Publications, Inc.
Published in the United Kingdom by AA Publishing.

Fodor's is a registered trademark of Random House, Inc.

ISBN 0-679-00472-6
Fourth Edition

Fodor's Exploring Australia

Author: **Michael Ivory**
Series Adviser: **Ingrid Morgan**
Joint Series Editor: **Susi Bailey**
Revisions: **Anne Matthews**
Revisions Editor: **Grapevine Publishing Services**
Cartography: **The Automobile Association**
Cover Design: **Tigist Getachew, Fabrizio La Rocca**
Front Cover Silhouette: **M. Berge/Photographers/Aspen**

Printed and bound in Italy by Printer Trento srl
10 9 8 7 6 5 4 3 2 1

How to use this book

ORGANIZATION

Australia Is, Australia Was
Discusses aspects of life and culture in contemporary Australia and explores significant period in its history.

A–Z
Breaks down the country into regional chapters, and covers places to visit, including walks and drives. Within this section fall the Focus On articles, which consider a variety of subjects in greater detail.

Travel Facts
Contains the strictly practical information vital for a successful trip.

Accommodations & Restaurants
Lists recommended establishments throughout Australia, giving a brief summary of their attractions.

ABOUT THE RATINGS
Most places described in this book have been given a separate rating. These are as follows:

▶▶▶　Do not miss

▶▶　　Highly recommended

▶　　　Worth seeing

MAP REFERENCES
To make each particular location easier to find, every main entry in this book has a map reference to the right of its name. This comprises a number, followed by a letter, followed by another number, such as 176B3. The first number (176) refers to the page on which the map can be found, the letter (B) and the second number (3) pinpoint the square in which the main entry is located. The maps on the inside front cover and inside back cover are referred to as IFC and IBC respectively.

Contents

5

*Above: Palm Valley, Finke Gorge
National Park
Left: Yachts moored in Hobart*

Bright flowers of the bottlebrush

Michael Ivory has written extensively about the lands of Eastern Europe—his books include Fodor *Exploring Prague* and Fodor *CityPack Prague*. He welcomed the chance to write a guide to Australia, a place which has always intrigued him. This book reveals something of his pleasure in experiencing this fascinating, diverse country.

My Australia

Crossing the interminable Nullarbor Plain aboard the Indian Pacific train, I made the Englishman's mistake of heading for an empty table in the dining car. The steward was shocked: "Hold on a minute, mate! Why don't you sit over here with these folk? I'm sure you'll have plenty to talk about." He was right of course. Australia is a place where human contact is easy. Indeed, Australian friendliness is proverbial; first names are used freely and "mates" are easily made, especially if you show yourself ready to join in, say what a wonderful country it is (not difficult!), and refrain from invidious comparisons with wherever you come from.

I won't forget that train ride eastward from Kalgoorlie across the Nullarbor Plain, where the scenery doesn't change from one day to the next and it was a real relief to have entertaining companions at the dining table. Australians have long since overcome what one of them called "the tyranny of distance," the impossibly vast spaces which faced early explorers and travelers. Nowadays half the enjoyment of Australia lies in the many different ways there are of getting around. It was a special thrill to get up into the cab of the big diesel heading for the Indian Pacific to marvel at the aching emptiness of the scene and at the single track heading ruler-straight to the far horizon. In utter contrast was the bumpy ride up the Bloomfield Track in Far North Queensland, with rain forest to either side. Rather more relaxing was a trip through the same kind of landscape aboard an amphibious DUKW, which took jungle, rivers, and snake-filled pools in its stride. I also joined bushwalkers in their wanderings among the beautiful bush country and eucalypt forest which surrounds most of the big cities. Here, perhaps more than anywhere else, flying comes into its own. Not by comfortable airliner, but in a light plane, tossed around by the thermals bubbling upwards from the hot surface of Ayers Rock, or in a little seaplane skimming the surface of Tasmania's Gordon River gorge. And the most sublime moment of all? Not in the air, but whizzing across Sydney Harbour in a powerboat, "tinnie" of lager in hand, at the moment when the Opera House came into sight beneath the great span of the Harbour Bridge, and I felt I'd really arrived "Down Under."
Michael Ivory

Australia Is

Australia occupies a lonely place on the globe. Aside from the frozen Antarctic, it is the only continent to lie wholly within the southern hemisphere; though Papua New Guinea is only just over the horizon on the far side of the Timor Sea, New Zealand is more than 1,240 miles across the Tasman Sea, and the Asian mainland at Singapore is 1,865 miles distant.

Girded by nearly 23,000 miles of coastline, the "island continent" has a simple threefold structure.

THE WESTERN PLATEAU Almost two-thirds of the land surface belongs to the Western Plateau, a vast and arid tableland covering most of Western Australia, South Australia, the Northern Territory and part of Queensland. Mostly flat and low-lying, it is interrupted by spectacular individual features like Ayers Rock

Mount Warning National Park, New South Wales

(Uluru) and the Olgas (Kata Tjuta), by rocky strongholds like the Kimberley and Arnhem Land, and by rugged ridges like those of the MacDonnell, Flinders and Hamersley Ranges.

The plateau is an ancient land whose fertility was leached away by rains that fell millions of years ago, leaving arid wastes with evocative names like the Nullarbor Plain or the Sturt Stony Desert. Similarly, winds that ceased to blow long ago left repetitive patterns of sand dunes. Except in the tropics, rainfall is not only minimal but also irregular; none may fall for years, then sudden down-pours will fill the normally vacant river beds, though the rainwater soon disperses to the great salt lakes.

Much of the area is uninhabited or very thinly settled, with a population measured in hundreds of square miles per person. Only to the west of the Darling Range, on the relatively fertile coastal plains around the great city of Perth, are there extensive farmlands and a network of settlements linked by roads and rail-roads. Elsewhere, settlements exist in isolation as ports, mining towns and staging posts along endless high-ways, or, increasingly, as centers for Outback tourism.

THE GREAT DIVIDING RANGE This mountain range runs down the whole of Australia's eastern coastline from Cape York in the far north to the hills and highlands of New South Wales and Victoria in the south. Where it leaps the Bass Strait to re-appear in the mountains of Tasmania the continent's highest peaks are found: Mount Kosciuszko in New South Wales (7,316 feet), Mount

Bogong in Victoria (6,516 feet) and Mount Ossa (5,305 feet) in Tasmania.

However, much of the area is not made up of mountains but of high plateaus, from which rivers run eastward across the coastal plain. The bulk of the country's population lives here, clustering for the most part in the metropolitan areas around the great coastal state capitals of Sydney (New South Wales), Melbourne (Victoria), Adelaide (South Australia) and Brisbane (Queensland). Rural settlement is relatively dense in the valleys between the uplands and all along the fertile strip extending into the tropics along the Queensland coast. The only inland city of any size is Canberra, the artificially implanted federal capital.

CENTRAL EASTERN LOWLANDS
Between the Western Plateau and the Great Dividing Range the Central Eastern Lowlands slope down gradually from the east toward the interior. A series of broad basins succeed one another, from the southern rim of the Gulf of Carpentaria through Queensland's Channel Country to the area drained by the country's greatest river system, the Murray/Darling/Murrumbidgee.

Here in the Outback, grazing animals outnumber people by a factor of several hundred to one, and rural life depends as much on unreliable rainfall as on the state of world markets. Mineral wealth has created a small number of towns like Broken Hill and Mount Isa, which are linked by interminably long roads and railroads to the coast.

South Australian opals

❏ The world's driest continent after Antarctica has a surprisingly small range of climates. The highest rainfall is in the tropical or subtropical north, where temperatures stay high all year round (84°F in summer and 75°F in winter). Unlike the north, where the rain falls during the summer, temperate southern Australia experiences its highest rainfall in winter and spring, and there is more variation in average temperatures (75°F in summer to 50°F in winter when snow falls on the higher peaks). Much of the interior is arid, with little rain, and temperatures here soar to scorching heights—a maximum of 127½°F was recorded at Cloncurry in Queensland in 1889—although nights can be in the low 60°F. ❏

11

Australia's 40 million years of isolation from the rest of the world resulted in plants and animals that are unique to the continent. Over this long period, both fauna and flora evolved in response to local conditions quite independently of developments elsewhere, resulting in the array of strange creatures and plants that so delighted Joseph Banks as he accompanied Captain Cook aboard the Endeavour *in 1770. Despite subsequent development that had little regard for environmental side effects, Australia was quick to create national parks, some 2,000 of which await today's visitor.*

12

FORESTS The richest habitat in Australia is that of the rain forest. Tropical rain forest is best seen in northern Queensland (see page 222), but also lies in parts of the northern coastlands in the Northern Territory and Western Australia. Temperate rain forest, of great fascination and beauty, spreads over much of the wild country of southwestern Tasmania. This is the domain of the **southern beech** and of one of the longest-lived trees on earth, the **Huon pine**.

Great forests still cloak some of the less accessible areas of the southeast and southwest, but all of Australia's woodland has suffered grievously at the hands of the timber-cutters. The majority of the country's trees are variations on the theme of **eucalyptus** (also referred to as eucalypts and gum trees); they include some of the tallest trees on earth, like the mountain ash of the Victorian coastal forests or the karri of southwestern Western Australia.

SCRUBLAND AND DESERT Away from the coast, the pioneers found impenetrable **mallee** (a dense scrub of low-growing eucalyptus) or more open, park-like woodland. Most of these original plant communities have been cleared for grazing land, while native grasses and herbs have given way to exotic, high-yielding varieties. The desert is perhaps the

The rainbow lorikeet

most intriguing of all Australian ecosystems, where **saltbush**, **spinifex** and the occasional **desert oak** provide shelter for creatures like scorpions and spiders, themselves food for snakes, lizards and **goannas**. The seeds of many small plants lie in wait for the sparse rain, flowering spectacularly when nourished.

FROM POUCHES TO PLATYPUSES Of all the marsupials that inhabit the island continent, the macropods— **kangaroos** among them—seem to need little introduction, having long

been familiar as one of the country's best-known emblems. But there's a whole world of roos out there; as well as the red kangaroo (reaching over 6 feet), there are some 50 other varieties, ranging from the equally large Forester kangaroos to the quokkas (mistaken for rats by early explorers) and brush-tailed bettongs. Kangaroos live in most parts of the country, even occasionally on the fringe of towns.

After the kangaroo, it is the endearing **koala** that every visitor wants to see. Koalas spend most of their time asleep and the rest chewing on the leaves of certain eucalypts. The population is recovering after being hunted for its fur, but it is still subject to disease and loss of habitat. As a result, you're more likely to see koalas in one of the country's excellent wildlife parks than in the wild alongside of **wombats**, burrowing marsupials, and **possums**, some of which are able to glide from tree to tree thanks to their flight membrane.

Another creature that you are more likely to see in an artificial environment is the **platypus**. This shy, egg-laying mammal with its soft bill was thought to be a hoax when a

The kangaroo—one of Australia's best-known marsupials

specimen was first sent to Britain for examination. The spiny anteater, or **echidna**, is less timid, being well defended by its ability to burrow below ground or present an attacker with its array of sharp spines.

NATIONAL PARKS Australia declared its first national park (Sydney's **Royal National Park**) as early as 1879. Today more than 2,000 such areas are protected and managed in order to conserve their natural beauty, protect their wildlife, and make them accessible to visitors. The outstanding quality and global importance of the country's natural treasures has also been recognized by the designation of no fewer than eleven World Heritage Areas.

Visitors to national parks will generally find a high standard of management in evidence, with good information services and lots of walking trails that have been created to encourage people to experience and explore the landscape. Always seek the advice of park rangers about local conditions.

It's quite possible you'll meet a stereotypical Australian male while Down Under. You've probably imagined him already: tall, sun-burned, probably blond and blue-eyed, short on words but long on ability to sink the stubbies (get drunk) with his mates, unhurried, an enemy of pretentiousness, and unrecon-structed in his chauvinism. The stereotype exists, of course, but few Australians can be quite so easily categorized these days.

For many thousands of years the Aborigines alone inhabited this vast continent. They had arrived during the Ice Age, before Australia became isolated from the rest of Asia by the rising sea levels. Then, in the 1770s, British captain James Cook reached Botany Bay and claimed Australia for the Western world.

EARLY IMMIGRANTS The story of Australia's earliest European settle-ment is bizarre, to say the least. After James Cook's 1770 voyage of discov-ery, the British government came up

14

> ❑ Although rather romantically labelled "convicts", most of Australia's earliest immigrants were neither noble political pris-oners nor dashing highwaymen. The majority of the First Fleeters were transported for relatively minor offences—receiving stolen goods, forgery, and petty theft— that ranged from the pathetic (pilfering a packet of snuff) to the tragic (the hunger-driven crime of stealing two hens, worth a total of fourpence). ❑

A classic Aussie "character"

with an ambitious—many would say outrageous—solution to the "dis-posal" of its felons and criminals. In May 1787, 11 ships carrying over 1,400 people, including 759 male and female convicts, set sail from England for the long and arduous journey to the virtually unknown southern continent. On their arrival in Sydney in January 1788, they became Australia's first, albeit unwilling, immigrants.

The 19th- and early 20th-century non-British immigrants to Australia were very conspicuous and often resented, although the pious and hardworking Germans who helped settle South Australia fitted in well enough. Gold rushes brought thou-sands of Chinese, who were treated with extreme prejudice, and South Sea Islanders known as Kanakas were kidnapped and enslaved to work the sugar plantations of Queensland, until they were repatri-ated under anti-slavery legislation.

15

WAR REFUGEES The postwar boom led to a demand for more workers than Britain could supply, and the country opened its gates to a Europe crowded with "reffos" (refugees) and displaced persons. Australia accepted hundreds of thousands of immigrants from northern and central Europe, the Netherlands, Germany, Scandinavia, Czechoslovakia, and the Baltic states.

When this source of labor began to dry up, the emphasis changed to southern Europe, and the next wave of "New Australians" consisted of Italians, Greeks, Maltese, Croats and Serbs. A tacit "White Australia" policy was followed; non-Europeans were rarely admitted, excluded sometimes by means of the infamous dictation test that allowed an immigration officer to give the would-be immigrant a test in a language of his (the immigration officer's) choice. An undesirable applicant of Chinese origin could thus have been examined on his knowledge of Gaelic, and, not surprisingly, fail.

A MULTI-CULTURAL SOCIETY A continuation of this policy became unsustainable with an increasing

Greek deli in Melbourne

awareness of Australia's geopolitical position and of its social ties with Asia. A continuing, though fluctuating, demand for workers resulted in a huge influx of Cambodian, Vietnamese, Filipino and other Asian immigrants—a fact that is instantly verifiable on the streets of any of the state capitals.

Total assimilation of the newcomers has been abandoned in favor of preserving immigrant culture. Of the two state-funded television channels, S.B.S. specializes in programs in a variety of different languages. Australia is now one of the most racially diverse countries in the world. More than half of all Australians were either born overseas themselves, or have at least one parent who was born overseas.

In the midst of this multi-culturalism, the Aborigines—who are, after all, the only Australians who are neither recent settlers nor descended from immigrants—strive to retain their traditions and culture (see pages 24–25). Only in recent times have Australians begun to accept their different way of life.

"No worries" seems to sum up much of the average Australian's attitude to life. Work doesn't play the central role here that it does in some societies around the Pacific Rim or even in Europe. Life is to be made the most of, preferably out in the open, enjoying food and drink, watching sports with passionate intensity, or swimming, surfing, bushwalking, and simply lazing around in the great outdoors of the "best country in the world."

Celebrating at the Melbourne Cup

The founding period of convicts was once a source of shame but is now looked back on with pride. It can be seen as a positive factor contributing to the way Australians are today. Australian "mateship" has its roots in shared oppression and in the importance of comrades in making a life in a harsh and empty land. The land posed a tough physical challenge, in which the conventional qualities of "manliness" were directly related to success or even survival. Work was originally performed under duress and for someone else, after which you were free to lead your own life. Authority was exercised by prison wardens and governors, and consequently resented, but there was no old ruling class or complicated code of manners. Strangers were seldom seen, but if they needed help they could be sure of getting it.

EVERYONE IS EQUAL So Australia has long been a land where people feel themselves to be basically equal and as good as the next person. Money and the making of it are admired, but this does not mean that the monied become beings apart. There is an openness about social contacts that is surprising to many visitors. When Australians say "How are you?" there's a good chance that they actually mean it, and will enjoy hearing your answer (especially if you reveal to them how much you like their country). If you expect to be deferred to, you could be in for an unpleasant surprise; Australians don't like pretension, and will prickle if they detect it.

THE OUTDOOR LIFE Given the character of the country, with its space, climate, the grandeur of its natural landscapes and the fact that the vast majority of the population lives close to a beach, it's hardly surprising that people seem obsessed with outdoor life and sport. Everyone loves a "barbie" (a barbecue) and a session on the beach, whether sunbathing or surfing. The great days of lifesaving clubs and parades are certainly not over, and neither is the allure of the beach; surfing is indeed a way of life for quite a number of people.

Gambling is also a national passion, taking place indoors in front of endless ranks of "pokies," at the casino

❑ Even though women got the vote at an early date, Australia was always a man's country. The male-female ratio among the transportees brought by the First Fleet was hardly a balanced one, and the scenes that took place when the first cargo of women was discharged were said to be "indescribable." "Sheilas" (women) were kept in their place longer here than in most other countries, both at home and behind the bar, where they filled the glasses while the men on the other side got on with the serious business of drinking. Big changes came during World War II, however, and then later with the growth of feminism, one of the key works of which, *The Female Eunuch*, was by the Australian writer Germaine Greer. ❑

17

Lifeguard at Bondi Beach

or outdoors at the racetrack. On the first Tuesday in November life stops across the nation for the big horse race, the Melbourne Cup.

SPORT Most Australians have a favorite sport, to watch if not to play. A passion for cricket is shared with other members of the British Commonwealth, and has been made less stuffy by innovations like one-day matches, floodlighting and the wearing of colored clothing instead of the traditional white. Rugby Union exists and Rugby League is played in N.S.W. and Queensland. The really big football game, however, and certainly in its Melbourne stronghold, is that known as Australian Rules. It originated on the goldfields, a crude version of Gaelic football played by prospectors taking time off from the diggings, and has been described as "a kind of organized mayhem remarkable for its lack of obvious rules." Up to 100,000 spectators gather to watch the grand final at the M.C.G. (Melbourne Cricket Ground) every September. The year 2000, however, will place Australia on the world's sporting map, when Sydney plays host to the XXVII Olympiad.

Australian culture goes back far longer than the 200-odd years of white settlement. Visitors will be fascinated by the evidence of at least 40,000 years of uninterrupted civilization in both the dot and x-ray style rock- and cave-paintings, and in the haunting stories of the creation legends of the Aboriginal Dreamtime.

Australians today have a high regard for culture and talent, and take pride in the international success of Australian artists, film-makers and writers. Most Aussies cannot resist a good performance, and visitors who demonstrate their enthusiasm will be much appreciated.

LITERATURE AND FILMS Drama has developed from such elegies for lost youth as Ray Lawlor's *Summer of the Seventeenth Doll* to the plays of David Williamson. Judith Wright and Les Murray are poets of world status, weaving together the personal and the public, while managing to capture the elusive character of the Australian environment.

Three classic Australian books are Robert Hughes's convict-era history, *The Fatal Shore*, Jill Ker Conway's childhood memoir, *The Road from Coorain*, and Bruce Chatwin's rendering of the Aboriginal relationship with the earth, *The Songlines*. Also

Tongue-in-cheek Crocodile Dundee

look for Barry Hill's *The Rock*, an illustrated multicultural history of Uluru (Ayers Rock).

Aussie novels that comment poignantly, sometimes humorously, on Australian life, history, and landscape are Nobel Prize-winner Patrick White's *Voss*, Peter Carey's spirited *Oscar and Lucinda*, David Malouf's *Remembering Babylon*, and Thomas Keneally's *The Playmaker*. Elizabeth Jolley sets her novels in her native state, Western Australia.

Since the 1970s, Australian film-makers have produced an increasing variety of internationally known work. The tragic *Breaker Morant* and Peter Weir's *Gallipoli* and *Picnic at Hanging Rock* are in a class of their own. *My Brilliant Career*, about an aspiring young writer on a sheep station, is another stand-out. *Crocodile Dundee's* bushwhacking swagger has its place in Australian mythology, as does the apocalyptic *Mad Max 2/The Road Warrior*, for different reasons, of course. More recent Aussie favorites include *Strictly Ballroom*, *A Cry in the Dark*, *Muriel's Wedding*, the side-splitting *The Adventures of Priscilla, Queen of the Desert*, *Babe*, *The Castle*, and *Shine*.

PAINTERS Marvelous light and scenery have contributed to a tradition of outstanding painting. The early dreamy landscapes of McCubbin and the Heidelberg School, lending the Australian scenery a European beauty, gave way to the more distinctively Australian works of painters like Sidney Nolan with his series of pictures depicting the fatal defiance of outlaw Ned Kelly. Arthur Boyd's and Brett Whiteley's enlargements of

their own dreams and obsessions sometimes achieve a vast scale, and Fred Williams' wonderful evocations of the arid Australian landscape rival the originality of Aboriginal art, which is now much sought-after by collectors all over the world.

Aboriginal paintings are well represented in museums, and the outdoor rock art that can be found all over the country is an undeniable cultural achievement.

MUSIC Australia also has much to offer musically. The golden voice of Joan Carden makes her a worthy successor to Dame Nellie Melba and Dame Joan Sutherland ("La Stupenda"). Each state capital boasts an Australian Broadcasting Commission symphony orchestra of world standard, with internationally recognized conductors and repertoires including music by contemporary Australian composers such as Colin Brumby, John Antill and Peter Sculthorpe. Aboriginal music is increasingly entering the mainstream of the country's culture, and the growing international reputation of Yothu Yindi, the Aboriginal rock band, was recognized by the 1992 "Australian

The Sidney Nolan painting Dog and Duck Hotel

of the Year" award given to its lead singer, Mandawuy Yunupingu. The country is also a hotbed of good jazz (James Morrison), folk (Archie Roach and Ruby Hunter), and country and western (Lee Kernaghan), all competing for listeners.

THE MEDIA In contrast, most Australian newspapers and T.V. channels are owned by two media moguls—Murdoch and Packer. Their content is dominated by personality trivia, sports, sentimental "bush-whacker" pap, and investigations into the private lives of public figures, often making the Australian press as sensationalist as any other.

The Australian Broadcasting Commission's radio and television programs, on the other hand, gain many international awards for quality and interest, particularly in the fields of science, environment and religion. Especially outstanding is the current-affairs weekly *Four Corners*, which for 20 years has exposed big business and government scandals that have been ignored by the commercial media.

The six states that came together on the first day of the 20th century to create the nation of Australia had all developed outward from the isolated footholds of their port-of-entry capital cities, with very different characteristics and cultures. In contrast with the slow evolution of a national consciousness, the states maintain a vigorous political and economic competition both with each other and with the Federal Government.

Since 1940 Commonwealth control of tax revenues and appointment of Supreme Court judges has guaranteed the Federal Government victory in most disputes with individual states. This included the 1983 prohibition of damming of the World Heritage-listed Franklin River in Tasmania and the 1990 exclusion of logging from the unique tropical rainforests of northern Queensland. In these matters, the Commonwealth Government has been influenced by a Green movement that commands a disciplined voting block—generally estimated at between eight percent and 15 percent of the electorate.

The political parties After 13 years in power (an unprecedented six terms of office), Australia's Federal Labor Government was heavily defeated by the right-wing coalition of the Liberal Party (representing the urban middle classes and employers) and National Party (the traditional voice of rural interests) in the March 1996 elections. The current Liberal Party Prime Minister is John Howard, who is best known for his extremely conservative approach.

A large proportion of the population was delighted by this transfer of power after Labor's long, and perhaps increasingly complacent, rule. But many Australians are concerned, for example, about the future of the proposed Australian republic, free of constitutional ties to the reigning British monarch, who is still the official head of the country. There is also an ongoing debate regarding a new and more appropriate flag.

Aboriginal, immigration, and arts policies have also changed, with John Howard and his supporters expressing little interest in these issues, and there is strong opposition from many quarters to the government's plans to introduce a GST (Goods and Services Tax). For the foreseeable future, the challenge to the Liberal/National Party coalition will be spearheaded by the Leader of the Opposition, formerly the Deputy Prime Minister, Kim Beazley.

Economic development The "Lucky Country" cannot now find enough markets for its wool, wheat, beef, or mineral exports to pay for its insatiable appetite for expensive imports. The tariffs that previously protected small local industries from being swamped by European and Asian manufacturers have been drastically cut in the interests of economic rationalism, unemployment is around 7.5 percent and, despite some economic growth in recent years, the overseas debt increases each year. Governments hope that growth in international tourism will help save the economy.

There is now bipartisan political agreement on the need to develop manufactured goods for export, though the current government policy of reducing tariff barriers has had the opposite result and has caused unemployment. However, there can be no argument about the need to integrate better with the economies of both Europe and Southeast Asia and the Pacific Rim—Australia's closest neighbors.

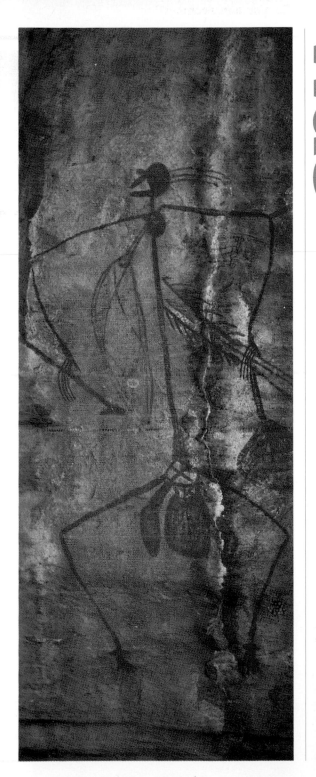

Australia Was

In some parts of the globe vigorous land-shaping processes are obviously hard at work. Ice and snow attack alpine peaks, glaciers grind through valleys, torrents and waterfalls erode, while elsewhere geysers boil and lava pours from beneath the earth. In contrast, Australia is a quiet continent, much of whose active geological history ended long ago.

ANCIENT TECTONICS Some 50 million years ago Australia was part of Gondwanaland, the great southern supercontinent that slowly split into the separate fragments we know today as Antarctica, South America, Africa, and India, as well as Australia and New Zealand. But its geological evolution goes back much farther; Precambrian rocks more than 600 million years old are exposed over much of the continent, among them the ancient iron ore deposits of the Pilbara in Western Australia. Subsequently, much of the heart of the continent was periodically submerged beneath the sea, leaving deposits of sands, shells and grits, or the limestone of the Nullarbor Plain. Great coral reefs were also formed, which, when uplifted, became the basis of the extensive cave systems of New South Wales and Queensland,

The Great Dividing Range

or the great bastion that today guards the southern rim of the Kimberley. The Great Artesian Basin came into being at this time too, and the water pumped from it continues to support life in much of the Outback.

MORE RECENT CHANGES About 2 million years ago, what is now the arid Red Centre of the continent enjoyed a far higher rainfall and carried a rich vegetation of tropical forest, traces of which can still be seen in the palms and other plants that have found a refuge in the gorges penetrating the area's harsh ranges. In the east, the Great Dividing Range was thrown up as the result of convulsive earth movements; its southern, alpine area, together with the Tasmanian highlands, is the only part of the continent to have been subjected to glaciation in the last Ice Age (10,000 years ago). As the ice melted, the sea

22

level rose, creating a wonderful natural harbor for the future city of Sydney. At the same time, the land bridges with Tasmania and New Guinea were cut. Later still (some 5,000 years ago), an outburst of volcanic activity covered the plains of southwestern Victoria with lava, leaving a legacy of cones and crater lakes and of deep fertile soil.

Right: Tessellated rock formation on the Tasman Peninsula
Below: Australia in 1848—note the dearth of information on the unexplored interior of the continent

23

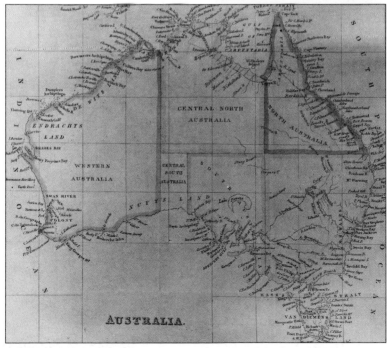

European explorers and educated early settlers tended to romanticize the black people they encountered on the shores of the unknown continent. Aborigines were seen by some as typifying the "Noble Savage" dreamed up by the imaginative powers of 18th-century thinkers. The first Australians were an endlessly fascinating subject for artists and draftsmen and were sometimes depicted in the heroic poses of ancient Greek statuary.

24

VICTIMS OF THE WHITE MAN The Aborigines failed to correspond to the European stereotypes. In what now seems an entirely appropriate response, albeit one doomed to failure, some groups put up a vigorous resistance to the encroachment of white settlement on the lands that had formed the basis of their lives since time immemorial. Others fell

Ritual and ceremony are central to Aboriginal culture

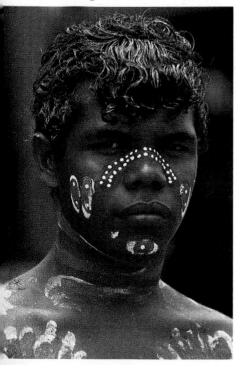

easy victim to the diseases and vices of their conquerors. Only a few decades after the arrival of the First Fleet, the Aborigines of the Sydney region had been decimated by drink and influenza, and before the 19th century had run its course, the Tasmanians had almost virtually disappeared. For much of this century Aborigines have been seen as second-class citizens—it was not until after a referendum in 1967 that they were given the right to vote.

It is only in relatively recent times that white Australians have begun to appreciate the richness and subtlety of the life that their appropriation of the continent all but destroyed, but which sustained the first Australians in material and spiritual harmony with the Australian environment for at least 40,000 years.

DREAMTIME Aboriginals inhabited the land in a way remote from European concepts of ownership and property. Rather than "own" land, they inhabit it in sacred trust on behalf of ancestral beings who created it during the Dreamtime. The land itself was part of the spiritual realm of the whole of creation, in which all creatures, animals as well as humans and the dead as well as the living, had their being. The landscape was venerated by individuals, large family groups or clans, with certain places—"sacred sites"—having a particularly intense meaning.

A deep understanding of the spiritual significance of the land was passed on by highly refined and diversified traditions of song and

dance. Never codified in writing, many of these oral traditions tragically have been lost. Ritual gatherings, sometimes known as *corroborees*, took up large amounts of time, with men and women often having strictly separate ceremonies. Visual arts, like cave- or wall-paintings, or designs executed on the ground had a ceremonial or storytelling role, and were ephemeral or subject to periodic renewal.

LIFESTYLE Virtually all Aboriginal groups were nomads, living a Stone-Age lifestyle of hunting, gathering, and fishing based on the seasonal availability of game, seeds and fruits. Controlled burning of the bush took place in order to encourage regrowth and thus attract animals to the area. Material belongings were kept to an absolute minimum, and consisted of baskets and nets, digging sticks, shelters of brushwood, weapons of carved wood and sharpened bone, canoes of bark, and boomerangs. Clothes were also minimal, except in the colder, wetter areas of south-eastern Australia, where skins and furs were worn.

Each clan had its own distinct territory, defined orally by song rather than marked out on the ground. For another group to cross such an

Aboriginal rangers are happy to share their knowledge of the land with visitors to the national parks

invisible but nevertheless definite boundary might have involved complex negotiation.

The whole of Australia can now be mapped in terms of these traditional territories, but at the time of European settlement no such map existed, except in the hearts of its inhabitants. This allowed legalistic Europeans to appropriate the land with a more or less clear conscience.

❑ Some 200 Aboriginal languages existed, related to one another but not necessarily mutually intelligible. Most people were multilingual, speaking perhaps five or six tongues. The language of the Aborigines around the future site of Sydney was, of course, unknown to Europeans, and the cry of "*Warra! Warra!*" they were greeted with was not understood. Even if it had been, would they have taken any notice? "*Warra! Warra!*" means "Go away!" ❑

The first people to explore Australia were the ancestors of today's Aborigines, who may have crossed the still intact landbridge linking the continent to New Guinea well over 40,000 years ago. At first they lived along the coasts and in other areas where food was easily obtainable, and eventually spread all over the country, learning to live even in those regions where survival seemed all but impossible to later explorers.

THE PORTUGUESE AND DUTCH EXPLORERS

The European discovery of the island continent began in a tentative, almost accidental way in the 16th century, as Portuguese mariners looked for routes to the eastern Spice Islands. But the first definite landfall was made in 1606 by the Dutch ship *Duyfken* ("Little Dove") sailing out of the Dutch colony of Batavia (now Jakarta). Her captain, Willem Jansz, was unimpressed by what he saw of the desolate western coast of Cape York and what he called its "wild, cruel black savages."

A little later, Dutch skippers on their way to Java found that they could cut weeks off their journey by making use of the Roaring Forties until they made a northward turn well short of the coast of western Australia. Some sailed straight on, like Dirk Hartog in 1616 (who left an inscribed pewter plate nailed to a post on the island that bears his name), and Frederik de Houtman, who landed on the Houtman Abrolhos islands in 1619.

Under the command of a captain whose name is unrecorded, the *Leeuwin* ("Lioness") sighted the southwestern tip of the continent in 1622. Subsequently, more systematic attempts were made by the Dutch East India Company to survey the coastline. The most famous of them was the voyage of Abel Tasman in 1642–43 in the *Heemskerck* and *Zeehaan*; put ashore on Tasmania's Blackman Bay, his pilot heard voices coming from the bush, but the natives failed to show themselves. Tasman had the flag run up, and named the island after the Governor

W. R. Stott's painting shows William Dampier being attacked by Aborigines when he landed in 1699

of the Dutch East Indies, Van Diemen, a name changed to honor the actual discoverer in 1855.

In the course of a second voyage, Tasman failed (as had all his predecessors) to find the gap between New Guinea and Australia, subsequently called the Torres Strait, but mapped 1,865 miles of the north coast instead. By this time, the coast had been explored by Dutchmen from the tip of Cape York around Western Australia to the archipelago in the Great Australian Bight. Although the Dutch did not take the continent under their control, they did name it—New Holland.

THE BRITISH ARRIVE The first Englishman to set foot on the shores of New Holland was the adventurer William Dampier, who landed twice on its northwestern coast, first in 1688, then again in 1699. It was Captain Cook, however, who not only found the unknown east coast, but sailed the length of it and identified the spot where British settlement was to take place. He completed his mission in spite of the fact that his ship the *Endeavour* ran aground on the Barrier Reef (see page 214). The name that Captain Cook gave to the land he claimed for the British Crown was New South Wales.

Even after British settlement had been well and truly established around Sydney Harbour (by Captain Phillip in 1788), many uncertainties remained as to whether the three known fragments added up to a continent. Part of the answer was provided by two truly intrepid men, George Bass and Matthew Flinders, who by 1798 had confirmed the existence of a channel between the mainland and Van Diemen's Land. Governor Hunter, impressed by this great discovery, named the channel Bass Strait after the explorer.

Aboard the *Investigator*, Flinders went on to explore the south coast with great thoroughness, meeting the French survey ship *Geographe* in what came to be known as Encounter Bay.

Early settlers—Captain Phillip arriving at Sydney Cove in 1788

The master of the *Geographe*, Nicolas Baudin, behaved impeccably, though Flinders was suspicious of the intentions of a servant of France, a country with which Britain had recently been at war. His suspicions of the French were justified when, later, having sailed around Australia in 1802–03, he was arrested by the Governor of French Mauritius on his way back to England, unaware that war had broken out again. Held for six years by the French, he returned to England a prematurely aged 40-year-old, barely able to complete his *A Voyage to Terra Australis* before dying in 1814.

❏ Non-Europeans also made contact with Australia. Chinese junks may have sailed to Australia's northern coast as early as the 15th century, and there were exchanges between the Aborigines and the warlike inhabitants of New Guinea. From about 1700 onward, fishermen from Macassar in the Celebes frequented the north coast in search of trepang (sea-cucumbers), an activity that continues today. ❏

The map of Australia is scattered with surnames attached to natural features or to settlements, honoring governors and other leaders. But there are others, like the Sturt Stony Desert, which commemorate a different kind of fame—that earned by the inland explorers, a breed of men who explored, with varying degrees of success, the new country's uncharted interior.

28

Straightforward curiosity may have impelled some adventures into the interior, but another factor was the hunger for land as the colony grew and needed to be fed. In addition, industrial England developed an insatiable appetite for wool, which the merino crossbreeds so successfully developed by John Macarthur could satisfy if only enough pastures could be found. For many years, the Blue Mountains seemed to bar the way from Sydney to the interior, but in 1813 this obstacle was overcome by William Lawson, William Charles Wentworth, and Gregory Blaxland. Governor Macquarie had a road built across the mountains in record time, and settlers rushed into the rich grazing lands beyond.

STURT'S JOURNEY For many years the puzzle of what became of the rivers flowing westward from the

Many lost their lives in the exploration of Australia's interior

mountains perplexed authorities and explorers alike. Did they perhaps feed a great inland sea? A partial answer—no!—was given in 1829–30, when Charles Sturt hauled a whaling boat over the hills and sailed down the Murrumbidgee to its confluence with the Murray. From there he continued downstream to wide Lake Alexandrina and the river mouth (in South Australia), which had so far been concealed from maritime explorers behind a sand bar. Sturt's return, rowing upstream against a swelling current, was an epic of endurance. It nearly ended in disaster as food for his party ran out and their strength ebbed.

❏ Explorers of several nationalities contributed to the exploration of Australia. In 1839–40 a Polish adventurer, self-styled "Count" Paul Strzelecki, underwent hardships almost equal to those suffered by Sturt as he traversed the uplands to which he gave the name Gippsland, and from which he was only extracted by the skills of his Aboriginal guide. An impetuous and quarrelsome Prussian, Ludwig Leichhardt, was less lucky, though in 1844 his first journey succeeded in covering an amazing 2,983 miles from Brisbane to Arnhem Land. An even more ambitious foray that was intended to carry him right across the center from Sydney to Perth failed. Leichhardt and his companions simply disappeared into the void. ❏

Above: Burke and Wills leave Melbourne in August 1860

BURKE'S EXPEDITION Another great failure, but a fully documented one, was the expedition that set out from Melbourne in 1860 under the impatient leadership of Robert O'Hara Burke. The expedition did reach its objective, the mangrove swamps of the Gulf of Carpentaria, but when the party returned to base camp at Cooper Creek, they found that it had been abandoned a mere seven hours previously by their support group. Both Burke and his deputy Wills perished, though another man, John King, was fed roots and fish by the Aborigines and survived to return and tell the tale.

Before successfully crossing Australia's center, Stuart had reached Alice Springs

EYRE AND STUART The names of highways spanning the great emptiness of the center and the west commemorate the epic treks undertaken by two explorers whose persistence has an almost legendary quality. In 1840–41, with the support of his Aboriginal guide Wylie, Edward Eyre reached Albany, having crossed the waterless desert across the top of the Great Australian Bight. In 1862, John McDouall Stuart, almost blind and with hair turned white, finally reached the coast near what was to become Darwin. His previous attempts to cross the center from south to north had been frustrated by spinifex and scurvy, though he had planted the British flag on a hilltop near Alice Springs. His return to Adelaide, where he was mobbed by the ladies of the city, was made partly on a stretcher.

In the first half of the 19th century Australia developed at a steady but unspectacular pace. Free settlers soon outnumbered convicts, and each colony won its right to a separate existence from New South Wales. But the discovery of gold transformed the country, drawing in a mass of enterprising folk who helped lay the foundation of Australia's essentially urban civilization.

GOLD FEVER The news of early gold finds was suppressed by the authorities, who were fearful of the disruption that such an announcement might cause. But there was no stopping Edward Hargraves, a veteran of the Californian gold rush of 1849, who struck gold near Bathurst in N.S.W. in February 1851.

The rush began, draining the cities of population and making Melbourne so fearful for its prosperity that city officials offered a prize to whoever found gold within a certain distance of the city. One James Esmond obliged, and his find at Clunes in July 1851 was followed by others at Castlemaine, Bendigo, and

Prospectors in the mid-19th century

Ballarat. Melbourne was emptied of able-bodied men and ships stood crewless in the harbor as sailors hurried inland to make their fortune.

Life in the goldfields was tough, raw and dangerous. Many of the prospectors longed for nothing more than solid respectability. They founded farms and businesses after striking lucky, or returned to seek their fortune among the seemingly limitless opportunities offered by "Marvelous Melbourne."

More rebellious spirits took a stand at the Eureka Stockade (see page 110), and even though this revolt failed, their gesture helped create a new democratic atmosphere in which representative government was to thrive. Victoria's population rose in 10 years from less than 100,000 to more than half a million, and the whole country received an injection of energy that carried it through a boom lasting until the 1890s.

FORTUNE-SEEKERS Prospectors came flooding in from all over the world, including the gold miners of California and hopeful fortune seekers from Britain. The largest minority were the Chinese, many of whom disembarked in South Australia and walked overland to the Victorian goldfields rather than pay the £10 landing tax at Melbourne. They were much resented by the other settlers for their willingness to work hard, for keeping to themselves, and for their sheer numbers. At the time of the Palmer River gold rush in the 1870s in North Queensland, Chinese diggers formed a majority of the male population in the state.

FROM BOOM TOWN TO GHOST TOWN

In Victoria, the rip roaring days were soon over. By the late 1850s, most of the gold that was available on the surface or by shallow diggings had been worked out. Individual miners could not afford the equipment that was needed for the excavation and maintenance of deeper mines, and the initiative passed from the self-sufficient pioneer to companies able to raise the necessary capital. Ballarat ceased being a muddy chaos and turned itself into the most respectable of Victorian cities.

In the second half of the 19th century gold strikes were made all over Australia, many of them ephemeral and leaving a poignant legacy of ghost towns. The last great rush was to the Eastern Goldfields of Coolgardie and Kalgoorlie-Boulder in Western Australia in 1892–1893. This gave a similar boost to the languid economy of the colony, and transformed Perth into a real city. Large-scale operations continue in this area today, based on vast opencast pits worked by huge machines, in total contrast to the primitive hand tools and hard manual labor of the prospectors of early days.

Sovereign Hill at Ballarat in Victoria is a re creation of gold rush days

❑ Highway robbery had been practiced in the colony for as long as highways had existed, and increased in appeal as the wealth created by the gold rush was moved around. Australia's bushrangers were just as fearsome as the legendary outlaws of the American West, their exploits winning them a heroic status among a population traditionally hostile to the police. The most notorious of them all, and a symbol of Australian defiance and sheer cussedness, was Edward "Ned" Kelly, son of an Irish ex-convict. After a series of exploits, which included holding up whole towns, the Kelly gang was cornered in June 1880 at Glenrowan, a small town in north-eastern Victoria. Kelly emerged from the pub wearing his famous homemade suit of armor, but was shot in the legs, brought to trial and hanged in Melbourne on November 11, 1880. ❑

The Australian landscapes that the early European settlers first cast eyes upon lacked the ordered character of the scenes they had left behind. Much of the European effort in Australia was to impose a rational and productive discipline on this unfamiliar and seemingly chaotic scene. This was sometimes at a cost to habitats and natural beauty that is only now being calculated.

In Europe, the conversion of the forest into farmland began in neolithic times and took some 5,000 years to complete. In the wooded southeastern and western areas of Australia, the same process was virtually complete after only a single century. The replacement of the bush by productive fields was one motive, but in many areas the timber itself was highly valuable and logging quickly developed into a major industry.

The removal of the native forest or its replacement by exotic tree species like radiata pines continued into the 20th century, but a partial halt has now been called. Today no visitor should miss seeing such glories of the Australian landscape as the tropical rain forest of Queensland, its temperate equivalent in the southeast and in Tasmania, the blue gums that have given their name to the Blue Mountains, or the splendid karri forests of Western Australia.

THE FARMERS MOVE IN Once the bush was cleared, squatters and sheep farmers parceled out their land, erecting fences, and planting European trees to give the place a more homely look. They built themselves homesteads with whatever degree of architectural elaboration they could afford. Australian country properties ranged from elegant stone mansions to shacks that were made of corrugated iron.

This attempt to impose order often faltered in the face of the capricious nature of the land. Rainless years ruined many a farmer who had tried to push the frontier of agriculture too far inland. Australia has as many

forgotten farmsteads as it has ghost towns abandoned by prospectors when mineral wealth ran out.

As settlement advanced, native animals retreated, displaced in many cases by flocks of sheep grazing on the imported grass species sown by farmers. Kangaroos and other animals, often shot as pests, sometimes profited by the irrigation of otherwise arid landscapes, and became a greater nuisance than ever.

CONFLICTS OF INTEREST The effect of these and other changes converted a seemingly formless scene into one that made economic and visual sense to the Europeans, and one that could be controlled and managed. It also meant that the landscape became uninhabitable by the Aborigines in any traditional way. Such basic differences of viewpoint probably contributed more than anything else to a conflict between settlers and the Aborigines, in which the latter were the inevitable losers.

❑ Rabbits were imported as game in the 1850s. Within a few years, the population exploded, and rabbits advanced at the rate of 60 miles a year, destroying much of the native herbage for ever. Supposedly rabbit-proof fences were built, one running 1,240 miles across a large part of Western Australia. But the rabbits found ways round them, and were only curbed when myxomatosis spread among them in the 1950s. ❑

A-Z
Australia

How to tackle Australia

The first thing to remember about Australia is that it is a continent. Planning a vacation here is like traveling across Europe or the United States—Australia is comparable in size to the U.S., excluding Alaska, and approximately 24 times as big as the British Isles—you could get an overall idea of the country in one trip, but you need time and money if you want to get to know it really well.

THE EXTENDED VISIT An absolute minimum for an extended trip that takes in all major sights is three months. In this time you could visit all the states, including Tasmania, and cover most of the highlighted attractions of this guide, especially if you were able to do most of your traveling—and some of your sightseeing—by plane. If you have more time, so much the better; you could stay in some places and absorb their atmosphere in a relaxed way rather than just hitting the principal sights. Now that you can drive right around the continent on paved roads, many retired Australians are getting to know their own country in a leisurely way, usually by driving an R.V. or camper-van.

THE SHORTER TRIP Most visitors to Australia have only limited time at their disposal, and choices must be made. As well as seeing something of city life, if you want to enjoy what Australia has to offer you will need to get out into the country, drive along the unsurfaced roads of the Outback, leave your car behind and walk through the bush or along the beach, wander around one of the old

34

Camper-vans are ideal for exploring the country, particularly for those on a tight budget

gold-rush townships, sit at the bar of an Outback pub, or sample the excellent diving or snorkeling.

Australians take great pleasure in inviting you to join in: you can take part in all kinds of activities, from riding a camel in the desert to digging for witchetty grubs in the company of an Aboriginal ranger. Not only are there probably more museums per head than anywhere else in the world (from the impeccably professional to the endearingly amateur), but all kinds of industries and enterprises open their gates to visitors. Wineries without tastings are unheard of, farms make you welcome and there are plenty of accommodations available on country properties with the chance to take part in rural activities.

PLANNING AN ITINERARY Within the confines imposed by a conventional vacation of a few weeks, setting definite limits on what you can reasonably undertake is very important. Though vast, nearly all the Australian states are dominated by their respective capital city, each with its own character and attractions. This is where colonial life began and where its traces are thickest on the ground. Wild landscapes start just beyond the suburbs; no big city lies out of sight of the hills or mountains of a national park.

One solution would be to choose one city or town as a base and then make excursions, some involving overnight stays, in order to appreciate the extraordinary contrasts between city and rural life that are such a feature of Australia. An overland trip by rental car, train, bus or organized tour beginning at one point and taking your time to reach another is a good way of getting the feel of the country; your round-trip airline ticket can usually be arranged to accommodate this.

But many Americans have far less time for their Australian vacation than visitors from the UK. If you only have a week, you could just about take in Sydney, Cairns, the Barrier Reef, Darwin, Alice Springs, and Uluru by flying between sites.

The Outback is uniquely rewarding, but before you head off in your rental car or camper-van, contemplate the distances involved. Remember that Cairns is 1,675 miles from Sydney, Alice Springs is 1,830 miles via Adelaide distant, Darwin 2,750 miles via Adelaide and Alice Springs and Perth a staggering 2,600 miles from Sydney—no short hop! You don't have to go all the way out and back overland; if time is short, you can fly to one of the many bases for Outback tours and start from there.

Australia now has a well-developed and very varied tourist infrastructure, mostly staffed by people who go out of their way to be helpful. Aside from accommodations and restaurants to suit a range of budgets, there are also many tour operators. However, check that the tours offered are exactly what you want—the ingredients of a package may have been put together to suit the operator's convenience rather than yours.

Far out in the Pacific, Lord Howe Island (over 480 miles northeast of Sydney) and Norfolk Island (another 620 miles farther on) are favorites with Australians in search of something different. Some 15 square miles in size, Norfolk was a prison island where offenders from Sydney were sent to suffer under a notoriously brutal regime, and the remains of convict-era buildings give it something of the atmosphere of Tasmania's Port Arthur. The climate is subtropical and as well as rainforest, there are stands of the famous Norfolk pines and rolling pasturelands. Lord Howe Island is less than half the size of Norfolk Island and is dominated by mountain peaks, with unique vegetation and birdlife that have led to its designation as a World Heritage Area. There are hardly any cars, and when not snorkeling you will have to get around by bike.

35

Drivers: beware of camels!

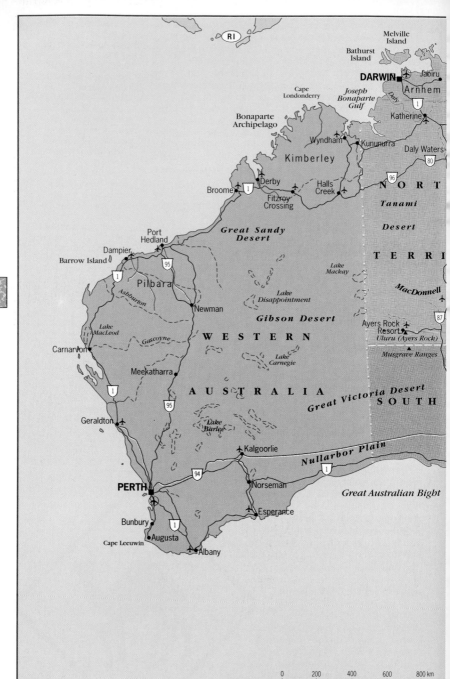

RI

Melville
Island

Bathurst
Island

DARWIN ■ Jabiru

Arnhem

Cape
Londonderry

*Joseph
Bonaparte
Gulf*

Katherine

Bonaparte
Archipelago

Wyndham Kununurra

Daly Waters

Kimberley

96

80

N O R T

Broome Derby

Fitzroy
Crossing

Halls
Creek

Tanami

Desert

T E R R I

Port
Hedland

*Great Sandy
Desert*

Lake
Mackay

Dampier

Barrow Island

95

Pilbara

MacDonnell

87

Ashburton

Newman

*Lake
Disappointment*

Ayers Rock
Resort

Gibson Desert

Uluru (Ayers Rock)

Lake
MacLeod

Gascoyne

W E S T E R N

Musgrave Ranges

Carnarvon

Meekatharra

Lake
Carnegie

A U S T R A L I A

Great Victoria Desert

S O U T H

95

Geraldton

Lake
Barlee

Kalgoorlie

Nullarbor Plain

PERTH

94

Norseman

Great Australian Bight

Bunbury

1

Esperance

Cape Leeuwin

Augusta

Albany

| 0 | 200 | 400 | 600 | 800 km |
| 0 | 100 | 200 | 300 | 400 | 500 miles |

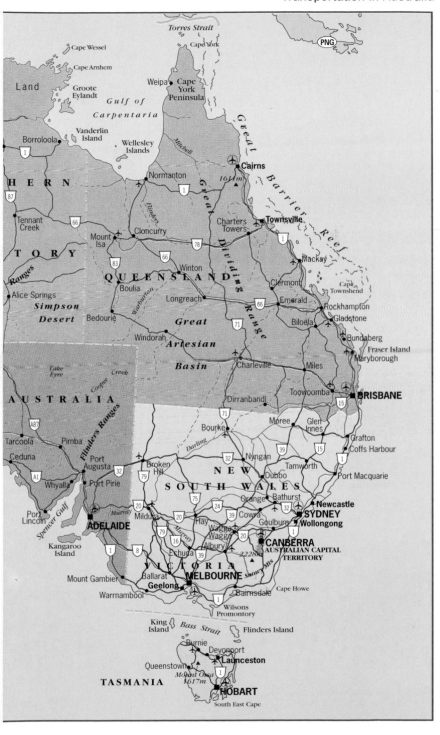

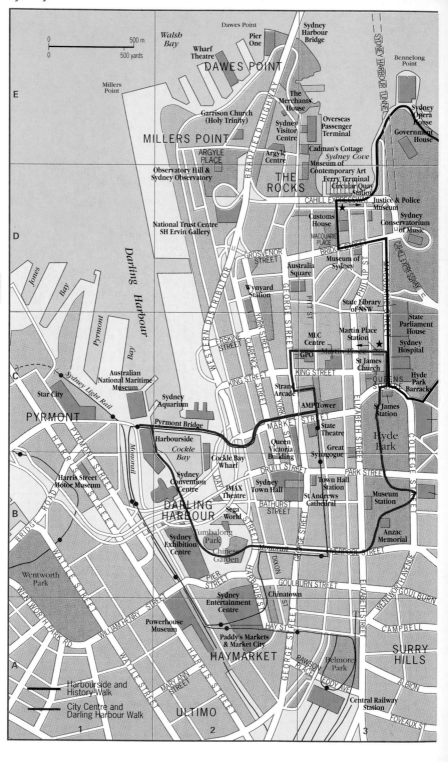

Sydney

0 — 500 m
0 — 500 yards

Walsh Bay
Dawes Point
Pier One
Sydney Harbour Bridge
Wharf Theatre
DAWES POINT
Bennelong Point
Millers Point
The Merchants' House
Garrison Church (Holy Trinity)
Sydney Visitor Centre
Overseas Passenger Terminal
Sydney Opera House
Government House
MILLERS POINT
ARGYLE PLACE
Argyle Centre
Cadman's Cottage
Sydney Cove
Observatory Hill & Sydney Observatory
Museum of Contemporary Art
Ferry Terminal
Circular Quay Station
THE ROCKS
Justice & Police Museum
Sydney Conservatorium of Music
National Trust Centre SH Ervin Gallery
CAHILL EXPRESSWAY
Customs House
MACQUARIE PLACE
GROSVENOR STREET
Australia Square
Museum of Sydney
State Library of NSW
Darling Harbour Bay
Jones Bay
Pyrmont
Wynyard Station
GEORGE STREET
PITT ST
State Parliament House
Sydney Hospital
ERSKINE STREET
YORK STREET
CLARENCE STREET
KING STREET
MLC Centre
GPO
Martin Place Station
Martin Place
Sydney Light Rail
Australian National Maritime Museum
Star City
KING STREET
St James Church
QUEENS SQUARE
Hyde Park Barracks
PYRMONT
Sydney Aquarium
Strand Arcade
AMP Tower
Pyrmont Bridge
St James Station
Harbourside
Cockle Bay
Cockle Bay Wharf
Queen Victoria Building
State Theatre
Great Synagogue
Hyde Park
Harris Street Motor Museum
Sydney Convention Centre
DRUITT STREET
Sydney Town Hall
IMAX Theatre
Town Hall Station
St Andrews Cathedral
PARK STREET
Museum Station
DARLING HARBOUR
Sega World
BATHURST STREET
DIXON STREET
Anzac Memorial
Sydney Exhibition Centre
Tumbalong Park
Chinese Garden
PIER STREET
HARBOUR ST
GOULBURN STREET
LIVERPOOL STREET
WENTWORTH AVENUE
GOULBURN
Wentworth Park
Sydney Entertainment Centre
Chinatown
CAMPBELL
SURRY HILLS
BRIDGE ROAD
WATTLE STREET
Powerhouse Museum
Paddy's Markets & Market City
HAY STREET
RAWSON PLACE
Belmore Park
ALBION
WENTWORTH PARK RD
WILLIAM HENRY STREET
HARRIS STREET
HAYMARKET
MARY ANN STREET
Central Railway Station
EDDY AVE
FOVEAUX ST
ULTIMO

Harbourside and History Walk
City Centre and Darling Harbour Walk

38

E
D
C
B
A

1   2   3

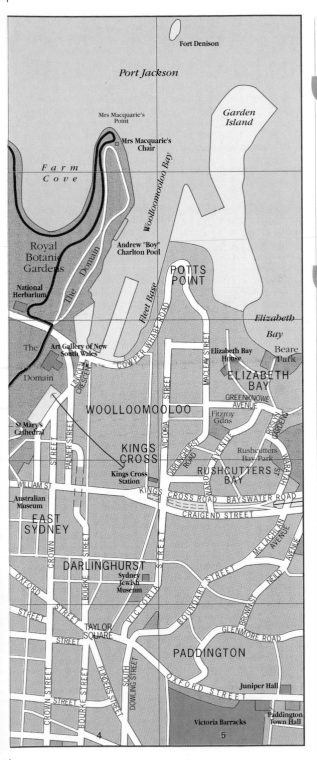

Sydney

THE FIRST SYDNEYSIDERS

The area around Sydney seems to have been inhabited by three main Aboriginal groups, numbering several thousand people, when the 11 ships of Britain's First Fleet sailed in. Large numbers of Aboriginal carvings survive in the sandstone plateaus to the north and south. The Aborigines' response to the invaders was a mixture of indifference, resentment, and curiosity, but they were in no position to resist, and by the early 1800s those who remained in the area had been reduced to drunkenness and begging.

SYDNEY Curling seductively around its sparkling harbor, Sydney has a superb setting. It is one of the world's great cities, with nearly a quarter of the population of the continent in its metropolitan area, and still seems in the first flush of youth—enthusiastic, welcoming, vibrant, and open to growth and change. Two of its famous landmarks, the Harbour Bridge and Opera House, became icons the day they were completed. Seen from across the water, the new glamorous buildings constructed in the city center in the last 20 years add further drama and excitement, while all around the 150 miles of harbor foreshore, waterfront suburbs of dream homes mingle with the remains of wild bushland.

Sydney, then, is beautiful, almost extravagantly so. There is also a fair measure of what has been called "the Australian ugliness." The skyscrapers make no attempt to harmonize with their immediate surroundings; close up, much of the city center appears chaotic. Beyond the often charming Victorian suburbs sprawls an almost horizonless sea of red-roofed bungalow suburbs. But the monotony of this urban sprawl is compensated for by magnificent natural surroundings: the heaths and forests of **Ku-ring-gai Chase** and **Royal National Park**, the high wall of the **Blue Mountains** and the string of beaches along many miles of Pacific coastline. The climate, despite a fair amount of rain, gives hot summers and bright winter days that enhance the visitor's enjoyment.

EARLY DAYS In January 1788, a favorable climate played no part in Captain Phillip's choice of Port Jackson as a landing place for his motley cargo of convicts. The First Fleet had originally anchored in Botany Bay and it was the first site chosen for the colony. Subsequently it was

40

found that the area around today's Circular Quay had fresh water, which Botany Bay did not. And so the British flag was run up. The name given to the landing place, Sydney Cove (after the British Home Secretary of the time), was soon transferred to the disorderly settlement that grew up around its shore.

As the colony became established, free settlers moved in, and the population of the city increased sharply when gold was found to the west of the Blue Mountains in the 1850s. Handsome villas were built in the outskirts, while in the later years of the 19th century middle- and working-class suburbs like Balmain and Paddington unrolled their streets of humble cottages and superior terraces over the countryside nearby, leaving areas like The Rocks to a life of drink, vice and violence.

By the time the population of the city had reached the million mark in the late 1920s, Sydney was a confident, swaggering sort of place, where a strong trade union movement helped insure one of the highest living standards in the world for its members.

UP TO DATE World War II brought the city into abrupt contact with a wider world, which came even closer in the postwar period, when Sydney became the recipient of waves of New Australians, first from devastated Europe and later from Lebanon, Vietnam, China, the Philippines, and other Asian countries. Once resolutely Anglo-Celtic, it is now a thoroughly multicultural city.

Sydney is a great tourist destination: its charms are not hidden away, but put boldly on display; its intriguing history is readily accessible; and it has all the museums, galleries, stores, restaurants, and entertainment that you would expect in a metropolis.

PENETRATING THE DEFENSES

One of Sydney's earliest fortifications, on Observatory Hill, was built to protect the colony's Establishment against a possible convict uprising; later, it was potential foreign invaders who became the worry, and by the mid-19th century virtually every promontory had been fortified. In World War II, despite a boom across the harbor's mouth, a Japanese midget submarine crept up as far as Garden Island. Here it launched its torpedoes at the cruiser U.S.S. *Chicago*; they missed. Depth-charges dealt with the brave and ingenious submariners; their vessel was recovered and is on display in an annex of the Australian War Memorial in Canberra.

41

Many consider Sydney "the best address on earth"

PLAYGROUND OF THE PACIFIC

This was the name given to Bondi Beach, and the early days of Australia's exuberant beach culture are celebrated with gusto in the Australian National Maritime Museum. Within living memory, the sands were scoured by inspectors who insured that no male swimmer went topless. But what emerges from the posters, photos and videos here is the sheer joy Australians have always had in stripping down and letting sea and sun work on their bodies. A somber note is struck by recalling Black Sunday, February 6, 1938, when what was described as an avalanche of waves took five lives in spite of the efforts of 60 lifesavers.

The Australian Museum houses ethnographic displays from all over the world

►►► Art Gallery of New South Wales   39C4

Art Gallery Road

This dignified classical sandstone edifice was opened in 1887 and expanded several times over the years, most recently and lavishly to mark the 1988 Bicentennial. Its generous interior houses what can fairly be described as the country's greatest art collection, even though the national collection is now at Canberra. It covers the evolution of Australian art up to the present day, and has major sections on Aboriginal (in the exciting Yiribana Gallery), Asian, American and European art; the collection of British 20th-century painting is outstanding. In addition the gallery hosts world-class visiting exhibitions. But it is the painters of Australia and their response to the people and places of the strange new land who most fascinate; they are all here, from John Glover's Tasmanian landscapes to Grace Cossington Smith's metamorphosis of the Harbour Bridge and Sidney Nolan's interpretation of the Ned Kelly saga.

►►► Australian Museum   38B3

Corner of College Street and William Street

Australia's largest natural history museum is a lively place, expanded and altered in recent years so that its Victorian architecture almost becomes part of the intriguing displays on earth history, animals, insects and birds, and the life of the sea. Exhibits include human rituals of the present as well as of the past and the evolution of Aboriginal culture over tens of thousands of years. There are also sections on Indonesia, Papua New Guinea, and the Pacific, as well as the "Planet of Minerals," featuring Australia's extraordinary mineral wealth. There are stuffed animals but they are always shown in context rather than as lifeless specimens, and there are plenty of "hands-on" computer displays. (See also page 49.)

►►► Australian National Maritime Museum   38C1

Darling Harbour

Looking more like a ship of the future than anything so conventional as a museum, this extraordinary structure houses an equally extraordinary array of objects that tell the story of the island continent's intimate relationship with the seas surrounding it.

There are many real vessels in the museum's huge interior, from Aboriginal canoes to high-tech yachts, but the emphasis is as much on people as on things. There are displays on explorers, convicts, settlers, refugees and other immigrants, on whalers and wharfies who made their living from the sea, on swimmers and surfers who simply enjoyed it, and on maritime "neighbors" like the Americans and Japanese. Tied up at the dock outside are more boats, including the Vietnamese *Tu' Do*, which arrived in Darwin in 1977, a World War II commando boat and the destroyer H.M.A.S. *Vampire*.

► Cadman's Cottage   38E3

George Street, The Rocks

This modest two-story Georgian house has the distinction of being the city's oldest surviving building. It was erected in 1816, getting its name from the pardoned

convict John Cadman who lived in it from 1827 to 1845. A lintel carries the initials G.R. for England's King George III in immaculately carved lettering. Some 55 yards inland from the shore, the cottage houses the Sydney Harbour National Park information center.

Over two hundred years on, Sydney Cove, the First Fleet's landing site, would be unrecognizable to those early pioneers

► Chinatown 38B2

Immigrants from China first arrived as part of the gold rush and took up residence in The Rocks or around Botany Bay. Sydney's Chinese citizens are now scattered around the suburbs, but the city's Chinese heart beats strongest along Dixon Street, behind whose ornamental gateways is an array of exotic stores, food centers, and restaurants. A few steps away is the **Chinese Garden of Friendship►►**, part of the redevelopment of Darling Harbour. Laid out by landscape architects from Sydney's sister city of Guangzhou in southern China, the gardens are a calm retreat of sensitively designed planting, lakes, bridges, and waterfalls, with a traditional tea house overlooking a tranquil lily pond.

►►► Circular Quay 38D3

Sydney's "chief people-watching site" (Jan Morris) is also one of the city's most historic places, since it was here at Sydney Cove that the First Fleet dropped anchor on January 26, 1788. It is still the epicenter of daily life, with a continuous stream of people pouring out of the railroad station, taxis, buses, and the busy ferries that bustle in and out of the quays taking commuters to destinations around the bay. Trains and traffic roar by overhead, ignored by those with time enough on their hands to stop and listen to the street performers on the broad promenade. Landward are the cliff-like buildings of the city center, while toward the water are alluring and ever-changing glimpses of the Harbour Bridge and Opera House. A map on the quayside shows the colony in 1808.

LOVELY HOMES
Not all Sydney's early houses were as unassuming as Cadman's Cottage, though the first Government House (see page 45) was damp and suffered from inexplicable smells. The aspirations of successful citizens were expressed in such delightful dwellings as Elizabeth Bay House, a splendid 1830s classical mansion in white stucco that turns its back on its sleazy neighbors in adjacent Kings Cross (see page 59). Further to the east is another highly desirable residence, Vaucluse House, whose battlements and verandas were created for the explorer William Charles Wentworth in the 1830s.

►►► Darling Harbour
38D1

The deep inlet on the western side of the city center was called Cockle Bay by the early colonists. Like so many docklands of its kind around the world, it eventually lost its commercial functions but is now enjoying a vigorous new lease on life as a tourist center, with major exhibition and entertainment facilities.

The Harbour is an exciting place, an extraordinary medley of old and new, defined to the east by glittering office towers, with expanses of water and pavement framing some of the city's most stimulating new buildings. The parkland at the southern end seems none the worse for its overhead expressways, while the whole area is linked to the center of Sydney by a controversial monorail that glides over Pyrmont Bridge, the oldest swing bridge of its kind in the world.

For details on attractions in the area other than the Australian National Maritime Museum (covered on page 42), see panel.

►► The Domain
39D4

The Domain extends inland from Mrs. Macquarie's Point to the large green space fringed by fig trees that serves as one of the city center's most important parks. This is where orators challenge their audiences along the lines of London's Speaker's Corner, where joggers jog and office workers eat their sandwiches.

Open-air opera and classical music concerts are also held here, particularly during the January Sydney Festival. The Domain has, however, suffered from the incursions of the Cahill Expressway, the Eastern Suburbs Railway and from the construction of an underground parking garage.

► Garrison Church
38E2

Millers Point

Hacked through the central ridge of The Rocks area, **Argyle Cut** was one of the colony's early engineering feats. It leads to **Argyle Place**, which has been frequently described as Sydney's sole village green, though not many village greens benefit from such close proximity to a multiple-lane expressway (the Harbour Bridge approach). Nevertheless, it is a pleasant enough place, lined with attractive mid-19th-century cottages. Holy Trinity Church, near the entrance to the Cut, was given the name Garrison Church because of its use by the red-coats manning Dawes Point Battery. Built from the stone quarried from the Cut, its squat appearance isn't helped by its lack of a spire, but it has a spacious interior and some of the city's finest stained-glass windows.

► Hyde Park
38C3

Like its London namesake, this fine park once marked the very edge of town, but today it has become one of those central city oases where people retreat from the heat, fumes and noise of the street. Its avenue of majestic Moreton Bay fig trees is particularly fine, and there is a splendid imitation-baroque fountain, but the park's centerpiece is undoubtedly the **Anzac Memorial►►** (see panel). This solemn but sumptuous essay in art deco forms the focal point of the Anzac Day (April 25th) march.

▶▶ Hyde Park Barracks   38C3

Queens Square, Macquarie Street

This splendid three-story edifice with pediment and pilasters is one of the city's finest classical buildings. Standing in dignified seclusion behind its grand gates, it was designed on Governor Macquarie's orders by the brilliant ex-convict Francis Greenway, whose architectural skills transformed Sydney. It provided accommodations for up to 1,000 convicts, who until then had had to find their own lodgings. It is now a museum of social history, with excellent displays on the early history of the colony and the life-style led by its former inmates.

▶▶ Museum of Contemporary Art   38D3

140 George Street, The Rocks

The rather forbidding-looking brown sandstone building facing Circular Quay used to be the offices of the Maritime Services Board. Designed at the very end of the art deco period, it is an incongruous setting for the country's major collection of contemporary art.

▶▶ Museum of Sydney   38D3

Corner of Bridge and Phillip streets

Built on the site of the first (1788) Government House, this museum offers a portrayal of life in colonial Australia. The house was demolished in 1846, but excavations have revealed the foundations, part of which can be viewed through the paving. Using state-of-the-art technology, the museum takes you on a journey of discovery—from the story of the local Aborigines to the Sydney of the 19th century. One of the museum's highlights is outside in the forecourt. The "Edge of the Trees" sculpture consists of poles, some of which "speak," representing Sydney's original inhabitants and the early settlers.

OBSERVATORY HILL AND SYDNEY OBSERVATORY
With commanding views over the harbor, Millers Point was the site of a citadel, a windmill, and then an observatory. The latter survives, established in 1858 to survey the hitherto unknown southern skies, and functioned until 1982. With its time-ball tower and domes, the observatory building has now been renovated as a museum of astronomy with plenty of intriguing hands-on features.

45

Sydney Observatory, a colonial building constructed from the local sandstone

One of the great privileges of life in Sydney is excellent access to the beaches of the Harbour and the Pacific Ocean. Astonishingly, until the early years of this century swimming during daylight hours was prohibited by "decency laws." Then, finally, the flamboyant editor of a Manly newspaper strolled fully clad into the surf in the middle of the day, defying the prosecution that, in fact, was never made.

CHECK BEFORE YOU SWIM

Few big cities are entirely free of water pollution problems, and some of Sydney's beaches occasionally suffer contamination by sewage. Measures are taken to remedy the situation, and conditions can be checked locally.

THE HARBOUR BEACHES

These hardly compare with those on the ocean, but there are plenty of good spots for picnicking and sunbathing. On the south shore at Vaucluse are Nielsen Park and Parsley Bay; the north shore has beaches around Manly, as well as Mosman's Obelisk and Balmoral.

Surfers and surfboat crews make good use of Sydney's beaches

To the north, **Manly** is the city's shore resort *par excellence*, "seven miles from Sydney, but a thousand miles from care." Lined with stores, take-out stands, cafés and pubs, a broad concourse called The Corso channels you from the ferry landing to the curving sandy beach with its double line of Norfolk pines facing the ocean. It was here, in 1915, that the art of surfing was born in Australia, and a big surf competition is held here every year. Manly has many other attractions, including the fascinating Oceanworld aquarium and the old Quarantine Station, once used to protect Sydney from contagious diseases, but now open daily for tours.

World-famous **Bondi**, to the south, has another magnificent beach, stretching between two headlands, though its setting of cafés, pubs, and apartment buildings has a tacky look about it. Bondi is suburban and popular, once connected to the center by a famous tramway whose cars would make the final descent to the beach at breakneck speed, giving rise to the expression "to shoot through like a Bondi tram."

Eighteen other beaches, equally fine if less famous, stretch north from Manly up the Warringah Peninsula to delightful Palm Beach. Some, like Narrabeen, are urban in character, while others, like Freshwater and Whale beaches, are still largely undeveloped. Similarly, a string of beaches runs south from Bondi, ending at 6-mile-long Cronulla, the only beach accessible by suburban train.

▶ **Parliament House**   *38C3*
Macquarie Street
Like the nearby Mint building, the home of the New
South Wales legislature was once part of the "Rum"
Hospital that was built in 1816. The Legislative Council
Chamber is a prefabricated iron structure, sent out from
England to serve as a goldfields church. Parliament
House is open to the public, even when in session.

▶▶▶ **Powerhouse Museum**   *38A2*
Harris Street, Ultimo
The cavernous boiler halls and other generous interior
spaces of the old power station and tram depot on the
edge of Darling Harbour are now home to the vast collections of Sydney's Museum of Applied Arts and Sciences.
The array of objects in Australia's largest museum is quite
astonishing. The decorative arts are strongly represented,
as is social history, with stimulating displays on the life of
the local Aborigines, traditional women's work, and
brewing. There are hands-on features as well as audiovisual presentations, sound effects, and holograms.

▶▶ **Queen Victoria Building**   *38C2*
George Street
This many-domed late-Victorian shopping gallery occu-
pying an entire city block was completed in 1898; in recent
years a thorough renovation has restored all of its original
features. With its many levels, stained glass and mosaics,
it is a cathedral to conspicuous consumption.

▶▶▶ **The Rocks**   *38D2*
Named after the sandstone peninsula ending in Dawes
Point, this is the site of Australia's first European settlement. For many years, it had a reputation as a place of
brawling, hard drinking, whoring and villainy, but this
murky past does no harm whatsoever to The Rocks' present status as a tourist mecca (see panel). In fact, the area
has long since been tamed, first by wholesale demolition
of many of its unsanitary dwellings after the outbreak of
bubonic plague in 1900, and then by another swath of
destruction preceding construction of the Harbour Bridge.

▶▶▶ **Royal Botanic Gardens**   *39D4*
These luxuriantly planted 74-acre gardens are the perfect
counterpoint to the high-rise buildings and bustle of the
city center. They benefit enormously from their proximity
to the harbor, looking onto the long curving promenade
of Farm Cove, which is set between twin promontories,
one crowned by the Opera House and the other by Mrs.
Macquarie's Point. Once the site of the first government
farm, the gardens contain a visitor center, the National
Herbarium (with more than a million plant specimens), a
fernery under a slatted steel dome, and the extraordinary
shapes of the Pyramid and Arc greenhouses, which shelter tropical plants from many countries.

▶▶▶ **Sydney Harbour Bridge**   *38E3*
Not just a symbol of Sydney but of Australia itself, the
Harbour Bridge leaps in a great arch between its granite
pylons to span the narrows between Dawes Point and
Milsons Point to the north. Opened in 1932, after almost

*The highly entertaining
Powerhouse Museum is
one of the best places for
kids to visit*

47

THE ROCKS TODAY
The area is now a place to
wander at leisure and
savor the almost medieval
atmosphere—quite
absent elsewhere in
Australia. You may wish to
start your visit at the informative Sydney Visitor
Centre at The Rocks, at
106 George Street.

DE GROOT'S DARK DEED
The opening of the Harbour Bridge on March 19, 1932, was the excuse for the biggest carnival Sydney had yet known, attended by one million people. As the crowds waited for the Labor Premier of N.S.W., Jack Lang, to cut the tape, a uniformed horseman darted forward and slashed the tape with his sword. Irishman Francis de Groot couldn't bear the thought of a socialist politician getting all this glory.

AMP TOWER
The view from the observation deck of this 1,000-foot-high structure—Australia's tallest building—is nothing short of spectacular. With a 360-degree vista that takes in the entire metropolitan area, it's the ideal place to familiarize yourself with Sydney's layout.

A DRAMA OF AN OPERA
In spite of the brilliance of its design, the Sydney Opera House is not an ideal building for opera, with acoustics inferior to those of Melbourne's Arts Centre. A local joke has it that Australia has the world's best opera house, the outside in Sydney, the inside in Melbourne.

The Sydney Harbour Bridge, completed in 1932, still functions as a major link between north and south

nine years of complicated construction, the bridge carries eight traffic lanes, a double-track railroad, a cycleway and a footpath. Its broad deck is the widest in the world and rises 196 feet above water level (the top of the arch is 439 feet up). Since the early 1990s the congestion-prone bridge has been supplemented by the Sydney Harbour Tunnel, which passes beneath the harbor.

There are several ways to 'experience' the bridge—take the footway from Cumberland Station in The Rocks and visit the southeastern pylon's observation platform, or take a thrilling guided walk to the very top with a company called Bridge Climb.

▶▶▶ Sydney Opera House   38E3
Bennelong Point

Once the site of a ramshackle tram terminus, since 1973 Bennelong Point has been crowned by this spectacular building, which is the inspired and outstanding creation of Danish architect Joern Utzon, born in 1918 and educated at the Royal Danish Academy. The construction of this world-famous landmark was plagued by both technical and political problems, leading Utzon to resign from the project before the building's completion. The complex curving shapes of the exterior are spectacular and have been compared to billowing sails, shells, or the hoods of nuns' habits. The elegant, soaring roofs are covered in over a million Swedish ceramic tiles. The interior houses the auditorium of the opera and four other performance spaces, including a concert hall and two conventional theaters, plus restaurants, bars, gift stores, and a library. Outside are large-scale steps and a promenade around the point. (Guided one-hour tours of the interior are available on most days, generally from 9–4, but times vary according to rehearsal schedules.)

Walk

Harborside and history

See map on pages 38–9.

This 3-mile walk gives magnificent harborside views, leads through the splendid botanic gardens, and then returns to Circular Quay past many fine early buildings.

The landward approach to the **Opera House** may lack some of the drama of the waterside approach but is still impressive, made part of the way underneath a canopy, then up gigantically scaled flights of steps. The fine trees of the **Royal Botanic Gardens** and Government House sweep down to the path leading around Farm Cove to the promontory of Mrs. Macquarie's Point, a popular harborside viewpoint. Do not miss the Botanic Gardens Tropical Centre with its "Arc" and "Pyramid" greenhouses.

The bridge leading to the **Art Gallery of New South Wales** over the Cahill Expressway has views over the city and east suburbs. Macquarie Street leads northward, bounded to the west by mostly modern structures, and to the east by an unparalleled sequence of fine historic buildings. Bridge Street penetrates westward, modern buildings vying with old. Macquarie Place makes a green interlude before you reach the 1885 **Customs House**, opposite Circular Quay. This is now the home of the **Djamu Gallery**, with a display of the Australian Museum's collection of indigenous Australian and Pacific art and cultural material.

Walk

Sydney city center and Darling Harbour

See map on pages 38–9.

This walk takes you through tightly built-up streets to the revitalized Darling Harbour and back through the calm and dignity of Hyde Park.

From Martin Place Station, walk to Martin Place, Strand Arcade, and Pitt Street Mall, pedestrian-friendly in their different ways. As you cross Pyrmont Bridge look up to see the monorail and back to enjoy the city skyline.

An amazing array of new and varied facilities clusters around **Darling Harbour**. A rest in the **Chinese Garden** could precede the final leg of this walk: across Dixon Street leading to **Chinatown**, then up into **Hyde Park**, with its splendid avenues of fig trees and the imposing **Anzac Memorial**, from where a visit to the nearby **Australian Museum** is recommended.

The Chinese Garden, designed by landscape architects from China

WHERE TO STAY?

In many ways, it's an advantage to be right in the city center, but Sydney's suburbs offer some excellent alternatives. Kings Cross has a wide range of hotels and price brackets, and is just one train stop from the city center. You can stay on the beach at Bondi, Coogee, and Manly, and the inner east suburb of Double Bay offers sophisticated surroundings—albeit at a price.

Luxury epitomized—one of the city's best hotels

Accommodations

There is a tremendous variety of accommodation in the Sydney area, though the city is not renowned for being cheap, except in the area of backpacker-style lodges. Hotels range from first-rate—like the super Park Hyatt or The Observatory—to modest, and there are also serviced apartments, motels, hostels, campsites, and bed and breakfast accommodation. An important factor is location, since there are places that are extremely remote unless you have a car, and others whose distance from the sights is compensated for by good public transportation links. Advance reservation is advisable for peak vacation periods like Christmas and the January school holidays.

Hotels The city center has an excellent range of first-class hotels, as do a number of inner suburbs like Manly, Kings Cross, and North Sydney. Whatever your price bracket, Manly is worth considering for its vacation atmosphere and its link to the center—by conventional ferry in 30 minutes or in about half that time by JetCat. The heart of town also has medium-priced and budget hotels, with a particular concentration around the Central Railway Station; Kings Cross also has a variety of such places, many of them in streets of relative tranquility.

Budget Kings Cross is a backpacker's paradise, with many lodges in Victoria Street. The scene here is in constant flux, so it is wise to check at the time whether a particular establishment is for you. Demand is often heavy, and it might be a good idea to start your tour of inspection early in the day. There is another cluster of accommodation at Bondi and Coogee—intriguing temporary addresses! The emphasis here is on affordable lodgings, with plenty of places offering rooms with cooking facilities. Bed and breakfast establishments are scattered all over the city. Details are obtainable from a number of agencies (see also Accommmodations and Restaurants on pages 268–281), and again, accessibility is a key factor. Camping sites are a long way out of the city.

Food and drink

Sydney's excellent brasseries and bistros are deservedly popular

Eating out Even more so than in the rest of Australia, eating in Sydney has been revolutionized in recent years, largely because of the huge influx of immigrants. *The Sydney Morning Herald's Good Food Guide* covers no fewer than 50 categories of cuisine, beginning with African and ending with Vietnamese. New restaurants continue to open, ingredients are good and chefs are increasingly skilled, particularly in the popular, internationally acclaimed style of cooking known as "Modern Australian"—a fusion of culinary styles and ingredients. Prices are extremely reasonable. The better restaurants often offer a fixed-price lunchtime menu at a considerable saving. Prices are kept even lower because of the Bring Your Own phenomenon (this, though primarily a feature of cheaper unlicensed restaurants, is sometimes available at licensed establishments). Remember that a small corkage charge may be made. The highest prices are reserved for restaurants that offer something extra, like a harborside setting or a panoramic view.

EXCLUSIVE EATING
Given Sydney's extensive shoreline, there are plenty of expensive restaurants with harborside settings, from The Rocks to Watsons Bay near South Head. The most stunning view is from the restaurants on top of the AMP Tower.

Ethnic restaurants These are scattered all over the city, though there are concentrations in particular neighborhoods that have been settled by different nationalities. Thus **Greek** restaurants cluster around Elizabeth and Liverpool Streets, **Chinese** restaurants are found in Chinatown, **Italian** in Leichhardt and Newtown, and **Vietnamese** in the southwestern suburb of Cabramatta. Restaurants of different kinds keep company in certain parts of town, along Darlinghurst's Oxford Street and on Stanley and Crown Streets in East Sydney, or to the west of the center, along Glebe Point Road, in King Street, Newtown, or Darling Street, Balmain. Manly and Bondi have an array of restaurants, cafés, and take-out facilities.

REFRESHMENTS
Sydney has plenty of cafés featuring excellent Italian-style coffee. The tourist may also be pleasantly surprised at the quality of food and refreshments available at the various museums and galleries.

Drink There is no shortage of places to drink in Sydney. The basic "hotel" or pub is still much in evidence, while others have been renovated and offer a more varied experience, which might well extend to food and entertainment. Farther up the scale of sophistication are the many hotel and cocktail bars; the locally famous **Marble Bar** can be found at the Hilton hotel.

Queen Victoria Building, a shopping wonderland in historic surroundings

THE ROCKS MARKET
A visit to The Rocks on a Saturday or Sunday has the added bonus of the lively market—held in Upper George Street. In addition to the 100 or so stalls that sell jewelry, homewares and unusual gifts, you'll find free entertainment and a carnival atmosphere.

DUTY FREE
Duty- and tax-free merchandise is available to those with an international air ticket, with substantial discounts on electrical goods, jewelry and watches, liquor and perfume. City center outlets are sometimes even cheaper than those at the airport.

Shopping

Sydney's C.B.D. (Central Business District) has all the temptations a shopper might reasonably expect in the center of a metropolitan city. There are department stores like **David Jones** and elegant 19th-century galleries like the **Strand Arcade**, or its modern equivalent, the shopping complex inserted into the lower floors of an office block. With its 200 boutiques and cafés on several levels, the immaculately restored **Queen Victoria Building** (see page 47) is a visitor attraction in its own right.

Souvenir hunting Souvenirs are plentiful in places where tourists congregate. Faced with the problem of what to bring home from Australia (apart from the inevitable stuffed koala or kangaroo—often made in Taiwan), you might consider a stylish Akubra hat or tough outdoor clothing to go with it, like a bush shirt or an oilskin coat. Sheepskin products, opals, or surfing gear are other possibilities. Australians are great readers, and bookstores are well-stocked with a good range of Australiana, albeit quite expensive, while newsagents (newsstands) sell an incredible range of periodicals catering to every taste.

First-rate maps are difficult to come by in Australia, so a visit to the **Travel Bookshop** (Liverpool Street) could be helpful here. Aboriginal artifacts of varying quality— paintings, carvings, boomerangs, fabrics, and didgeri- doos (a large wooden wind instrument)—are widely available, but are better bought from a specialty store than from a souvenir stall. Try the souvenir stores run by the main museums and galleries; the **Australian Museum's** stuffed platypus actually looks like the real thing!

Markets Outside the center, the shopping streets of the more colorful suburbs such as Paddington and Balmain are good places to browse, while Sydney's markets offer a memorable shopping experience. Usually held on a Saturday or Sunday, they take place in The Rocks, Bondi Beach, Balmain, Glebe, Manly, and in Paddington. The famous **Paddy's Market** in the Chinatown area is good for fresh produce, and the vast and lively fish market at Pyrmont is a daily spectacle well worth watching.

Nightlife

Concerts and theater With several auditoriums, the **Opera House** is a major site for classical concerts, ballet and drama. Classical music can also be heard at the **Town Hall** and, performed by student musicians, at the **Conservatorium of Music**. Some 20 theaters offer a choice of musicals, mainstream or alternative plays in a variety of locations, some—like the **Wharf Theatre** (near The Rocks) or **Ensemble Theatre** (on the north shore)—in an attractive waterside setting. A visit to the beautifully restored 1928 **Capitol Theatre** in the Haymarket area is highly recommended. The exciting **Sydney Dance Company** and the **Aboriginal and Islander Dance Theatre** appear at various locations.

Film City center movie theaters show the latest blockbusters, and there are a number of houses specializing in second runs and foreign films in Paddington (Academy Twin) as well as in the center (the two Dendy cinemas). The **State Theatre**, with its extravagant décor, is the home of the city's June Film Festival.

Music Sydney has a lively jazz scene–the best venue is the long-running Basement, near Circular Quazy. Rock is also well represented, with mammoth concerts held in the **Entertainment Centre**. Discos, cabarets and nightclubs abound, catering to all tastes and pockets. There are probably more gays in Sydney than in the rest of Australia put together, with the bars, clubs and pubs of Darlinghurst's Oxford Street the main focus of the gay scene.

INFORMATION
The wealth of distractions available in this exhilarating city are detailed in the Friday edition of *The Sydney Morning Herald*, while various free publications also provide comprehensive entertainment listings. A good way of sampling Sydney's nightlife is to take one of the several guided tours available, although these can be tourist traps.

STAR CITY
Sydney's first, temporary, casino opened in the mid-1990s, and has now moved to its permanent site to the west of Darling Harbour. This vast complex includes a hotel and theater, as well as restaurants, bars, 1,500 poker machines, and 200 gaming tables that offer roulette, blackjack, baccarat, Asian games such as *pai gow* and the Australian favorite, two-up (which is essentially betting on which way two coins will fall).

53

The bright lights of Sydney's Star City casino

THE SYDNEYPASS

This combined ticket gives unlimited bus (including Airport Express, Sydney Explorer, and Bondi & Bay Explorer) and ferry travel for three, five, or seven days, and is a bargain well worth thinking about.

Taxis are numerous, and can be hailed on the street, picked up at a cab rank, or ordered by telephone. Don't get worried if the driver has to consult his street directory!

SYDNEY LIGHT RAIL

Sydney's newest transportation system recreates the days of trams. The Light Rail track runs from Central Station to Chinatown, Darling Harbour, the casino, and the Sydney Fish Market, covering the major city south and west attractions. At peak times trams run every five minutes.

The Monorail

Practical points

Tourist information The following will provide all the help you need: **Sydney Visitor Centre**, 106 George Street, The Rocks (tel: 9255 1788); **Transport Infoline** (tel: 13 1500) for all metropolitan bus, rail, and ferry inquiries.

Getting around Probably the best way of familiarizing yourself with the layout of the city and its sights is to take a guided bus tour, most of which pick up and drop off at central hotels. Alternatives are the bright red **Sydney Explorer**, which trundles around a 19-mile circuit of the principal attractions, allowing you to get on and off at will for a set fare, and the blue **Bondi & Bay Explorer**, which travels to the harborside Eastern Suburbs, Bondi, Bronte and Coogee beaches, and Paddington on the same basis.

Buses run a comprehensive scheduled service in the city center and suburbs. They connect with ferries and trains at Circular Quay and with trains at Wynyard and Central Stations. Airport Express buses run from Circular Quay and a few stops in the center, as well as from Kings Cross, Bondi Beach, Glebe, and Darling Harbour.

Ferries travel at frequent intervals between Circular Quay and a number of destinations such as Manly and Taronga Zoo on the north shore, or Balmain and Hunters Hill upriver. There are also daily ferries east to Double Bay, Rose Bay, and Watsons Bay.

Double-decker electrified trains run on an extensive network of suburban lines as well as on a City Circle linking a number of stations in the C.B.D. such as Town Hall, Central Station, and Circular Quay. There's a useful spur from Central Station and Town Hall to Kings Cross and Bondi Junction (continue by bus to the beach). The line to North Sydney includes a trip over the Harbour Bridge. A novelty is the overhead **Monorail**, which runs between the southwestern part of the city center and Darling Harbour.

What Captain Cook named Port Jackson and Captain Phillip called "the finest harbour in the world" is still alive with freighters, ferries, and pleasure craft. The glorious stretch of water forming the harbor is Sydney, the reason for the city's existence, the source of its distinct identity and special glamor.

One of the world's largest harbors Sydney Harbour has a complex outline of inlets, tributary rivers, bays, coves, and promontories, so that many city residents have some sight of the water from where they live, though competition is fierce and prices astronomical for those dwellings that enjoy the best views. Much of the 150 miles of shoreline has been preserved as national park land. Added interest is given by an array of islands, including Fort Denison, where the skeletons of the executed once swung, and Goat Island with its old shipyards west of the Harbour Bridge.

How to explore Undoubtedly, the best way to explore the harbor would be an unhurried cruise, taking all day, on a friend's yacht! Water taxis would do the same kind of job, albeit expensively. The variety of commercial cruises are a more realistic choice. But perhaps the most authentic way, enjoyed everyday by many city commuters, is the ferry. Now that the tramcar has all but vanished from the streets, the ferry is the city's only remaining traditional means of conveyance.

An assortment of vessels plies Sydney Harbour from the central hub of Circular Quay. In a matter of minutes you can slip across the water in the shadow of the Harbour Bridge to Kirribilli, or chug upstream in the afternoon with uniformed schoolchildren returning to their pleasant suburban homes on the promontory of Hunters Hill. Or you could take the 50-minute journey by RiverCat upriver, via Sydney Olympic Park, to the historic city of Parramatta, where you can see some of Australia's very first buildings (see pages 60–61).

The magnificent harbor and its twin symbols of Sydney—and Australia

A STROLL AROUND THE ROCKS
The Museum of Contemporary Art contrasts with Cadman's Cottage of 1816 and the other old buildings above it in well-restored George Street, where the visitor center dispenses useful information. Old and new come together around Campbells Cove, while Dawes Point Park, crouching at the feet of the Harbour Bridge, was the first fortified position in Australia. The way back is via the high-level Gloucester Walk and Argyle Street.

The Blue Mountains Drive

Palm Beach and West Head Drive

56

E

Ebenezer

Cattai National Park

Cattai

Hawkesbury Heritage Farm

Wilberforce

Freemans Reach

Maraylya

Glenorie

Arcadia

Butterfly Farm

Pitt Town

Hawkesbury

North Richmond

Richmond

Galston

Windsor

Mulgrave

John Tebutt Observatories

Vineyard

Box Hill

Agnes Banks

Rouse Hill

Round Corner

D

Castlereagh

Schofields

Kellyville

Castle Hill

South Creek

Marsden Park

Quakers Hill

Baulkham Hills

Featherdale Wildlife Park

HILLS MOTORWAY

Emu Plains

Penrith

St Marys

Doonside

Seven Hills

Northmead

Old Government House

C

Panthers World of Entertainment

Rooty Hill

Blacktown

Eastern Creek

Pendle Hill

Parramatta

GREAT WESTERN HIGHWAY

Wonderland Sydney

Blue Mountains, Wentworth Falls, Cliff Drive, Echo Point, Govett's Leap Lookout

4

WESTERN MOTORWAY

The Australian Wildlife Park

Prospect Reservoir

Experiment Farm Cottage and Elizabeth Farm

Merrylands

Guildford

Erskine Park

Prospect Creek

Smithfield

Fairfield

Chester Hill

Cecil Park

Cabramatta

31

B

Kemps Creek

Wallacia

Bonnyrigg

Warragamba

Luddenham

Badgerys Creek

Warwick Farm Racecourse

Liverpool

Milperra

Hoxton Park

SOUTH WESTERN

East Hills

Rossmore

Bringelly

Glenfield

Harris Creek

A

5

Nepean

Ingleburn

Military Reserve

Lucas Heights

0   5   10 km

Gledswood Homestead

31

HUME HIGHWAY

SOUTH WESTERN FREEWAY

Minto

George's

Minto Heights

0   5 miles

Australiana Park

1

2   Southern Highlands

Campbelltown

3

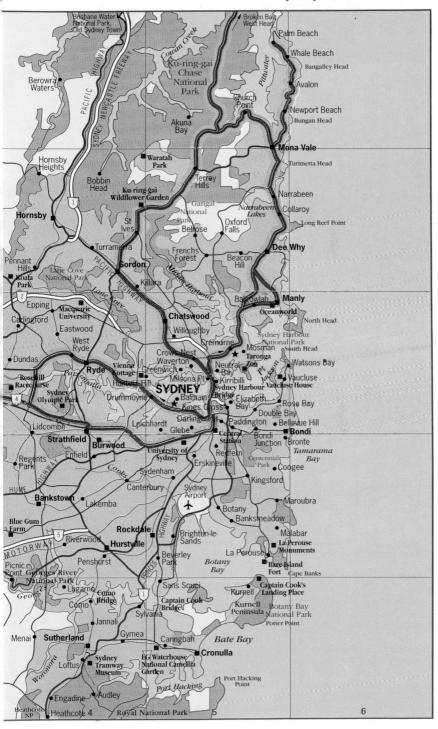

Drive

The famous Three Sisters pillars

58

The Blue Mountains

See map on pages 56–57.

The truly spectacular cliffs, canyons, and forests of the Blue Mountains can be seen in a day trip.

The fastest exit from Sydney is via Parramatta Road, which connects to the Western Motorway near Strathfield. The route then crosses the plain past Penrith to begin the climb up into the mountains, running parallel to the railroad. Several places of interest are marked by signs off the freeway; these are described below.

Wentworth Falls are probably the grandest waterfalls in the region. Pretty little Leura marks the start of the **Cliff Drive**, which skirts the 984-foot drop into the valley below. **Echo Point** is, deservedly, the most famous viewpoint in the mountains. Not far from the visitor center, viewing platforms offer panoramas over cliffs, eucalyptus forest and the Three Sisters sandstone columns. There are designated walks from here, or you can ride the Scenic Railway or Scenic Skyway further along the Cliff Drive.

Stops can be made at Katoomba, "capital" of the Blue Mountains, and northeast of Blackheath at the Blue Mountains Heritage Centre. **Govett's Leap Lookout** offers amazing views of the canyon.

Return on the Western Motorway, via Parramatta and Homebush Bay, where you will see the main venue for the 2000 Olympics—**Sydney Olympic Park**. The International Aquatic Centre and some of the other sporting facilities are open to the public, and informative bus and walking tours of the impressive site are available.

Drive

Palm Beach and West Head

This drive goes from Sydney to the splendid Northern Beaches and headlands. *See map on pages 56–57.*

Beyond the Harbour Bridge, Route 14 (Military Road) leads northeastward, crossing Middle Harbour by the Spit Bridge. A detour can be made to Manly (better visited by ferry from Circular Quay), or continue northward past the fine beaches of Long Reef, Collaroy, Narrabeen and Whale Beach.

The road narrows and winds as it approaches **Palm Beach**. To the west are fine views over the Pittwater inlet, a contrast to the crashing surf of the ocean beach to the east. On its headland to the north, is the **Barrenjoey Lighthouse**.

Return to Mona Vale and follow the road around the southern end of Pittwater, turning right through the greenery of the **Ku-ring-gai Chase National Park** to **West Head**. The head offers a completely different but equally spectacular view over Pittwater and Broken Bay. There are many well-marked trails through this section of the national park, and it is a short walk to see bushland, Aboriginal paintings, and perhaps some wildlife.

Return via Mona Vale Road (Route 3) and the Pacific Highway.

The suburbs

There is a great deal to see and do in the various historic inner suburbs of the city.

Sydneysiders seem proud of the red-light district of **Kings Cross►►**, which has its fair share of hookers, strip joints, and adult bookshops. But there are also lots of places to eat and drink and plenty of shops for the local community. A stroll along Darlinghurst Road between Kings Cross Station and Fitzroy Gardens with its El Alamein Fountain is sure to entertain day or night. The genteel, neighboring suburb of Elizabeth Bay holds a contrasting attraction—1830s **Elizabeth Bay House►**. This elegant mansion, built for the N.S.W. Colonial Secretary, stands as a reminder of the area's 19th-century opulence.

Built in the heady days of the Victorian-era gold rush, then proletarian and now gentrified, **Paddington►►**, or "Paddo," has had a checkered career as it has passed in and out of favor. Its glory is its delicious row houses with their fine ironwork and their subtle adaptation to the contours of the slopes falling northward toward the harbor. Built between the 1860s and 1890s, most have been carefully restored. Also here are **Juniper Hall** (1824), the **post office** (1885), and **Paddington Town Hall** (1891). Opened to mark Sydney's 100th birthday, **Centennial Park** supports a varied birdlife as well as offering outdoor activities.

The population of **Balmain►** used to work in its shipyards, but its delightful terraces and little detached timber cottages have been colonized by a middle-class population generally more left-leaning and artistically inclined than Paddington's inhabitants.

Hunters Hill► is a tranquil place of expensive, fine stone houses and humbler cottages. Many of the former were built in French style in the 1850s. One of the 19th-century tradesmen's abodes, Vienna Cottage, has been restored by the National Trust and houses a local museum.

SYDNEY JEWISH MUSEUM
A short stroll from Kings Cross brings a very different experience. The excellent Sydney Jewish Museum (corner of Darlinghurst Road and Burton Street, Darlinghurst) traces Australia's Jewish connections, from the First Fleet convicts to post-World War II arrivals, and serves as a poignant memorial to the millions of Jews who perished in the Holocaust.

EASTERN SUBURBS
Sydney's Eastern Suburbs are the country's most desirable and expensive real estate and at Double Bay it shows, with plenty of designer labels and a discreet lack of price tags in its exclusive shops. There are lots of pleasant cafés too, where shoppers can be seen relaxing after making their choices.

See how the other half lives in exclusive Hunters Hill

UP THE HAWKESBURY

The area around Richmond and Windsor along the upper reaches of the Hawkesbury River was settled within a few years of the arrival of the First Fleet. The winding lower river is best explored in a leisurely way; a unique experience is to board the mail boat at Brooklyn and accompany the letters, packages and much more on their journey to isolated little places along the tranquil river.

THE LOSS OF LA PEROUSE

Jean-François de Galaup, Comte de La Perouse, had brushed with the British before his meeting in Botany Bay with Captain Phillip. He was taken prisoner after the battle of Quiberon Bay in 1759 and later fought in the American wars. His ships *Astrolabe* and *Boussole* had reached Australia after a long search for the elusive North West Passage. On quitting Botany Bay La Perouse disappeared for ever, though wreckage assumed to be that of his ships was discovered off the New Hebrides in 1826.

Captain Cook's landing place memorial

Excursions

Easy-to-reach sights from Sydney are covered alphabetically on these two pages.

Broad **Botany Bay►** (7 miles south of the center), where Captain Cook's *Endeavour* dropped anchor on April 28, 1770, was given its name in recognition of the array of Antipodean plants collected here by Joseph Banks. Oil installations, industry, and the airport now dominate the scene, but to commemorate Cook's historic landing on the Kurnell Peninsula, the national park contains monuments, a visitor center, and a museum. At the northern edge of the bay, La Perouse, named after the commander of the French expedition that arrived just after the First Fleet, is the site of a museum and one of Sydney's principal Aboriginal settlements.

With splendid coastal and river scenery, **Brisbane Water National Park►** (47 miles north) resembles Ku-ring-gai Chase, its sandstone foundation supporting the same spectacular range of flowers and wildlife. There are woodlands of eucalyptus and pockets of rain forest, and Aboriginal carvings can be viewed at the Bulgandry site.

A visit to Parramatta (by road—see page 61) can easily encompass a tour of **Homebush Bay►►** and Sydney Olympic Park—the main site for the 2000 Olympic Games (see page 58).

Ku-ring-gai Chase National Park►► (19 miles north of Sydney) remains in its wild state thanks to its designation as a national park as far back as 1894. The rugged sandstone plateau is deeply incised by the deep sheltered waterways of the Hawkesbury River. From West Head there are spectacular views across Broken Bay and the broad expanse of Pittwater. The Ku-ring-gai (Guringai) Aborigines who once lived here traced many carvings in the sandstone. There is a useful visitor center at Bobbin Head, with interesting displays on the area's varied animal and bird populations.

A short train ride away from today's glittering metropolis is the meticulously researched reconstruction of **Old Sydney Town►►** (stop at Gosford Station), showing what life might have been like as the city struggled to establish itself. Among buildings that re-create the atmosphere of the pre-1810 period, characters in authentic costume ply their trades, fight duels, or endure the barbaric punishments prescribed by harsh judges. At the very tip of the Warringah Peninsula, 25 miles north of the city center, lies the exclusive residential area of **Palm Beach►►**. To the east, the ocean surf crashes on the beach, and to the west the tranquil surface of the beautiful **Pittwater** inlet is a windsurfers' paradise. The lighthouse on Barrenjoey headland offers a terrific view over Broken Bay and inland up the drowned valley of the Hawkesbury River.

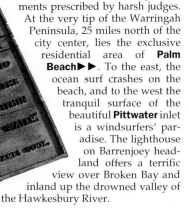

A room inside 1835 Experiment Farm Cottage, Parramatta

Parramatta▶ ▶ was founded only a matter of months after Sydney itself, because of the fertility of the surrounding area. Now the focal point of the sprawling western suburbs 15 miles from the city center, it has been redeveloped, although many traces remain of early days, including some of the nation's very first buildings.

Beyond the mock-Tudor gatehouse to Parramatta Park stands Australia's most venerable public edifice, **Old Government House**, which was built in 1799 though much expanded early in the 19th century. For many years the official Vice-Regal residence, it contains early Australian furniture. **Elizabeth Farm** in Alice Street is even older, begun in 1793 by the agricultural pioneers John and Elizabeth Macarthur. Its veranda is the prototype of countless others that adorn dwellings all over Australia. It too has been refurnished in the style of that period, as has the interior of **Experiment Farm Cottage** in Ruse Street. The land on which this house stands belonged to one of the few convicts with any farming experience; in 1789, James Ruse was the first man in Australia to sow a crop of wheat successfully.

Australia's first national park, proclaimed in 1879, the **Royal National Park**▶ ▶ consists mostly of a rugged sandstone plateau with a varied vegetation of heathland (which has a brilliant show of wildflowers in spring), fine forests of blue gum, and patches of rain forest. Eaten into by the sea, the park has a coastline of spectacular cliffs interspersed with sandy coves. About 22 miles from Sydney, it has long been a favorite of serious bushwalkers, and is now a popular place to go for weekend outings of all kinds.

Reached by ferry from Circular Quay, the splendid **Taronga Zoo**▶ ▶ benefits from its superb site almost directly opposite the city center and is worth visiting for the view alone, particularly if you take the cable-car ride. Taronga doesn't limit itself to native animals, but it is the Australian fauna that most visitors want to see.

THE ROAD TO PARRAMATTA
A road was built from Sydney to Parramatta as early as 1794, but for years it was easier to bring people and goods up the river than along the highway. Partly superseded by an expressway, today's Parramatta Road is neither lovely nor efficient, though a trip along it reveals a cross section of Australian suburbia. In spite of interminable traffic lights and shabby shopping centers, there remains something indefinably romantic about it, a whiff of the days when it alone pointed to the interior of the unknown continent.

Sunset on Black Mountain, Canberra, capped by the Telstra Tower

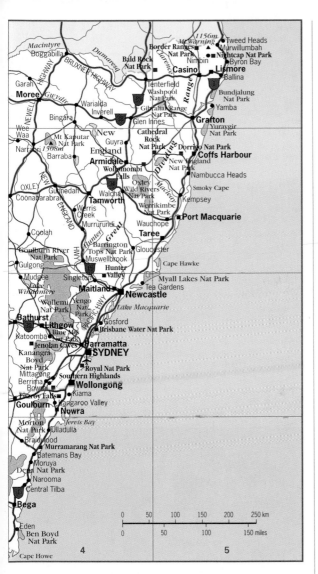

NEW SOUTH WALES This state *was* Australia in the early days of European settlement. Today it is still the country's most populous state, and its capital, Sydney, is the country's greatest city. If time is short, some travel planners advise tourists to concentrate on this state alone; a vacation spent entirely within New South Wales' far-flung borders can be very rewarding for both urban pleasures and the delights of wild nature.

THE COASTAL LOWLANDS The "Premier State" can be divided into four regions, which encompass many facets of the Australian experience. Most of the population lives in the Coastal Lowlands, a fertile strip of country of varying width running some 870 miles from Victoria to Queensland. Apart from glamorous Sydney, the region is

CLINGING TO THE COAST
Between them, the cities of Sydney, Newcastle, and Wollongong are home to around 4.5 million people—a very large proportion of the state's 6.3 million. The remainder of the population lives mostly in coastal towns, far from the inhospitable interior.

home to the industrial cities of **Newcastle** and **Wollongong**, as well as a glorious chain of little ports and shore settlements like Ulladulla (directly east of Canberra). White Australia's history began here, when Captain Cook's charts led the First Fleet to Botany Bay, and where, after a shaky start, the process of colonization gradually got under way with the founding of townships and the clearing of the bush for farmland.

The area has also been the focus of much of the country's modern history, its industrial heartland and stronghold of the Labor movement that has played an often decisive role in Australian government and politics. It is here that the foundation was laid for Australian beach culture, as love of the sun, surf and sheer physical well-being overcame the remnants of Victorian prudery in the early decades of this century—a process that owed much to the incomparable beaches, which are still one of the state's main tourist attractions.

THE GREAT DIVIDING RANGE In places the Great Dividing Range drops almost directly into the sea. It provides a constant backdrop to the coast, with its hill peaks and tablelands also running the length of the state. Despite their low altitude, the forested hills remained an impregnable barrier to exploration until 1813, when the spectacular **Blue Mountains** were successfully crossed for the first time.

The highlands are as wonderfully varied as the coast: to the south, in the Snowy Mountains, they include the country's highest peaks and most extensive snowfields; to the north lies the high-level plateau of New England, named after the old country for its misty cooolness and vivid green. In places, as in the **Southern Highlands**, the

WHAT'S IN A NAME?
Between 1768 when he set out for Tahiti, and 1779 when he was hacked to pieces on a Hawaiian beach, Captain Cook probably named more places than anyone else in history. Some recall people (Port Jackson), some are a lively evocation of events (Cape Tribulation, where Cook's ship was holed by a reef), some characterize a quirk of topography (Mount Dromedary in Tasmania has two humps). Inspiration seems to have failed him when confronted with the task of finding a suitable name for the whole of the eastern coast of Australia, even given the supposed resemblance of part of it to the coastline of southern Wales. But perhaps New South Wales, as a name, is one up on such masterpieces of inventiveness as South Australia.

ranges are interspersed with broad plains that were converted early on into attractive farmland. Here there is a wealth of old buildings in town and country, as well as a 965-square-mile tract carved out of the state to form the Australian Capital Territory (A.C.T.), the site of the nation's capital, Canberra.

Most of the rivers of southeastern Australia have their source in the uplands, with their relatively abundant rain and snowfall. Some, like the Hawkesbury and Hunter, are quite short, running east to the Pacific; others, much longer, form part of the huge Murray/Darling system, flowing slowly westward.

THE WESTERN SLOPES Beyond the mountains and tablelands, the Western Slopes fall gradually toward the interior. Settled in the early 1800s, the area today consists mostly of unspectacular wheat and wool country, and there are several substantial towns and even small cities in this region such as Moree, Dubbo, Orange, Wellington, Bathurst, and Wagga Wagga. To the south, in the Riverina, the waters of the Murray and Murrumbidgee have been used to create huge irrigated areas that now support a variety of crops.

65

THE WESTERN PLAINS This area stretches to the borders with South Australia and Queensland. It is the New South Wales Outback, with vastly more sheep than people. Here the township of **Bourke** has given its name ("back of Bourke") to utter remoteness, the Outback beyond the Outback. In the harsh landscape, the city of **Broken Hill** has grown up based on the world's richest lode of silver, lead and zinc; it is a place that attracts many visitors for its sheer strangeness.

Attractive Canberra, a modern planned city that is like nowhere else in Australia

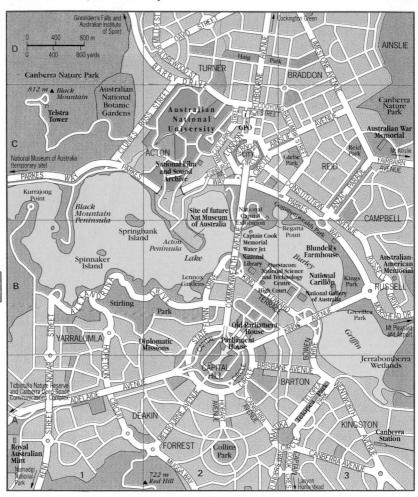

Canberra

The home of foreign embassies

Australia's capital comprises the prestigious buildings that house the nation's central institutions, all in a setting of broad boulevards and cozy neighborhoods and framed by glorious mountain scenery. As well as being the country's only major inland city, Canberra is unique in having been planned in every detail from its very beginnings.

At the time of Federation, in 1901, the bitter dispute between Sydney and Melbourne about which should become the country's capital was finally resolved by choosing neither. Instead, the new Constitution stipulated that a site should be found in New South Wales, no closer than 100 miles to Sydney. After much debate the present location was chosen, and in 1911 some 965 square miles of land south of the Goulburn Plains became the Australian Capital Territory. Over 130 hopefuls took part in the international competition for the design of the new city, the American landscape architect Walter Burley Griffin, a pupil of Frank Lloyd Wright, emerging as winner.

Griffin had never seen Canberra when he drew up his plans for a new city thousands of miles from his Chicago base, but his experience enabled him to interpret maps and diagrams, and to appreciate the potential of the chosen location. His design is very much of his period, a combination of great vistas framing noble buildings, and self-contained residential neighborhoods.

The target population for the country's capital was 25,000, but Canberra's growth was painfully slow and this total was only reached in the years following World War II. Growth took off in the 1960s, and today the city is home to over 300,000 people. Around half of its workforce has always consisted of public employees, not necessarily a sound basis for a satisfactory social balance. In its infancy and adolescence, the city was seen as a place of exile, populated by bored civil servants longing for the fleshpots of Sydney or Melbourne. Nor is its contemporary image among Australians a particularly happy one; many think of it as a privileged place of parasitic politicians and cosseted bureaucrats. In recent years, though, Canberra's dining, entertainments, and nightlife scene have become far more lively than they used to be.

The city of Canberra has been described with some truth as a collection of suburbs in search of a city, but what it lacks in urbanity it more than makes up for with easy access to national parks, wildlife, wineries, sheer spacious beauty, and convenience (there are no gridlocks!). It certainly is nothing like any other city in Australia and is well worth visiting for that reason alone, with an array of splendid modern buildings in the immaculately landscaped setting planned for them in the early years of the nation's foundation.

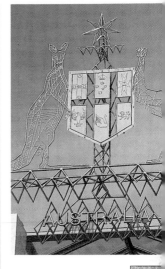

The extraordinary Parliament House (completed in 1988) is rich in national symbolism

67

The 266-foot flagpole on top of Parliament House and Capital Hill

▶▶ Australian National Botanic Gardens   66C1

These attractive gardens situated on the lower slopes of Black Mountain present a wonderful range of native Australian plants—some 6,000 species in all. A network of paths leads through a series of contrasting environments, each with its fully labeled array of trees, shrubs, and other plants. This is *the* place to appreciate Australia's flora.

▶▶▶ Australian War Memorial   66C3

Limestone Avenue, Campbell

Flanked by massive stone pylons, the dome of the War Memorial stares somberly from the lower slopes of Mount Ainslie down Anzac Parade toward Capital Hill on the far shore of Lake Burley Griffin. With its great courtyard containing the Roll of Honour and the Eternal Flame, it was opened in 1941 and redeveloped in 1998/1999. It is not just a great monument, but a world-class museum that attempts to make some sense of the senselessness of war. Beyond the carefully crafted symbolism of the exterior are extensive galleries and displays evoking the many conflicts in which the country has been involved, from the Maori Wars of the 1860s to 1970s Vietnam. As well as the hardware of war, such as guns and airplanes, there are superb paintings, photographs, huge dioramas, film and sound recordings, and documents and papers.

▶ Diplomatic Missions   66B2

One of the most fascinating tours in Canberra is to the suburb of Yarralumla. Here many foreign countries have built their embassies, free from any of the constraints of fitting into a long-established city. National self-expression takes a variety of forms: the American embassy is a handsome, Williamsburg-style edifice, Greece's has classical columns, that for Papua New Guinea has an exuberantly gabled longhouse, and Indonesia's has a Balinese temple for its diplomats.

▶▶ Lake Burley Griffin   66B2

Burley Griffin included a beautiful lake in his visionary plan for the new city, but it was not until 1964 that the great body of water bearing his name came into being, with an area of more than 23 square miles and a varied shoreline 22 miles long. A number of islands enliven the scene, which is further enhanced by lakeside landscaping, as in the **Commonwealth Park**. The **Captain Cook Memorial Jet** waterspout reaches 460 feet in calm weather.

Dating from 1860, **Blundell's Farmhouse** near the lakeshore is one of the few old buildings in Canberra. Rising over the weeping willows on Aspen Island are the crisp white concrete shafts of the **National Carillon**, a gift from Britain to mark Canberra's 50th anniversary in 1963. Its 53 bells play Australian melodies as well as hymns and popular songs. Designed to be the focal point of this city, the lake makes a splendid setting for many of its most prominent buildings; an excursion aboard one of the cruise vessels is a pleasant way to make the most of it.

The slender **Australian-American Memorial** close to the lake's eastern shore, commemorates the role that American forces played in the defense of Australia during World War II.

A CAPITAL MUSEUM
The National Museum of Australia, which is expected to open in 2001, is still in the early stages of development. Its plans are presented in a visitor center on Lady Denman Drive, Yarralumla, and some exhibitions are now being held in Old Parliament House.

An Aussie "digger" (soldier) runs up the flag outside the Australian War Memorial

►► National Capital Exhibition   66C2
Regatta Point, Commonwealth Park
Boasting "the best view of the national capital," this is a good place for appreciating the meticulous and sometimes controversial planning of the new city. The exhibition features models, plans, photographs, and audiovisual displays.

► National Film and Sound Archive   66C2
McCoy Circuit, Acton
Australia was an early leader in the development of the motion picture, and this center presents an intriguing selection from the nation's contribution to the delights of the silver screen, including a short film of the 1896 Melbourne Cup. Radio and T.V. are also represented.

►►► National Gallery of Australia   66B3
Parkes Place
The national art collections are housed in an imposing structure of sandblasted concrete. Its neighbors on the banks of Lake Burley Griffin are also of national significance, like the glass and concrete cube of the High Court. The National Gallery has an excellent array of Australian art, beginning with Aboriginal artifacts and ending with canvases on which the paint seems hardly dry. There is much else besides, displayed to advantage in well-lit and varied spaces, including a good selection of European and American art—particularly of the 20th century—as well as works from Asia and the Pacific. Sculpture benefits from the attractive setting of the Sculpture Garden, which also serves as a venue for outdoor events.

The National Botanic Gardens are renowned for their splendid collection of Australian native plants

CAPITAL VIEWS
Canberra's ring of uplands provides splendid viewpoints over the carefully planned city in its superb setting. The spike of Telstra Tower rises from the top of Black Mountain (2,664 feet), giving panoramic vistas from its viewing galleries. Mount Ainslie (2,762 feet) rises through bushland behind the War Memorial and has equally spectacular views, as does Red Hill, 1¼ miles south of Parliament House.

Parliament House, one of Canberra's most popular attractions

CAPITAL COINAGE
As well as a gallery enabling visitors to see the country's money being made, the Royal Australian Mint has a public coining press where you can mint your own coins or tokens.

CAPITAL PUNISHMENT
Justice has moved on in Australia since the early days when the jail was sometimes the most prominent building in town, but modern Australians are second only to Americans in their fondness for litigation. The imposing High Court has an exhibition explaining the workings of the country's legal system.

A SPORTING CAPITAL
Sports fans should not miss a tour of the Australian Institute of Sport (A.I.S.) in the northern suburb of Bruce. The institute, set up in 1980, features top-class facilities and an interesting Visitors Centre with displays and entertaining hands-on exhibits. Tours are conducted by the A.I.S.'s élite athletes.

▶ **National Library of Australia**   *66B2*
Parkes Place
In addition to several million books, this rather severe neo-classical building houses other unique collections relating to the history and evolution of Australia. The interior is adorned with fine tapestries and stained glass.

▶▶ **Old Parliament House**   *66B2*
King George Terrace
This beautifully renovated 1927 building, made redundant by its much larger replacement in 1988 (see below), is now the home of the **National Portrait Gallery**, a collection of likenesses of famous and lesser-known Australians. There is a guided tour round the building, and you can also watch an intriguing sound and light presentation, appropriately entitled "Order! Order!."

▶▶▶ **Parliament House**   *66B2*
Capital Hill
The truly spectacular structure of Parliament House was completed in time for Australia's Bicentenary in 1988. Home to the House of Representatives and the Senate, it has also become a major visitor attraction in its own right, rich in artworks and national symbolism. Over three million cubic feet of soil was removed from the top of Capital Hill to make way for the new building, then replaced to form its green roof. This superb viewpoint over the city is topped by a 266-foot flagstaff of stainless steel flying what must be the biggest flag in the world. Below is a complex of beautifully designed internal spaces, adorned with the creations of Australian artists like Arthur Boyd, whose gloriously colorful tapestry graces the far wall of the Great Hall. The 48 marble columns of the foyer recall the country's eucalyptus trees, whose cool green color appears again in the chamber of the House of Representatives.

▶▶ **Questacon**   *66B2*
King Edward Terrace
The National Science and Technology Centre in its exciting modern building has around 200 hands-on displays in six different galleries. This informative and interactive center brings the world of science alive, to even the most non-technical, and is worth an extended visit.

By air A comprehensive network of international and domestic air services operates from Sydney's Kingsford Smith Airport, 7 miles south of the city center. Buses and taxis link the separate domestic and international terminals. As of 2000, they will also be connected by the new Airport Link Railway, which will transport passengers to the city's Central Station in 8–10 minutes. The frequent Airport Express buses are currently the most economical way to reach the city center and inner suburbs. There are flights to the N.S.W. Outback and many coastal resorts, to Cooma (for the Snowy Mountains) and to Canberra.

By bus The network of long-distance bus services is far-flung, although schedules can be inconvenient to remote townships. On the main routes there is likely to be a choice of operator and times. Many places can be visited by organized bus tours from Sydney. Most major towns have a well-developed network of local bus services.

By train N.S.W. has a widespread rail network, and of those towns that have lost their train service, many are connected to a railhead by Countrylink buses operated by the State Rail Authority (Countrylink). Multiple-unit express trains (XPTs and XPLORERS) ply between many major towns. Interstate trains run to Brisbane and Melbourne, and the legendary *Ghan* now runs from Sydney to Alice Springs via Adelaide. Broken Hill is visited by the *Indian Pacific* on its way to and from Western Australia, and has its own weekly XPT link to Sydney. The Greater Sydney region is well served by frequent CityRail services, which extend as far as Newcastle and Dungog in the north, the Blue Mountains in the west, Goulburn and the Southern Highlands, and Nowra on the south coast.

By car Driving is not recommended in the Sydney area, unless you are heading out of town to places like Palm Beach or the Royal National Park. Here, public transportation and the occasional taxi should get you anywhere you are likely to want to go. However, many remote parts of the state are accessible only by car.

SAVE TIME AND FLY
Unless you have plenty of time to spare and are happy to drive, flying to the more distant parts of the state is highly recommended. Qantas, Ansett, and their subsidiaries cover most major N.S.W. destinations.

A LONG WAY BY CAR
New South Wales is comprehensively crisscrossed by a web of named highways, very helpful in planning an itinerary, though they tend to be of variable quality. Driving the Pacific Highway north along the coast can get tedious, and many prefer the inland and more scenic New England Highway.

71

Renting a 4WD makes sense if you plan to go off road

One of the grand old buildings in the pleasant city of Bathurst

THE WAY TO THE WEST
Just visible from Sydney, the dark escarpment of the Blue Mountains, which rises abruptly (the highest point, near Mount Victoria, is just over 3,500 feet) from the Sydney plains, blocked the way westward to the early colonists. Some convict escapees were convinced that China lay just beyond the mountains as they headed toward what they hoped would be freedom. The puzzle of how to cross the mountains, by keeping to the ridges rather than to the valleys, was solved by Blaxland, Lawson, and Wentworth in 1813, and within two years Governor Macquarie had a road built by convict labor on the route still followed by the modern road and railroad. This marked a great leap forward in the development of the colony, promising an opening up of the immense potential of the then unknown interior.

▶▶ **Armidale**   63C4
Unofficial capital of the cool uplands of New England in the northeast of the state, Armidale is the nearest thing Australia has to a university city. There are a number of higher education colleges and several private schools as well as the University of New England in its parkland campus. A couple of cathedrals, plus a number of venerable public buildings and delightful old houses further enhance the refined atmosphere. The modern **New England Regional Art Museum**▶ has a reputation as the best provincial collection of Australian art, and there is a Folk Museum housed in a building dating from 1863.
   Armidale is the ideal base for exploring this part of New England (whose Scottish settlers tried and failed to make the name New Caledonia stick); within easy reach are a number of spectacular waterfalls, including the highest in Australia, **Wollomombi Falls**▶ in the Oxley Wild Rivers National Park.

▶ **Batemans Bay**   63A4
This fishing port and popular tourist resort on the estuary of the Clyde River is the closest open beach to Canberra, only 93 miles away over the mountains. There are fine oysters and lobsters, and a penguin colony on the Tollgate Islands Nature Reserve.

▶▶ **Bathurst**   63B4
At the end of the Great Western Highway from Sydney, Bathurst was founded by Governor Macquarie in 1815, making it the country's oldest inland settlement. It was the point of departure for many expeditions farther into the interior, and in 1851 this area was the scene of Australia's first gold rush. Those days are recreated in the open-air museum called **Bathurst Goldfields**, and the town itself is full of interest. The scenic drive around Mount Panorama forms part of what is considered to be Australia's finest motor-racing circuit.

▶▶▶ **Blue Mountains National Park**   63B4
Sheer cliffs dropping into deep canyons and glorious eucalyptus forests make up some of the most spectacular landscapes to be seen in Australia. The grandeur of the natural scene is all the more impressive because of the proximity of the manicured residential and retirement areas clustered along the main road and railroad from Sydney, 90 minutes away.
   The Blue Mountains are not really mountains, but a vast sandstone tableland, deeply incised by watercourses like the Nepean and Cox's rivers. Their color is real, however, as a vaporous emanation from the leaves of the eucalypts hangs in the air as a blue haze. Since the early part of this century the mountains have attracted serious bushwalkers as well as sightseers, and they offer all kinds of pleasures today, from antiques hunting in sophisticated little townships, to real escape into wild country. The following main sights could just about be seen in the course of a day trip from Sydney, but it would be far better to stay at least a couple of days.
   A good place to start is at the excellent **National Parks and Wildlife Service's Heritage Centre**▶ 1¼ miles to the east of the main highway at Blackheath. A short distance

away is one of the most spectacular lookouts in the whole National Park, **Govett's Leap**▶▶, with views of the Grose Valley and Bridal Veil Falls. A panoramic walk leads along the clifftop to other vantage points, while a steep track (for experienced hikers) descends into the forest of blue gums far below.

The other great viewpoint in the park is **Echo Point**▶▶ just to the south of **Katoomba**, the "capital" of the municipality known as City of the Blue Mountains. Here there is another visitor center whose glass wall looks straight out into the treetops, while projecting platforms give giddy views of the famous sandstone pillars of **The Three Sisters**. A number of popular walks fringe the clifftop or descend into the valley. Just to the west are two exciting forms of tourist transportation, the Skyway, a cable car dangling over the abyss, and the Scenic Railway, a modernized inclined plane dropping steeply into the valley bottom.

To the east are the famous **Wentworth Falls**▶▶, the highest in the area with a drop of 886 feet. Wentworth Falls village is the location of the charming 1888 house, Yester Grange, now containing tearooms and period antiques; nearby Faulconbridge is the home of the **Norman Lindsay Gallery and Museum**▶, which commemorates this well-known artist and writer. Westward are the truly spectacular **Jenolan Caves**▶▶ and the charming late-Victorian guesthouse associated with them, while one of the country's great feats of railroad engineering, the **Zig Zag Railway**▶ (see panel) can be experienced first-hand at Clarence, near Lithgow.

Dramatic sandstone cliffs and densely forested valleys around Katoomba in the Blue Mountains

THE GREAT ZIG ZAG
In 1866, the engineers building the railroad line to the west were faced with the problem of how to lower it from the top of the Blue Mountains down the sheer cliff face into Lithgow. Their solution was to construct a line in the form of a letter Z down the cliff face, with reversing stations at two points. This was replaced by the present main line, which takes a long way round but eliminates the need for reversing. The Zig Zag has been restored as a tourist railroad, an impressive spectacle as powerful engines haul their coaches up the steep slope.

Wentworth Falls lookout in the Blue Mountains

National parks

New South Wales, with its long coastline, mountains and extensive Outback, has wonderful examples of many of the continent's characteristic natural landscapes.

In the far west On the fringes of Australia's Red Centre and well over 600 miles from Sydney are two superb arid wildernesses. In **Sturt National Park** summer temperatures can reach 122°F for days on end; grassy plains alternate with claypans and pebbly desert from which rise flat-topped mesas (rocky tableland). In the extreme west are the ruddy sand dunes of the Strzelecki Desert. **Kinchega National Park** has vast plains of red sand as well as the strange saucer-shaped overflow lakes of the Darling River. Both areas are home to emus and the large red kangaroo.

To the east The land gradually rises through the western slopes of the Great Dividing Range to the range itself, the backbone of the state. On the border with Victoria is one of the world's great national parks, centered on Australia's highest peak, **Mount Kosciuszko**, after which the park itself is named. Glacial lakes, wild heathlands, alpine flowers, and glorious forests of snow gums make a superb setting for summer hiking, while the area becomes the nation's winter playground during the ski season, from early June to early October each year. The forested highlands that extend from near Newcastle through New England to the Queensland border have a rich vegetation that includes much undisturbed rainforest; here 16 separate parks and reserves have been grouped together to form one of Australia's World Heritage areas, the **Australian East Coast Temperate and Subtropical Rainforest Parks**. Old volcanoes give rise to dramatic landforms here and at **Warrumbungle National Park** farther inland, a weird world of rocky crags and natural skyscrapers. **Bald Rock National Park**, near the Queensland border in the far north, is another extraordinary landform, a great granite dome rising 656 feet out of the bush.

Mount Kosciuszko: good walking country

Bourke
62C2

This Outback town 485 miles northwest of Sydney seems utterly remote. It is the center of a vast and semi-arid area supporting large numbers of sheep and cattle as well as some crops on land irrigated with water from the Darling River. Originally a wooden stockade built in 1835 against Aboriginal attack, Bourke has a number of buildings dating from the latter part of the 19th century. Its main attraction, however, lies in its usefulness as a base for penetrating farther into the New South Wales Outback.

▶▶ Broken Hill
62C1

Founded on a 4¼-mile lode of silver, lead and zinc, the richest of its kind in the world, the unique "Silver City" now faces an uncertain future as down-grading measures take place against a background of low world prices for its products.

Thanks to the water piped in from its recreational reservoir at Lake Menindee 68 miles away, Broken Hill is a surprisingly green and leafy spot in what is one of the world's harshest environments: bitterly cold in winter, intolerably hot in summer, with a negligible rainfall that is only a tiny fraction of the evaporation rate. Nearly dead from thirst, the explorer Sturt gave the hump-backed ridge its name in 1844, but it was not until the 1880s that a German-born boundary rider, Charles Rasp, founded the Broken Hill Proprietary Company (see panel), which exploited the underground wealth in uneasy partnership with the workforce for many years. A great strike of 1919 ended in a historic compromise; the companies were insured their profits and the workers granted conditions far in advance of the time, such as a 35-hour week. A confederation of labor unions effectively ran the town, not always on what today would be regarded as progressive lines. Broken Hill has always been a long way from the government in Sydney, and its ties are closer to South Australia, with smelters at Port Pirie, union beaches at Adelaide, clocks that keep South Australian time—half an hour behind that of Sydney—and a South Australian region telephone prefix code.

Continued on page 78.

**WHAT TO SEE
"OUT BACK"**
From Broken Hill you can travel to many Outback locations. Lying within the relatively small distance of 124 miles are the opal-mining village of White Cliffs and Mutawintji National Park, Kinchega National Park and the Menindee Lakes, and Wilcannia, a quiet Darling River town with a large Aboriginal population.

BROKEN HILL PROPRIETARY COMPANY
B.H.P., as it is universally known, had its roots in Charles Rasp's discovery in 1883 of the immensely rich silver, lead, and zinc lode at Broken Hill. It is now Australia's largest company, having long since diversified into iron and coal, gas and oil, and steel-making. Its profits are taken by many as an index of the prosperity of the country as a whole.

Born the son of a farm laborer at Marston in Yorkshire, England, in 1728, James Cook became the greatest explorer of his age. He was educated at the expense of his father's generous-minded employer, then learned seamanship aboard a Whitby coal vessel. In 1755 he joined Britain's Royal Navy, where he refined his navigational and other skills in the course of the Seven Years' War. The achievement for which Lieutenant (as he then was) Cook is best remembered is his masterly voyage of exploration along the previously unknown east coast of Australia in 1770.

AHEAD OF HIS TIME
Cook was well in advance of his time in seeing beyond his own culture and background to the deeper harmony of the Aborigines' way of life. He wrote: "they are ... wholy (sic) unacquainted ... with the superfluous ... Conveniences so much sought after in Europe ... the Earth and sea of their own accord furnishes them with all things necessary for life."

1770: Cook takes possession of N.S.W. for Britain...

As Cook had documented an eclipse of the sun off the coast of Newfoundland, he was a natural choice when the Royal Society wished for an accurate observation to be made from Tahiti of the transit of Venus across the face of the sun. Accompanying him on this mission aboard the barque *Endeavour* was an astronomer, Charles Green, together with two eminent botanists, Daniel Solander and Joseph Banks, still a young man of 25.

East coast sighting On July 3, 1769, the transit of Venus was duly observed and Cook opened the sealed orders given him by the Admiralty. These instructed him to investigate the existence or otherwise of a great southern continent and to survey and take possession of New Zealand. Having completed a thorough exploration of the New Zealand coast, Cook decided to return via the hypothetical "East Coast of New Holland." This was sighted on April 19, 1770, when Cape Everard (originally called Cape Hicks in honor of Cook's sharp-eyed second in command) came into view.

Sailing northward along the coast, Cook found a convenient harbor where the ship could drop anchor and he and

CAPTAIN COOK'S LANDING PLACE

his men could investigate local conditions. The crew feasted on fresh fish, and the delighted botanists discovered an extraordinary array of plants, birds, and animals previously unknown to science. In deference to their serious purpose, Cook altered his original name for the anchorage, Stingray Harbour, to Botany Bay.

Grounded on the Barrier Reef Farther north, Cook noted the existence of what seemed to be a fine natural harbor and named it Port Jackson. The wonderful setting for the future city of Sydney had to await full discovery until the arrival of the First Fleet 18 years later. Feeling his way into "the labyrinth of coral islands, shoals, rocks and lee shores" of the Barrier Reef, even Cook with his superb seamanship couldn't fend off a grounding, and the *Endeavour* struck a reef.

Although the crew re-floated the vessel at high tide by jettisoning some of its equipment (including a cannon that is now in the National Library in Canberra), the barque needed repairs and was beached for a month near today's Cooktown at the base of Cape York. Once more the scientists had a field day, making their first acquaintance with kangaroos and turtles. When the *Endeavour* was seaworthy again, Cook sailed north to the tip of the cape where, on Possession Island, he hoisted the flag and formally declared the whole of eastern Australia to be British, giving it the unremarkable name of New South Wales.

The end of the road Promoted to captain, Cook went on in 1772–1775 to become the first to sail within the Antarctic Circle, finally putting paid to the idea of the great southern continent. In the course of an attempt in 1779 to find the elusive northern passage between the Atlantic and Pacific, he landed on Hawaii. As he was mediating in a relatively trivial dispute with the islanders, one of his men stupidly discharged his firearm; enraged, the islanders fell upon Cook, who had turned his back on them to restore order, and he collapsed beneath blows from clubs and daggers.

BANKS THE BOTANIST
Australia's 73 species of *Banksia* commemorate Joseph Banks, the wealthy botanist who sailed with Cook and who has been described as "the father of Australian botany." On the voyage out he listed 230 plant species at Madeira, 316 at Rio, 104 at Tierra del Fuego and 400 in New Zealand. Later, Banks was president of the Royal Society for 32 years.

...having made his mark in Botany Bay

Guess what grows at this Coffs Harbour plantation!

SILVER SCREEN SILVERTON

About 16 miles west of Broken Hill is the ghost town of Silverton, whose population moved to the bigger town when mining became unprofitable here in the late 1880s. With its restored buildings seeming to typify the spirit of the Outback, it has taken on a new lease of life as a stage set for a number of films, including *A Town Like Alice* and one in the *Mad Max* series.

OUR BANANA'S THE BIGGEST

The improbably oversized fruit known as the Big Banana dominates the scene on the Pacific Highway Just to the north of Coffs Harbour. Made of concrete rather than peel and fruit, it marks the entrance to a banana plantation that welcomes visitors. Here you can see bananas growing, eat bananas in every imaginable form, buy banana-shaped souvenirs, and find out everything you always wanted to know about bananas but never dared to ask.

Continued from page 75.

Protected from dust storms by extensive tree belts, Broken Hill is laid out on a grid of streets with names like Chloride, Mica, and Cobalt. The excellent Tourist Information Centre is close to the old Sulphide Street Station, now a mineral and train museum. **The GeoCentre** is an interactive earth sciences museum, but it's more exciting to go down a former mine, like Delprat's Mine or Day Dream Mine. The town is also a base for the **Royal Flying Doctor Service** and the **School of the Air**, both of which are open to the public. The strange environment of the city and its surroundings seems to have acted as a stimulant to a number of artists, and there are several galleries, of which the best known is that run by Pro Hart.

►► Byron Bay   63D5

Cape Byron is the easternmost point of the Australian mainland, capped with a powerful lighthouse. Byron Bay itself, with wonderful beaches and a gloriously scenic hinterland of forests and mountains, has been a focal point of alternative lifestyles since the late 1960s. A major attraction here is the town's lively dining, shopping, and nightlife scene, as well as adventure activities such as sea kayaking and hang-gliding. The beaches on either side of the headland vary in character, from secluded coves to great stretches of sand. Surfing is well established; the first lifesaving club was founded here as early as 1907.

► Cobar   62C2

This copper-mining town on the fringe of the Outback straddles the Barrier Highway on its way west to Broken Hill. Founded in the early 1870s as a typical mining city of tents and huts, it soon reached its peak population of some 10,000. Among the buildings that date from the town's early days are the Great Western Hotel with its extraordinarily long veranda and the mining company's office, now the **Cobar Outback Heritage Centre**. After a long decline, the place prospered again in the 1960s.

▶ Cockington Green, A.C.T.   66D3

The original Cockington in the southwest of England, a picture-postcard village with thatched cottages, a pub, a forge and other items of rusticity, is reproduced on the outskirts of Canberra in miniature form. There are also scaled-down versions of Stonehenge and other quaint features of the country Australians once called "home."

▶▶ Coffs Harbour   63C5

Roughly halfway between Sydney and Brisbane, this old timber port is famous for its beaches and banana plantations (see panel opposite). A string of fine beaches runs northward from the town's Park Beach, some with good surf. There is rafting on nearby rivers, while manmade attractions for vacationers include the Pet Porpoise Pool, with seals, penguins and sharks as well as amiable porpoises. The harbor is protected by a headland to the south, and by Muttonbird Island (reached by the old timber jetty) named after the species of burrowing sea birds that nest there. The town center, with its **Historical Museum** and **North Coast Regional Botanic Garden**, is some distance inland. Coffs Harbour is a popular place for craftsmen and handicraft stores.

▶ Dubbo   62C3

At the junction of the Newell and Mitchell Highways, Dubbo is the flourishing center for a large part of N.S.W.'s Central West area. First settled in the 1840s, it became a stopping point for those in search of "better land, farther out." Overlanders driving their cattle southward to the markets of S.A. and Victoria used to cross the Macquarie River near here. There are a number of fine old buildings in the town center, among them the 1876 bank, which now houses a good local museum and the jail, complete with gallows. But most visitors come here for the **Western Plains Zoo▶** which features animals from all over the world roaming freely over its parkland.

▶ Eden   63A4

The last place of any size on the N.S.W. coast before the border with Victoria, this little port and resort began life as a whaling station, recalled in the **Killer Whale Museum▶**. On Twofold Bay are the remains of Boydtown, begun around the 1840s by the English entrepreneur Benjamin Boyd and vaingloriously intended to rival Sydney as the colony's capital. More recently, Eden has been the focus of the battle to save Australia's forests from the woodchip industry.

▶ Forbes   62B3

Almost deserted after the gold rush of the 1860s, this western town survived as the center for a rich agricultural area. Some fine late 19th-century buildings, such as the imposing Town Hall, still grace the wide streets. Just outside town is a recreated settlement of pioneer days, **Lachlan Vintage Village▶**, where you can pan for gold or watch sheep being shorn. The bushranger Ben Hall met his end in Forbes in 1865, an event recalled in some detail in the old music hall that houses the town's **Folk Museum.**

79

These days, whale-watching is popular at Eden's Twofold Bay

WATERING THE WILDERNESS

The explorer John Oxley reckoned no white man would ever want to take up residence in the "barren and desolate" country he glimpsed from Mount Binya in 1817. But in the early 1900s, the N.S.W. government, enthused by private successes with irrigation experiments, built the Burrinjuck Dam and encouraged settlement in the Murrumbidgee Irrigation Area. Many settlers were out-of-work miners from Broken Hill; later, returned servicemen and Italian immigrants with important agricultural skills moved in, and in spite of many disappointments and technical difficulties, the area produces crops of fruit (including grapes), vegetables, cotton, and rice. Together with similar projects in the region, a total of 2,317 square miles of near desert has been made to bloom.

All of the 60 or so wineries in the Hunter Valley welcome visitors; most are around Cessnock and Pokolbin

▶ Glen Innes   63D4

This high-altitude town in northern N.S.W. is at the center of a prosperous farming area, once named the "Land of the Beardies" after two pioneers. The region is well known for the sapphires and other gemstones that are extracted commercially (amateur fossicking or searching is also possible). The town center has several well-cared-for late 19th-century buildings; the old hospital houses the **Land of the Beardies History House Museum▶**, one of Australia's most comprehensive small historical museums.

▶ Goulburn   63B4

The second oldest inland town in Australia straddles the Hume Highway some 125 miles southwest of Sydney and is the focal point of the well-tended farmlands all around, whose specialty is proclaimed by another one of those Australian "big ones"; 50 feet high, the Big Merino guards the town's western approach. Goulburn is a "real" city, with two cathedrals, a long main street and a number of imposing 19th-century buildings. On the edge of town is Riversdale, a coaching inn dating from the late 1830s, authentically restored and furnished.

▶ Grafton   63D5

Center of the Clarence River district, Grafton was "green" before its time. The town council initiated a policy of tree-planting as early as the 1860s, and today's citizens are benefiting from the many jacarandas and other flowering species that grace its broad streets. The bend of the Clarence was only bridged in 1932, when the present double-decker structure was built. Grafton is a good base for tours, with several national parks within easy reach.

▶ Griffith   62B2

Designed by Walter Burley Griffin, the American architect responsible for the planning of Canberra, this model township was built to act as the main urban center for the

Murrumbidgee Irrigation Area. Its conception on the drawing board can be seen in its radial street pattern and in the decorative use of irrigation water in its gardens.

▶ Gundagai 62B3

The name of this township along the Hume Highway is derived from an Aboriginal word meaning "up-river;" in spite of warnings from the local Aborigines, the first settlers built their houses on the floodplain of the Murrumbidgee, and were duly swept away when the river broke its banks in 1852, causing the country's worst-ever flood disaster. The Murrumbidgee is crossed here by the longest wooden viaduct in Australia.

▶▶ Hunter Valley 63C4

The broad valley of the Hunter River, which ends in the sea at Newcastle, has contrasting landscapes created by mines and wines. The coalfield has been exploited for a century and a half, and has been the making of the city of Newcastle. The vineyards were first planted here in the 1830s and, after periods of decline, are flourishing once more. A day trip or, better still, one lasting a couple of days is a favorite outing for Sydneysiders, not least because of the excellent food offered in the area.

The landscape of the Hunter is one of its attractions, in its framework of wooded hills running down from the Brokenback Range to the southwest of the valley. Grapevines benefit from the rich soil, which has its origin in the outpourings of ancient volcanoes. The wineries range from family-sized concerns to large-scale commercial enterprises. Australia's oldest wine-press is on display at the **Golden Grape Estate**. The vineyards of the Wyndham and Rothbury Estates are well worth visiting, while the McGuigan Hunter Village has a complex of attractions including restaurants, playgrounds, stores, and a superb cheese shop and factory. Other wineries are situated in the Upper Hunter Valley, some 56 miles farther on.

A DOG'S LIFE
The teamsters traveling along the rough roads of early Australia were inevitably accompanied by various breeds of dog, one of which seems to have committed an unspeakable act while sitting on his master's tuckerbox (lunch box) by the side of the road. This and other deeds were recorded in the crude ballads of the time, refined somewhat in a version by the poet Jack Moses, and commemorated in a sculpture just outside Gundagal. This is the work of one Frank Rusconi, who was also responsible for the amazing model cathedral of marble on show in the Tourist Information Centre.

81

This part of the Great Dividing Range is the roof of Australia, much of it a highland plateau from which rise a number of peaks more than 6,500 feet high. Parts of it feature several well-equipped ski resorts. But the mountains are glorious in summer as well as in winter; a carpet of alpine wildflowers unrolls as the snow retreats, and there are superb paths and trails offering some of the most exhilarating hiking in the whole of Australia.

The region is popular with winter sports enthusiasts

82

THE SNOWY MOUNTAINS SCHEME
This was a visionary project to alter the course of rivers to irrigate the parched agricultural areas farther west and generate hydroelectric power in the process. Many dams were built, of which the largest, at Lake Eucumbene, holds back more water than is contained in Sydney Harbour. There are 50 miles of aqueducts, 93 miles of tunnels and seven power stations, the latter providing a good proportion of the electricity consumed in southeast Australia. Some of the impressive installations (like Murray 1 on the Alpine Way, or Tumut 2 north of Cabramurra) are open to the public.

History Aboriginal interest in the mountains was more recent than in many parts of Australia, dating only from the end of the last Ice Age some 10,000 years ago. This is one of the few Australian landscapes with glacial lakes, cirques, and moraines, all the result of the action of the ice sheets that were absent throughout most of the country.

The mountains attracted graziers (sheep farmers) from early on in the days after white settlement, and a few determined bushwalkers between the two world wars, but it was only after the start of the Snowy Mountains Scheme in the late 1940s, when roads were driven through the wilderness and many other facilities created, that the area became accessible and visitors were able to come here in large numbers.

A popular starting point for exploring the mountains is the town of **Cooma** at the junction of the Monaro and Snowy Mountains highways. It was from here that the Snowy Mountains Authority oversaw what was to be one of the greatest 20th-century engineering projects in the world. There are two tourist offices that provide information about the mountains and the great project that transformed them: the visitors information center in town, and the Snowy Information Centre on the Canberra road.

The resort town of **Jindabyne** on its lake provides plenty of lodgings for winter sports enthusiasts heading for the snowfields farther west. The National Parks and Wildlife Service has a useful visitor center here, at Kosciuszko Road, before visitors head for the skiing areas in the heart of the mountains.

Popular resorts include the delightful alpine-style village of Thredbo on the southern side of the range, and the mega-resort of Perisher Blue, which encompasses the ski regions of Smiggin Holes, Mount Blue Cow, Guthega, and Perisher Valley—the latter reached by the underground railroad known as the Ski Tube.

At the end of the northern road is Charlotte Pass, with superb views of the mountain peaks. This is the starting point for a number of wonderful walks, including the Summit Walk to the top of **Mount Kosciuszko**, at 7,310 feet the highest peak in Australia.

Jindabyne is also the terminus of the **Alpine Way**, the splendid scenic highway that leads to the 5,190-foot pass at Dead Horse Gap. From here the partly unsurfaced road descends into the valley of the Murray River and on to Khancoban. This is the starting point for a fair-weather highway leading to **Mount Selwyn**, a winter sports resort on the north side of the peaks, and to the remains of the old gold-mining township of Kiandra.

Farther north still are **Yarrangobilly Caves**. Of the 60 caves so far discovered, four are open to the public.

SKIING
Although the snow isn't always as abundant as resort operators would like, the Snowy Mountains offer ideal conditions for cross-country skiing and some excellent downhill facilities. The main resorts are in the vast Perisher Blue region, which incorporates four ski areas and offers 50 lifts and T-bars, and the smaller and more charming alpine village of Thredbo. The ski season runs from early June to early October.

Murray 1 hydroelectric power station

A souvenir of your visit to Kangaroo Valley

THE KIAMA COAST
Kiama's beaches are pleasant enough—and excellent for surfing. Farther south lie Gerroa and Gerringong (which also offer great surfing), and then the spectacular wave-pounded expanse of Seven Mile Beach, part of a national park.

84

BLACK IS BEAUTIFUL
The Lightning Ridge black opals are not quite unique, but this is the only place in the world where this unusual stone occurs in quantity. It has been described as combining "the iridescence of the dewdrop with the colour of the rainbow, set in the blackness of night." The biggest stone ever found was given the name "Queen of the Earth."

MUTAWINTJI HISTORIC SITE
Located within the National Park, this extraordinary site represents one of the state's greatest collections of Aboriginal art and cultural relics. Some of the 20 rock shelters and 15 engraving sites can be visited in the company of an Aboriginal ranger.

► Kangaroo Valley   *63B4*

This is a delightful old township tucked away in an upland valley on the beautiful scenic road leading inland from Nowra, 62 miles south of Sydney. Apart from being the starting point for bushwalks, its main attraction is the **Pioneer Settlement Reserve**, a faithful reconstruction of a dairy farm of the 19th century.

► Kiama   *63B4*

The most famous feature of this pleasantly situated port and resort on the "Kiama Coast" south of Wollongong is the **Blowhole**, which gushes a 197-foot spout high into the air. With its rocky headlands and fine beaches, Kiama has long been popular with visitors. To the west is the Minnamurra Rainforest Reserve, with its palms, fig trees and other rainforest plants; rare red cedars; and exquisite lyrebirds. The reserve can be explored via its two marked and interpreted walking tracks.

►►► Kosciuszko National Park   *62A3*

See pages 74 and 83.

►► Lanyon Homestead, A.C.T.   *66A3*

This fine building on the Murrumbidgee River near Canberra was built in 1859 and added to around the turn of the century. Now in the care of the National Trust, both buildings and gardens have been restored with care. There is a gallery housing a collection of the works of Sir Sidney Nolan, one of the best places to get to know this idiosyncratic Australian artist.

►► Lightning Ridge   *62D3*

Just off the Castlereagh Highway before it quits N.S.W. for Queensland, this far northwestern township is famed for its black opals, mined here since 1902, in recent years by machine rather than by hand. Amateur fossickers (searchers for gold or gemstones) are welcome, provided they don't trespass on professionals' rights, and there are many old mines to visit and cutting demonstrations to watch, as well as artesian baths to relax in.

►► Mount Warning National Park   *63D5*

This 3,796-foot peak is the plug of an ancient volcano, given its name by Captain Cook to mark the reefs off

Point Danger, on which the *Endeavour* almost came to grief. It is the first place on the Australian mainland to receive the rays of the rising sun, and the view is well worth the 2,460-foot climb from the parking lot and visitor center. The steep but well-made path rises through splendid woodlands that change from subtropical rain forest to temperate rain forest and finally to open bush.

►► Mutawintji National Park 62C1

Beyond Broken Hill, in N.S.W.'s farthest northwest, are the rugged sandstone ranges of this remote national park, which is nevertheless accessible on gravel roads. Arid sandy plains and pebble deserts contrast with pools and watercourses fringed with river red gums and other lush vegetation. Aborigines occupied the area for countless years, leaving a wealth of rock paintings and engravings.

►► Myall Lakes National Park 63B4

These tranquil lakes (37 miles north of Newcastle), separated from the Pacific Ocean by windswept sand dunes, are best reached from the township of Tea Gardens by boat up the Myall River. There is little development along the shores, though the fishing village of Seal Rocks on the coast at the eastern end of the park is popular with visitors who want to get away from it all. You can rent everything from canoes to houseboats to explore the magnificent lakes.

► Nambucca Heads 63C5

Subtropical crops now grow in this attractive and popular resort, 31 miles south of Coffs Harbour, where the cedar forests were cleared last century. There are fantastic views from various lookout points, of which Yarrahapini is the most spectacular. You can take tours inland to the rugged ridges and deep forested valleys of the New England and Dorrigo national parks.

MYALL LAKES FLORA AND FAUNA
The Myall Lakes, fringed by splendid forest, which includes rain forest species like cabbage palms, make up the largest such lake system in the state. The lakes are also famous for the shrimp that breed in them. Waterbirds abound, as well as sea eagles, and the area is rich in other wildlife, too.

85

Swim or surf from the beach at Nambucca Heads

Attractive Lake Macquarie, Australia's largest saltwater lake, near Newcastle

AUSTRALIAN COUNTRY
Far inland from Port Macquarie, halfway between Sydney and Brisbane on the New England Highway, is the town of Tamworth. This sizeable place claims fame as the capital of Australian country music. An annual festival, held in January, draws thousands of fans to hundreds of performances; other attractions are the Country Collection (wax-works), and the Hands of Fame Park (handprints). More enduring stars can be contemplated at the Pyramid Planetarium to the north of town, where the solar system is repro-duced in miniature.

▶ **Newcastle**   *63B4*
Dominated by the B.H.P. steelworks, industrial Newcastle is the largest city in Australia that's not a state capital. Its fortunes, like those of its namesake in England, were founded on the abundant coal reserves of the Hunter Valley; Newcastle coal constituted the country's first export.

But there's much more to Newcastle than industry. The Foreshore Park, Queen's Wharf, and Customs House Plaza make a fine setting for festive occasions. **Fort Scratchley▶** is one of the few forts in Australia to have seen active duty—soldiers stationed there in 1942 fired on a Japanese submarine. The old stronghold gives a good panorama over the city in its setting, and houses the **Maritime Museum** and **Military Museum**. The city center has some imposing 19th-century buildings and more museums and galleries. The "Bogey Hole" on the city beach below beautiful King Edward Park was built as a saltwater bath in convict days. To the south of the city, **Lake Macquarie▶** offers all kinds of watersports. The country's largest saltwater lake, four times the size of Sydney Harbour, it is also the home of a koala colony and a delightful flora and fauna reserve.

▶ **Nimbin**   *63D5*
Set among the natural splendors of northern N.S.W., Nimbin developed as a center for artists and bohemians in the early 1970s. Today, its crafts shops and cafés attract the curious as well. It is close to **Nightcap National Park▶▶**, whose 2,953-foot peaks form part of the outer walls of the huge extinct volcano of which Mount Warning is the core. The park, with its glorious rain forest and diverse wildlife, is now part of N.S.W.'s World Heritage Area protecting the temperate and subtropical forests of the north.

▶ **Nowra** 63B4

Nowra is just upstream from the mouth of the Shoalhaven River. It is an extremely busy tourist resort, largely because of the beaches that extend north and south along the coast, one of them (Hyams Beach on Jervis Bay) boasting the whitest sand in the world.

▶ **Orange** 62B3

Lava flows from the extinct volcano of Mount Canobolas —the highest point between the Great Dividing Range and the Indian Ocean—have broken down over the millennia into fertile soils that today support great tracts of orchards growing apples, pears, cherries, and grapes for wine—but no oranges! The town of Orange has prospered from the fertility of its surroundings and is a busy but pleasant place, leafy with parks and trees. The first goldfield to be exploited in Australia was at nearby **Ophir**, where two prospectors made a sizable strike in 1851. You can try your luck at searching for gold today in picturesque surroundings along Summer Hill Creek.

▶ **Port Macquarie** 63C5

At the mouth of the Hastings River, Port Macquarie has turned from trade and commerce to tourism and retirement with considerable success. **St. Thomas' Church** is a reminder of these early days; one of the first churches to be built in Australia (1824-1828), it has box pews and a view from its tower. The **Hastings District Historical Museum▶** has good displays on the evolution of the town and its hinterland, and nature is on show at the **Billabong Koala and Wildlife Park**, and **Sea Acres Rainforest Centre▶** with a boardwalk through the rain forest. Good beaches stretch southward from the town.

▶▶ **Southern Highlands** 56A2

Easily accessible by train and by the Hume Highway, this is one of the great rural playgrounds of Sydneysiders. The district was opened up early in the colony's history, in the 1820s, and much of it has a pleasant air of maturity, with lush landscapes recalling those of Tasmania. Recreational facilities cater to every possible desire.

Among the towns in the area, Bowral is a leafy place with a number of fine old buildings along its main street. **Berrima▶▶** retains even more of its past; founded in the 1830s, it still has many sandstone buildings dating from that period, though the inns have dwindled in number from the original 13. The 1834 Surveyor General Inn claims to be the oldest continuously licensed premises in the country. Popular **Bundanoon** acts as the gateway to the Morton National Park, a starting point for energetic bushwalks or casual strolls up Glow Worm Glen.

▶▶ **Tidbinbilla, A.C.T.** 66A1

There are two important visitor attractions at Tidbinbilla, 25 miles southwest of Canberra. The **Canberra Deep Space Communications Complex▶** is a combined U.S./ Australian deep-space tracking station; it is not open to the public, but the visitor center features multi-media displays and model spacecraft. Back on earth, **Tidbinbilla Nature Reserve▶** is a vast tract of countryside with bushwalks and an array of Australian wildlife.

MORTON NATIONAL PARK

This high sandstone plateau into which rivers have cut deep gorges is one of the most beautiful attractions of the Southern Highlands. Waterfalls pour into the depths from high cliffs, as at Fitzroy Falls, where there is a visitor center. Scenic highways connect the area to the coast (one of them goes via Kangaroo Valley), making an interesting round trip from Sydney possible.

87

Rugged Morton National Park is popular with Sydneysiders

The long list of Australian creatures able to cause you harm, in some cases fatal, is particularly impressive. Still, you are much more likely to come to grief at the hands of a local driver or suffer heatstroke than you are to fall victim to them.

88

Marine hazards Of the 85 species of **sharks** around the coast of Australia, a few are man-eaters. Attacks are extremely rare, and the average number of fatalities per year is just one person. The highest risk occurs in summer when the water temperature is in excess of 72°F, and during this time it might be advisable to swim only from one of the many beaches protected by systems of netting. More dangerous are **saltwater crocodiles** (salties—see page 183), and on no account should you swim (or stand close to the water's edge) in the northern areas frequented by these formidable creatures. Their numbers have also increased dramatically since they have been given the status of protected species.

Box jellyfish breed in river estuaries and infest the coastal waters of Queensland and the N.T. from October to May. Practically invisible, they deliver a sting that can be fatal. Stay out of the sea at this time! Some of the beautiful corals can also deliver a mild sting, as can the crown-of-thorns starfish that is attacking the Barrier Reef. Much worse, however, is the **stonefish**, which looks like a rock as its name suggests; wear shoes when walking on a reef, and avoid rockpools. There are also sea snakes, which become active at the same time as the box jellies.

Terrestrial hazards Snakes also inhabit the land, and there are some 170 species, the venomous ones outnumbering the harmless—in Tasmania, for example, *all* snakes are venomous. Rangers and bush folk are fond of detailing their degree of poisonousness in terms of the number of mice a bite could kill; this figure can get into the hundreds of thousands, and is quite enough to fell the strongest human. However, even the most lethal of snakes—like the taipan, tiger snake, death adder, or brown snake—will get out of your way if it possibly can.

SPIDERS AND INSECTS

Spiders can reach an alarming size, and their bite can be unpleasant. Avoid the redback (or black widow), a small black spider with red patches on its back, and the larger funnel-web, at all costs—tourist information centers can give further information on how to recognize them. The funnel-web, unlike most of its kind, is aggressive and rears up for the attack. It's also a Sydneysider, so don't think you are safe in that city. Insects abound in Australia, but flies, mosquitoes, wasps, ticks, ants, and even scorpions are more of a nuisance than a real hazard.

Steer clear of the deadly taipan

► Wauchope   63C5

Among the forests of the Hastings River district, Wauchope has long been a center of the logging industry, a fact made much of in **Timbertown ► ►**. This ambitious re-creation of a late 19th-century pioneer settlement has a whole range of buildings (shops, houses, church and sawmill), demonstrations of all the activities associated with logging and processing, as well as rides around the area aboard a cart or a steam train.

Kempsey ►, 16 miles north of Wauchope, is home to the world-famous Akubra hat. Akubras (believed to be an Aboriginal word for hat) are made from rabbit pelts—as imported rabbits pose a serious environmental threat, many see this as a good use for them.

Australia's famous Akubra hats are made in Kempsey, near Wauchope

► West Wyalong   62B3

In the harsh countryside at the junction of the Mid-Western and Newell highways, West Wyalong was N.S.W.'s busiest goldfield at the turn of the century. Now the center for an extensive wheat-growing area, it also produces and exports that quintessential Australian fluid, eucalyptus oil. However, visitors may be more interested in the model of a gold mine in the District Museum.

WAGGA WAGGA OR WOGGA WOGGA?
More famous for its name (pronounced Wogga) than for its tourist amenities, Wagga (150 miles south of West Wyalong) is a fair-sized town that has profited from its location on the Murrumbidgee River and Sydney–Melbourne railroad line to become the thriving center of N.S.W.'s Riverina district.

► White Cliffs   62C1

This old opal-mining settlement more than 620 miles northwest of Sydney is a place to experience life in the Australian Outback. A small, highly individual population of opal miners lives here, some of them underground, where they won't need air-conditioning—elsewhere a must because of the sometimes intolerable climate. There are plenty of opportunities to see opals in their various states, as well as one of Australia's largest solar power stations, which can be toured.

► Wollongong   63B4

The life of New South Wales' third largest city is based on heavy industry and there are few conventional tourist attractions. But, not far away, the rugged Illawarra Coast has wonderful beaches while inland there are splendid hills and forests. Mount Keira and Mount Kembla in the **Illawarra State Recreation Area ►** offer fantastic vistas.

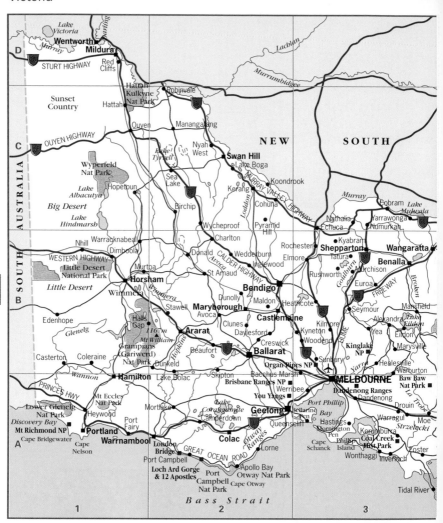

The Dandenong Ranges
harbor a rich profusion of
native flora

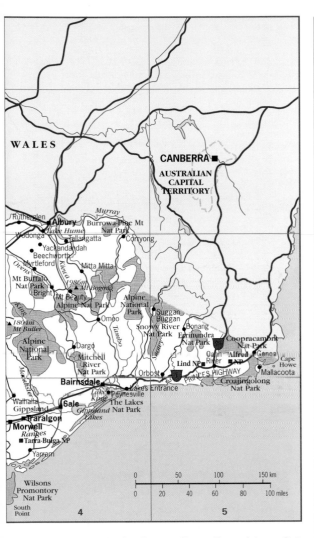

WALES

CANBERRA
AUSTRALIAN
CAPITAL
TERRITORY

Murray

Rutherglen Albury Burrowa-Pine Mt
Lake Hume Nat Park
Wodonga Tallangatta Corryong
Yackandandah
Beechworth
Myrtleford
Ovens Mitta Mitta
Mt Buffalo
Nat Park 1986m Mt Bogong
Bright Mt Beauty Alpine
Alpine Nat Park National
Omeo Park Suggan
Buggan
Snowy River Bonang
180m Nat Park Errinundra
Mt Butler Nat Park Coopracambra
Alpine Nat Park
National Dargo Cann Alfred Genoa
Park Mitchell River Lind NP NP
River Orbost Cape
Nat Park Howe
Bairnsdale PRINCES HIGHWAY Mallacoota
Croajingolong
Lakes Entrance Nat Park
Lake Paynesville
Walhalla King The Lakes
Gippsland Sale Gippsland Nat Park
Traralgon Lakes
Morwell
Ranges
Tarra-Bulga NP
Yarram

0   50   100   150 km
0   20   40   60   80   100 miles

Wilsons
Promontory
Nat Park
South
Point   4   5

VICTORIA The Garden State is the smallest of Australia's mainland states. However, it is comparatively densely populated and highly industrialized, with about a quarter of the country's inhabitants living on what amounts to only 3 percent of its land surface, a substantial proportion of which is agriculturally productive. Out of the state's total of 4½ million or so people, just over 3 million live in the metropolitan area of Melbourne, whose area of more than 2,300 square miles makes it one of the largest cities in the world.

Beyond the metropolis, Victorians live in a variety of settlements, many of considerable charm and historic interest. There are delightful little ports and several well-established resorts along the 745-mile coastline, a multitude of places founded in the mid-19th-century rush for gold such as charming Yackandandah, old river ports along the Murray, and prosperous agricultural centers quietly getting on with their own lives.

▶▶▶ REGION HIGHLIGHTS

Old Victorian building in Melbourne

92

The state's landscapes are diverse; with varied and spectacular coastal scenery, high mountains and extensive forested uplands, rich farmlands and semi-desert, Victoria has been described as a microcosm of Australia, though true Outback lies beyond its border. Agriculture takes many forms. The rolling hills of Gippsland feed dairy cattle, sheep graze on the vast pastures of the plains stretching to the west, and fruit grows in profusion along the Goulburn and Murray rivers, thanks to irrigation works carried out on a huge scale at the turn of the century.

For the tourist, the presence of such variety in close proximity to the state capital makes a stay particularly rewarding; few places are more than half a day's drive from Melbourne.

AS IT WAS Victoria belonged to a new phase of European colonization of the continent. The coast had been sighted from aboard the *Endeavour* in the course of Captain Cook's 1770 voyage; in 1803, Lieutenant David Collins attempted to found a settlement on the shores of Port Phillip Bay but gave up and went on to Tasmania instead. For decades, only whalers and sealers landed along the coast. Then, in 1835, one John Batman from Tasmania sailed into the bay again and signed a treaty of dubious legality with the local Aborigines that gave him title to 600,000 acres of land. In spite of official attempts from Sydney to discourage settlement on the bay, Batman and others persisted; his famous phrase "This will be the place for a village" marked the founding of Melbourne.

The new settlers wanted nothing to do with the convict system, sending any ships that arrived with prisoners on

BUCKLEY'S CHANCE
One of the members of Lieutenant Collins' party, which tried and failed to establish a settlement at Sorrento on the Mornington Peninsula in 1803, was the British-born convict William Buckley. Taking a chance, he decamped and fled around Port Phillip Bay to the Barwon area, where he lived with the local Aborigines. Decades later, in 1835, some of John Batman's associates were amazed at the emergence of "a wild white man" at their encampment, hardly able to speak English any more. Buckley earned a pardon, a government pension, and a place in the language ("Buckley's chance" means no chance at all).

to Sydney, and petitioning for separation from New South Wales. This was granted in 1851, and the new colony was given the Queen of England's name. It was only weeks after this event that gold was found near Ballarat and at Clunes; other finds followed, the rush was on, and Melbourne and Victoria changed utterly in the process. Handsome new towns arose from the tent cities erected by the prospectors, and Melbourne boomed, fitting itself out with fine new buildings paid for by the profits made from the precious metal.

Melbourne has been eclipsed by Sydney as the financial capital of the nation; Sydney gets more migrants and has a more racially diverse character. But Melbourne is now one of the most cosmopolitan of Australia's major cities, while other places within the state retain a pleasing atmosphere of more stately and sedate times.

OUTDOOR VICTORIANS In spite of (or is it because of?) their unpredictable weather, the people of Victoria embrace the outdoors with fervor, igniting the barbecue or flocking to the beaches at the slightest opportunity. The big event in the racing calendar is the Melbourne Cup, which takes place on the first Tuesday of November, when not only Victoria but the whole country comes to a stop. Australian Rules football is followed with passion by people of all ages and both sexes.

The accessibility of fine scenery brings out the bushwalkers in summer, while in winter the roads to the snowfields of the Alps are crowded with the cars of skiers. Skiing began in the 1930s, when the first lift started taking people up to the plateau country beneath Mount Buffalo.

SKIING IN VICTORIA
Mount Donna Buang and Mount Baw Baw are accessible to day-trippers from Melbourne. Mount Buller, farther on in the Alps, is Australia's most popular winter resort. The resort at Mount Hotham is the highest in the country, with an award-winning, environmentally friendly complex at Dinner Plain, while Falls Creek in its sheltered bowl in the Alpine National Park has slopes suitable for every kind of skier.

93

Morning Star Creek, still with one foot in the past

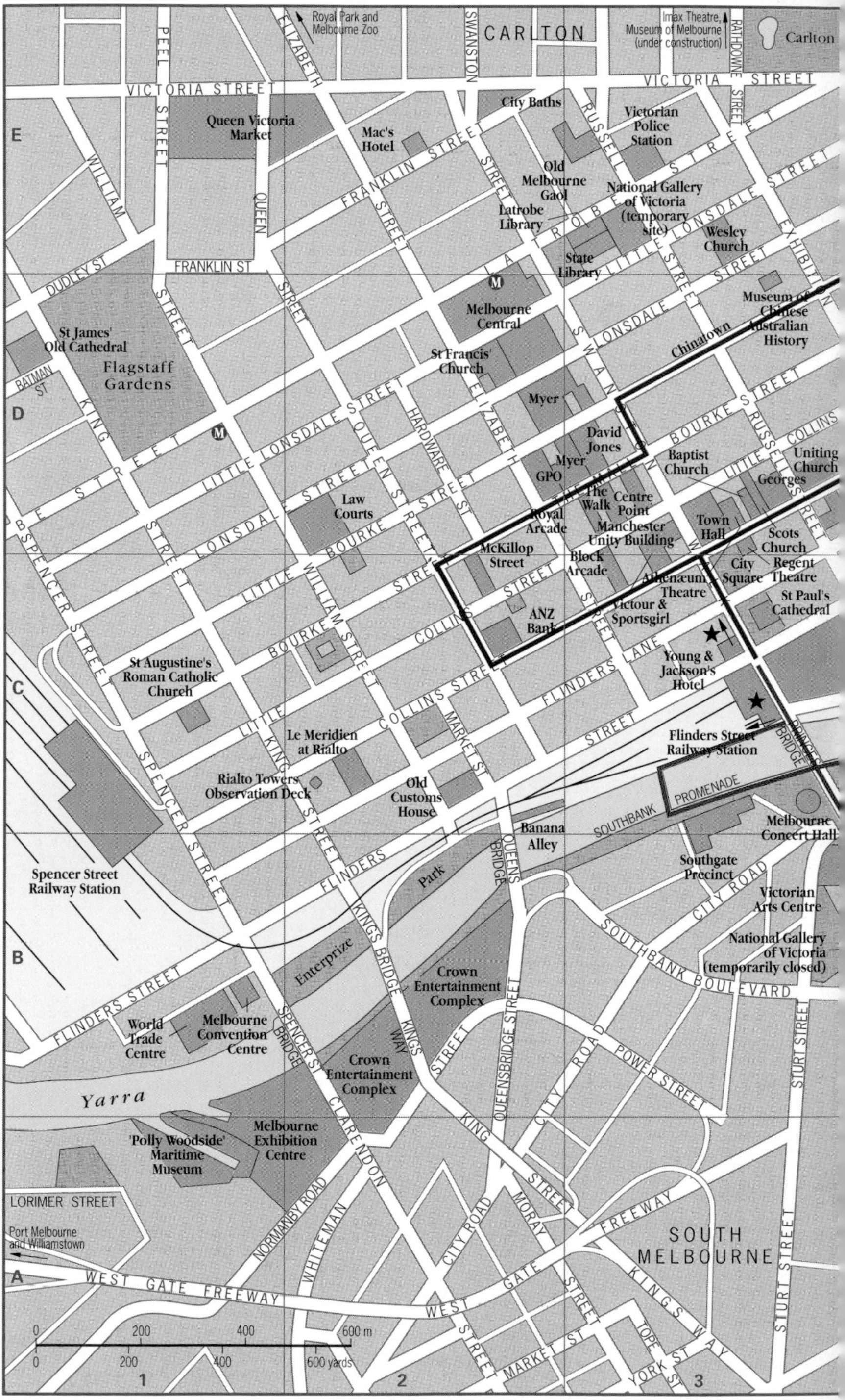

CARLTON

Royal Park and Melbourne Zoo

Imax Theatre,
Museum of Melbourne
(under construction)

Carlton

VICTORIA STREET

VICTORIA STREET

City Baths

Victorian
Police
Station

E

Queen Victoria
Market

Mac's
Hotel

Old
Melbourne
Gaol

National Gallery
of Victoria
(temporary
site)

Latrobe
Library

Wesley
Church

FRANKLIN ST

State
Library

Museum of
Chinese
Australian
History

St James'
Old Cathedral

Flagstaff
Gardens

Melbourne
Central

St Francis'
Church

Chinatown

D

Myer

David
Jones

Baptist
Church

Uniting
Church
Georges

Myer
GPO

The
Walk

Centre
Point

Law
Courts

Royal
Arcade

Manchester
Unity Building

Town
Hall

Scots
Church

McKillop
Street

Block
Arcade

Athenæum
Theatre

City
Square

Regent
Theatre

ANZ
Bank

Victour &
Sportsgirl

St Paul's
Cathedral

St Augustine's
Roman Catholic
Church

Young &
Jackson's
Hotel

C

Le Meridien
at Rialto

Flinders Street
Railway Station

Rialto Towers
Observation Deck

Old
Customs
House

PROMENADE

Banana
Alley

SOUTHBANK

Melbourne
Concert Hall

Spencer Street
Railway Station

Park

Southgate
Precinct

Victorian
Arts Centre

B

Enterprize

Crown
Entertainment
Complex

National Gallery
of Victoria
(temporarily closed)

World
Trade
Centre

Melbourne
Convention
Centre

Crown
Entertainment
Complex

Yarra

'Polly Woodside'
Maritime
Museum

Melbourne
Exhibition
Centre

LORIMER STREET

SOUTH
MELBOURNE

Port Melbourne
and Williamstown

A

WEST GATE FREEWAY

0   200   400   600 m

0   200   400   600 yards

1   2   3

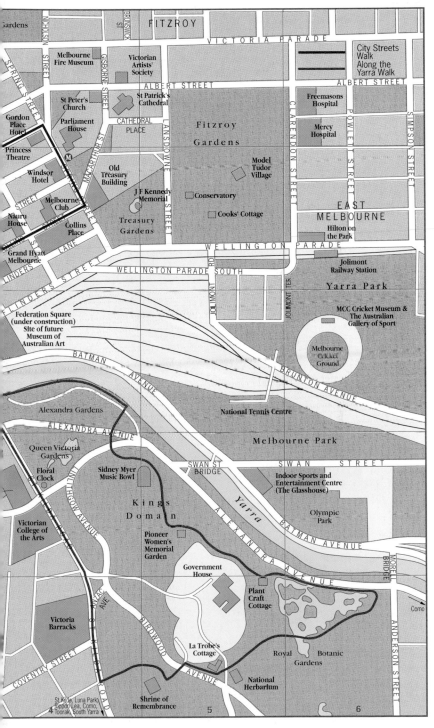

Queen Victoria Market

MOOMBA
The Melburnians' ability to let their hair down is demonstrated every March in the huge carnival known as Moomba, an Aboriginal word that can be translated as "let's get together and have fun." Ten days of festivities culminate in a monster multicultural procession.

BATMAN'S BARGAIN
In exchange for 600,000 acres of Aboriginal land, John Batman delivered 40 blankets, 30 tomahawks, 100 knives, 50 pairs of scissors, 30 mirrors, 200 handkerchiefs, 100 pounds of flour, and 6 shirts. The understanding that a similar quantity of useful items would be handed over annually was soon consigned to oblivion.

Outside the 1856 Parliament House

Melbourne

Australia's second great metropolitan city sprawls around the head of Port Phillip Bay at the outlet of the muddy Yarra River. Hardly a generation ago, Melbourne was almost a synonym for dull respectability of a peculiarly British flavor, but since the 1960s Melbourne and its population have undergone a startling transformation. Much of the city center has been redeveloped with glittering office towers, to which the remaining treasures of 19th-century architecture act as a wonderful foil. Massive immigration, from southern Europe and Asia, has enlivened the city's social scene. In addition to countless galleries, museums, theaters and movie houses, the city now has a thriving nightlife of bars and discos, cabaret and comedians, jazz, rock, and a casino. Melbourne offers a multitude of different types of cuisine, from "Mod Oz" to Vietnamese. The shopping is a treat too.

THE EARLY YEARS Once John Batman's illegal treaty of 1835, by which he acquired 600,000 acres of land, had been accepted as a *fait accompli* by the authorities in Sydney, his "village" above the Yarra soon became a city laid out on the usual grid pattern by an army surveyor. Within a few years, the wealthy were buying estates to the southeast of the river where they could set themselves up as country gentlemen and build elegant houses. Due to gold and land speculation, Melbourne boomed for most of the second half of the 19th century, leading a roistering kind of life that was then characterized as "American" in contrast to Sydney's staid "Britishness." A great slump in the 1890s ended the era of "Marvelous Melbourne," and the city entered the long period of middle-aged respectability from which its recent renaissance has so triumphantly rescued it.

ATTRACTIONS TODAY Melbourne is a wonderfully green metropolis with an abundance of parks and trees, but it is also renowned for its excellent 19th-century architecture. The best view of the city—and probably one of the finest panoramas in Australia—is from the south bank of the Yarra, particularly from Alexandra Gardens or the Southgate Precinct.

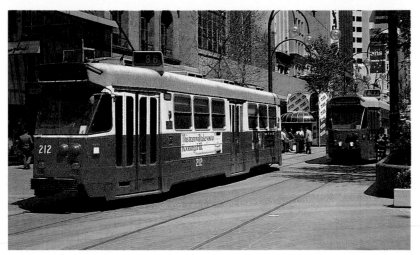

The city's inner suburbs have a strong and varied identity that makes them well worth exploring.

Carlton, just north of the city center, is home to the University of Melbourne and the huge 1870s Royal Exhibition Building. The adjacent Carlton Gardens area is being developed to include an IMAX theatre (already open) and the new Melbourne Museum, opening during 2000 (see page 100).

Once regarded as "rough," **Fitzroy** has now turned Bohemian, its original inhabitants supplemented by students and artists. Brunswick Street is a fascinating mixture of cheap restaurants and alternative bookstores.

East Melbourne is a charming enclave of carefully restored row houses within walking distance of the city center via Fitzroy Gardens.

The suburb of **St. Kilda** became Melbourne's seaside in the 1880s, when the pier and the substantial villas of the rich were built. These days St. Kilda is very colorful, and Acland and Fitzroy Streets are hard to beat as restaurant strips. The beaches stretching from here around to Port Melbourne are still popular, and the bay has been cleaned up in recent years. On Sundays, St. Kilda hosts a big arts and crafts market.

South Melbourne has one of the most attractive of all inner city residential areas; in St. Vincent's Square, fine houses in a variety of styles were laid out around central gardens from the 1860s onward.

One of the wealthiest inner suburbs east along the Yarra, **Toorak** is synonymous with trendiness, and neighboring South Yarra, the location of the historic Como House, is famous for its restaurants, shopping, and nightlife.

Beyond the Yarra to the west, **Williamstown** has a superb view of the city center across the water. A stroll along the Strand is well worthwhile, and railroad buffs enjoy the Railway Museum. On the way here, at Spotswood on the western side of the Westgate Bridge, is the highly entertaining Scienceworks, an annex of the Melbourne Museum. It has an amazing array of interactive exhibits on the theme of science and technology in the past, present, and future.

Melbourne is the only Australian city with an extensive system of tramways

MELBOURNE'S TRAMS
One of the emblems of the city, the network of green and yellow trams covers much of the Melbourne metropolitan area. The older trams are classified by the National Trust, while a new line speeds commuters and workers between the city center and Port Melbourne. Visitors can make good use of the free City Circle Tram service, and you can even dine aboard a vintage model; the Colonial Tramcar Restaurant is fitted with specially smooth suspension to keep your Yarra Valley red in its glass. It has one-way windows to maintain your privacy while you glide gondola-like through the streets.

COLLINS STREET

This has always been the best address in town, ever since professional men set up here in the late 1840s. The upper, eastern end of the street, tree-planted and close to parklands and government buildings, was more salubrious than the western end, down by the railroad tracks of Spencer Street Station. Not quite all the buildings from the era of "Marvelous Melbourne" have been replaced by developments like twin-towered Collins Place (No. 45) or the harsh precast concrete panels of Nauru House (No. 80); the Melbourne Club, most exclusive of such institutions, still stands (No. 36), as do a number of dignified banks, office buildings, churches and theaters.

►► A.N.Z. (Australia and New Zealand) Bank 94C2

386 Collins Street

One of the finest examples of Gothic revival architecture in the country, the building of what used to be the English, Scottish and Australian Bank is more Venetian than the Doges Palace in Venice, with a magnificently elaborate interior whose blue décor is enhanced by lavish use of gold leaf.

The A.N.Z. Banking Museum has changing exhibitions on the history of Australian banking.

► Chinatown 94D3

Centered on Little Bourke Street, Melbourne's Chinatown has existed ever since Chinese prospectors joined the rush to the goldfields in the 1850s. It expanded later in the 19th century as the goldfields contracted and miners drifted back to the big city. Today it still flourishes as a haven for the Chinese community and for diners in search of cheap and excellent food and groceries, and has been fitted out with the usual archways that boldly proclaim its identity.

An interesting addition to the area is the **Museum of Chinese Australian History►►** in an old warehouse in Cohen Place, just off Little Bourke Street. Its displays bring alive the considerable Chinese contribution to Australian history. Star exhibits include a life-size replica of a warrior-general of the 2nd century BC and Dai Loong, the 328-foot, 100-legged dragon that emerges once a year for the Chinese New Year parade. Fascinating guided heritage walks of the Chinatown area depart from the museum daily.

►► Como 95A6

Como Avenue, South Yarra

Begun in 1847, this delicious white mansion crowning the rise in the middle of its richly landscaped gardens is a wonderful example of the gracious buildings of

The gateway to Chinatown

Melbourne's pre-boom period. Behind the well proportioned facade in South Yarra are a series of furnished rooms evoking the comfortable and very sociable life lived here in the 19th century; to the side are outbuildings containing the original laundry. Como's unselfconscious elegance was not imitated by the nouveau-riche owners of the next generation of villas to be built in the suburb of Toorak; they preferred something more ostentatious, usually combining a number of architectural styles. Most of these pompous residences have now given way to apartment buildings, but Como, thankfully, passed into the hands of the National Trust in 1959.

►► Fitzroy Gardens   95E5

Just to the east of the city center and a favorite place for lunchtime sandwiches and assignations are the sweeping lawns and splendid trees of these 19th-century gardens, complementing the spires of St. Patrick's Cathedral in the background. Toward the southern end of the park is **Cooks' Cottage►►**. A modest stone building of the mid-18th century with the characteristic Yorkshire pantiled roof, this was the home of the great navigator's parents; it was dismantled and brought here in 1934 to mark the centenary of the founding of Melbourne. It is open to the public, as is another reminder of Anglo-Australian ties, the miniature Tudor Village, a gift from the citizens of the London borough of Lambeth in thanks for World War II food parcels.

►► Kings Domain   95B5

A splendid tract of parkland sweeps southeast along the Yarra from the city center through Victoria and Alexandra Gardens to the Kings Domain and beyond to the Royal Botanic Gardens (see page 101). Alexandra Gardens has a fine riverside view of the city center, and Queen Victoria Gardens has an elaborate floral clock. Altogether more functional is the **Sidney Myer Music Bowl**, whose soaring canopy shelters all kinds of open-air musical events. Crowning the higher ground in the Domain is the great white **Government House**, the fourth to be built on this site (see panel). Its square tower rises above the trees and is a well-known city landmark. In contrast to this magnificence is the very first Government House, **La Trobe's Cottage**, a prefabricated two-story cottage brought from England, erected in nearby Jolimont in 1839, and moved here in 1963.

► Melbourne Cricket Ground   95C6

Jolimont Terrace, Jolimont

To the southeast of the city center at Jolimont, divided up by roads and railroad tracks, are sports grounds of all kinds, many of them laid out for the 1956 Olympics. The central site for the games was the great M.C.G.—the Melbourne Cricket Ground—a vast stadium with a capacity up to 100,000, just as much associated with football ("Aussie Rules") as with cricket. Here, too, are the M.C.C. Cricket Museum, the Australian Gallery of Sport, and the Olympic Museum, recalling the triumphs and disappointments that have attended the modern games since their revival in 1896. A guided tour of this large complex is a very worthwhile experience.

GOVERNMENT HOUSE
Built by government architect William Wardell in the 1870s, the present Government House was modeled on Queen Victoria's Osborne House on England's Isle of Wight. That monarch is supposed to have been rather miffed that Government House's ballroom was twice as big as the one in Buckingham Palace.

99

One of the world's greatest stadiums, the Melbourne Cricket Ground at Jolimont creates an incredible atmosphere

THE SYDNEY SNEER
The rivalry between Sydney and Melbourne is long-standing and will probably never go away, though these days the tone of exchanges between Sydneysiders and Melburnians is bantering rather than bitter. The 1955 painting by John Brack entitled *Collins Street, 5 o'clock*, showing grim-faced commuters marching along Melbourne's main artery, has given much pleasure to Sydneysiders by confirming their view of Melburnians as archetypal killjoys.

The carefully restored barque Polly Woodside *at the Maritime Museum*

The National Gallery of Victoria is also the site for international traveling exhibitions

▶ Melbourne Museum

Other than its science and technology sections, now located at Scienceworks (see page 97), Melbourne's main museum is closed until the year 2000 when it will reopen adjacent to the Royal Exhibition Building in Carlton. Pride of place is still likely to be given to Phar Lap, famous racehorse of the 1930s, preserved for posterity.

▶▶ Melbourne Zoo 94E2

Elliott Avenue, Parkville
This vast zoo with its progressive approach is located in Royal Park, just 2½ miles from the city center and the city's largest tract of open space. Visitors move easily through large enclosures simulating the native habitat of the creatures within—including an African rain forest and a butterfly house. A range of Australian fauna is also on show, from birds in their giant aviary, to fur seals in their tank, and platypuses in their platypusary.

▶▶▶ National Gallery of Victoria 95B4

Russell Street
This gallery houses some of the finest artworks to be seen in Australia. It is currently being refurbished and so most of the collection has been temporarily relocated to the old Museum of Victoria site (Russell Street) until late 2001. The international collection will then return to the St Kilda Road gallery and Australian artworks will move to the new **Museum of Australian Art**, being built at Federation Square, adjacent to Flinders Street Station. The collection of Australian art includes John Glover's charming scenes of colonial Tasmania, the story pictures of the later 19th century, and the works of Sidney Nolan and Jeffrey Smart. In addition, there is a good selection of European Old Masters, as well as pre-Columbian, Aboriginal, and American art, and the courtyards contain a number of fine modern sculptures.

▶▶ Old Melbourne Gaol94E3
Russell Street
Of all the countless jails that are such a feature of
Australian townscapes, this grim bluestone building with
its chilling interior seems to sum up the harshness of 19th-
century concepts of justice and punishment. Here you can
see the death mask of Ned Kelly, made in 1880. The most
notorious and defiant of Australia's bush-rangers looks
peaceful enough, his wayward spirit expressed perhaps
more strongly by the homemade suit of armor that is
displayed alongside.

▶ Parliament House95E4
Spring Street
Begun in 1856, this great neo-Grecian palace of government was planned on such an ambitious scale that it has
never been completed. The state government was moved
from its grandiose home here in 1901 to make way for the
newly established Federal Parliament, which sat in
Melbourne until finally persuaded to make the move to
Canberra in 1927.

There are guided tours of the splendid interior when
parliament is not in session; the Legislative Council
Chamber was described by poet and connoisseur of
Victorian architecture John Betjeman (1906–84), as "the
best Corinthian room in the world."

▶ Polly Woodside Maritime Museum94A1
Lorimer Street East, Southbank
Built in Belfast in 1885, the sailing barque *Polly Woodside*
ended her working days as a rusty, dilapidated, coal hulk
in the Port of Melbourne. Fortunately she was immaculately restored and is now moored in an old dock basin at
Southbank, as the proud centerpiece of this maritime
museum, which has numerous other exhibits evoking the
age of sail.

▶▶ Queen Victoria Market94E1
Victoria Street
Melbourne's sole surviving 19th-century market, exuberantly multicultural, is an exciting place to store or just
wander. Trading has been carried on here since 1859, and
more than a thousand stalls sell everything imaginable at
affordable prices.

▶▶ Rialto Towers Observation Deck94C2
525 Collins Street
From this viewing area on the 55th level of Melbourne's
highest building the views of the city, Port Phillip Bay,
and many of the city's outlying regions are stupendous.

▶▶ Rippon Lea95A4
192 Hotham Street, Elsternwick
Begun in 1868 by the London-born Frederick Thomas
Sargood, this two-tone brick house is perhaps the most
splendid late-Victorian mansion to have survived in the
Melbourne suburbs. When it was completed in 1887 it had
no fewer than 33 rooms. The gardens are both opulent
and extensive.

Continued on page 103.

101

*The Botanic Gardens:
a fine example of
19th-century English
landscaping*

Early European Australia was not distinguished by its architecture. No architect sailed with the First Fleet, and the very first structures were primitive affairs of sticks, mud, thatch, bark, or any materials that came quickly and easily to hand. Some prefabricated structures were shipped out from England and reassembled on site, sometimes by guesswork.

102

The first proper edifice in Sydney was Government House, a two-story brick dwelling that amazed the Aborigines when they found people walking around above their heads. A sense of restraint and emphasis on good proportion contributed toward simple but effective structures like Elizabeth Farm at Parramatta, built in 1793. Its veranda, destined to become a persistent motif in Australian building, was derived from British practice in India. But architecture capable of making some kind of civic statement had to await the rule of Governor Macquarie and his forger-turned-architect, Francis Greenway. Thanks to buildings like **Hyde Park Barracks** and **St. James' Church**, Sydney began to take on the airs of a real city for the first time.

The development of the terrace Gold was the making of Melbourne, and of many architects, too. Melbourne is still one of the world's great 19th-century cities in terms of building, with grand self-confident edifices in a variety of revived styles—Gothic for churches, Romanesque and Venetian for offices and banks, and classical for public buildings. This was the period when row houses reached a high point of development, their elegance and cast-iron decoration helping to make the inner suburbs of both Melbourne and Sydney some of the most livable of their kind in the world.

AUSTRALIA'S OWN
What has been described as the most original local contribution to Australian architecture is the tropical house of Queensland. Raised above ground for ventilation, it is liberally provided with verandas and with a roof of corrugated iron—handsome, cheap and durable.

An Aussie style The row house was replaced after the turn of the century by the detached villa, built for a decade or so in a wealth of varied forms and with features like terracotta kangaroos on the roof line and eucalyptus leaves in the barge boards.

The later, 20th-century suburbs are undistinguished. The interwar California bungalow has given way to brick veneer dwellings and bizarre neo-Grecian palaces. Similarly, the redeveloped city centers do not seem to have embraced Australian style either.

Right: renovated Victorian building in downtown Melbourne

Continued from page 101.

▶▶▶ Royal Botanic Gardens 95A6

The jewel in the crown of parkland: extending along the Yarra River from the center of town, these superb, lush, and beautifully landscaped gardens rank among the finest in the world.

The site was chosen as early as 1845, and the gardens were laid out and stocked with an incredible range of plants by successive directors. Ferdinand von Mueller (Director, 1852–1873) preferred a formal layout, while his successor, William Guilfoyle, redesigned the gardens in a more romantic, English style with sweeping lawns, informal lakes, and curving pathways.

Plants from many parts of the world thrive in Melbourne's kind climate; here there are more than 6,000 tree species, ranging from cool temperate regions through to subtropical areas. English elms and oaks contrast with grass trees and river red gums. The Australian Lawn is planted with eucalypts from all over the country, and the Australian Border features a fine modern rockery, designed by the aptly named landscape architect, Ellis Stones. There is also the Oak Lawn, the Rose Garden, a cactus and succulent garden and a bulb garden. There are a number of buildings in the garden, which complement the plantings; they include the classical Temple of the Winds and the 1930s Visitor Centre and Herbarium with its excellent modern extension. A good way to familarize yourself with at least some of the riches that these wonderful gardens have to offer is to take one of the guided walks that start at the visitor center (11 AM and 2 PM daily except Sat).

▶ St. Patrick's Cathedral 95E4

Cathedral Place, East Melbourne

Less hemmed in by modern buildings than the Anglican Cathedral (see page 104), the 338-foot central spire of this great Roman Catholic cathedral features in many city views (see panel). It was designed by William Wardell, the state's official architect, who also built the fabulous Venetian-style A.N.Z. Bank.

One of the inhabitants of the highly acclaimed Melbourne Zoo

THE SEPARATION TREE
This is the name given to one of the fine river red gums in the Royal Botanic Gardens, since it was beneath its branches that the grand public celebration took place in 1851 to mark the independence of Victoria from New South Wales.

INSIDE ST. PATRICK'S
St. Patrick's has a splendidly soaring interior, with magnificent stained-glass windows. Long regarded as an Irish stronghold, it also has a statue of Daniel O'Connell—the great 19th-century Irish patriot known as "the Liberator"—in the churchyard.

On guard at the impressive Shrine of Remembrance

ARTS TOUR
The Victorian Arts Centre complex is adorned inside and out with numerous works of art, many of them specially commissioned. The Centre's guided tours are an excellent way of getting to grips with them all.

NELLIE MELBA'S MELBOURNE MEMORIAL
Born in the Melbourne suburb of Richmond in 1861, world-famous soprano Helen Mitchell changed her name to Nellie Melba to honor her native city. Like so many Australian artists of the period, she made her reputation abroad, her association with London's Covent Garden lasting for three decades. The Performing Arts Museum has much Melba memorabilia.

▶ St. Paul's Cathedral   94C3
Corner of Swanston and Flinders Streets
No longer the dominant element in the cityscape, this fine Gothic Revival-style church still has a commanding presence. Standing on the site where the first official church service in Melbourne took place in 1836, the cathedral was built in 1880–91 to a design by the British architect William Butterfield, also responsible for the Chapter House and Diocesan Offices in the cathedral complex.

▶▶ Shrine of Remembrance   95A5
Off St. Kilda Road
This huge temple to the dead forms a dramatic terminus for the long vista that starts in the city center. Modeled on the Parthenon, the shrine sits massively on top of a rise in the ground in Kings Domain. It was completed in 1934 to honor the 114,000 Victorians who served in World War I, of whom 19,000 died. The central chamber has a Stone of Remembrance illuminated by a shaft of light at 11 AM every November 11. Deep below is the crypt, displaying regimental colors, and high above is a gallery with fine panoramas over the city and its environs. The immaculate grounds have been laid out to commemorate those who fell in other wars.

▶▶▶ Victorian Arts Centre   94B3
100 St. Kilda Road
No cultural ghetto, but a vibrant part of city life, the modern Arts Centre, completed in 1984, comprises a complex of exciting buildings on the south bank of the Yarra.

Next to the National Gallery is the **Theatres** building, topped by a stunning 377-foot-high spire and one of Melbourne's cultural landmarks. The three theaters themselves are below ground: the State Theatre is the home of the Australian Ballet; the Melbourne Theatre Company performs in the Playhouse; and the third is a highly adaptable studio space. The spectacular interior of the **Concert Hall** is done in mineral colors that reflect the geology of the Australian continent. The center also embraces two restaurants, the Arts Centre store, a Sunday market, the entertaining Performing Arts Museum (see panel) and, in Kings Domain, the Sidney Myer Music Bowl. Guided tours take place from Monday to Saturday.

Melbourne's city streets

See map on pages 94–95.

From the traditional meeting place of Melburnians—"under the clocks" at Flinders Street station—to grandiose Parliament House, this walk of about 1¾ miles covers the civic and commercial aspects of Melbourne.

The station steps open onto the bustle of the city center. Cleared of motor traffic, Swanston Walk is a calm setting for the Gothic grandeur of **St. Paul's Cathedral**. Modern City Square, with its elaborate water features, marks the junction with Collins Street, dominated by the splendid Town Hall. Commercial dynamism has taken many shapes along this prestigious artery, from American deco of the 1930s to Victorian Gothic.

In Queen Street the elaborate Safe Deposit Building (Nos. 88–92) is dwarfed by the **A.N.Z. Tower** shooting skyward. Trams and shoppers throng Bourke Street Mall, off which runs the city's oldest shopping gallery, Royal Arcade, with its 1870 figures of Gog and Magog. Colorful archways signal the entry to Chinatown.

The grid of city streets ends where Little Bourke Street emerges into Spring Street, overlooked by the imposing colonnade of Victoria's **Parliament House**, and the Windsor Hotel of 1883. Nearby stands the **Old Treasury Building**, built in 1857, which contains the Melbourne Exhibition on the city's social and architectural history.

You can call a halt here, or return to Flinders Street station via the eastern, "Paris," end of Collins Street.

Along the Yarra

See map on pages 94–95.

A 3-mile walk along Melbourne's River Yarra into the green spaces of Kings Domain and the Botanic Gardens.

Downstream from Princes Bridge, the Yarra is crossed by a new footbridge. Avoiding the tempting riverside cafés of the Southgate Precinct, you are rewarded with a stunning view of the city skyline from Southbank Promenade on the far side of Princes Bridge.

Negotiate the crossing of Alexandra Avenue with care and enjoy the calm of **Kings Domain**, with its various focal points like the Sidney Myer Music Bowl and the Pioneer Women's Memorial Garden. The far bank of the lake in the **Royal Botanic Gardens** marks the outermost point of the walk, excuse enough for a pause at the lakeside café. Beyond the Herbarium and Visitor Centre is the **Shrine of Remembrance**, whose outside gallery gives a wonderful vista back to the city center.

The return to Flinders Street station can be made on foot or by tram along St. Kilda Road.

The Yarra River: locals' playground

THE BIRDS OF WYPERFELD

Much of this national park is alive with great flocks of birds: white and pink cockatoos, galahs, and regent parrots. The most curious bird, though, is the mallee-fowl, builder of underground nests in which its young are hatched in meticulously controlled incubation conditions.

PEAKS AND BEACHES

Although Victoria cannot lay claim to any of Australia's World Heritage regions, this small state encompasses an extraordinary variety of national parks and wilderness areas. Aside from the alpine regions, Victoria's favorite park is probably the superb coastal region of Wilsons Promontory (see page 121).

At Point Nepean on the Mornington Peninsula— the entrance to Port Phillip Bay

National parks

From high alps to rolling downlands, from luxuriant rain forests to desert scrub and from the spreading floodplains of the Murray River in the north to some of the country's most dramatic coastline in the south, Victoria's landscape is as varied as its climate. A high rainfall over much of the state contributes to the luxuriance of the forest cover as well as to the productivity of grasslands and other farmed areas; by contrast, the far northwest is extremely arid.

Victorian Alps The dominating physical feature of the state is its mountain backbone, the southernmost stretch of Australia's Great Dividing Range. Majestic alpine summits rise to almost 6,560 feet, while foothills and lower ranges stretch southward and westward to form a hilly backdrop to the metropolitan area of Melbourne. Many of the highest and most spectacular parts of the Victorian Alps are protected as national parks; they include **Mount Buffalo** (5,646 feet), whose characteristic hump-backed shape was first seen by the explorers Hume and Hovell in 1824. Beneath the summit stretches a vast upland plateau bounded by cliffs falling abruptly to the plains below. Used for skiing in winter, the plateau is embroidered with wildflowers in spring.

The vegetation cover varies with altitude, the dense wet forest of the valleys becoming more open farther up the slope, with peppermint gums giving way to alpine ash and finally to snow gums. In the early days of white settlement, cattlemen drove their beasts high into the uplands to feed off the summer pastures, building stone huts for shelter. Many of the huts remain, but grazing has been forbidden because of erosion. A number of physically separate national parks—Bogong, Cobberas-Tingaringy, and Wonnangatta-Moroka parks—have since been grouped together to form the exhilarating **Alpine National Park**, which is Victoria's largest at 1,596,000 acres.

Southeastern Victoria Along the border with New South Wales lies some of the most unspoiled scenery in the state. Inland are a number of national parks. **Errinundra National Park** encompasses a large tract of cool, temperate woodland, and there are other pockets of rain forest at **Lind** and **Alfred National Parks**. The splendid gorges along the course of the **Snowy River** offer exciting white-water canoeing; this park is also the habitat of the rare brush-tailed rock wallaby. Running from Sydenham Inlet to the N.S.W. boundary is one of the country's finest coastal reserves, the **Croajingolong National Park**, with savage cliffs and headlands protecting pristine beaches and tranquil inlets. In complete contrast are **The Lakes** to the west, where the seemingly infinite Ninety Mile Beach is backed by lagoons and waterways.

As well as the Dandenongs (see page 114), day trips from Melbourne can take in **Point Nepean** at the tip of the Mornington Peninsula, the **Brisbane Ranges**, the forests and fern gullies of **Kinglake National Park** to the northeast, and the basalt columns of **Organ Pipes National Park** to the northwest. The rugged **Grampians (Gariwerd) National Park** in the west is one of Victoria's highlights. This reserve with its Aboriginal sites, stunning scenery and abundant wildlife—more than 900 wildflower species, 200 species of birds, and 30 species of native mammals—is reachable in a day, but merits a longer stay.

Victoria's southwestern coastline The best can be seen in two contrasting parks: between Lorne and Cape Otway the high ranges of the **Otways**, still covered in glorious rain forest, rise steeply from the sea; farther west, the breakers are constantly resculpting the cliffs of the **Port Campbell National Park**, creating some truly spectacular coastal scenery. Inland, volcanic activity has given rise to fertile farmland interspersed with crater lakes and worn-down volcanic cones, as at **Mount Eccles**. Far from the coast and the wooded uplands is **Wyperfeld National Park**, a complex system of normally dry lakes and lagoons, with mallee (see panel) stretching to the horizon.

The basalt columns of the aptly named Organ Pipes National Park

107

MASTERING THE MALLEE
Much of northwestern Victoria was once covered in mallee, "a blue and level sea stretching to the horizon." Mallee is an Aboriginal word describing the fire-resistant scrub composed of 20 or so species of low-growing eucalyptus. The mallee burns fiercely, but quickly regenerates from the surviving roots, making it difficult for farmers to clear. Its demise came about with the invention of mullenization; a heavy roller was dragged through the scrub by oxen, followed by an ingenious "stump-jump" plow. Years of burning and cropping finally eradicated the troublesome mallee, except in areas like Wyperfeld, itself threatened with clearance as late as the 1960s.

Victoria's relatively small size and excellent roads make driving the ideal way to explore the state

THE GREAT OCEAN ROAD
One of Australia's most famous drives, the Great Ocean Road stretches 186 miles from south of Geelong toward the South Australian border, and takes in beaches, charming ports and villages, forested hillsides and, around the town of Port Campbell, dramatically eroded coastline (see page 119).

THE UNPREDICTABLE STATE
The weather in Victoria is notoriously changeable; desert influences may be felt one moment, with searing dry winds and high temperatures, giving way suddenly to cold and wet air from the ocean to the south. If you don't like our weather, say Melburnians, just wait a minute—it's bound to change!

How to travel

By air Melbourne's Tullamarine Airport is 13½ miles northwest of the city center and is connected to many overseas destinations as well as to all major cities in Australia. Domestic and international flights share the same terminal. Frequent Skybus services link the airport to Spencer Street station downtown, from where a shuttle distributes passengers to city center hotels.

By bus Express buses travel to major destinations in Australia and within Victoria. Because of the (relatively!) small size of the state, public transportation is a reasonable proposition for most journeys. Many places in Victoria are accessible in a day's outing from Melbourne. There is the usual excellent range of organized bus tours —shop around for the one that suits your requirements.

By train Greater Melbourne's comprehensive public transportation network is marketed under the name of **The Met**. Electric suburban railroads that travel as far afield as the Dandenong Ranges and Mornington Peninsula are supplemented by one of the world's most extensive systems of tramways and by urban buses. Through-ticketing is based on a zoning system, and there are a number of special deals like day tickets or weekly passes that are worth considering. The principal station is Flinders Street, and most trains travel around the underground loop that circles the city center with useful stops at Flagstaff Gardens, Melbourne Central, Parliament and Spencer Street.
   Quite a number of towns in Victoria can be reached by **V-Line train** (sometimes supplemented by a V-Line bus). There are interstate services to Adelaide and Sydney as well as to Perth (changing at Adelaide or Port Pirie), and Alice Springs on the famous *Ghan*.

By car Highway conditions in Victoria are generally good. The grandiose freeway plan for Melbourne was only partly implemented, but traffic still seems to flow much more freely than in Sydney. To visit the more inaccessible national parks renting a car is recommended.

►► Apollo Bay   90A2

This little fishing port about 116 miles to the west of Port Phillip Bay has magnificent beaches and makes an excellent base for exploring the superb forests of the Otway Ranges. The hills reach the sea at Cape Otway, the "fearful coastline" described by the explorer Matthew Flinders, with a lighthouse rising from 328-foot cliffs.

► Ararat   90B2

This town (125 miles northwest of Melbourne) owes its foundation to the gold strike of 1857, when 3,000 ounces of alluvial gold were found in the space of three weeks. Then Ararat's population was more than double its present total; now sheep outnumber people by about 150 to one. To the north is the world-famous **Seppelt Great Western Winery**, where the champagne is stored in underground galleries originally dug out by the gold miners.

► Avoca   90B2

On the Pyrenees Highway between Ararat and Castlemaine, Avoca was once a gold town and is now the center of an agricultural area. Since the 1960s, vineyards have been replanted on the north-facing slopes of the foothills, making this one of the state's newer wine districts. The solid Court House complex with bluestone jail, powder magazine and police residence dates from the mid-19th century.

►►► Ballarat   90B2

No bigger than in its gold-rush heyday, Ballarat has preserved much of its 19th-century townscape and the atmosphere of those heady times.

Gold was first found in 1851, and within a few months thousands of ill-assorted diggers were frantically prospecting in spite of mud, cold, and frequent bitter disappointment. Surface deposits were soon exhausted, and individual miners were succeeded by companies with sufficient clout to dig deep mines and buy the machinery to run them. Gold may have made Melbourne, but it made Ballarat too; profits seem not to have been gambled or drunk away, but to have been invested respectably in bricks and mortar, giving the town as splendid an array of fine 19th-century building as can be seen anywhere in the country. Banks, churches, a synagogue, clubs, a mining exchange, a splendid town hall, and an art gallery all demonstrate how quickly the raw life of the diggings was transmuted into civic respectability.

109

The gold-rush town of Ballarat contains many grand buildings that date from the 19th century

EUREKA!
By 1854, passions were running high in Ballarat's goldfields. Grim working and living conditions and encroachment by bigger mining companies were compounded by high license fees, extracted from resentful diggers by heavy-handed and much hated special police. Eventually, a band of Irish-led miners staged the only major revolt by whites in Australian history. Licenses were burned in a joyous conflagration, and the rebels, armed with pikes, assembled in the Eureka Stockade under the banner of the Southern Cross. But in a savage example of overkill, they were swiftly overcome by govern-ment soldiers, who left 30 dead. Australia's "Civil War" lasted 15 minutes; it is convincingly recreated, using advanced *son et lumière* techniques, at Sovereign Hill.

A statue of Queen Victoria presiding over formal gardens in Bendigo

BRED IN BALLARAT
Ballarat Wildlife Park has a wonderful selection of mostly Antipodean animals in its park-like setting. It is one of the few places where Tasmanian Devils are suc-cessfully bred; if you are so inclined, you can see these thugs of the animal world being fed their daily ration of white mice.

Sovereign Hill▶▶▶ is a superb re-creation of life and work on the goldfields in the 1850s. It is popular with its visitors, who can pan for gold, ride Cobb & Co.'s stage-coach, store in the emporiums of Main Street, savor the unique world of the Chinese Village, or even spend the night in 1850s-style accommodations at the Sovereign Hill Lodge. Other features include the Mine Museum, with 1,970 feet of underground workings, and the Gold Museum, which has displays showing the history of the precious metal.

▶▶ Beechworth   91B4
This exceptionally well-preserved gold town in the foothills of the Australian Alps, 168 miles northeast of Melbourne, has a fine array of old buildings, many of them constructed from warm, honey-colored stone. As well as the post office, with its imposing tower, and the 61 hotels dating back to gold-rush times (the carriage house of one is home to a coach museum), there is also the Burke Museum. Named after the ill-fated explorer, the museum is packed with memorabilia, including mementoes of Ned Kelly who spent a night in the cell beneath the town hall.

▶▶ Bellarine Peninsula   90A3
Stretching eastward into Port Phillip Bay, this broad peninsula, with its fine surf beaches and popular resorts like Ocean Grove and Barwon Heads, has become the summer playground for the inhabitants of Geelong. One of the peninsula's greatest attractions is the charming resort town of Queenscliff (see page 119), known for its fort, lighthouse, and grand old hotels.

▶▶ Bendigo   90B2

Like Ballarat, Bendigo began as a gold-rush town, expanding rapidly from 1851 onward to become one of the state's largest inland towns. Many of its fine late 19th-century buildings, erected with the wealth won from the ground, remain in peak condition. These include the vast Shamrock Hotel, a number of imposing churches and a fine group of public buildings. The work that paid for all this architectural splendor is celebrated in the completely preserved **Central Deborah Goldmine**▶▶, with its impressive underground galleries, while the special contribution of Chinese miners is recalled in the delightful **Joss House** at Emu Point. The best way to get acquainted with this fascinating town is to take the "Talking Tram," which runs along a 5-mile route and gives a full commentary on all the sights.

▶ Brisbane Ranges National Park   90A2

This extensive block of slate and sandstone has been eroded in places to form deep defiles like Anakie Gorge, a favored spot for not-too-demanding bush walks. Gold was once mined in quantity at the ghost town of Steiglitz, now a historic park.

▶ Camperdown   90A2

This township is located on the sweeping plains formed from lava and ash that run from the South Australian border to Port Phillip Bay and have long been the basis of a prosperous grazing industry. Now silent, the volcanic cones responsible for all this fertility are scattered over the area. Mount Leura and Mount Sugarloaf are to the southeast of town, while to the west there are two examples of crater lakes—Lake Bullen Merri (fresh water) and Lake Gnotuk (salt water).

▶▶ Castlemaine   90B2

Once gold had been discovered here in Specimen Gully by a shepherd, 25,000 diggers joined the rush, although Castlemaine declined fairly quickly because of the lack of reef gold. Today it is an attractive township, popular with Melbourne folk and full of interesting old buildings. Most striking is the classical market hall, an almost exact reproduction of a Greek temple that now contains the local museum. Castlemaine is also home to an excellent art gallery, some fine botanic gardens and the mansion known as Buda, begun in 1857.

The Castlemaine and Maldon Railway is a steam train ride that is very popular with children. It is based at Maldon station, 11 miles west along Highway 122 (see also page 117).

▶▶ Coal Creek Historical Village, Korumburra   90A3

The railroads of Victoria used to run on Korumburra coal, and after the last mine had been closed down in the late 1950s it was decided that the days of coal and steam should be recreated at Coal Creek Mine just outside town (about 62 miles southeast of Melbourne). As well as the gallery of the mine, the popular 99-acre site has a railroad station, tradesmen plying their crafts, old stores, and settlers' cottages.

THE GIPPSLAND WHOPPER
Of the 100 or so species of Australian worms, *Megascolides australis* is easily the biggest, measuring up to 12 feet long and 1 inch thick. This extraordinary creature has its own worm-shaped museum near the turn-off for Phillip Island on the Bass Highway.

Castlemaine is a former mining town about 25 miles north of Daylesford

For much of its 1,615-mile length, the Murray forms the boundary between Victoria and New South Wales. The longest river in Australia rises in the Great Dividing Range near Mount Kosciuszko, flowing past stands of red gums and irrigating the land around Mildura before entering the sea at Encounter Bay.

For thousands of years the rich wildlife of the Murray and its tributaries gave sustenance to the Aborigines who lived along its banks. It was discovered by Hume and Hovell in 1824, and explored more thoroughly by Charles Sturt in the course of his expedition of 1829–1830. As settlers arrived, in the beginning strongly opposed by the Aborigines, the river took on great importance as a transportation route. A spirited contest took place in 1853 between the *Mary Ann* and the *Lady Augusta*, to see which would be the first steamboat to make it up the Murray as far as Swan Hill. With the prize money of £4,000, the master of the winning steamboat founded the Murray River Navigation Co., whose sternwheelers dominated river traffic for many years until the coming of the railway rendered them obsolete.

The greatest handicap to navigation was the irregularity of the Murray's flow; for many months of the year there would not be enough water to float a boat of any size, and the risk of running aground was constant. A number of proud vessels survive to carry cargoes of nostalgic tourists rather than the bales of wool that filled the holds in their 19th-century heyday.

Attractions Upstream from the twin towns of Albury (N.S.W.) and Wodonga (Victoria) is **Lake Hume**, several times the size of Sydney Harbour. Built to regulate river flow, it is now an ideal location for watersports. Downstream are the wineries around **Rutherglen**, while **Yarrawonga**, thanks to Lake Mulwala, has become a major inland water recreation area. Around **Cobram** are dozens of fine sandy beaches.

Echuca was once Australia's busiest inland port, with a truly magnificent wharf more than a mile long built from the timber of red gums. The people of the town are very proud of its heritage, and have taken pains to preserve it for the pleasure of visitors. The port area has been fully restored and has a whole series of visitor attractions, including the Cargo Shed with life-like dioramas. The Bridge Hotel is full of period furniture,

BARMAH FOREST
Spreading for 116 square miles over the floodplain of the Murray upstream from Echuca is this magnificent forest of river red gum trees, some of them 500 years old. Australia was largely built on the timber milled from these majestic trees, which was used for railroad construction, bridges, mines, fences, and wharves. When the river spills over its banks during exceptionally rainy spells, the forest comes alive with the calls of more than 200 species of migrating birds.

A journey to the past aboard a paddle steamer...

...stopping at Echuca, Swan Hill, Mildura, and other places along the Murray

and the old Customs House has been put to use as the information center. It is rare to see so many steamboats, either under restoration or in action.

To the northwest of the Kerang Lakes is another river port, **Swan Hill**, named by explorer Thomas Mitchell who was kept awake at night by the swans on a nearby lagoon. The town's outstanding attraction is the **Swan Hill Pioneer Settlement**, a painstaking riverside re-creation put together using original buildings as well as accurate replicas, and brought alive by the presence of craftspeople practicing traditional trades. In addition to its daytime attractions, the Pioneer Settlement offers an illuminating sound and light show that concentrates on the early pioneers. A strong sense of the past can also be experienced in two fine old properties, the **Tyntyndyer Homestead** to the north, and **Murray Downs** to the east, the latter designed to repel attack by Aborigines.

Red to green At the heart of the irrigated area, **Mildura** was originally laid out on the American pattern, with streets given numbers rather than names. In the language of the Kulkyne Aborigines, Mildura meant "dry red earth," but here red has turned to green—the Chaffey brothers, who arrived in 1885 from North America, brought advanced irrigation techniques (see panel). Avocados, melons, oranges and grapes—both for the table and for wine-making—are all grown here, as is a whole range of fruit for drying. A number of establishments are happy to share their production secrets with you, among them Orange World and the Lindemans Karadoc Winery. Alternatively, you could take a trip upriver aboard one of the paddle steamers that operate from here.

THE CHAFFEYS
Canadians George and William Chaffey pioneered artificially irrigated settlements in California before being invited to bring their expertise to the Murray. They both succeeded and failed; from the 1880s on, thousands of new settlers flocked to the newly irrigated areas around Mildura, and the town itself prospered, but there were floods, problems with leaching and salinity, and the great slump of the 1890s. By 1896 George had had enough and borrowed his fare home, but William stayed on, helping to put the area's economy on a firmer footing once the railroad arrived in 1903. The water pumps that George had designed continued to work into the 1950s.

The lovely Rhododendron Gardens at Olinda in the Dandenong Ranges

A FEATHERED PHILANDERER
The forests and gullies of the Dandenongs provide a habitat for *Menura novae-hollandiae*, the superb lyrebird, a wonderful singer and mimic of the calls of other birds. The rather ordinary-looking male of the species comes into his own in winter, when he senses that female lyrebirds are ready to respond to his advances. Having built a series of mounds throughout his territory, the male mounts one and undergoes an extraordinary transformation, fanning out his lyre-shaped tail-feathers so that his body disappears in a froth of plumage, at the same time pouring forth a cascade of song. The more impressive the display, the greater the bird's chances of winning his way with a succession of females.

▶ **Colac**   90A2

Colac is the market town for the agricultural wealth of the surrounding basalt plains. This southwestern area incorporates a lake district of some 50 to 60 water bodies. Those that have formed in deep craters contain fresh water, while the shallower lakes contain salty water because the rate of evaporation from them exceeds the rate of replenishment; Lake Corangamite is a saline lake, and is also Victoria's largest.

▶▶ **The Dandenong Ranges**   90A3

Melbourne is fortunate to have these magnificently wooded hills on the eastern edge of the metropolitan area, a wonderful destination for a day's outing. The highest point is **Mount Dandenong**▶▶ (2,077 feet), with fantastic views over the sprawling city to the west and the further hills to the east.

Because of their accessibility, the Dandenongs have long been a favorite residential area, and there are pretty townships and many fine mansions, some of which have been converted into hotels and restaurants. There are lush gardens, too, like the **Rhododendron Gardens**▶ at Olinda, whose exotic shrubs contrast with the native vegetation of towering mountain ash trees, massive tree ferns and rampant creepers. At Belgrave is the terminus of **"Puffing Billy"**▶▶, the vintage narrow-gauge steam locomotive that pulls trainloads of tourists on a scenic 8-mile trip through the forest.

▶▶ **Daylesford**   90B2

Between them, Daylesford (62 miles northwest of Melbourne) and Hepburn Springs contain half of Australia's mineral springs. The supposedly therapeutic waters were discovered in the course of gold mining in the 1850s and 1860s, and by the turn of the century the place had taken on the character of the spa resorts so common in Europe, perhaps because many of the early inhabitants were originally immigrants from the Swiss canton of Ticino. At the Hepburn Spa Complex, the old spa building is still intact; you can acquire bottled water, take various treatments and enjoy relaxing walks. The excellent **Daylesford Historical Society Museum▶** is housed in the old School of Mines, and there are attractive botanical gardens. To the north is the old volcanic cone of Mount Franklin with a fine view from its summit.

▶ Dunolly 90B2
The area around Dunolly, 108 miles northwest of Melbourne, yielded more nuggets than any other Australian goldfield, including the Welcome Stranger, weighing 2,505 ounces. Reproductions of this and other mega-nuggets can be seen in the quiet little town's Goldfields Museum.

▶ Geelong 90A2
This industrial port city, Victoria's second largest, once saw itself as a rival to Melbourne, but has long since given up the struggle, though its harbor still exports the rich produce of its agricultural hinterland. In spite of much redevelopment, there is plenty of evidence of 19th-century grandeur; imposing public buildings adorn the city center and the prosperity of Geelong's merchant class is reflected in the many elegant properties, such as Barwon Grange overlooking the Barwon River. Corio Villa above Eastern Beach was prefabricated in Scotland and re-assembled here by guesswork after the plans and instructions had been destroyed. One of the fine old bluestone woolstores has been splendidly restored to house the excellent **National Wool Museum▶▶**. This is the place to come if you want to understand how Australia "rode to prosperity on the sheep's back."

▶▶ Gippsland 91A4
Named in the 1840s by Polish explorer Count Strzelecki after the Governor of N.S.W., Gippsland is the loosely defined region comprising most of southeastern Victoria between the highlands of the Great Dividing Range and the coastline of Bass Strait. The superb temperate rain forest that once blanketed the area has mostly been cut down to yield rich dairying and fruit-growing land, though fine tracts of woodland remain in the state forests and national parks along the N.S.W. border in the far east. This is one of the areas where protest action by conservationists has focused public attention on the fact that the glories of Australia's natural heritage are not inexhaustible. The La Trobe Valley in the heart of Gippsland has the world's biggest deposits of brown coal, burned here in power stations to provide something like 90 percent of the state's electric power, while oil and gas is extracted in quantity from offshore wells in Bass Strait.

The scale of contemporary opencast mining can be appreciated in the course of tours from the **Morwell Visitor Centre▶**, while more traditional activities can be contemplated in the **Gippsland Heritage Centre▶** at Moe, with its collection of old buildings from many parts of Gippsland. Inland is some of Victoria's most attractive countryside, running up into the alpine foothills of the Great Dividing Range, while the Gippsland Lakes (see panel) lie landward of Ninety Mile Beach.

GIPPSLAND LAKES
Sometimes described as "the best example of a coastal lagoon in the world," and with a near-Mediterranean climate, this area offers unrivaled opportunites for sailing, cruising, fishing or just taking it easy. Both beach and lakes are protected as national parks.

115

Rich dairy lands make for fine Gippsland cheeses

Victoria

OUR PEOPLE
Following the 1988 Bicentenary, Australia's indigenous people decided to try to replace the overall term "Aborigine" with names from their own languages. "Koori," meaning "our people," is now widely in use in southeastern Australia. The Grampians are an outdoor gallery of Koori art, to be seen in the Billimina, Larngibunja and Ngamadjidj shelters, and at Flat Rock.

YARRA VALLEY
An hour away from Melbourne, Australia's fastest-growing wine region is located among the rolling hills and rich soils of the Yarra Valley. There are almost 30 wineries to visit, particularly around the town of Yarra Glen. The valley is becoming famous both for its fine dining and its excellent range of rustic bed and breakfast accommodations.

▶ **Goulburn Valley**   *90B3*

The Goulburn River runs northwest from artificial Lake Eildon in the foothills of the Victorian Alps through a rich fruit- and vine-growing area to join the Murray River near Echuca. With an indented shoreline more than 300 miles long, Lake Eildon is an immensely popular place for watersports of all kinds. There is also some good walking in this area. The lake is fringed by Eildon State Park and Fraser National Park—forested environments that are also rich in wildlife. To the west of the river, Rushworth is a fine example of a gold-rush town of the 1850s.

▶▶ **Grampians (Gariwerd) National Park**   *90B1*

The Aborigines, who left many traces of their rock art here, knew the Grampians as Gariwerd. Forming the largest national park in Victoria, the region consists of a succession of sandstone ridges sloping gently to the west, ending in sheer cliffs and jagged rock formations to the east. The area is rich in wildlife and is carpeted with wildflowers in summer.

The park has an excellent network of trails and paths, and can also be appreciated by car thanks to a series of scenic roads. There are any number of spectacular viewpoints; **Boroka Lookout▶▶** gives a fine panorama over the town of Halls Gap, where there is a visitor center and the **Brambuk Living Cultural Centre▶**, which is intended to bring the history and culture of local Aborigines to life. To the west are two of the most spectacular sights of the ranges; the rock formation known as the **Balconies** and the grandiose water staircase of the **Mackenzie Falls**.

▶ **Hamilton**   *90A1*

Focal point of much of the prosperous agricultural plains of central western Victoria, Hamilton likes to style itself the "Wool Capital of the World." Its outstanding attraction is the **City of Hamilton Art Gallery▶**, with a large and varied collection including wonderful examples of the

The huge overhanging rocks in the Grampians National Park known as the Balconies

applied arts of many countries, plus a splendid array of the watercolors and etchings of the British topographical artist Paul Sandby.

►► Healesville 90B3

Nestling among its green hills in the Yarra Valley, this attractive township is a good place for walks and picnics, but it is mostly visited now for the **Healesville Sanctuary►►**. A visit to this wildlife park is an excellent way to appreciate the strange and wonderful fauna of the Antipodes, in a range of cleverly re-created habitats and walk-through enclosures. The local Aboriginal cultural center, **Galeena Beek►►**, includes displays on artifacts and ritual dances, and offers walking tours.

►► Lorne 90A2

Protected from the north by the steep forested slopes of the Otways, this charming little place facing onto the curving beach of Loutit Bay has enjoyed a high reputation as a Great Ocean Road beach resort for over a century. There are also delightful walks in the forest park.

►► Maldon 90B2

Among the many old gold-rush townships of central Victoria, Maldon is outstanding—"the best preserved town in Australia of the gold-mining era" according to the National Trust. It is certainly full of charm; the scale of the place is modest and the tone is set by delightful cottages, many of them with pretty gardens.

► Marysville 90B3

Pleasantly located in the foothills of the Victorian Alps, the township of Marysville has long been favored by weekending Melburnians. In summer there is wonderful bushwalking to the Steavenson Falls, some of the highest in Victoria, or to the Cumberland Valley where the state's tallest trees grow, while in winter there is good cross-country skiing, particularly on the popular snowfields of Lake Mountain.

Maldon's wide main street slopes gently downhill and features some typically Australian country architecture

DUCKBILLED DENIZEN
Even the normally bashful platypus can be observed going about its daily life at Healesville. The sanctuary has the distinction of being the first place to successfully breed this reclusive egg-laying mammal in captivity.

PENGUINS ON PARADE
The endearing little fairy penguins that live along the coasts of southern Australia are the smallest of the species in the world, being only about a foot in length. They spend their days feeding at sea, then as evening falls they gather in groups to waddle to their burrows at the back of the beach on Phillip Island. They maintain this routine with apparent indifference to the floodlighting and to the countless tourists huddled in the stands watching them.

The dramatic Twelve Apostles coastline near Port Campbell, on the Great Ocean Road

▶▶ Mornington Peninsula   90A3

Melbourne's favorite weekend and vacation area embraces Port Phillip Bay in a great curve of sheltered beaches before ending at Point Nepean, overlooking the dangerous currents of the narrow entrance to the bay known as The Rip. Much of the peninsula is suburban in character, with dwellings crowding along the main road and spreading out from the residential and resort towns like Frankston and Mornington, but there are over 100 wineries to visit. In the season, the foreshore is crowded with campers and R.V.'s. Toward the tip, refined Sorrento and exclusive Portsea have retained the feeling of early days, when paddlesteamers plied across the bay from Melbourne. Once off limits as a naval base, Point Nepean is now part of the Mornington Peninsula National Park, reached from the visitor center by shuttle. The "front" beaches facing the bay tend to be calm but busy, while the "back" beaches looking out onto the Bass Strait are rough—no place for inexperienced swimmers. Former Australian Prime Minister Harold Holt disappeared here in 1967, and was presumed drowned.

The peninsula's importance in Victoria's history is recalled by the graves of the "early settlers" at **Sorrento**, and by the 1844 **McCrae Homestead▶**, the home of the first permanent settler family. The best overall view is from 1,000-foot high **Arthur's Seat**, reached by road or, more excitingly, by chairlift.

▶▶ Phillip Island   90A3

Bounded to the west by the Mornington Peninsula, the great tidal estuary of Westernport bay is broken up by a number of islands. French Island and Little Churchill Island are rich in wildlife, but the most famous of the

islands is Phillip Island, whose irresistible **Fairy Penguin Parade** pulls in hundreds of thousands of onlookers.

Reached by bridge and about 80 miles from Melbourne, Phillip Island has a varied coastline that includes rugged cliffs and long surf beaches. Muttonbirds nest on **Cape Woolamai**, the island's highest point; the **Koala Conservation Centre** features a large koala colony; and Seal Rocks is home to the world's largest Australian fur seal colony. This is also the location of the new **Seal Rocks Sea Life Centre**, which aims to interpret the island's abundant wildlife. **Cowes** is the main resort, with boat trips to see the seals and French Island.

▶▶▶ Port Campbell National Park 90A2

Backed by the Great Ocean Road running west from Geelong, this park comprises 19 miles of some of the world's most spectacular coastal scenery, a succession of high cliffs, headlands and strange rock formations standing out to sea. Cookie-like beds of limestone, sand, mud and seashells formed beneath the sea and then uplifted 25 million years ago are now being eaten away by the breakers rolling in from the Southern Ocean. Because the rock varies in strength and texture, the sea advances more rapidly in some places than others, leaving behind isolated features that have been given evocative names like the Twelve Apostles (at Port Campbell). In a dramatic demonstration of the rate of erosion, the arch of "London Bridge" collapsed into the surf in 1990, stranding the walkers who had ventured onto it. Quickly rescued, they were luckier than the many passengers and crewmen who perished along what was named the "Shipwreck Coast" in the days of sail (see pages 242–243).

▶▶ Port Fairy 90A1

This delightful little Great Ocean Road fishing port and beach resort at the mouth of the Moyne River is one of the oldest settlements in Victoria, having been home to sealers and whalers in the early years of the 19th century. There are 50 buildings classified as historic by the National Trust, including Mott's Cottage and a wooden house erected by a whaling skipper in the 1830s.

▶ Portland 90A1

Founded in 1834, this busy deep-water port is the oldest permanent settlement in Victoria. To the southwest are the spectacular seascapes of Cape Nelson and the blowholes and petrified forest of Cape Bridgewater.

▶▶ Queenscliff 90A3

Separated from Point Nepean on the Mornington Peninsula by the treacherous waters of The Rip, Queenscliff is an old-fashioned kind of place, with a harbor, a fort (1882), grand hotels, and the Black Lighthouse, prefabricated in Scotland and shipped here in 1863.

▶▶ Strzelecki Ranges 91A3

The best way to see these forested ridges is to follow the Grand Ridge Road from Nyora, southeast of Melbourne, to Carrajung (about 80 miles), passing through some of Victoria's finest upland scenery and numerous pretty towns and villages.

Queenscliff on the Bellarine Peninsula— where Melburnians come to get away from it all

119

COUNT THE CONSONANTS
The Polish explorer Paul Edmund de Strzelecki styled himself "Count," a claim with little apparent substance. Although it was Angus McMillan who had first blazed a trail through the almost impenetrable rain forest jungle of southeast Victoria, it was not his name for the area ("New South Caledonia") that was adopted, but Strzelecki's "Gippsland." Strzelecki's own venture into Gippsland was only saved from disaster by the skill of his Aboriginal guide, Tarra, after whom the Tarra Bulga National Park has been named.

Gum trees or, to give them their more correct name, eucalypts, are the trees most closely identified with Australia. They comprise more than 500 different species, and grow in most parts of the country; some three-quarters of all Australian trees are eucalypts, many of them with wonderfully descriptive names like peppermint, iron-bark, bloodwood or blackbutt.

EUCALYPTUS LEAVES
All eucalyptus leaves contain a fragrant oil that is used for various medicinal purposes. Their indigestible look doesn't deter the koala either, which in fact depends entirely on one eucalyptus species for its food source.

WORLD-BEATER
The confusingly named mountain ash (*Eucalyptus regnans*) is the tallest flowering plant in the world, reaching an extraordinary height of up to 328 feet in the forests of Victoria and Tasmania.

The great river red gum forest at Yarrawonga

Early settlers didn't much like the look of the unfamiliar eucalypts, with their pale grayish-green or peeling, untidy bark hanging in strips and tatters and the unseasonal failure of their dull gray leaves to fall at the proper time of year. Many farmers and sheep ranchers brought cuttings of other trees from home, and elm, oak, willow and poplar grace many a rural scene. The same was true of townsfolk, who preferred the more orderly European trees for their parks.

Forests and felling But eucalypts have their own distinct allure, individually or in mass, forming magnificent forests or growing with other trees, shrubs, and grasses to form the surprisingly park-like landscapes of many parts of the interior. Over the millennia, eucalypts have also learned to live with fire, regenerating almost miraculously after the all-too-common bushfires from buds concealed within their bark. Many species, like jarrah and messmate, yield first-rate wood, and in consequence were felled ruthlessly until quite recently. Others are logged, somewhat demeaningly, to be turned into woodchip for foreign pulp mills.

Varieties There are many types of eucalypts, from the Tasmanian blue gum that provided the wood for railroad ties, to the river red gum of semi-arid areas, the ghost gum of deserts, and the hardy, cold-resistant snow gum, symbol of the Australian Alps.

▶ Walhalla 91A4

Tucked away in the deep wooded valleys north of Moe, isolated Walhalla boomed in the late 19th century when more gold was extracted here than from any other area in Victoria. By the time the railroad reached here in 1910 via a series of spectacular tunnels and trestle bridges the gold had more or less run out. A stroll along the crooked main street recalls some of the atmosphere of former days, and you can visit the Long Tunnel Extended Mine. You can also ride on the restored Walhalla Goldfields Railway through this magnificent upland scenery.

▶ Wangaratta 90B3

The Hume Highway is the main route north from Melbourne to Sydney. About 150 miles from Melbourne is Wangaratta, a service center for the surrounding agricultural area. The body of the notorious bushranger Daniel "Mad Dog" Morgan is buried here minus his head, the latter having been sent to Melbourne in order to establish whether he really was mad, or just plain bad. The town's other attraction is the **Airworld Museum▶ ▶**, with a splendid collection of vintage aircraft.

▶ Warrnambool 90A1

The biggest town on Victoria's southwest coast, Warrnambool benefits from superb beaches. Founded by whalers in the 1840s, it is still frequented by southern right whales, which come here in winter to calve (see panel). **Flagstaff Hill Maritime Museum▶ ▶** is a conscientiously re-created port village with several historic vessels and other fascinating displays.

▶▶ Wilsons Promontory National Park 91A4

The southernmost point of mainland Australia, this wild and mountainous granite peninsula protruding into Bass Strait is perhaps Victoria's favorite national park. Many of its rocky headlands, splendid beaches and dense forests are only accessible on foot, and in spite of its popularity it is always possible to find whatever degree of isolation you want (except for kangaroos, of course). The only settlement is at Tidal River, where the road ends and a network of wonderful hiking trails begins.

Southern right whales playing off Warrnambool

121

THE WARRNAMBOOL WHALES
Between May and August southern right whales gather off Logan's Beach to bear their young. A special viewing platform has been built from which you can observe these magnificent creatures, once hunted to near-extinction, as they dive and play, making spectacular fountains from their blowholes or leaping bodily from the waves.

"THE PROM"
Discovered by maritime explorer George Bass in 1798 and named after a friend of Bass's colleague Matthew Flinders, Wilsons Promontory attracts all kinds of nature-lovers. In summer the area is great for scuba diving and snorkeling; there are wonderful walks; and the hundreds of species of plants make the park a botanist's dream.

The Dandenong Ranges

Less than an hour from the center of Melbourne, the "Blue Dandenongs" are a favorite recreation area and summer retreat for the inhabitants of the city.

Canterbury Road leads to Montrose at the northern end of the Dandenong Tourist Road. If you have time, continue another 19 miles to **Healesville**

Sanctuary in the Yarra Valley, one of the best places in which to see Australian wildlife at close quarters.

Mount Dandenong, at 2,077 feet the highest point of the range, and the sculptures of the **William Ricketts Sanctuary** are accessible from the Tourist Road. The route to the village of Kallista passes the Nicholas Memorial Gardens and **Sherbrooke Forest Park**, where you can see the tree-ferns and the magnificent mountain ash trees for which the area is famous.

Belgrave is the terminus for the irresistible "Puffing Billy," a restored steam train that hauls delighted passengers through the forest along its narrow-gauge track.

Mornington Peninsula

The 62-mile drive to Point Nepean National Park at the tip of the Mornington Peninsula passes through resorts and residential areas with access to the beaches of Port Phillip Bay.

Frankston marks the end of the commuter railroad line from Melbourne. Beyond **Dromana** with its excellent Tourist Information Centre the coast is lined with vacation homes and campsites, while above the town **Arthur's Seat** rises 1,000 feet to give a fine panorama over bay and ocean. On its northern slope is the little **McCrae Homestead**, built in 1844 and still evocative of pioneer days.

With its broad main street, **Sorrento** has a charm all of its own, while posh **Portsea** does its best to maintain its exclusivity. On the outer rim of the peninsula, the "back beaches" face the ocean surf of Bass Strait. For a long time off limits as defense land, the **Point Nepean** section of the **Mornington Peninsula National Park** can now be visited. With 25 miles of rugged coastline, this park and its adjacent marine reserve encompass excellent surfing beaches and diving spots, and wildlife that features dolphins from November to March. Other Mornington Peninsula attractions include about 30 wineries, acclaimed golf courses, and a growing reputation for boutique guesthouses and dining.

From Frankston, the Mornington Peninsula Freeway and South East Freeway can be used to speed your return to Melbourne.

Right: Port Phillip Bay begins at the tip of the Mornington Peninsula

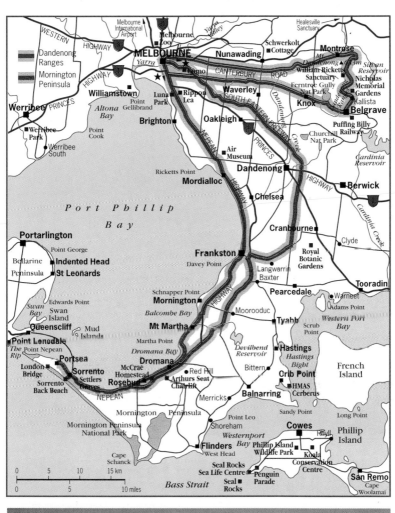

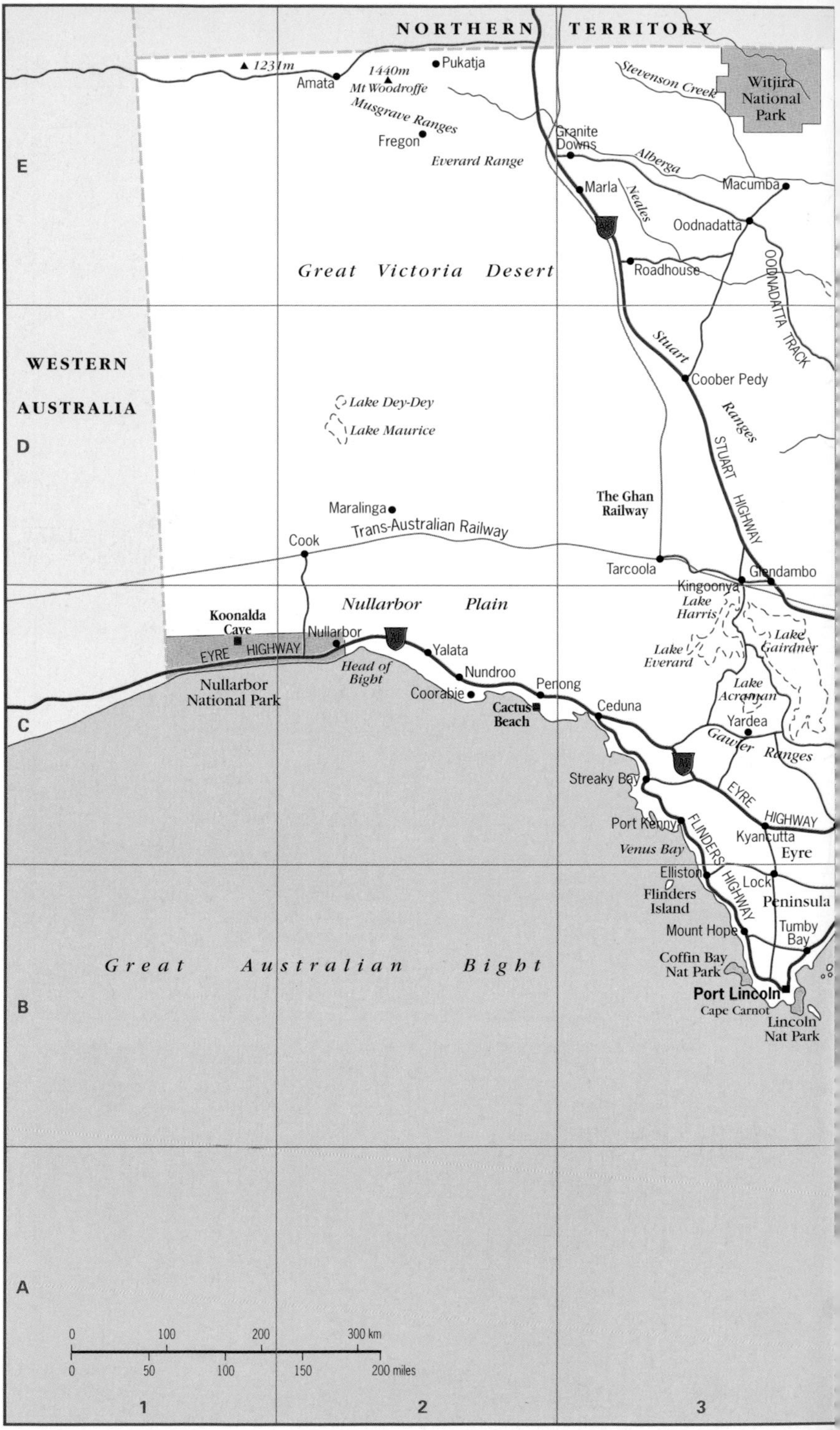

NORTHERN TERRITORY

▲ 1231m

Amata
1440m
Mt Woodroffe
Pukatja

Stevenson Creek

Witjira National Park

Musgrave Ranges

Fregon

Everard Range

Granite Downs

Alberga

E

Marla

Needles

Macumba

Oodnadatta

Roadhouse

Great Victoria Desert

OODNADATTA TRACK

Stuart

Coober Pedy

WESTERN

AUSTRALIA

D

Lake Dey-Dey

Lake Maurice

Ranges

STUART HIGHWAY

Glendambo

Maralinga

Trans-Australian Railway

The Ghan Railway

124

Cook

Tarcoola

Kingoonya

Koonalda Cave

Nullarbor Plain

Nullarbor

Lake Harris

Lake Gairdner

EYRE HIGHWAY

Yalata

Lake Everard

Nullarbor National Park

Head of Bight

Nundroo

Lake Acraman

Coorabie

Perlong

Ceduna

Yardea

Cactus Beach

Gawler Ranges

C

Streaky Bay

EYRE HIGHWAY

Port Kenny

Kyancutta

FLINDERS HIGHWAY

Venus Bay

Eyre

Elliston

Lock

Flinders Island

Peninsula

Mount Hope

Tumby Bay

Great Australian Bight

Coffin Bay Nat Park

Port Lincoln

B

Cape Carnot

Lincoln Nat Park

A

0   100   200   300 km

0   50   100   150   200 miles

1   2   3

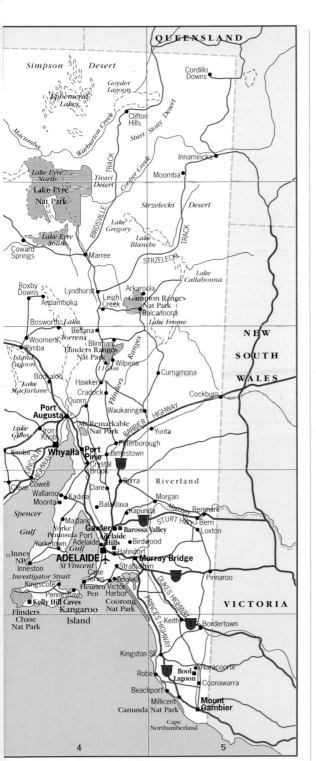

REGION HIGHLIGHTS ▶▶▶

DRY DOCK
Australia's driest state covers an eighth of the continent's total area, but has a population of less than 1.5 million. South Australia also has the distinction of being the only state established without the aid of convict labor—a fact of which it is particularly proud.

126

WOWSERS NO MORE
A wowser originally meant someone who didn't know how to enjoy himself. The epithet was maliciously applied to the good citizens of Adelaide because of their supposed piety and apparent aversion to letting their hair down. The visitor to South Australia is unlikely to see much trace of this today, least of all in Adelaide. It may still be a city of churches, but it is now also a city of restaurants, watered by the products of its wineries. And it was in South Australia that the country's first nudist beach was opened, at Maslins on the coast south of Adelaide.

SOUTH AUSTRALIA Virtually all the inhabitants of Australia's third largest state live along the fertile coasts of its gulf lands and southeastern plains, three-quarters of them in Greater Adelaide. Northward from this tamed littoral with its almost Mediterranean climate stretches an immense and arid area of Outback and desert, some of it bearing the traces of failed European settlement, and huge tracts of it returned to the Aborigines. This is a land of sharp differences, with a capital that is the most elegant and obviously cultured of all Australian cities.

IN THE BEGINNING South Australia was not a prison colony but a "province," settled by free people (mostly from the south of England, but many also from Germany) under the auspices of the South Australia Company. The first group landed from the *Buffalo* in 1836, but the true founding father was Colonel William Light, a brilliant and unorthodox character whose visionary plan for Adelaide has shaped the city to the present day. The development of the colony was erratic. Within a few years of its foundation it was only saved from economic collapse by the discovery of copper at Kapunda and Burra. Attempts to push the frontier of agriculture north were defeated by long years of drought, although the peninsula's corn lands flourished.

For many years Adelaide remained simply the center of a vast agricultural and mining area, its affairs conducted by merchants who lived sober lives ("wowsers" to other Australians—see panel). Much of the tone of South Australian life was indeed set by the seriousness with which its Nonconformist (British) or Lutheran (German) citizens took their religion; not for nothing was Adelaide known as the city of churches.

The vulnerability of what was an almost entirely rural economy became apparent in the years of the great Depression, and following World War II the state underwent an industrial transformation, with shipyards at Whyalla and car factories at Adelaide's satellite town of Elizabeth. In the 1970s, these activities showed themselves to be vulnerable in their turn, and South Australia, along with much of the rest of the country, has its share of economic and financial troubles.

Given the state's range of landscapes, it is not surprising that tourism is of increasing importance. Adelaide attracts visitors with its biennial Festival of Arts (even-numbered years), as well as by the elegance of its townscape and its reputation for good living. A relatively new attraction is the Womadelaide Festival—a biennial (odd-numbered years) celebration of world music. It is no longer possible to take a luxury cruise from Port Adelaide around the two great inlets, Spencer Gulf and Gulf St. Vincent, but an immensely long coastline offers endless opportunites for water-based activities of all kinds at unspoiled towns such as **Robe**, south of the spectacular Coorong National Park. Coastal landscapes vary from the wild isolation of rugged headlands to delightful little fishing ports and resorts. Offshore islands invite those with a taste for escapism; the biggest of them, **Kangaroo Island**, offers sea lions, koalas, kangaroos, pelicans, sea eagles, and fairy penguins in their native environment.

South Australia is the starting point for many of the country's great tourist itineraries. Outback Tarcoola is the junction for two trains of almost legendary reputation— the *Ghan*, on its way north to Alice Springs in the Red Centre, and the *Indian Pacific*, pausing here on its transcontinental run westward across the Nullarbor.

Bethany's Lutheran church and hall in the Barossa Valley

127

DASHING DON'S DERRING-DO
South Australia's Premier from 1967–1968 and again from 1970–1979, Don Dunstan not only cultivated a progressive and dynamic image, but was also instrumental in dragging his state into the late 20th century. Under his leadership, South Australia passed legislation outlawing racial and sexual discrimination. Pastor Sir Douglas Nicholls, a distinguished Aborigine, became Governor, while a police chief who refused to reveal who had instructed him to keep secret files on M.P.s and other potential subversives was dismissed. Sadly, the popular ex-premier died in 1999.

It is possible to tour some of the World Heritage listed Naracoorte Caves

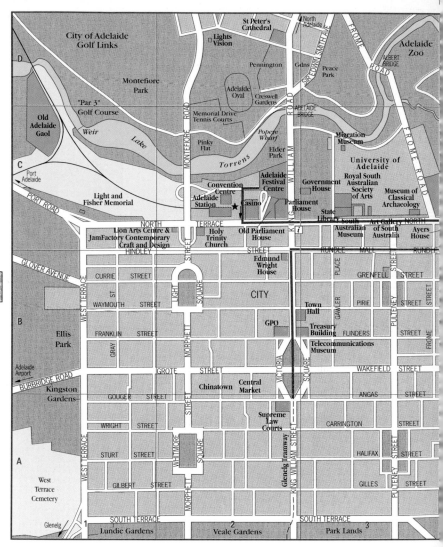

LIGHT WAS RIGHT

"The reasons that led me to fix Adelaide where it is I do not expect to be generally understood or calmly judged at the present. My enemies, however, by disputing their validity in every particular, have done me the good service of fixing the whole of the responsibility upon me. I am perfectly willing to bear it; and I leave it to posterity, and not to them, to decide whether I am entitled to praise or to blame."

Adelaide

Australia's fifth largest city likes to be known for its biennial Festival of Arts, its restaurants, and its generally high cultural tone. Many of its early citizens were religious dissenters escaping from persecution in their home countries; they pursued both work and recreation with what seemed from the outside a kind of earnest dullness, in rationally planned surroundings of dignified elegance.

These surroundings were the vision of one man, Colonel William Light, who, as South Australia's Surveyor-General, drew up a brilliant plan in 1836, to which the city has adhered ever since. Having found a suitable site on the banks of the little River Torrens, he set out a square-mile grid of streets on the south bank. The central thoroughfare was impressively wide, and the whole was

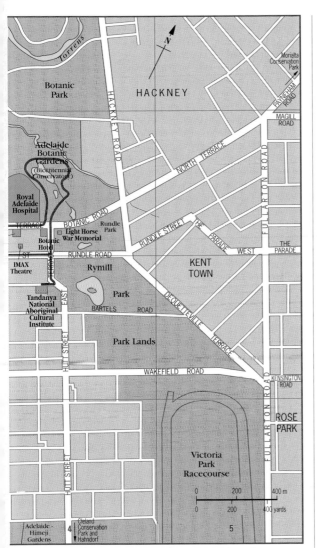

SHOP 'TIL YOU DROP

Adelaide offers a good range of shopping opportunities. The Central Markets are excellent for food and produce, the JamFactory Contemporary Craft and Design Centre sells fine art and crafts, North Adelaide and King William Road (south of the city) are the perfect places for designer clothing, while Unley and Port Adelaide are known for their antiques.

SON OF A GUN!

Most Australian cities developed in a totally chaotic way. It was left to an army officer, illegitimate offspring of the English founder of Penang in Malaysia and a Eurasian woman, to conceive and implement the ambitious plan for Adelaide. William Light had served as an intelligence officer with the Duke of Wellington, gaining his rank of colonel on a temporary posting in Spain; he reveled in the commission to survey and plan not only the site of Adelaide but much of the rest of the new province. Married to the daughter (also illegitimate) of the Duke of Richmond, he left his wife at home in England, and when he died (probably from overwork) in 1839, was refused the last rites because he had been "living in sin" with another lady.

enlivened with a series of squares. A green belt around the city was to remain parkland in perpetuity, a fit setting for public buildings such as Government House; on the far bank of the river was the fine suburb of North Adelaide. In spite of opposition at the time, in spite of the building boom of the 1970s and 1980s, and in spite of the automobile, all these elements are in place today, helping make Adelaide a delightful city.

It is rare in a metropolis to be able to live in a Victorian villa looking onto splendid parkland, walk or cycle to work in the city center, spend the evening at the theater, then walk home again—but here the residents can do exactly that. The majority of people, however, live in the suburbs that have spread across the coastal plain between the magnificent beaches along the gulf and the Adelaide Hills to the east.

Sailing is a popular pursuit at Port Adelaide, the city's harbor town

FESTIVE SEASON
They say in Adelaide that the Adelaide Festival Centre cost less to build than it did to carpet Sydney's Opera House. The center is busy all year round, with two major theaters and two outdoor performance areas. Its plaza, designed by the German environmental sculptor Otto Hajek, has been described as Australia's biggest outdoor art work.

Adelaide's Festival of Arts is held in even-numbered years for three weeks in February/March. Warm days and mild nights help create the right atmosphere for a wonderful choice of events—opera, ballet, concerts, theater, exhibitions, children's activities, the Fringe Festival, and a literary festival—all of which are within walking distance of each other.

►► Adelaide Botanic Gardens 129C4
North Terrace
Founded in 1855, these 49 acres of trees, shrubs, lawns, and lakes glitter with an array of heritage buildings. As well as the Museum of Economic Botany, there is the Simpson Shade House, the 1868 Victoria House with its giant waterlily, and the wonderful Palm House, brought out from Germany in the 1870s and completely restored in 1996. But most extraordinary is the soaring **Bicentennial Conservatory**, an environmental capsule of great sophistication, within whose high-tech skin there flourishes a profusion of plants from the tropical rain forests of North Australia and its neighbors.

►►► Art Gallery of South Australia 128C3
North Terrace
Behind its classical portico this refined building houses one of the country's most important collections of Australian, European and Asian art. Some of the paintings by Australian artists are familiar, seeming to encapsulate key aspects of the country's character, like the stampeding sheep in Tom Roberts' *The Breakaway* of 1891 or the subtle beach flirtation depicted in Charles Conder's *Holiday at Mentone* (1888). The Aboriginal section is particularly good, and the gallery also features a large collection of Rodin's works.

► Glenelg 128A1
Once Adelaide's most popular seaside center, with splendid sandy beaches stretching far in either direction, suburban Glenelg still has plenty of charm, epitomized by the 1920s trams that link it to the city's Victoria Square (a 30-minute trip). It was here that Governor Hindmarsh and the first band of settlers landed in 1836.

►► Migration Museum 128C3
82 Kintore Avenue
Housed in the restored buildings of the city's Destitute Asylum, this innovative institution presents the story of the immigrant groups who founded South Australia. The museum tells stories of courage and hope—such as the successful adaptation to life in a new country—as well as those of disappointment and difficulty. An essential visit for understanding how Australia has evolved.

▶▶ North Adelaide   128D3

Adelaide's classiest and oldest suburb has many fine houses. Melbourne Street has shops, restaurants and boutiques, while O'Connell Street is famous for its restaurants and al fresco wining and dining. St. Peter's Cathedral boasts the heaviest bells in the southern hemisphere, and at Light's Vision lookout, a statue of the good colonel surveys the city he created.

▶▶ Port Adelaide   128C1

Some 6 miles northwest of the landlocked city center, Adelaide's harbor town has been deserted by most of its maritime traffic, leaving it free to concentrate on its fascinating past; it has South Australia's largest collection of distinguished 19th-century buildings. Among the long quayside sheds is the bright red 1869 lighthouse, overlooking a number of historic ships when they are in dock. A short distance inland on Lipson Street are a couple of first-rate museums, each on its own well worth the bus or train trip out from the city center. The main building of the fascinating **South Australian Maritime Museum▶▶** is an old bond store, while the **Port Dock Station Railway Museum▶▶**, featuring 26 locomotives and steam train rides, is the biggest of its kind in the country.

▶▶▶ South Australian Museum   128C3

North Terrace

This is the state's museum of natural history, with geological and zoological displays, but its main attraction is probably its outstanding collection of Aboriginal artifacts. These are presented in an imaginative and accessible fashion, making the museum the best such place in the country to study the past life of the original Australians.

▶▶ Tandanya National Aboriginal Cultural Institute   129B4

253 Grenfell Street

This exciting addition to Adelaide's vibrant East End offers an exceptional opportunity to learn about contemporary Aboriginal culture. There are dance and theater performances, meetings, talks, and celebrations, constantly changing exhibitions, and demonstrations and sales of arts and crafts.

OTHER ADELAIDE SIGHTS
The 19th-century Ayers House with its curving bays is perhaps the most elegant structure in North Terrace. Seven times premier of South Australia, Sir Henry Ayers used his home for state functions; the hub of city life, its ballroom was washed down with milk to give it a smooth and fast surface.

Not to be confused with Parliament House up the street (still lacking the dome planned for it), the Tudor-style Old Parliament House in North Terrace was home to South Australia's first parliament.

131

NGURUNDERI'S DREAMING
An extensive display in the South Australian Museum tells the story of Ngurunderi, one of the great ancestral dreaming figures of the Ngarrindjeri people. His travels from high up the Murray River to Kangaroo Island in pursuit of his miscreant wives are said to explain many of the features of the river and coastal landscape. The bends of the Murray were made by the giant cod Ponde sweeping his tail, while Long Island near Murray Bridge is Ngurunderi's spear, which missed its target. Another spear thrust created the islands off Victor Harbor, while his abandoned club became the Bluff. As his wives fled west along the causeway that then connected Kangaroo Island to the mainland, Ngurunderi caused the waters to rise and drown them. They turned into the rocky Pages Islands, while Ngurunderi rose to become a star in the Milky Way.

Impressive Ayers House, now open to the public

The Tandanya National Aboriginal Cultural Institute in Adelaide's East End

Walk

Green spaces and old buildings

See map on page 128.

Linking some of Adelaide's splendid green spaces with North Terrace, the city's boulevard, this walk passes through the central shopping mall before ending in Victoria Square, the geographical heart of the city.

A walkway leads to North Terrace from the **Adelaide Festival Centre** complex overlooking parkland along the River Torrens. Stay on the north side of North Terrace to admire the sequence of historic buildings and monuments revealed as you walk eastward. The post-modern forecourt of the Hyatt Hotel contrasts with the grandiose railroad station building now housing the city's casino. The **Old Parliament House** of 1855 seems very modest compared with the ultra-conservative design of its successor, completed in 1939. **Government House** behind its garden wall gives way to the State Library (1884), the **South Australian Museum** (1898), and the **Art Gallery of South Australia** (opened in 1881). The south side of the Terrace has both imposing edifices and modern buildings, ending with the fine colonial mansion of **Ayers House** and the Botanic Hotel with tiers of verandas.

The detour into **Adelaide Botanic Gardens** should take in the elegant old Palm House and the remarkable Bicentennial Conservatory. Rundle Street is the heart of Adelaide's lively East End region. Here you will find the IMAX Theatre, plenty of shops, historic pubs, and dozens of excellent cafes and restaurants, most of which offer al fresco dining. Take a short detour to the excellent **Tandanya National Aboriginal Cultural Institute** in Grenfell Street just to the south. Rundle Mall is a cheerful pedestrian precinct, the main focus of city shopping. It leads into King William Street, Adelaide's main north–south route. The General Post Office and Town Hall stand at the northern end of Victoria Square, where the city's last surviving original tramway waits to take its passengers down to the sea at **Glenelg**.

National parks

Dry as dust The interminable flatness of the interior is broken only by two mountain ranges. Part of the vast Pitjantjatjara Aboriginal Lands, the Musgrave Ranges in the far northwest parallel the other ridges of the Red Centre just over the boundary with the Northern Territory. The ancient Flinders Ranges run some 300 miles from near the head of Spencer Gulf toward Lake Eyre, their most spectacular single feature being the magnificent natural fortress of **Wilpena Pound**, a 30-square-mile natural ampitheater. Northward are the interminable sand ridges of the **Simpson Desert**, laid down by winds that ceased to blow in prehistoric times. In the rare bouts of rain, its sparse cover of spinifex supplemented by a sudden tapestry of wildflowers, while its inhabitants include unique creatures like hopping mice and marsupial moles. The Sturt Stony Desert is a virtually impassable plain of wind-polished stones known as gibbers, while, much farther south, **Mount Remarkable** has deep gorges.

The wildlife-rich south Toward the sea, the near-total aridity of South Australia's interior gives way to a Mediterranean-type climate, whose hot summers are relieved by relatively cool and moist winters. A century and a half of settlement has converted much of the area into productive farmland. There is still plenty of wilderness left, along the coast from Coffin Bay and Lincoln national parks at the tip of the Eyre Peninsula in the west to **Coorong National Park** in the far southeast. In between are the dunes and cliffs of **Innes National Park** on the toe of Yorke Peninsula and the scenic and wildlife wonders of **Kangaroo Island**. The extraordinary Coorong begins at the mouth of the Murray where the great river reaches the sea. A 90-mile beach stretches southeastward, backed by sand dunes and a long, shallow lagoon. This is one of the best places for observing the pelican.

AUSTRALIA'S DEAD SEA
Much of the huge expanse of Lake Eyre is below sea level. When filled with water, an event that has only occurred three times in living memory, the lake becomes alive with birds. On the map it appears to be fed by rivers over 600 miles long, but their waters usually run dry long before they reach the lake. Its salty surface, flat and featureless, made it ideal for Donald Campbell's successful attempt on the world land-speed record in 1964.

133

The Remarkable Rocks on Kangaroo Island are famous for their strangely weathered granite shapes

THE GHAN
One of Australia's most famous railway lines runs from Adelaide to Alice Springs in the Northern Territory. The route is named after the Afghan (and other) camel drivers that the railroad superseded in the late 19th century. (See also page 189.)

BY CAR
Roads in the relatively densely populated coastal area are good and the main interstate highways are all paved, including the Stuart Highway north to Alice Springs. In the Outback, roads are of variable quality and you must check conditions first and take adequate provisions (see page 143).

BY WATER
You can take the car or passenger ferry to Kangaroo Island from Cape Jervis at the tip of the Fleurieu Peninsula.

A diesel commuter bus on Adelaide's "O-Bahn" line

How to travel

By air Only 3¾ miles from the city center, Adelaide's airport is served by both international and domestic flights, linking it to all important destinations in Australia and many overseas. The size of South Australia makes flights within the state an attractive proposition. There are frequent flights between Adelaide and places on the Eyre Peninsula such as Port Lincoln and Ceduna, or to Kangaroo Island and Mount Gambier. Other flights serve Coober Pedy and Broken Hill in N.S.W., though most people heading into the Outback get there by road.

By bus Adelaide has a comprehensive metropolitan transportation system with integrated ticketing, mostly based on buses, but also including suburban trains. The free City Loop and Bee Line buses run frequently between the main railroad station and the Glenelg tram terminus in Victoria Square. The Passenger Transport InfoCentre in King William Street is helpful in planning tours around Greater Adelaide. The Glenelg Tram (a vintage 1929 model) and the replica Adelaide Explorer tram, which tours the principal attractions on a 2¾-hour circuit, are an excellent introduction to the sights.

Long-distance buses operate express services to all major destinations, and even quite remote places in the Outback may have a bus service of some kind, albeit an infrequent one. If you have a little time to spare, a fun way to travel between Adelaide and Melbourne or Alice Springs and take in many of the good things en route is by the very reasonably priced **Wayward Bus** (three days to Melbourne and eight to Alice).

By train Long-distance trains leave Keswick terminus at the southwestern edge of Adelaide city center for Perth, Alice Springs, Melbourne, Broken Hill, and Sydney. There are also services to Port Pirie and Mount Gambier. Adelaide's suburban network based at the main station on North Terrace is quite extensive, with services to places of interest like Port Adelaide.

Visitors and cuddly residents at Cleland Conservation Park

▶▶ Adelaide Hills   125B4

Sprawling over the coastal plain, Greater Adelaide is defined to the west by the beaches of Gulf St. Vincent and to the east by the gorges and steep slopes of these beautiful hills. Laced with scenic drives and hiking trails through wild bushland, this is an area of richly varied landscapes—vineyards, avenues of tall conifers, towns of rough-hewn stone—with some of the oldest settlements in South Australia. The forest has regrown since "Black Sunday" of January 2, 1955, when an uncontrollable bush fire raged for days. As well as many vineyards, there are market gardens, orchards, and any number of recreational attractions. The latter include the **Toy Factory**, its emblem the biggest rocking horse in the world, the animals of the **Cleland Wildlife Park** on the slopes of Mount Lofty, 12½ miles southeast of Adelaide, and the superb **Warrawong Sanctuary** at Mylor.

▶▶ Arkaroola   125D4

Formerly a vast sheep station, the Outback resort and wildlife sanctuary of Arkaroola is now the center for exploring the northern parts of the spectacular Flinders Ranges. The rugged ridges of the **Gammon Ranges National Park**▶▶ glint and glitter in the piercing light with quartz, fluorspar, and other minerals. There are hot springs, a vast salt lake, an observatory and an abundance of wildlife.

▶▶ Birdwood   125B4

The National Motor Museum is a good excuse for a 30-mile leisurely drive through the Adelaide Hills. Australia's biggest collection of vintage, veteran and classic cars is housed in the stone-built Birdwood Mill of 1852.

▶▶ Burra   125B4

In the 1840s, the discovery of rich copper deposits in Kapunda and Burra rescued the ailing South Australian economy. Miners flocked to Burra, 96 miles north of Adelaide, and within 10 years had created the Monster Mine, 8 miles long and 3¾ miles across. Today, a 7-mile heritage trail includes a museum, a mine captain's cottage, and the extraordinary riverbed dugouts in which as many as 2,000 miners once lived.

DEUTSCHLAND DOWN UNDER
Germans sailed into Sydney Harbour with the First Fleet, and many thousands have come since. South Australia was the destination in the 1830s and 1840s for whole communities from Brandenburg and Silesia suffering religious intolerance at the hands of the Prussian authorities. The first settlements were Klemzig, now overwhelmed by Adelaide's suburbia, Hahndorf and Lobethal in the Adelaide Hills, then in the Barossa Valley, originally called Neuschlesien (New Silesia).

HOLDEN'S HEROES
Australia became one of the world's major car-owning nations from early on; by the beginning of the 1960s there was one car per family. Sir Edward Holden's car body firm merged with General Motors in 1931, initially assembling British and American vehicles. "Australia's Own Car" rolled off the Holden production line in 1948, the millionth in 1962. With the advent of the inexpensive and reliable Japanese cars Holden faltered, but in recent years has made something of a comeback.

The lives of the first "opal gougers" on display at Coober Pedy's Old Timer's opal mine

136

THE AUSSIE WAVE

When you're watching an Australian game of cricket on T.V., why do the spectators always seem to be waving casual greetings to unseen friends? It's not friends, but the persistent flies—as noted by Dutch Commander Pelsaert in 1629: "Such a host of flies came to sit in the mouth and eyes that they could not be beaten off." This early observation would seem to disprove the theory that the plague is due to the dung dropped in quantity by all those cattle in the Outback. Australians protect themselves from this nuisance with door and window screens at home and, outside, with insect repellant and as nonchalant a wave as possible, since frantic swatting seems only to encourage the fly. No one (except gullible tourists) wears a hat with dangling corks to keep the flies away.

▶▶ Coober Pedy   124D3

The search for opals has created a landscape of mounds and holes in the ground which greets travelers on the Stuart Highway some 536 miles northwest of Adelaide. The name Coober Pedy comes from the Aboriginal *kupa piti* meaning something like "white fellow's burrow": ever since opals were first discovered here in 1915, enterprising folk from all over the world have been hacking away in the hope of making their fortune, living underground in order to escape the sweltering conditions on the surface. As well as comfortable troglodyte homes, there are underground shops, restaurants, hotels, and even a couple of churches. Several working mines in the area can be visited.

▶ Eyre Peninsula   124B3

This vast triangle faces the breakers of the Great Australian Bight to the west and the sheltered waters of the Spencer Gulf to the east. The northern base of the triangle is formed by the uninhabited Gawler Ranges, while its southern apex is near the deep-water harbor of Port Lincoln. The sandy soils of the peninsula support wheat and sheep, while the subsoil yields iron ore, converted into steel at Whyalla, South Australia's second city.

The Eyre Highway runs from Port Augusta at the head of the Gulf toward the Western Australian border. The journey south on the Lincoln Highway reveals a magnificent coastline of cliffs and white sandy beaches, dotted with fishing towns and holiday resorts. There are seals and dolphins around **Tumby Bay**, while **Port Lincoln▶** is home to Dangerous Reef, sea lions and white pointer sharks. To the south, **Lincoln National Park▶** is famous for its beaches and scenic drives. Beyond here the unspoiled coastline stretches northwestward to remote **Ceduna**, from where migrating whales can be seen between June and October.

▶▶ Fleurieu Peninsula   125B4

Rolling countryside, vineyards and a superb coastline of wild cliffs and fine beaches provide a wonderful vacation region right on Adelaide's doorstep. Within half an hour's drive south of the city is the **McLaren Vale wine district▶▶**, centered on the township of McLaren Vale amid delightful hills. Farther south, around Willunga, the crop changes to almonds, with a froth of blossom in July. Studded with sandy beaches, including the country's first official nudist one, Maslins, the coast runs southwestward along the gulf to terminate in rugged terrain around Cape Jervis. The far shore of Backstairs Passage belongs to Kangaroo Island, reached from here by ferry.

Around the corner of the Cape the scenery is no less spectacular, particularly at **Deep Creek Conservation Park▶** where the land falls sheer into the ocean. The pleasant resort of **Victor Harbor** (see page 142) is guarded by the massive lump of rock known as Rosetta Head. From here the vintage Cockle Train chuffs eastward past the breakers crashing on the beaches of Port Elliot to the charming town of **Goolwa** near the mouth of the Murray River (see page 138). The story of the Murray, including its current problems, is told at the impressive interpretive center at Signal Point (see page 138).

►►► Flinders Ranges 125C4

These ranges are made up of some of the world's most ancient rocks, marking the landscape northeast of Port Augusta with steep ridges and rugged gorges. These peaks have been cracked, folded, and sculpted by millions of years of rain and sun. Of no great height, the ranges owe their popularity to their vivid mineral coloring, dramatic landforms, and fascinating plant and animal life. One of the gateways to the main part of the ranges is the township of Quorn, once an important railway junction, but now a small town of 1,500 or so people; here is the terminus of the **Pichi Richi steam railroad►**, part of the old Ghan line. Beyond Quorn, the road to Hawker passes close to the ruins of the old **Kanyaka Homestead**, constructed in the 1850s but long since abandoned, as well as the **Yourambulla Caves** with their Aboriginal rock-paintings.

The road to one of the country's great geological curiosities, the mighty natural stronghold of **Wilpena Pound►►►**, turns off at Hawker. The Pound is a great oval, 12½ miles long by about 5 miles wide, protected from the outside world by sheer 3,280-foot high walls, sloping steeply to a park-like interior where the flat floor is rich in sugar gums and, in spring, wildflowers. Like any great fortress, the Pound has only one way in, a narrow gorge cut by the Wilpena Creek, sometimes a torrent but usually just a trickle. A number of marked trails of varying difficulty lead from the tourist center near this entrance; anyone capable of walking 12½ miles lengthwise and 1,640 feet vertically should consider the trek across the Pound and up to its highest point, St. Marys Peak. The reward is a stunning panorama, including the dazzling white surface of salty Lake Torrens.

Beyond Wilpena on unpaved roads is the main part of the Flinders Ranges National Park. Its wildlife includes hosts of birds and two types of kangaroo, as well as the rare yellow-footed rock wallaby.

REPTILIAN RAMPARTS
Like so many features of the Aboriginal landscape, the walls of Wilpena Pound are perceived to be the petrified forms of the animal ancestors who assisted at their creation. Two giant serpents were lying in wait here for those who gathered to celebrate the very first ceremony of initiation of a young man into adulthood by circumcision. The serpents devoured them all, save for Wala the wild turkey, Yulu the kingfisher, and the young man himself, who all escaped and founded new tribes. The serpents expired, their bodies curling round to enclose the Pound

137

Typically dry, rugged scenery in the Flinders Ranges

Take time for a trip up the broad Murray River...

SIR HANS HEYSEN

Young Hans came to South Australia in 1884 at the age of seven. He is one of the best-loved painters of the Australian landscape, whose natural features, particularly its trees and the play of light on them, he studied with great meticulousness. His charming works grace many an Australian gallery, and can also be seen at his Hahndorf home, The Cedars (and its adjacent studio), where he lived from 1912 until his death in 1968. Sir Hans is honored by having the long-distance walking trail from the Fleurieu Peninsula to the Flinders Ranges, as well as part of the ranges themselves, named after him.

AUSTRALIAN SEALS

Of the three species of seal that inhabit Australian waters, two live around Kangaroo Island: the New Zealand fur seal and the Australian sea lion. The former were almost hunted to extinction in the 19th century; now protected, their numbers are recovering. Sea lions had an easier time, largely because they lack the warm coat of the fur seal.

▶ **Goolwa**   *125B4*

This little riverport on the lower reaches of the mighty Murray River is the terminus for two trips in time: the old-timer Cockle Train that runs along the coast, and the paddlesteamer *Mundoo* that heads upriver. The **Signal Point Interpretive Centre▶** has comprehensive displays on the theme of the Murray River yesterday and today.

▶ **Hahndorf**   *125B4*

South Australia's second-oldest German settlement (1839) can be found in a pretty location in the Adelaide Hills. Conveniently close to the South Eastern Freeway, Hahndorf is full of Teutonic tradition, with German-style architecture and cafés serving traditional foods. Other attractions are the fine artworks of the Hahndorf Academy, an antique clock museum, and The Cedars (see panel). You can still see how the first settlers laid out their homes in orderly fashion along the main street.

▶▶▶ **Kangaroo Island**   *125B4*

Separated from the Fleurieu Peninsula by the deep straits known as Backstairs Passage, this is Australia's third largest island, a paradise for lovers of nature, with wild coastal landscapes and a particularly rich animal life. The island was named by the redoubtable Matthew Flinders; when the *Investigator* called here in 1802, his crew shot a few of the locals, members of the subspecies of gray kangaroo still present in large numbers.

Most visitors arrive by ferry from the mainland at the little fishing port of Penneshaw on the Dudley Peninsula at the eastern end of the island. Fairy penguins frequent Christmas Cove just to the west of the harbor. Situated on Nepean Bay, Kingscote preserves some traces of its past in its oldest building, Hope Cottage of 1859. A paved main road heads past the airport into the interior, but the island's unique sights lie on the south coast.

Seal Bay Conservation Park▶▶ is home to the country's largest colony of sea lions, seemingly indifferent to their many human visitors. Further west is the spectacular underground world of **Kelly Hill Caves**, discovered by a horse of that name that disappeared for ever into their still unexplored depths (Kelly's rider was saved). The surging waters around Cape du Couedic at the island's southwestern tip are often visited by another marine mammal, the New Zealand fur seal. At the cape itself is awesome **Admirals Arch**, a natural bridge hollowed out in the limestone cliffs, while to the east are the aptly named **Remarkable Rocks▶▶**. Crowning a smoothly planed promontory, great blocks of granite have been eroded into strange shapes as if by the chisel of an abstract sculptor at his most imaginative.

Flinders Chase National Park▶ in the west is a reminder of how most of the island once looked—a wilderness of low-growing eucalyptus and shrubs. The headquarters of the park is at Rocky River, where friendly kangaroos, wallabies and emus are likely to pester you for your sandwiches. Koalas can be seen in the trees nearby, and platypuses sometimes reveal themselves to the patient observer. The northwestern tip of the island is marked by the isolated lighthouse at Cape Borda. To the east, accessible by a rough road, stretches a spectacular coastline of cliffs sometimes rising to over 650 feet and relieved by the occasional sandy bay.

▶ Mount Gambier　　　125A5

The most important town in the southeast of South Australia had a turbulent volcanic past that only came to an end in relatively recent times. This has left a legacy of cones and craters, with one water-filled hole in the very center of town. Blue Lake, just outside town, changes color mysteriously according to the season.

▶ Murray River　　　125B5

The sluggish Murray (see pages 112–13) meanders into South Australia near Renmark. From here to where it meets the sea at Lake Alexandrina, the river has become a mecca for vacationers. Houseboats are particularly popular, and can be rented at Renmark, Berri, Loxton, Murray Bridge, and several other towns.

ALONG THE MIGHTY MURRAY
Massive irrigation projects have transformed the area into a vast orchard and vineyard, producing oranges, apples, pears and some 40 percent of the state's grape harvest. Loxton Historical Village recreates life as it was in the difficult early days of settlement. Many of the places along the river have a poignant feel about them, now that the great days of river trade have gone. There is another evocation of bygone times at the Old Tailem Bend Pioneer Village, and the paddlesteamer *Marion* moored at Mannum has been transformed into a passenger boat and floating museum.

139

...it's a wonderfully relaxing way to travel and view the striking scenery

Vine cuttings were among the plants imported with the First Fleet, though the very first attempts to produce an Australian wine met with failure. However, persistence has paid off, and today Australian wines enjoy a high reputation at home and abroad.

AMBER FLUID IN ICE-COLD TUBES
Despite the rise in wine consumption, Australians remain some of the most committed beer drinkers in the world. A century ago, most beers tended to be top-fermented on the model of British ales and stouts, but these have steadily been displaced by bottom-fermented, lager types. These were first brewed by Melbourne Germans as well as by the Foster brothers, originally from New York, who gave their name to Foster's Lager. Americans used to six-packs may be surprised at the standard-sized "slab" (a 24-pack).

A winery at Nuriootpa in the Barossa Valley

In the early days, the colonists preferred rum; later it was the country's beer that was rated highly, in contrast to its wines, which foreigners wrote off as crude imitations utterly failing to fulfill the promise of their labels.

Since the 1960s things have changed as a result of increased prosperity and greater sophistication. A visit to a well-stocked wine merchant reveals a whole world of home-grown wine; like other great wine countries, Australia has no real need to import. In fact exports of wine are expected to reach AU$1b by the year 2000.

New South Wales This state has the most venerable vineyards, in the highly reputed Hunter Valley only a short journey north of Sydney. Wine has been produced in this area since the 1830s, and the valley's 60 or so wineries include some of Australia's best. Quality is the keynote here, whereas far to the southwest, in the irrigated valley of the Murrumbidgee River, producers concentrate on making as great a quantity as possible for the inexpensive wine casks that are Australia's "vin ordinaire."

Victoria Here there were once as many vineyards as N.S.W. and S.A. had put together, but most were wiped out by phylloxera in the last century and later replaced by

phylloxera-resistant American root stock. Victorian wines could now be described as up and coming; there are many "boutique" wines, some of the best from the **Yarra Valley** near Melbourne. The Great Western area is famous for sparkling wine.

Western Australia This state has its old vineyards too, planted along the Swan Valley in the early days of settlement. Exciting (and expensive) wines come from the **Margaret River** area.

Tasmania Lying closer to the South Pole, Tasmania is benefiting from a fashion for growing vines over a long ripening period in a cool climate, and there is an increasing number of vineyards (mostly around Hobart and Launceston) producing wines of fine quality.

South Australia This is the heartland of Australian wine, contributing about two-thirds of the country's total production. Most of the original vineyards of the Adelaide Plains have disappeared, and the huge quantities of grapes grown along the Murray are the basis of Australia's bulk wine trade, but other districts make wines of the highest reputation. Far-off **Coonawarra** in the southeast produces wonderful reds on a tiny band of volcanic soil, while **Adelaide Hills** is the most successful of the newer, cool climate regions. The boutique wines made among the rolling hills of the **McLaren Vale wine district** are much in vogue and the **Clare Valley's** cool-climate vintages are excellent, but perhaps the best of all wine districts is the **Barossa Valley**, north of Adelaide. The combination of suitable soils, summer sun, and reliable winter rain makes for an excellent product, grown amid a delightful landscape of old-established towns and well-ordered countryside.

Tastings Australian vintners welcome visitors. Tastings have become a popular pastime, though choosing can be difficult. The name of a reputable vineyard is generally considered a good starting point.

A RUM CORPS
Historical records show that in the early days of N.S.W. coinage was short; in its absence Bengal rum took over many of the functions of currency. Its sale was controlled by the officers of the New South Wales Corps, perhaps the least prestigious of the British regiments of the time. With little to occupy them in the way of genuine military activity, these gentlemen devoted their time to enriching themselves by all possible means, only stirring into martial action when their monopoly on rum was threatened by Governor Bligh. Their march on Government House on January 26, 1808, and arrest of the governor has become known disparagingly as the "Rum Rebellion."

141

Petrel Cove at Victor Harbor

▶ Naracoorte   125A5

This southeastern town celebrates the prosperity of its pastoral surroundings in the excellent Sheep's Back wool museum. But most visitors come to marvel at the beauty of the World Heritage-listed **Naracoorte Caves▶**. Only a few of the 60 or so known caves are accessible; there are guided tours into Blanche Cave and Alexandra Cave. In 1969, the bones of hitherto unknown marsupials, giant kangaroos, and wombats were found in Victoria Cave. To the south, Bool Lagoon forms an important wetland region that attracts thousands of waterbirds and other wildlife.

▶ Strathalbyn   125B4

Strathalbyn, at the neck of the Fleurieu Peninsula, has something of Scotland in its dignified public buildings and neat public gardens on the banks of the Angas River. The town's past has been tidily gathered up and presented by the National Trust in two buildings, the 1858 police station and the 1867 court house.

▶ Victor Harbor   125B4

Victor Harbor's setting on Encounter Bay is superb, protected as it is from the ocean by both Rosetta Head ("The Bluff") and Granite Island, the latter reached across a causeway by horse-drawn tram. The island's colony of fairy penguins generally puts in an appearance in the evening, and whale watching is a popular winter activity.

▶ Yorke Peninsula   125B4

Some 150 miles long, this boot-shaped peninsula projects southward, bounded by Spencer Gulf on the west and Gulf St. Vincent to the east. South Australians come here for quiet vacations, fishing, boating, and all kinds of water activities. Because there were few good roads in the past, little ports and landing places were dotted all along the coast, and you are sure to find an appealing place. Toward the tip of the peninsula the coastline becomes more rugged, though there are still splendid beaches for swimming, surfing, and diving.

Strangely compelling, South Australia's 230,000 square miles of Outback include some of the least hospitable parts of the earth's surface. Distances are vast, water is sparse and summer temperatures are almost unbearable. Human life is spread thinly over cattle stations the size of small European states and "towns" no bigger than hamlets. But the Outback has its own fascination; its arid beauty is liable to sudden and miraculous change when rain falls, as salt lakes fill with water and wildflowers carpet the land.

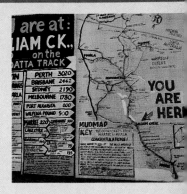

The great vastness of the South Australian Outback is penetrated by a small number of roads, tying together the isolated stations and settlements. Some are paved throughout, while others are still rightly referred to as "tracks" and set a challenge for the more adventurous.

The Oodnadatta Track This track is part of a route north from Adelaide to Alice Springs, an alternative to the Stuart Highway. Beginning at Marree near the southern end of Lake Eyre, it follows the route taken by the explorer John McDouall Stuart and subsequently by the Overland Telegraph and the original Ghan railroad line. Before the line was completed to the Alice, Oodnadatta was the railhead, goods being carried on from here on the backs of camels. The old station, now a museum, still stands.

The Strzelecki Track Named in honor of the Polish explorer Count Paul Strzelecki, this track runs northeast from Lyndhurst toward the Queensland border, following the trail used by the notorious Captain Starlight to drive stolen cattle down to southern markets in 1871. The track fringes the northern Flinders Ranges before crossing the interminable sandhills of the Strzelecki Desert and ending at Innamincka where the unfortunate explorers Burke and Wills finally expired.

The Birdsville Track Also a cattle-driving route, this track was traced out by stockmen possibly more law-abiding than Captain Starlight but equally tough. Like the Oodnadatta Track it begins at Marree, but this track ends up in Queensland's Birdsville some 320 miles later.

Above: William Creek, on the Oodnadatta Track

143

BIRDSVILLE TRACK SIGHTS
Along the track's course are hot springs, deserted homesteads, 30-foot-high sandhills and the wind-polished pebbles of the Sturt Stony Desert stretching to the horizon. The old frontier post of Birdsville with its famous pub comes alive when its annual horse races are held—an event that can yield up to 50,000 empty beer cans!

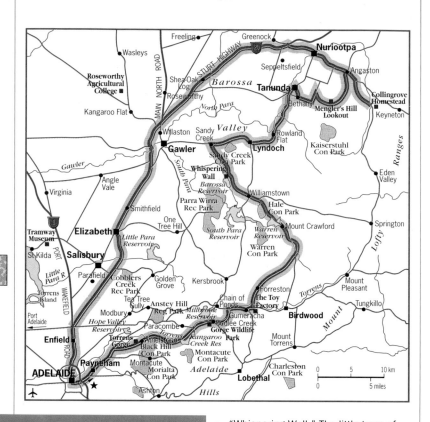

Drive

Barossa Valley

The world-famous wine-growing district of the Barossa Valley can be reached by this indirect but rewarding route through the varied countryside of the northern Adelaide Hills.

Adelaide's Payneham Road, then Gorge Road lead to the rocky defile followed by the River Torrens, and so into the orchard country around **Gumeracha**. Among the many dams built to take advantage of the relatively high rainfall of these uplands, the **Barossa Reservoir** is a popular stopping point because of the curious sound effects produced by its "Whispering Wall." The little town of Lyndoch is the gateway to the Barossa Valley, while **Tanunda**, with its informative Barossa Wine & Visitor Centre and charming main street, is the cultural center of what was Australia's major German-settled area. All around are inviting wineries. **Bethany**, founded in 1842, the valley's oldest village, sits beneath Mengler's Hill Lookout, with its splendid panorama over the neatly ordered countryside. It is worth taking a detour to Angaston's 1850s **Collingrove Homestead**, now managed by the National Trust but once the center of the million-acre estate belonging to the Angas family, early pioneers of South Australia.

The route back to Adelaide passes through **Nuriootpa**, the commercial heart of the Barossa, the prosperous agricultural center of **Gawler** and the satellite town of **Elizabeth**, home to many British immigrants in the post-war years.

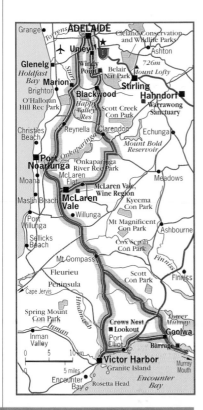

Bird-attracting banksias

Drive

McLaren Vale wine region and Fleurieu Peninsula

This drive leads through the attractive wine-growing countryside of the McLaren Vale wine region, across the rolling farmland of the Fleurieu Peninsula to the mouth of the Murray River and the dramatic ocean setting of Victor Harbor.

From Adelaide, Unley Road soon reaches the surrounding hills and climbs to the **Windy Point Lookout**, from where there is a fine panorama of city and suburbs sprawling over the coastal plain. The uplands are a favored residential area for the city's more affluent commuters, but the suburban housing soon gives way to farmland and forest, and to the vine-yards and welcoming wineries around **McLaren Flat** and **McLaren Vale.**

A beautifully engineered highway speeds you toward the coast through the broad "waist" of the **Fleurieu Peninsula** to the small town of Goolwa. Here the excellent **Signal Point Interpretive Centre** tells all you could want to know about the longest river in Australia, the Murray, which flows through the bird-thronged barrage to the east of the town. You can take cruises from here to the mouth of the Murray and the Coorong Rivers.

A short drive along the shore of Encounter Bay leads to **Victor Harbor** with its causeway linking the resort to Granite Island. The view of town and ocean is well worth the 330-foot climb up the **Bluff**, just to the west of the town. Return to Adelaide by the direct route to complete a 125-mile drive.

146

Perth's Swan River was named after the black swans that live here

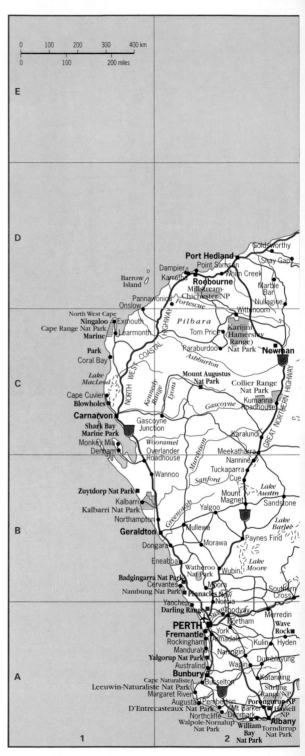

0 100 200 300 400 km
0 100 200 miles

E

D

Goldsworthy
Port Hedland Point Samson Shay Gap
Dampier Whim Creek
Barrow Karratha Roebourne Marble
Island Millstream- Bar
Pannawonica Chichester NP Nullagine
Onslow Fortescue Wittenoom
North West Cape Pilbara
Ningaloo Exmouth Karijini
Cape Range Nat Park Learmonth Tom Price (Hamersley
Marine Range)
Park Paraburdoo Nat Park Newman
Coral Bay Asbburton
Lake Mount Augustus
C MacLeod Nat Park Collier Range
Cape Cuvier Kennedy Nat Park
Blowholes Range Lyons Kumarina
Carnarvon Gascoyne Roadhouse
Shark Bay Gascoyne Karalundi
Marine Park Junction
Monkey Mia Wooramel Meekatharra
Denham Overlander Murchison Nannine
Roadhouse Tuckaparra
Wannoo Sanford Cue
Zuytdorp Nat Park Mount Lake
Kalbarri Magnet Austin
Kalbarri Nat Park Yalgoo Sandstone
Northampton Greenough Lake
B Geraldton Mullewa Barlee
Dongara Morawa Paynes Find
Eneabba Lake
Watheroo Wubin Moore
Badgingarra Nat Park Nat Park
Cervantes Moora Southern
Nambung Nat Park Pinnacles New Cross
Yanchep Norcia
Darling Range Toodyay Merredin
PERTH Northam Wave
Fremantle York Rock
Rockingham Armadale Kulin Hyden
A Mandurah Narrogin Dumbleyung
Yalgorup Nat Park Wagin
Australind Katanning
Bunbury Stirling
Cape Naturaliste Busselton Range NP
Leeuwin-Naturaliste Nat Park Porongurup NP
Margaret River Mt Barker Hassell
Augusta Pemberton NP
D'Entrecasteaux Nat Park Northcliffe Denmark Albany
Walpole-Nornalup William Torndirrup
Nat Park Bay Nat Park

1 2

Western Australia

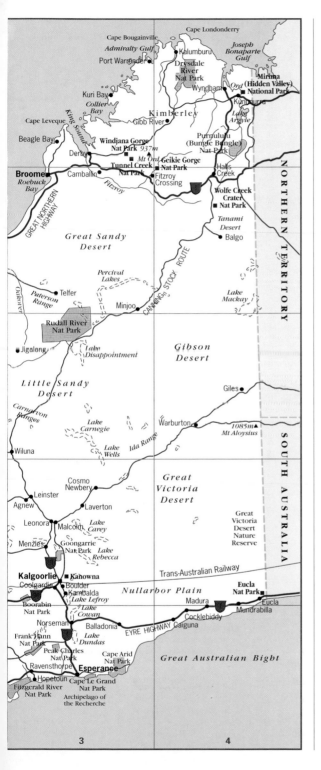

147

Virgin karri forests at Warren National Park, southwest of Pemberton

ON TOP OF THE STATE
The Stirling Range is the highest mountain range in southwestern Australia, and is carpeted by wildflowers during the spring (September through October). The area has numerous hiking trails, but don't forget your rain gear, because sudden storms are common.

TROPICAL NORTH
Parts of the Kimberley are subject to monsoonal rainfall; rivers that may have been reduced to a few pools in the Dry quickly fill and spill over the surrounding plains. In the far north are habitats of such biological value that their national park status, far from opening them up to the public, has led to the banning of all access.

WESTERN AUSTRALIA Devotees of this state, Australia's largest, are fond of producing maps showing how much of Europe or the U.S.A. might be fitted into its 965,250 square miles. Western Australia is undoubtedly *big*—larger than the combined area of Alaska and Texas. It is also very empty, much of it consisting of variations on the theme of desert—voids of various kinds extend from the desert beaches of the Indian Ocean in the far northwest to the cliffs of the Nullarbor being eaten away by the Southern Ocean. A further factor is its isolation. Perth is generally reckoned to be the most remote city on earth; its nearest neighbor, Adelaide, is 1,678 miles away and Sydney is 2,610 miles away. For all this, the West provides some of Australia's great vacation destinations.

Friendly, sunny **Perth** is every Australian's second favorite city, next to Sydney; until recently, this was the place other Australians migrated to in search of the good life at an affordable price. It certainly ranks high in the hierarchy of Australian cities, not least because of its stunning site on the beautiful Swan River just inland from its port of **Fremantle**, one of the country's most atmospheric historic towns.

Perth and its metropolitan region dominate the coastal plain spreading westward from the **Darling Range**, Western Australia's modest equivalent of the Great Dividing Range. With a Mediterranean climate, an often spectacularly rugged coastline, fine forests and the lion's share of fertile farmland, this is the most densely inhabited part of the state. Inland stretches the Wheat Belt, its yields of grain dependent on a variable rainfall, gradually merging into the scrublands that herald the desert itself. Straggling along the desert rim is a line of gold-rush towns, some defunct, some, like **Kalgoorlie–Boulder**, still with plenty of kick in them.

In the rest of the state, people are thinly spread. Towns, none of them of any size, are widely spaced along the immensely long coast. The old pearling base of **Broome** is enjoying a revival as a tourist center, while **Port Hedland** deals efficiently with the iron ore being extracted in huge quantities from its Pilbara hinterland. Here are strange new settlements of prefabricated buildings, erected quickly to create air-conditioned shelter from the fierce temperatures for miners and prospectors.

Visitors will want to experience the grandeur of Western Australia's natural landscapes far more than its urban amenities. The paving of the highways to the north and the northwest of the state has encouraged visitors to explore areas previously considered to be well off the beaten track. Even more than the harsh vastness of the **Hamersley Range** in the Pilbara, the far-off tropical **Kimberley** is attracting tourists to its wealth of natural wonders, sometimes as part of a trip to the adjoining Northern Territory.

HISTORY New Holland was the unlikely name bestowed in the early 1600s on the western rim of the unknown continent by Dutch seamen on their way to their country's possessions in the East Indies. They would race eastward across the Indian Ocean, then sail along the Australian coast toward Java. Sometimes they were traveling too fast, and Western Australia's earliest European history is studded with the names of famous ships such as the *Zeewijk* and *Batavia* wrecked on the reefs and shoals of its treacherous coastline.

The first British impressions were not favorable either; William Dampier's reports in 1688–9 on the barren northwest were distinctly discouraging. It was a (largely imaginary) French threat in the 1820s that impelled the British to add the west of the continent to the Empire; the port of Albany was founded on the south coast in 1826, and in 1829 Lieutenant-Governor Stirling and his band of free settlers established the Swan River colony where Perth now stands. Progress was fitful, and the colony was only saved by a massive infusion of convict labor in the 1850s and 1860s, then in the 1880s and 1890s by the opening up of the Eastern Goldfields, where the combined city of Kalgoorlie-Boulder still thrives on mining today.

In the early 20th century, Western Australia's adherence to the Federation was only secured by a promise to link it to the rest of the country by the construction of the Transcontinental Railway. Even as late as the 1930s, a referendum revealed a majority in favor of secession. Today, in spite of extraordinary financial mismanagement on the part of politicians and unscrupulous entrepreneurs, the west's position seems to be secure, based on massive postwar immigration and seemingly unlimited mineral wealth.

A LAND APART
Despite modern transportation and communications facilities, Western Australia is still very much a land apart. Anything east of the South Australian border—be it Adelaide, Melbourne, or Sydney—is often referred to under the blanket term "Eastern States," and West Australians are more likely to vacation in Bali than on the Great Barrier Reef.

149

The Stirling Range National Park near Albany in the southwest

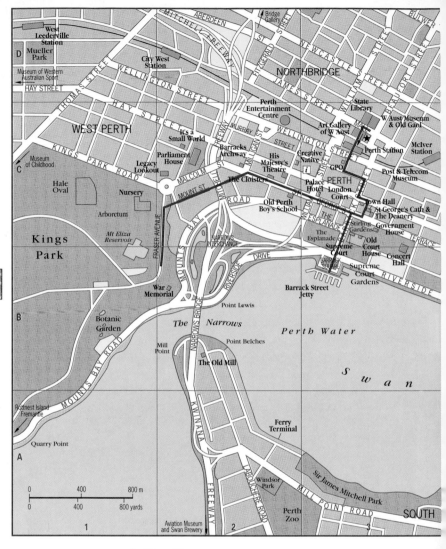

Perth

SUBURBS
The plush succession of waterside suburbs you pass if you take the ferry to South Perth (see panel opposite) may tempt you to sell up and move here without further ado. This is where the millionaires of the "Golden West" choose to live, with easy access to their yachts at the marina or yacht club.

Perth, like Sydney, is an inspired fusion of fine building situated in a splendid natural setting. The view eastward from **Kings Park** reveals one of the world's great urban panoramas—to the left are the office towers of the city center glittering in the constant bright sunlight; to the right lies the glorious stretch of Perth Water alive with pleasure craft.

The city seems to offer its citizens most of the ingredients of the good life: a Californian-style climate unspoiled by smog; attractive homes in every price category in suburbs that range from the merely pleasant to the opulent; and every kind of outdoor playground, from the sweeps of the Swan River and superb ocean beaches, to lavish parklands that bring the bush almost into the city center.

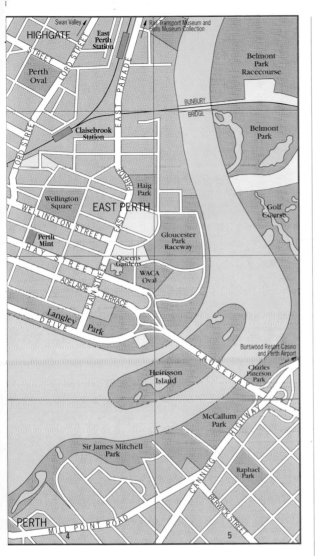

Covering a large area of bushland and parks, Kings Park in the center of Perth is an ideal place to relax

RIVERSIDE PERTH
True Perth is a synthesis of city and river, and you should make sure that you enjoy this not only from Kings Park but from the river itself. At the very least, take the ferry across to South Perth (and back again!), but better still travel by ferry to Rottnest Island or Fremantle. For much of the latter part of the journey, your eye will return again and again to the unforgettable image of the city's clustering towers rising over the functionally elegant Narrows Bridge.

CITY OF PLENTY Perth used to be known for its dullness. True or false at one time, this is no longer the case. Contrasting with the historic and lavishly restored **His Majesty's Theatre**, the home of Western Australian opera and dance, the **Concert Hall** and the **Entertainment Centre** are major recent additions to the city's cultural life. Another modern landmark is the white tower of the **Burswood Casino**, biggest in the southern hemisphere. Other buildings of high cultural significance (the Art Gallery and State Library) have been grouped together to form a new urban focal point. The city center is compact. A network of futuristic walkways straddles streets and tunnels through buildings, linking transportation terminals, shopping arcades, pedestrian precincts and civic plazas. Spectacular sights may be few, but there are a host of urban pleasures.

Perth, viewed from the Kings Park area—a most attractive city

SUN, SAND AND SURF
Perth's suburban beaches are the finest in Australia. The white sands and clear blue Indian Ocean waters of Cottesloe, Scarborough, Swanbourne, and many other beaches are far superior to those of more famous Bondi, Sydney's favorite strip of sand.

SIGHTSEE BY WATER
Ferries connect the jetty at Barrack Square in Perth with South Perth, Fremantle and Rottnest Island, and there are trips upstream, too, visiting the early colonial landscapes and wineries of the upper reaches of the Swan River. Cruise ships still occasionally call at Fremantle.

▶▶ Art Gallery of Western Australia   150C3
Perth Cultural Centre, James Street, Northbridge
This gallery is generously housed in a spacious modern building, and has a fine collection of mostly Australian artworks, including an acclaimed array of Aboriginal art. There are also collections of traditional and contemporary crafts, ceramics, textiles, jewelry, woodwork and glass. The museum extends its influence beyond its doors with sculpture gracing the plaza linking the city center to Northbridge. Free guided tours happen regularly.

▶ Aviation Museum   150A2
Bull Creek
Australia's largest collection of historic aircraft and aviation memorabilia is in the southern suburb of Bull Creek. The aggressive elegance of war winners like the Avro Lancaster and Supermarine Spitfire contrasts with the workaday lines of the famous Dakota, first built in the 1930s and still flying today. The museum has 28 aircraft, engines, models, photographs, and other memorabilia.

▶▶ Kings Park   150C1
Few cities in the world enjoy anything like this great swath of natural landscape on the very edge of the city center. From the founding of the colony in 1829 it was always intended that this area, known as Mount Eliza, should be kept as an open space. About two-thirds of the park is bushland, glorious with wildflowers in the spring, and accessible by scenic drive as well as on foot. Fraser Avenue, with its monuments, memorials and lines of lemon gums, gives an unequaled panorama of Perth in its Swan River setting, while the **Botanic Garden** encapsulates the incomparable floral wealth of Western Australia in a series of richly planted gardens.

▶ Perth Zoo   150A2
20 Labouchere Road, South Perth
An excellent reason for taking the ferry to South Perth, the city's zoo has a fine collection of exotic animals as well as

Australian creatures like emus, koalas, and kangaroos, which you can meet in the Australian Wildlife Park. The zoo is famous for its research and breeding programs for endangered species, and one resident of Western Australia now on the endangered list, the little termite-eating numbat, a small marsupial, is provided with its own quarters.

The zoo is constantly developing innovative features such as Harmony Farm (which demonstrates techniques for living harmoniously with Planet Earth), the Alinta Reptile Encounter, a Nocturnal House, and the African Savannah, which is a complete reconstruction of an African ecosystem.

▶▶▶ Western Australian Museum   150C3
Francis Street, Northbridge

This museum complex comprises a cluster of buildings of many different dates and styles contributing in their various ways to the attractive ambience of Perth's Cultural Centre. Half a day spent here is no substitute for a month spent exploring the natural wonders and human heritage of Western Australia, but it will go a long way toward it!

The centerpiece of the complex is the modern Francis Street building, which has a **Marine Gallery** dominated by the awesome 79-foot skeleton of a blue whale, as well as an **Aboriginal Gallery** that is a magnificent attempt to review in a comprehensive and sympathetic way the art, religion, and culture of the first Australians. Traditional displays of mammals and fossils are in the old Beaufort Street building, while the history of white settlement of the west is evoked in the cool spaces of the stone-built jail, the **Old Gaol**, Perth's original prison complex, which dates from the 1850s.

ALL THAT GLITTERS
Perth is home to several shops that sell precious and semiprecious stones. You can buy pearls from Broome, opals from Coober Pedy and, not least, pink diamonds from the state's own Argyle Diamond Mines.

SUBURBAN ATTRACTIONS
In the southern suburb of Canning Vale you can tour the famous Swan Brewery, while the northern coast offers the Underwater World aquarium and Hillary's Boat Harbour at Sorrento. The historic port of Fremantle lies downstream, and a cruise to the Swan Valley wineries is highly recommended.

153

The mock-Tudor London Court, built in 1937, runs between the Hay Street Mall and St. George's Terrace

Walk

Perth city center

See map on page 150.

This walk of about 2½ miles takes in many of the contrasts of old and new that make Perth such a stimulating capital city.

North of Perth's City Railway Station are the buildings and plazas of the **Cultural Centre** including the Western Australian Museum and Art Gallery of Western Australia. The pedestrian mall south of the station is dominated by the sandstone **General Post Office** (1925). The junction of Hay Street Mall with Barrack Street is overlooked by the tower of the **Town Hall**, behind which is **St. George's Cathedral** and the cottage-style **Deanery** (1859) facing onto **St. George's Terrace**.

Government House was built in the mid-19th century and enclosed in luxuriant gardens. Following the slope down toward The Esplanade fronting the Swan River are **Stirling Gardens**, laid out as a botanical garden in 1829, and **Supreme Court Gardens**, laid out on reclaimed land. Next to the Supreme Court itself is the city's oldest surviving building, the **Old Court House** (1837).

The mock-Tudor arcade known as **London Court** links St. George's Terrace with Hay Street Mall. Despite its ecclesiastical Gothic appearance, No. 139 St. George's Terrace is not a church but the National Trust listed **Old Perth Boy's School**. Farther west is **The Cloisters**, founded in 1858 as Perth's first secondary school and now tastefully converted to offices.

You can complete your walk here, or continue on foot or by free City Area Transit (C.A.T.) bus past **Barracks Archway** to the viewpoints in **Kings Park**. If you're walking, be sure to have a look at impressive **Parliament House** (which can be toured on weekdays) beyond the archway.

Drive

The southwest

This day's outing from Perth follows the coastline south of Fremantle toward the state's southwestern tip, an area rich in forests and vineyards.

Beyond the resort of **Mandurah**, the old coast road passes close to the lakes, swamps and woodland of **Yalgorup National Park**. **Bunbury** has fine beaches; between here and **Busselton** on Geographe Bay the highway runs through fine stands of tuart trees, some of the few remaining after the uncontrolled felling that took place in colonial days. The coastline of the **Leeuwin-Naturaliste National Park** stretches for about 75 miles between Cape Naturaliste in the north and Augusta in the south. The backbone of

the area is formed by a granite ridge capped by limestone; erosion by water has given rise to hundreds of caves, some of which are open.

Some two dozen vineyards cluster around the little township of Margaret River. To the south are the wonderful karri trees of the **Boranup Forest**, which are best seen from the forest drive and the **Boranup Lookout**. There are fine coastal views at Prevelly Park at the mouth of the Margaret River.

If time permits, the tour can be extended to **Augusta** and to **Cape Leeuwin**. The return to Perth is faster via the South Western Highway beyond Bunbury.

Drive

Mundaring Weir

This short excursion enters the heavily wooded Darling Range.

The Great Eastern Highway leaves the city behind as it winds up the Darling scarp. The **John Forrest National Park** is a recreation area, with streams, waterfalls and a pool, while the dam and reservoir of **Mundaring Weir** have an attractive bushland setting.

Return via Lesmurdie Falls and Kalamunda.

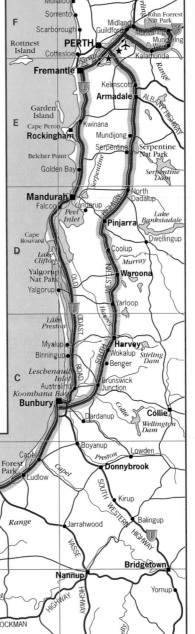

155

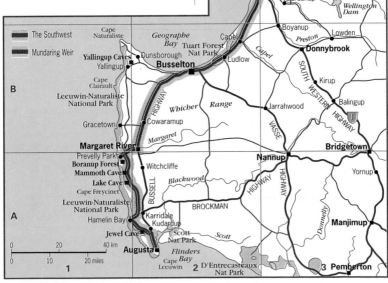

The eerie landscape of the Pinnacles, 152 miles north of Perth and located within Nambung National Park

GRASS-TREES
Among the oddest of Australian plants are the grass-trees. They used to be known as blackboys, from their supposed resemblance to an Aborigine brandishing a spear, but this term has been discarded, at least officially. Resin exudes from the blackened, stubby trunk above which flares a skirt of grass-like leaves and a spectacular flower spike (the "spear"). Grass-trees depend on fire for their growth, reaching a maximum height of about 16 feet.

National parks

The immense spaces of Western Australia include great swaths of unvarying country of little obvious interest, but there are also any number of landscapes well deserving of their national-park or special-interest designation. The state contains just one of Australia's 11 World Heritage registered sites—spectacular Shark Bay on the mid-north coast.

The southwest Facing the meeting point of the Southern and Indian Oceans, the southwest of the state enjoys a reasonably high rainfall that favors the growth of magnificent forests, notably of the karri tree. Its numbers much reduced by the 19th century's insatiable appetite for wood, this forest giant nevertheless survives in substantial patches in a number of national parks. In the southwest, these include the Stirling and Porongurup Ranges, the Boranup Forest in the Margaret River area, and the **Walpole-Nornalup National Park**, a coastal park beautifully sited around the Nornalup Inlet, where deep rivers wind seaward through heath-covered dunes.

Battered by breakers, these southwestern coasts have a rugged quality, well exemplified in the wild cliffs and rocky shoreline of the **Leeuwin-Naturaliste National Park**. On the shoreline farther north resorts mix with wildlife-rich lagoons and lakes, as at **Yalgorup National Park**. The backdrop to the coastal plain is formed by the escarpment of the Darling Range, covered with jarrah woods and bushland. The jarrah (a eucalyptus) is one of the characteristic trees of the southwest, much logged in the past and sawed up for railroad ties. The range is accessible at any number of points along its 186-mile length, from the **John Forrest National Park** east of Perth, or **Lane Pool** on the Murray River, to **Marrinup** and **Pinjarra**.

One of the privileges of life in Perth is easy access to unspoiled nature. Only 22 miles out of the city to the northeast is **Walyunga National Park**, an area of wild bushland where the Swan and Avon Rivers have cut through the Darling Range. Equally near the city, but due north, is **Yanchep National Park** where the bush is home to honey possums, kangaroos and bandicoots; a lake and limestone caves can be explored. Few sights are as compelling as the countless limestone pillars known as **The Pinnacles** in the Nambung National Park.

The northwest There is a great contrast of natural landscapes in the vast northwest. Some of the most stunning scenery is on the coast. Among the inlets and peninsulas of the World Heritage listed **Shark Bay Marine Park** is unique and dazzlingly white Shell Beach, 37 miles long and built up of a 33-foot depth of crushed and compacted shells. The North West Cape has twin parks of outstanding interest. To the east are the parched plateau and deep rocky gorges of the **Cape Range National Park**, descending to the west through fossil reefs and sand dunes to Australia's "other" barrier reef, the **Ningaloo Marine Park**, 162 miles of coral reef sheltering a shallow lagoon. Running inland from the tidal flats and mangrove swamps of the coast is the **Pilbara**, a spectacular upland deeply incised by river valleys and culminating in the vividly colored 328-foot deep gorges of the **Karijini (Hamersley Range) National Park**.

Between the Pilbara and the Kimberley, the Great Sandy Desert claims part of the coastline. Where it merges with the Little Sandy Desert, far inland, are the salt lakes of the **Rudall River National Park** (contact the Western Australian tourist office for information).

The Kimberley Beyond the desert, dramatic landforms include **Geikie Gorge**, **Windjana Gorge**, the world's second largest meteorite crater at **Wolfe Creek**, and the strange beehive rock formations of the **Bungle Bungles**. Plant life ranges from sparse spinifex to scenes of great luxuriance in spots with a guaranteed water supply.

A possum—part of the myriad wildlife of the state

A RARE BIRD
In 1894 Windjana Gorge in the Kimberley was the scene of a gun battle between heavily armed police and a band of Aborigines led by Jundumurra, known to his adversaries as Pigeon. A skillful horseman and tracker, Pigeon had been compelled to work for the police against his own people. Eventually turning against his masters, he shot a constable, set prisoners free, and for years waged a minor guerilla war. He was finally hunted down and killed at Tunnel Creek on April 1, 1897.

The fragile silica and sandstone forms of the Bungle Bungles are best seen from April through October

The rugged wilderness of Kalbarri National Park can be appreciated by helicopter

EYRE TRAVEL
The 1,043 miles of the Eyre Highway between Adelaide and Perth are less of an obstacle than might be supposed. Plenty of Australians refuse to be deterred by such distances and plan their driving accordingly, settling down to a steady pace and accepting the discipline of distance. At vacation periods it's wise to reserve ahead if you plan to stay in any of the motels along the route. Your vehicle should be absolutely roadworthy before setting out, since repair facilities are limited. Two hazards to remember: the sign "Road Train" identifies a truck with up to three trailers. Make sure the road is clear before attempting to overtake a road train; and when traveling west, you will have the setting sun to reckon with for long and disagreeable periods. One solution (reserve well in advance!) is to put the car on the train for the westward journey and drive back to the east.

By air The remoteness and sheer size of Western Australia mean that air travel is often used, not only for traveling between major cities but also to reach faraway places of interest or for day and half-day trips. Perth has direct connections to numerous overseas destinations, as well as daily flights to all state capitals and a number of other Australian cities.

By bus Express buses link Perth to the rest of the state, and to other Australian cities (given time!). The metropolitan area of Perth has a comprehensive network of buses, some of them operating out of the futuristic terminal near The Narrows. The capital also enjoys free services in the central area: City Area Transit (C.A.T.) buses circle the city center each day at regular intervals, a great boon once you've got the hang of their routes.

By train Perth has a three-pronged suburban rail service, connecting City Station with Guildford, Armadale and, usefully for the visitor, Fremantle. Fares are reasonable, and the service is generally efficient. Most of Western Australia's railroads now carry freight only, though there are passenger trains from Perth to Bunbury in the south (the Australind) and west to Kalgoorlie (the Prospector). One of the world's great trains runs from Perth Terminal Station, the twice-weekly *Indian Pacific* to Sydney via Adelaide. Linking west and east across the Nullarbor Plain, this train is the railroad experience of a lifetime—the journey to Adelaide takes 38 hours, and it is a two-and-a-half-day, three-night trip to Sydney.

By car The alternative routes north from Perth to Port Hedland, the **North West Coastal Highway** and the **Great Northern Highway**, are both paved, as is their continuation onward to the Kimberley and the Northern Territory. It's a long way, though. The road network around Perth and in much of the southwest is well developed, but many places can only be reached on unpaved roads, in varying states of upkeep. Some particular favorites, like the rough but very scenic **Gibb River Road** through the Kimberley, can definitely only be negotiated by 4WD, and this road is often closed during the December–April wet season.

►► Albany 146A2

Albany was the first European settlement in Western Australia, founded in 1826 by Major Edmund Lockyer to preempt any possible French interest in this quarter of the continent. It became an important base for whalers, then a coaling station for ships on the India–Sydney run; it is now a popular vacation town. The 19th-century buildings include the **Old Gaol; Patrick Taylor Cottage►** of 1832, constructed from wattle and daub and now a folk museum; the **Old Post Office►**, now the Inter-Colonial Communications Museum; and the excellent **Albany Residency Museum►**. Nearby is the *Amity* **Replica**, a full-size reproduction of Major Lockyer's brig, which was built from local timber in 1975.

The town nestles between Mount Clarence and Mount Melville, the summits of which give terrific views over coast and countryside. Further inland are the granite domes and karri forests of Porongurup National Park, and farther still the high Stirling Range. To east and west lies one of Australia's finest stretches of coastline, and protecting the sound to the south is the rugged peninsula of **Torndirrup National Park►►**, with spectacular features like the **Blowholes►**, **The Gap►**, and **Natural Bridge►**, a huge granite bridge-like suspension. The old whaling station on Frenchman Bay is now **Whaleworld►**, which claims to be the world's largest whaling museum.

► Augusta 146A2

Augusta is one of Western Australia's oldest settlements. This popular holiday resort overlooks the mouth of the Blackwood River and, founded in 1830, has some delightful beaches, plenty of good fishing spots, and offers river cruises. This region is perhaps best known for its remarkable series of caves, particularly the spectacular **Jewel Cave►**, with its strange rock formations that include an enormous straw stalactite and an underground river. In town, the Augusta Historical Museum is worth a visit, and there are panoramic views from lighthouse-capped **Cape Leeuwin►**, 5 miles to the south.

DIGGERS ON HORSEBACK
Australia's Desert Mounted Corps distinguished itself in the Middle East in the course of World War I. Albany was the port of embarkation for many of its troops, and they and their mounts are commemorated by the dramatic statue on top of Mount Clarence. This is a recast of the bronze erected on the banks of the Suez Canal in 1932, which came to a sorry end during the Suez crisis of 1956. The original of the horse's head was recovered, and is on view in the Residency Museum.

159

A LADY LION
The map of Australia reveals a number of names of Dutch origin. Perhaps the most famous of these is Cape Leeuwin, with its lighthouse overlooking the meeting point of the Indian and Southern oceans. Its name recalls the Dutch vessel that first put it on the map, the *Leeuwin*, or lioness, which passed this way in 1622.

The town of Albany viewed from the water

BROOME'S ZERO HOUR
It was not only Darwin that suffered Japanese air raids in World War II. On March 3, 1942, a squadron of Japanese Zero fighter planes spent a leisurely hour attacking a number of Allied flying boats moored off Mangrove Point. At very low tides, the remains of some of these machines can be seen in the bay.

A STAIRWAY TO THE SKY
Another effect of Broome's exceptional tidal range is the optical illusion known as "The Staircase to the Moon," visible only at certain times of the year when the rays of the moon are reflected off the exposed bed of the ocean.

The pleasant town of Bunbury is a major seaport and the center of the southwest

▶▶ Broome 147D3

The tourist's southwestern gateway to the Kimberley, Broome makes the most of its colorful past, when divers from all over Asia braved the bends and fierce rivalry to harvest precious mother-of-pearl from the sea bed (see page 161). Although only a few luggers still sail today, cultured pearls are farmed in the vicinity.

The authentic past can best be savored in the **Broome Historical Society Museum▶**, or in the **cemetery**, its graves a grim record of the dangers of life as a diver. The restored Japanese section is particularly impressive. The town overlooks the mud flats and mangroves of Roebuck Bay, a rich haven for birdlife.

The tidal range at Broome is exceptional, up to 33 feet, and at very low tide the footprints of dinosaurs can be seen at Gantheaume Point to the south of the town. From here the splendid white sands of Cable Beach stretch north for 14 miles.

▶ Bunbury 146A2

Bunbury's population of 25,000 inhabitants makes it one of Western Australia's largest settlements. The viewpoint known as Boulter's Heights provides a panorama over the town and its surroundings. As well as a port, Bunbury is a popular resort, with good fishing, a fine string of beaches along the 5-mile Ocean Drive and, a relatively recent phenomenon, a friendly school of dolphins that enjoy the company of visitors to Koombana Beach.

▶▶ Bungle Bungle (Purnululu) National Park 147E4

The soft sandstone of this part of the East Kimberley has been eroded into strange rock formations resembling domes, turrets, and beehives. Access to the national park is by 4WD only and there are no facilities: the region is closed from January to March to help prevent too much disturbance during the wet season. Most visitors prefer to view the park by plane or helicopter; the aerial perspective reveals nature's weird beauty and striking colors. The park also has numerous examples of the art of the tribes who lived here, plus a number of burial sites.

Pearl oysters thrive in the tropical seas from Cape York in northern Queensland right around to Shark Bay in the west of Western Australia, a distance of some 1,865 miles. There is a particularly large concentration of them between Derby and Cossack in the northwest. From early on, the pearls themselves were a bonus, the mainstay of the industry being mother-of-pearl shell, used for jewelry and, above all, for humble buttons.

Commercial exploitation This began in the 1880s, when Aborigines were more or less forced by pearling masters into diving for the shell on the sea bed, an often lethal task; even if they could avoid the danger of drowning, there were shark attacks, and many boats and their crews were lost in the frequent cyclones. With the expansion of the trade and the introduction of diving suits later in the century, there was an influx of Chinese, Filipinos, Malays, Koepangers from Timor, and the most expert of all pearlers, the Japanese. In the 1920s Broome, one of the world centers of pearling, had a population of about 3,000, some 1,200 of Japanese descent. A typical pearling lugger might have had a European master, a pair of Japanese divers, a Japanese engineer and a crew from Timor. The different races lived in sometimes uneasy proximity in Broome, with occasional outbreaks of violence. Each August during the famous Shinju Matsuri (Pearl Festival), Broome remembers its golden days.

Pearling today By the 1930s the shell beds had been seriously depleted and, later, mother-of-pearl was displaced by plastic in the manufacture of buttons. Nowadays a few luggers still set off for the oyster beds some 4 miles off the coast, but most of Broome's current output comes from cultured pearls, raised in "farms" away from public view. Pearling's colorful history is explained in the **Broome Historical Society Museum**, while an old pearling lugger can be seen outside the **Maritime Museum** in Fremantle. A real curiosity connected with this trade is the Catholic mission at Beagle Bay, 80 miles north of Broome, its altar shimmering with mother-of-pearl.

THE PEARL FARMER'S YEAR
From December through March there is little to do, for this is the region's wet season; from April through August the young oysters are seeded so that they produce pearls; during the remainder of the year the large oysters are removed and their shells used for mother-of-pearl.

161

Until recently, Broome relied on pearling for its livelihood

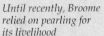

WESTERN ROCK

Mount Augustus, 280 miles inland from Carnarvon, may lack the unique beauty of Ayers Rock but beats it hands-down for size. This is the world's largest monocline, created—according to the Aborigines—when a man called Burringurrah was speared by his enemies in the Dreamtime. From a viewpoint southeast of the rock his form can still be made out, with the stump of the spear in his leg.

WATERING THE GOLDFIELDS

Extracting gold from the fields of Western Australia posed fewer difficulties than finding water in this utterly arid area. The Irish-born engineer Charles Yelverton O'Connor solved the problem. Already responsible for the construction of Fremantle Harbour and the building of much of the state's railroad system, this late-Victorian genius built one of the wonders of the age, known as the Goldfields and Agricultural Water Supply Scheme. Beginning at the splendid dam at Mundaring Weir near Perth, O'Connor's great pipe sucked water 340 miles eastward in sufficient quantities to quench the miners' thirst and leave some over to irrigate the farms of the Wheat Belt. Attacked by landed interests and ridiculed by critics, O'Connor lost heart, and he committed suicide a year before completion of the project.

Coolgardie—model of Ned Kelly

► Busselton   146A2

Busselton is a pleasant family resort with good beaches, facing north across Geographe Bay and sheltered from the west. Fishermen still frequent the Busselton Jetty, the longest (1¼ miles) wooden jetty in Australia. It has been fully restored after a battering from Cyclone Alby in 1978.

The approach to the town from the north passes through a splendid forest of tuarts, a tree unique to Western Australia. Just off the highway is the long and low tin-roofed 1830s colonial mansion known as **Wonnerup House►**, furnished in period style and open to the public, courtesy of the National Trust.

► Carnarvon   146C1

Only about 90 miles south of the Tropic of Capricorn, Carnarvon wears a tropical air, with palm trees lining its fascine promenade and hibiscus and bougainvillea blooming in its elegantly broad main street. Famous for its fishing industries (you can visit the shrimp and scallop processing plant), it is also the center of a prosperous fruit and vegetable growing area, the Gascoyne district.

The **Bibbawarra Bore►**, 10 miles to the north of town, produces a constant gush of water at 149°F. There is another demonstration of the power of water at **The Blowholes►**, 43 miles north, where jets of water spout 65 feet into the air.

► Coolgardie   147B3

A classic boom-and-bust town 348 miles east of Perth and 224 miles from Kalgoorlie–Boulder, Coolgardie was the center of Australia's most frantic gold rush, with a peak population in the 1890s of 15,000. The then residents' needs were catered to by two stock exchanges, three breweries, and a couple of dozen hotels. The population is now only a tenth of its former size.

Looking like an exceptionally grand railroad terminus, the old Government Buildings are now the home of the **Goldfields Exhibition►**, with extensive displays including a model of the town at its height. Opposite is the weird **Open Air Museum**, its scrapped machinery and statues of Australian heroes standing out surrealistically in the implacable sun. More abandoned machinery, rolling stock and a locomotive have been preserved in Coolgardie's **Railway Station Museum**, which is located in the 1896 railway terminal.

► Darling Range 146A2

The unbroken line of this wooded escarpment stretches far to the north and to the south of Perth, rising to a height of about 1,909 feet and defining the boundary of the coastal plain. Not far from the city are several popular recreation areas, like the bushland and streams of the John Forrest National Park or Mundaring Weir. The reservoir here was built in 1898–1902 to supply the far-off Eastern Goldfields with water; attractively landscaped, it is a favorite picnic spot. The **C. Y. O'Connor Museum▶** at the reservoir is named after the engineer who oversaw this vast project and tells the story of its construction (see panel opposite).

▶ Denmark   146A2
Rugged coastal scenery contrasting with the tranquil Denmark River and attractive farmlands makes the small town of Denmark in the extreme southwest a popular place for family vacations. Wilson Inlet is one of the largest areas of sheltered water on the south coast, with fine fishing, boating and other aquatic pleasures. To the west, **William Bay National Park▶** has sand dunes and pristine beaches, as well as heathland and karri forest.

▶ Derby   147E3
On the shores of King Sound to the north of the mouth of the Fitzroy River, and within striking distance of the West Kimberley, Derby likes to describe itself as the "Gateway to the Gorges;" indeed, Windjana Gorge is only about 87 miles east of the town. Nearer at hand (5 miles away) is a famous boab tree, popularly supposed to have served as a lock-up for a small part of its 1,000-year life.

▶ Esperance   147A3
This deep-water port on the south coast flourished and declined in parallel with the boom and bust in the goldfields to its north. Now tourism has discovered Esperance, not least because of the magnificent beaches and the islands of the Recherche Archipelago. A scenic drive takes in part of the fine coastline and leads to **Pink Lake▶**, an extraordinary salt lake, genuinely pink in color. Some of the best coastal scenery is some 30 miles to the east; here is the **Cape Le Grand National Park▶**, with stunning bays of blue water and white sand set between rocky headlands.

▶▶▶ Fremantle   146A2
Now part of the built-up area of Greater Perth, the old harbor town of Fremantle continues to serve as Western Australia's principal port. Founded in 1829, Fremantle owes some of its attractive appearance to the convict craftsmen shipped in to save the colony's faltering fortunes in the gold-rush building boom of the 1890s. These were Fremantle's great days, when the harbor was improved by the great engineer O'Connor (see panel opposite).

The center of town is compact, its venerable (by Australian standards!) townscape best enjoyed on foot. Good places to get your bearings include the viewing platform on top of the Port Authority Building or the **Round House▶**, erected in 1831 as the new colony's prison. The **Western Australian Maritime Museum▶▶** has a pearling lugger drawn up outside the old Commissariat Store in which it is housed; inside are some excellent maritime history displays.

The town's other major museum, the **Fremantle History Museum▶**, occupies a neo-Gothic edifice on the far side of town. In between are any number of places worth a visit, including the famous **Fremantle Markets**.

The fine port and city of Fremantle lies southwest of Perth, where the Swan River meets the Indian Ocean

163

HOW FREMANTLE GOT ITS NAME
Fremantle is named after the commander of the British naval force sent here to claim the west before anyone else. Captain Charles Howe Fremantle planted the Union Jack here on May 2, 1829, a month before the first settlers arrived to found the Swan River colony. An optimist, he believed that the colony would become "in time, a place of consequence," in spite of "its sandy and uncompromising appearance."

UNWILLING IMMIGRANTS
It was on the shores of Kalbarri that Australia's first known European settlers made their landfall, albeit an involuntary one. Wouter Loos and Jan Pelgrom had been among the mutineers of the *Batavia* (see page 242). After their arrest by Commander Pelsaert, they were put ashore at the mouth of the Wittecarra Creek in late 1629, where they are commemorated by a cairn. Their further story is unknown; ordered to look for them in 1644, Abel Tasman could find no trace.

Crumbling sandstone has created rugged cliffs around the resort of Kalbarri

▶▶ Geikie Gorge National Park   *147D4*

The tiny settlement at **Fitzroy Crossing** has grown up around the point where the Northern Highway traverses the 400-mile-long Fitzroy River that drains much of the Kimberley. Reduced to a series of pools in the dry season, the Fitzroy rises an extraordinary 53 feet in the Wet, flooding vast areas. The effects of this phenomenal difference in water level can be observed (in the Dry!) by taking a boat trip up nearby Geikie Gorge in the national park, where the lower parts of the sheer 100–165-foot cliffs have been dramatically scoured by the annual floodwaters. The gorge is home to many tropical aquatic life forms, including stingrays and freshwater crocodiles, and is fringed by reeds and dense forest supporting a rich range of birdlife.

▶ Geraldton   *146B2*

This prosperous harbor town to the north of Perth, noted for its export of locally caught lobsters, is popular with visitors year round but particularly in winter because of its excellent sunshine record. Some 35 miles off shore is the archipelago aptly named the Houtman Abrolhos (derived from the Portuguese for "Keep your eyes open!") Islands, notorious as a death trap for ships heading eastward across the Indian Ocean. Relics from famous wrecks are the mainstay of the Maritime Museum, part of the **Geraldton Museum▶**; natural history and other sections are housed in the nearby Old Railway Building.

▶ Halls Creek   *147D4*

Halfway through the Kimberley on the Great Northern Highway, Halls Creek seems the archetypal Outback town, center of a vast area thinly populated by cattlemen and mineral prospectors. A short distance away is Old Halls Creek, with its evocative remains of an 1880s gold rush. Between the two settlements is a natural curiosity, a vein of white quartz standing clear of its surroundings and inevitably named the China Wall. An 81-mile drive to the south brings you to the 2,625-foot-wide and 164-foot-deep Wolfe Creek Meteorite Crater.

Instead of horses, cars now front Kalgoorlie's often elaborate hotels

► **Kalbarri**   *146B1*

The gorges in the **Kalbarri National Park►►** are up to 50 miles long and 558 feet deep, cut into the vivid red and wonderfully named tumblagooda sandstone. A number of easily accessible viewpoints like Hawk's Head Lookout overlook this landscape in its setting of sandy plains. The coastal scenery has its drama, too, with high red cliffs dropping sheer into the ocean. The national park is also famous for its spring wildflowers, which bloom in a great diversity of colors and species.

►►► **Kalgoorlie–Boulder**   *147B3*

The classic gold-rush towns of Kalgoorlie and Boulder were amalgamated in 1989. Gold was first found at nearby Coolgardie; not long after, on June 10, 1893, Patrick (Paddy) Hannan and two mates made the greatest find of all—known for ever after as Hannan's Reward—and within a year tens of thousands of eager prospectors had swarmed to the "Golden Mile." In under a decade, both places had been transformed from ragged settlements to solid-seeming municipalities.

Hannan's slightly bemused statue sits outside the massive 1908 Town Hall on the sidewalk of the street named after him. This gently sloping roadway is of boulevard dimensions, wide enough to turn a camel train. On either side are monuments to the town's great days: canopied shopfronts; grandiose public edifices like the colonnaded government buildings; and the swaggeringly self-confident hotels, the **Exchange** (1894), the **Palace** (1897), the **Old Australia** (1896) and the **York** (1900).

►►► **The Kimberley**   *147E4*

See page 173.

► **Kununurra**   *147E4*

This town in the East Kimberley was created in the 1960s to act as an urban center for the Ord River Irrigation Scheme (see panel). A solitary relic of the past, the **Argyle Downs Homestead** was rescued when the land on which it stood was flooded, and is now a pioneer museum. Outside town at **Mirima (Hidden Valley) National Park►**, 300 million years of erosion have created spectacular patterns in the red sandstone.

THE WILD WEST
Kalgoorlie always was a rip-roaring kind of place, and even today takes a perverse pride in being labeled the most crime-ridden of Australia's smaller towns. In 1926, gold thieves hacked to death the detectives sent after them, and 10 years later anti-immigrant riots raged for two days before a train-load of police could be brought up from Perth. Many of today's misdeeds seem to be the result of enthusiastic weekend drinking getting out of hand rather than anything more serious.

165

OUT OF ORDER
Frustrated at seeing the floodwaters of the Ord River in the Kimberley running uselessly into the sea while for the rest of the year the land lay scorched and thirsty, the goverment spent huge sums on the Ord River Irrigation Scheme. Completed in 1972, its dams held back the muddy tide and distributed it among thousands of acres of irrigated cropland. But the desert, on the whole, failed to bloom. The cotton crop was killed by caterpillars, and other crops have been only partially successful, while D.D.T.-resistant insects come to enjoy life in the 380 square miles of the project's main water body, Lake Argyle.

"We can make this country a quarry to serve the whole world," enthused Henry Bolte, the Premier of Victoria (1955–1972). The prosperity of Australia's states and territories rests largely with the abundant mineral resources locked up in their ancient rocks.

Visitors can pan for real gold at the Sovereign Hill historical park in Victoria

IRONING OUT THE LANDSCAPE

Long suspected, the existence of unbelievably rich deposits of iron ore in the Pilbara were confirmed almost by accident in the 1950s. Forced by poor weather to fly low over one of the area's many gorges, Lang Hancock noticed that its walls gave off a metallic sheen. Subsequent investigation revealed what proved to be the world's greatest concentration of iron ore. The topography of whole tracts of land has been transformed by its removal, for example at the Mount Whaleback Mine near Newman, the biggest opencast iron ore pit in the world.

A wealth of minerals Western Australia really came alive with the discovery of gold in unprecedented abundance in the Eastern Goldfields at the end of the 19th century, but the state also has (or had) reserves of antimony, bismuth, asbestos, coal, tin, copper, iron, and nickel, as well as such rarities as tungsten, tantalite, and beryl. Exploration and prospecting are very much a matter of the present as well as of history. The world's biggest iron mountain was discovered by accident in the Pilbara in the 1950s (see panel); while the incredibly productive Argyle Diamond Mine near Kununurra, which produces exquisite white-, champagne-, and pink- colored stones, and is the world's largest producing diamond mine, only came on stream in the 1980s.

The first rush But it is the lure of gold that still catches the imagination most. The gold rushes, here as everywhere, were epic events, with their extraordinary mixture of greed, determination, and endurance amounting to heroism. The first rush in Western Australia was to Halls Creek in the Kimberley, in 1885, when Charlie Hall's Christmas present to himself was a 28-ounce nugget. Conditions in this utterly remote and harsh area were perhaps the worst anywhere; one devoted mate, Russian Jack, carted a sick friend 200 miles in a wheelbarrow in search of a doctor.

Halls Creek failed to live up to its promise, and the prospectors soon abandoned the Kimberley for the greater pickings to be found in the Eastern Goldfields. In 1892 Arthur Bayley rode into Southern Cross with 554 ounces of gold that he and his partner, Bill Ford, had found at Fly Flat 125 miles to the east; bars emptied as the news got around, and within hours the greatest rush in the colony's history had begun. Fly Flat was renamed

Coolgardie; within six months thousands were living in a city of tents, having trekked through the waterless waste on foot or horseback, while supplies were brought up by dray or camel train. A year later the biggest find of all was made at Boulder. The rush greatly increased Western Australia's population and was an immense stimulus to the colony's development. Terrible conditions endured for a while, with plagues of flies, outbreaks of typhoid, and water that sometimes cost as much as champagne. Before the completion of O'Connor's 340-mile pipeline from Perth in 1903 (see panel on page 162), traders in water often became richer than prospectors.

Companies move in Within the space of a few years, individual prospectors had scarred most of the Eastern Goldfields area with their shallow diggings ("specking") and extracted most of the alluvial gold. From now on it became necessary to mine more deeply, requiring the use of sophisticated machinery and the outlay of capital. Companies took over from rugged individuals.

Contemporary opencast methods of gold extraction and the extraordinary landscape they are creating can be observed from the viewing platform overlooking Kalgoorlie's **Super Pit**, which will eventually stretch for several miles and reach a depth of 1,640 feet.

PADDY'S PATTER
A "living" Paddy Hannan recounts the tale of the Eastern Goldfields at Hannan's North Tourist Mine in Boulder, a faithful reconstruction of a mine and its surroundings in its heyday. Here you can drop underground in the cramped miners' cage and have the mysteries and miseries of extraction explained to you by a veteran miner. Back on the surface, a railroad meanders around the extensive site with its many authentic old buildings.

Other mine museums in Kalgoorlie–Boulder are the School of Mines Museum and the Museum of the Goldfields.

Pilbara: giant trucks are used to transport the iron ore

167

The golden sandy beaches around the resort of Mandurah are always popular

168

RAILS THROUGH THE FOREST
In the early part of the century the jarrah forests inland from Mandurah echoed to the hiss of steam and the toot of whistles as narrow-gauge locomotives hauled timber to the mills. One of these forestry railroads, the Hotham Valley Tourist Railway, running between Pinjarra and Dwellingup, has been kept alive by enthusiasts, and steam trains meet passengers off the modern Australind train from Perth. The enthusiasm is such that an additional line, the Etmilyn Forest Tramway, was opened in 1986, leading deep into the heart of the atmospheric jarrah woodlands.

▶ **Mandurah** *146A2*
Less than an hour's drive south of Perth, Mandurah is deservedly popular with city weekenders. Vast areas of sheltered water along the Murray and Serpentine Rivers and the Peel Inlet, 25 miles of beaches, and an abundance of shady picnic spots help distribute the crowds and keep at least some of the town's tranquil atmosphere.

▶▶ **Margaret River** *146A2*
The township of Margaret River is the center of the attractive district named after it, where the manicured landscape of prestige wineries contrasts with the savagery of surf pounding a rugged coastline and with a mysterious underground world of limestone caves. Arts and crafts abound in the town itself, while music (of the highest caliber, but only once a year) is performed in the delightful grounds of the Leeuwin Estate winery.

Among the more sheltered places along the coast, most of which forms part of the Leeuwin-Naturaliste National Park, is **Prevelly Park▶**. This is one of Australia's premier surfing spots, and the Margaret River Classic surf competition is held in the area each November. Only a few of the hundreds of caves are accessible, among them Mammoth Cave▶ (named for its size) and Lake Cave▶. The **Boranup Forest▶** is a good place to see the extraordinary massed ranks of karri trees.

▶▶ **Monkey Mia** *146C1*
Some of the several hundred bottlenose dolphins living in Shark Bay mix with humans and accept fresh fish. To stand in the water of Monkey Mia beach and be nuzzled by a dolphin is an experience that few can resist, but the rangers at the Dolphin Information Centre ask that you check with them first. (See also page 174).

▶ **New Norcia** *146B2*
The Benedictines came to Western Australia as early as 1846, leaving the unmistakable imprint of Mediterranean Catholicism here in the bush 80 miles north of Perth, where they established a mission for the Aborigines. As well as the Abbey Church and Monastery, there is a fine museum and art gallery.

The "strangeness" of Australian plants—including eucalypts of all varieties, wattles, and banksias—fascinates visitors from the northern hemisphere. Australia's native vegetation provides a constant reminder that you're not in Kansas anymore.

Early settlers tackled the isolation of this unfamiliar land by manipulating its appearance to recall the landscapes left behind. Planted in uncountable numbers, oaks, elms, willows, and poplars transformed whole tracts of countryside—particularly in Tasmania—into a version of lowland England; the occasional eucalyptus looked like an intruder.

A great variety One of the joys of springtime is the abundance of wildflowers, particularly in Western Australia. Here a twofold isolation, not only from the rest of the world but from the rest of the continent, has resulted in flora of extraordinary variety. The state has some 8,000 named species, plus a further 2,000 that are still anonymous, three-quarters of them unique to the area though not necessarily unrelated to plants elsewhere in Australia. Some of Western Australia's most famous plants are the kangaroo paw, with its strangely shaped red or green flowers; a range of banksias, including the scarlet and acorn varieties; and the 60 species of tooth-leafed dryandras.

Springtime spectacular Wildflowers pattern the ground from north to south as springtime advances. At the **Kalbarri National Park**, 375 miles north of Perth, flowers begin to bloom in July. Some of the most spectacular displays occur in the heathlands of the southwest, where there are more species of plants than in the rain forest. In places like the **Stirling** and **Porongurup Ranges** spring arrives much later, with November being the most rewarding month. **Kings Park** in Perth features extensive areas of natural bushland and a special section devoted to Australian trees, shrubs, and wildflowers.

Below: trailing orchid in bloom

169

Wildflowers in coastal Western Australia

HAROLD HEIGHTS
Named after former Prime Minister Harold E. Holt, the joint U.S./Australian Naval Communication Station keeps in touch with what is going on around the oceans with an extraordinary cluster of tall towers, the central one of which, at 1,273 feet, is taller than the Empire State Building. American accents can be heard in the streets of Exmouth, founded in 1964 as the support town for the base, but visitors come here mostly for the excellent fishing; North West Cape is the nearest point in Australia to the teeming marine life of the continental shelf.

The lesser-known rival of the Great Barrier Reef, Ningaloo Reef is home to over 500 varieties of fish

►► Ningaloo Marine Park and Exmouth area · 146C1

A long detour leads off the North West Coastal Highway to far-off North West Cape, whose backbone is formed by the rugged **Cape Range**. This national park is made up of a high limestone plateau cut into by gorges and ravines, some containing deep pools. To the west stretch rarely visited dunes and beaches, protected from the ocean rollers by a barrier reef, 162 miles long and extending some 10 miles from the coast. The reef of Ningaloo Marine Park—with its 220 species of coral, whale sharks, the world's biggest fish, and more—is as yet hardly exploited; there is fishing, camping, diving, and swimming, and glass-bottomed boats operate from Coral Bay and **Exmouth**. The best place to begin your exploration of these natural wonders around Exmouth is at the innovative Milyering Visitor Centre in the Cape Range National Park.

► Northam · 146A2

An important road and rail junction and depot for the Goldfields Water Scheme, this Wheat Belt town is the regional center for much of the attractive Avon Valley. The railway up from Perth about 60 miles away used to terminate here, so Northam was the point at which prospectors would begin their thirsty trek to the Goldfields 280 miles to the east; the old railroad station is now a museum with displays of evocative memorabilia of those days.

► Northcliffe · 146A2

This tiny place lost among the magnificent karri forests of the extreme southwest began as one of the townships of the ill-fated Group Settlement Scheme of the 1920s, whose hopes and failures are documented in the excellent **Pioneer Museum►**. A good base for viewing the karris (some of the tallest of them grow in the nearby Forest Park), Northcliffe is also the starting point for a 17-mile road leading to Windy Harbour, the only readily accessible beach between Augusta and Walpole.

A forest of karris, the tallest of the eucalypts which can reach a height of 280 feet or more

THE GLOUCESTER TREE
It was difficult to build fire-watch towers of sufficient height to rise above the canopy of the giant karris. The answer was to wind a peg ladder around the trunk of a suitable tree and make a lookout cabin at the top. Planes perform the lookout function nowadays, but the Gloucester Tree near Pemberton has been kept for fearless tourists to climb its 153 rungs and be rewarded with a stupendous view over the treetops. It's the loftiest fire lookout tree in the world, but at around 195 feet, it is by no means the tallest karri.

► Nullarbor Plain 147B4
Renowned for its utter desolation, the world's largest flat surface stretches interminably eastward into South Australia, covering an area of more than 77,000 square miles. Few plants (other than saltbush) and fewer animals flourish in this unyielding environment—the name Nullarbor means "no trees."

The explorer Edward John Eyre survived his terrible journey across the plain from east to west in 1840–1841 by keeping close to the coast, where brackish water could occasionally be found beneath patches of sand dunes. The highway named after him also follows a southern route, while the transcontinental railroad strikes off boldly from the goldfields far inland. The landscape along the highway, which is coated entirely in asphalt, is not entirely without incident, since only a relatively short section traverses the Nullarbor proper, but the 90-mile continuous straight between Balladonia and Caiguna tests any driver's ability to stay alert.

►► Pemberton 146A2
Steeped in logging lore, the township of Pemberton in the southwest corner of the state is the best place to experience the magic of the magnificent karri forest. Its wonders can be appreciated in a variety of ways—by car, on foot, or aboard a 1907 replica tramcar of the Pemberton Tramway, which travels through the forest on a 22-mile railroad line. One tree can be walked through, another, the **Gloucester Tree►** (see panel) can be climbed. You can visit a restored 1865 sawpit, take a guided tour around a huge modern sawmill, or trace the area's history in the nearby **Manjimup Regional Timber Park►**. The beauty of the forest is enhanced by clear streams, pretty cascades, and a wealth of wildflowers in the spring.

RAILS ACROSS THE DESERT
Passengers on the Trans Australia Railway have the dubious distinction of taking part in one of the world's few railroad journeys where the view from your sleeping berth in the morning is identical to the one on which you closed the curtain the night before! Imposing-sounding stations turn out to be nothing more than a marker planted in the wilderness, or at the very most a huddle of railroad paraphernalia with a section of loop allowing trains to pass. The 297-mile "Long Straight" between Ooldea and Watson tests the patience of the most disciplined driver of the big diesel hauling its train of stainless steel cars.

There are several high peaks in Porongurup National Park in the Albany hinterland

KARRIED TO EXTREMES
One of the tallest of all eucalypts is the karri (*Eucalyptus diversicolor*), a magnificent tree reaching a height of 280 feet, and with a lifespan of up to 1,000 years. Growing together in the forest, the soaring stems of the karris create the stately atmosphere of a Gothic church. The finest tracts of karri forest are found in the well-watered south, inland from the coast between Augusta and Albany; much of it was cleared after both world wars to make small-holdings for returned soldiers. Most of these settlements failed, since the deep loamy soil preferred by the karris was good for trees but not for crops.

▶ **Pilbara** *147C2*

Until the 1960s, a few cattlemen were the only inhabitants of this wasteland in the northwest. The accidental discovery in the 1950s of what proved to be the world's largest deposit of iron ore (see page 166) was the stimulus for the construction of mining cities like Tom Price and Newman and the growth of deep-water harbors like Dampier and Port Hedland. Trains 6,550 feet long haul the ore from the huge opencast pits down hundreds of miles of track to the sea. Much of this exported raw material is later returned to Australia in the form of Japanese cars.

Tourists come this way for winter sun and for the stunning landscapes of the **Karijini (Hamersley Range) National Park▶▶**. The vividly colored rocks of this ancient plateau have been bitten into deeply by the action of rivers, forming splendid gorges where intensely cold water gathers in pools and where a surprisingly lush vegetation flourishes. Even more luxuriant plants are a feature of the **Millstream-Chichester National Park▶**, to the north, where there is a large colony of fruit bats and permanently flowing water, nourishing the palm trees of a relict rain forest.

▶▶ **The Pinnacles (Nambung National Park)** *146B2*

The thousands of limestone monoliths scattered around the sandy plain south of the coastal township of Cervantes were mistaken by Dutch sailors for the remains of an ancient city. Varying in size from 19-foot giants to finger-thick pieces of piping, they may well be the fossilized roots of long-dead trees and shrubs. Whatever their origin, they remain compelling in their desert setting. The Cervantes area boasts several beautiful beaches, popular with sailboarders and boaters.

▶ **Porongurup National Park** *146A2*

The ancient granites of this range of hills in the Albany hinterland have been eroded into domes and curious formations like Balancing Rock. Castle Rock (1,870 feet) gives stunning views over karri forest and the country beyond. In spring, the forest floor is brilliant with wildflowers.

This remote land in the far north of Western Australia was explored in 1879 by Alexander Forrest, who thought that some of it might sustain grazing animals. Million-acre stations still graze their stock on the sparse vegetation. There is diamond mining at Argyle, and tourists pass through on around-Australia trips or make the Kimberley their prime destination, drawn by the lure of a "last frontier."

East Kimberley The modern township of Kununurra is the gateway to the East Kimberley, a region of ancient volcanic rocks and sandstone ranges. Tropical rainfall fills the rivers in the Wet, supporting a rich pattern of vegetation and wildlife, while mangrove swamps clad the margins of estuaries. The Ord River Irrigation Scheme has attempted to harness the river's summer flow to irrigate vast areas of cropland, with only limited success; remote **Wyndham**, the state's northernmost harbor and a port town since the 1880s, exports cattle as well as whatever crops the project produces. Persistence will lead the determined visitor to natural wonders like the **Mitchell Falls**, or even (with a permit) along the Kalumburu Road to the far off Aboriginal Reserve and Mission near the mouth of the King Edward River. Some areas, like the Drysdale River National Park, of unresearched biological value, may not be visited at all.

West Kimberley Entered via Broome and Derby, the west has spectacular inland gorges, cut through the limestones of an ancient barrier reef, long since hoisted high above sea level. The river running through **Windjana Gorge**, composed of rocks that are part of a 350-million-year-old limestone shelf, is reduced to a series of pools in the dry season, while the mighty Fitzroy River manages to maintain an all-year flow through the much longer **Geikie Gorge**.

HOW TO GET THERE
Most traffic takes the long way around from Derby to Kununurra via the main highway. This gives access to Wolfe Creek Crater National Park as well as the magical Bungle Bungles (though both of these extraordinary natural phenomena are better seen from the air). The shorter route is the Gibb River Road, rougher but more rewarding, with well-vegetated creeks, gorges and waterholes.

173

The Argyle Diamond Mine, in the East Kimberley, produces high-quality stones

A NEST OF RATS

Rottnest Island, meaning rats' nest island, was named in 1696 by Dutchman Willem de Vlamingh who found the place infested with what he took to be large rodents. The rats were in fact the hare-sized marsupials known as quokkas, a kind of small wallaby, found here on "Rotto" and on parts of the mainland.

MARINE WONDERLAND

Shark Bay Marine Park's UNESCO World Heritage status was bestowed for its remarkable natural beauty and significance. The Monkey Mia dolphins are the region's best-known attraction, but the bay also contains stromatolites—fossilized layers of blue-green algae—at Hamelin Pool, and one of the last-surviving herds of dugongs, or sea-cows.

Some of the hundreds of dolphins that inhabit the warm waters of Shark Bay

▶ Rottnest Island   155E2

Situated 12 miles off the Fremantle coast, reached by air or ferry from Perth, and measuring a mere 7 miles long by a maximum of 3 miles across, Perth's weekend paradise has a special charm, enormously enhanced by the lack of cars; bikes are the main mode for exploring the delightful bays and white beaches along the rugged coastline. The extraordinarily clear turquoise waters are ideal for diving and snorkeling.

▶▶ Shark Bay Marine Park   146C1

Divided into a series of inlets by peninsulas and islands, and with 932 miles of coastline, World Heritage listed Shark Bay was named in 1699 by the adventurer William Dampier. The waters of the bay provide excellent swimming, fishing, and other watersports, and there are spectacular dunes of red sand, high limestone cliffs, and extraordinary beaches as well. Shell Beach, 37 miles long, is made up of countless shells to a depth of 33 feet; naturally compacted at this depth, this strange material can be cut into blocks and used in buildings. The little resort of Denham is the westernmost town in Australia; on the opposite side of the Peron Peninsula are the famous dolphins of Monkey Mia (see page 168).

▶ Southern Cross   146B2

The streets of Southern Cross, founded by gold prospectors in 1888, are still wide enough to turn a camel train. There are mementoes of the old days in the 1891 court house, now a local history museum.

▶ Stirling Range National Park   146A2

A scenic highway threads through this 40-mile-long range near Albany, whose peaks rise abruptly 3,250 feet above the surrounding country. As well as being southwestern Australia's highest mountains, with occasional snowfall, they are a botanical reserve of first importance and great beauty, with 1,000 wildflower species.

►► Wave Rock   146A2

Wave Rock remains forever a surfer's dream turned to stone. More than 325 feet long and 50 feet high, the petrified breaker's resemblance to the real thing is emphasized by the colorful vertical streaking, the result of natural chemicals in the granite reacting with rainwater.

Other curiosities near the little Wheat Belt town of Hyden (211 miles inland from Perth) include further odd rock formations with names like the Humps and the Hippo's Yawn. In Mulka's Cave the visitor can view genuine Aboriginal wall paintings .

► Yanchep   146A2

Days out from Perth often take in the coastline to the north of the city with its fine beaches, sand dunes and chain of lakes just inland. Yanchep itself is a resort, but around it stretches the **Yanchep National Park►**, with colorful limestone caves, a lake, eucalyptus woods, koalas and a wealth of wildflowers in the spring.

► York   146A2

With Northam and Toodyay, York is one of a trio of much-visited towns that are located in the picturesque Avon Valley 60 miles northeast of Perth. Western Australia's most historic inland town, York was founded in 1831, and many of its lovely old sandstone buildings have survived the ravages of time, including an earthquake in 1968.

The **Residency Museum►** evokes the early days of life in Western Australia, as does the **Balladong Farm►**, which is a living museum of agriculture with animals galore—a good place to take children. More than 200 vintage cars, motorcycles, and even some horse-drawn vehicles are on display in the **York Motor Museum►►**.

Wave Rock: another ancient geological curiosity

175

RIVER OF THE BLACK SWANS
The Avon is a tributary of the Swan River, given its name in honor of the black swans that make it their home. Both rivers formed a corridor for early settlement, and the area around Guildford includes many historic buildings like Woodbridge at nearby Midland, built in 1885 and now restored and authentically furnished (open to the public). The Swan Valley is famous for its wine. A tour of the wineries is always a popular excursion.

Hotel sign in the small, respectable town of York

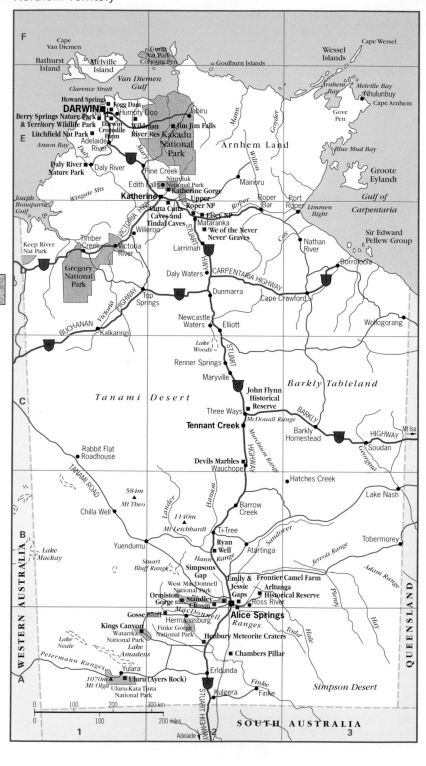

THE NORTHERN TERRITORY With the thin bitumen ribbon of the Stuart Highway as its backbone, the third largest territorial area in Australia stretches from the country's desert heart, the "Red Centre," to the coast and islands of the tropical north, the "Top End."

The cattle industry, once the basis of the Territory's economy has been overtaken by mining (bauxite, manganese, uranium) and by tourism; more and more visitors are drawn here, not only to the mysterious landforms of the desert, of which **Ayers Rock** is just one, but to Darwin; to the natural riches of the north; and, above all, to the incomparable World Heritage wilderness of **Kakadu National Park**.

FIRST SETTLEMENT The first European sighting of the coast of the Northern Territory seems to have been made in 1623 by the Dutchman Jan Carstenzoon on board the *Arnhem*. However, the process of colonization did not actually begin until the 1820s.

The first attempts to found settlements came to grief; Port Essington (1824) on the Cobourg Peninsula had no fresh water, Fort Dundas (1824–1829) on Melville Island suffered from attacks by hostile Aborigines, and Raffles Bay (1827), also on the Cobourg Peninsula, was abandoned after only two years. Victoria (on an inlet of Port Essington) was established in 1838, and in spite of cyclones and earthquakes, managed to last until 1849, when it too was given up.

The splendid natural harbor of Port Darwin was given its name in 1839 by Captain J. C. Wickham of the *Beagle*, thereby honoring Charles Darwin, a member of an earlier voyage. However, it was not until three decades later, in 1869, that the site of the present capital of the territory was surveyed and a start was made on building houses. The choice turned out to be a propitious one, and Darwin, which was originally named Palmerston, has survived and prospered in spite of numerous cyclones and Japanese air raids during World War I.

A ghost gum, easily recognizable by its white trunk

GREAT CASUAL DRESS OR... BUGGER ORF!

CONQUERING THE INTERIOR

The interminable and arid spaces of the center resisted attempts to cross them until 1862 when, undeterred by five heroic failures, John McDouall Stuart finally blazed a trail from south to north; Stuart's route is followed by the highway named after him. Before the road was built, the famous Overland Telegraph, spanning the unmapped wilderness between Port Augusta on the coast of South Australia and Darwin, had been completed in less than two years. Linked at Darwin to the submarine cable from Java in 1872, Australia was connected with the "grand electric chain that unites the nations of the earth." The repeater stations, constructed along its 1,800-mile length at Alice Springs, Tennant Creek, and other places, became focal points for travelers and townships later developed around these isolated outposts. Pastoralists then moved into the territory, and it became part of South Australia in 1863. The telegraph station at Alice Springs still stands, though the town itself has moved south.

INTO THE 20TH CENTURY

In 1911 the Northern Territory, a drain on the meager resources of South Australia, became the responsibility of the Commonwealth. Though self-governing since 1978, it has still not acquired full statehood, and some of its affairs (Aboriginal matters and uranium mining) continue to be handled by Canberra. For many years it stayed a backwater; few drivers braved the horrible surface of its unpaved roads and there were very few tourists. However, World War II changed all that. In a series of heavy raids, Japanese aircraft inflicted severe damage not only on Darwin but on the Australian psyche. Acutely aware of the country's vulnerability via the empty and remote north, government and armed forces paved the road from the railhead at Alice Springs to the coast, and built a chain of depots, bases and airfields, remains of which can be seen along the highway.

The Northern Territory was hauled bodily into the life of the nation by these events.

ROAD TRAINS

The first car to cross the desert center took 51 days on its arduous trip from Adelaide to Darwin, and signaled the beginning of the end for the horses, camels and buffalo-drawn carts that had served the Northern Territory's needs until then. In the 1930s, a cumbersome A.E.C. diesel and trailer formed what was called the Government Road Train, hauling supplies to isolated communities. After World War II, Kurt Johannsen used an old army tank transporter to pull no less than eight cattle trailers. Today's road trains are limited to a maximum of three "dogs" or trailers, a formidable sight as they roar along the highways of the Northern Territory, Queensland, and Western Australia.

One of the lovely gorges cut by the Katherine River

National parks

Traveling along the Stuart Highway between the arid Red Centre and tropical Top End you experience some of the most dramatic contrasts nature has to offer in Australia.

THE RED CENTRE Geological processes have shaped the red rocks of the center, creating an almost abstract world of crater and boulder, jagged ridge, and lonely monolith, starkly defined against a background of sandy plain or pebbly desert. Etched into this awesome pattern are the winding beds of watercourses, filled only when rare rainstorms rage. Ancestors of the present rivers were fed more generously, and they carved chasm, gorge and canyon niches in this hostile world for a surprisingly rich and varied wildlife. The rugged **MacDonnell Ranges** to the west and east of Alice Springs are breached by many a gap filled with ferns, palms, and other exotic plants, some of them descendants of the flora that flourished on the shore of the vast sea that once covered much of central Australia. Waterholes persist here long after rivers have dried up, creating a refuge for both animals and humans.

Experiencing the desert is not difficult (unless you want it that way!). Parks Australia North and the Parks and Wildlife Commission of the N.T. are improving facilities while preserving the landscapes entrusted to them. Their management of Ayers Rock is a model of its kind.

THE MORE VERDANT NORTH Toward the northern rim of the center, permanently flowing rivers are a reminder of a more abundant, monsoon rainfall (up to 63 inches a year compared with around 4¾ inches in the south). Many rivers have their source on the high plateau of Arnhem Land; the Katherine River has cut a series of spectacular gorges, while the **Kakadu National Park** teems with wildlife. The Top End has some of Australia's remotest places, while Darwin itself enjoys a superabundance of natural areas in its hinterland.

DARWIN'S TERRITORIAL WATERS
At Doctors Gully at the end of the Esplanade, thousands of fish and no small number of tourists come together at Aquascene during every high tide—the former to be fed and the latter to do the feeding.

Another place for seeing fish as well as a recreated coral reef is at the Indo Pacific Marine at the lively Darwin Wharf Precinct. The Precinct is also home to the Australian Pearling Exhibition.

179

RAINFOREST AND RIVERS
An easy day's outing from Darwin, Berry Springs has both a nature park with natural swimming pools and the splendid Territory Wildlife Park. This tract of bushland is aimed at introducing visitors to the N.T.'s varied wildlife.

Well off the beaten track down the Daly River Road, the Daly River Nature Park is a favorite spot for barramundi fishing and boating, although the large number of salties (saltwater crocodiles) precludes swimming.

The remote Gregory National Park has a spectacular gorge and there are boat trips along the Victoria River.

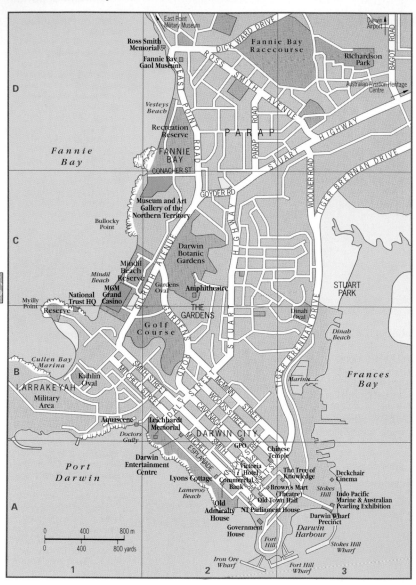

Darwin Airport

Ross Smith Memorial
Fannie Bay Gaol Museum
East Point Military Museum
Fannie Bay Racecourse
Richardson Park
BAGOT ROAD
DICK WARD DRIVE
ROSS SMITH AVENUE
Australian Aviation Heritage Centre

D

Vesteys Beach
Recreation Reserve
PARAP
PARAP ROAD
STUART HIGHWAY
WOOLNER ROAD
TIGER BRENNAN DRIVE

Fannie Bay

FANNIE BAY
CONACHER ST
GOYDER RD
EAST POINT ROAD

Museum and Art Gallery of the Northern Territory
Bullocky Point

C

Darwin Botanic Gardens

STUART PARK

Mindil Beach
Mindil Beach Reserve
MGM Grand Casino
GARDENS ROAD
Gardens Oval
Amphitheatre
THE GARDENS
Dinah Oval
Dinah Beach

National Trust HQ
Myilly Point Reserve

Golf Course

B

Cullen Bay Marina
Kahlin Oval
LARRAKEYAH
Military Area
MITCHELL STREET
SMITH STREET
MCMINN STREET
WOODS STREET
CAVENAGH STREET
Marina

Frances Bay

Aquascene
Doctors Gully
Leichhardt Memorial
DARWIN CITY
THE ESPLANADE
MITCHELL STREET
KNUCKEY STREET
SMITH STREET

Port Darwin

Darwin Entertainment Centre
Lyons Cottage
Lameroo Beach
GPO
Chinese Temple
Victoria Hotel
Commercial Bank
Brown's Mart
Old Town Hall
The Tree of Knowledge
Deckchair Cinema
Stokes Hill
Indo Pacific Marine & Australian Pearling Exhibition

A

Old Admiralty House
NT Parliament House
Government House
Fort Hill
Darwin Wharf Precinct
Darwin Harbour
Stokes Hill Wharf

Iron Ore Wharf
Fort Hill Wharf

0   400   800 m
0   400   800 yards

1   2   3

180

Darwin

The capital of the Northern Territory clings precariously to the peninsula protruding into Port Darwin, a superb natural anchorage that is approximately twice the size of Sydney Harbour.

Darwin has almost disappeared from the map no less than four times. Cyclones flattened the place in 1897, 1937, and again in 1974. In between, the aviators of the Imperial Japanese forces did their best to imitate nature at her most furious in the course of no less than 60 air raids. But Darwin's resilience is legendary; after each disaster, the evacuated population has returned to rebuild. In

GETTING AROUND
The best way to orient yourself is to take a trip on the Tour Tub, an open circulating minibus that allows you to get on and off at any point along its route.

1974, Cyclone Tracy destroyed nearly all the town's old buildings, including elegant old stilt houses; their replacements were conceived with cyclone-proofing in mind more than beauty.

1883 tropical-style Government House, Darwin's oldest building

DIVERSE COMMUNITY Advertised as Australia's front door, Darwin has looked for much of its life more like the country's back yard. Its appeal is that it is on the edge, a place in touch with other places. Founded in 1869, it became a base for "fabulous old-timers—pearlers, buffalo hunters, trepangers, prospectors, cattlemen and overlanders." The city's population is extraordinarily mixed; the number of ethnic groups varies between 49 and 61 depending on who is doing the counting. Many are Asians, and of all Australian cities, Darwin is the most conscious of the lands just to the north; Singapore is no further away than Sydney and Jakarta is closer.

Most visitors pass through Darwin with other destinations in mind, either abroad or in the Northern Territory, many of whose attractions are within easy reach. However, they should beware the place's allure, one based less on visual appeal than on a very relaxed, tropical lifestyle.

CITY SIGHTS AND ORIENTATION Small enough to walk around, the center of the city has a number of surviving (or reconstructed) buildings from early days. Some of these face the parkland of the west-facing Esplanade; here is **Government House** of 1883 as well as **Old Admiralty House**, a fine example of a tropical building on stilts dating from the 1920s. Among the grid of streets further inland is the much rebuilt **Victoria Hotel**, the **Chinese Temple** or Joss House and, in the courtyard of the Civic Centre, an ancient banyan, the **"Tree of Knowledge,"** one of Darwin's most resilient landmarks. These venerable structures contrast strongly with the new, hugely expensive, Northern Territory Parliament House, which can be toured. Other sights lie farther afield, many of them overlooking beautiful Fannie Bay to the north. Here is the MGM Grand Casino, close to Mindil Beach where a famous sunset market is held from May to October.

SHIP OF BREWS
The tropical heat provides the people of Darwin with an excellent excuse to drink more beer than anywhere else in what is a country known for its fondness for the beverage. Discarded beer cans once used to litter the streets and highways, but an ingenious solution has been found for the disposal of the cans in which the amber fluid comes—the Beer Can Regatta. Held every August at Mindil Beach, this weird event featuring bizarre craft ingeniously constructed from the humble "tinnie" has become one of the highlights of Darwin's social calendar, attracting thousands of spectators. Beer consumption during the festivities helps provide the raw material for the following year's event.

Meet the awesome crocodile Sweetheart at the Museum and Art Gallery

A FAST LADY
Darwin lies in the path of cyclones, none of which have raged as fiercely as Cyclone Tracy on Christmas Day, 1974. In the space of four hours, two-thirds of the city's buildings were destroyed and most of the rest severely damaged. The death toll was put at 66. No one knows exactly how much puff Tracy had in her—the windspeed indicator at the airport broke showing 135 m.p.h., but the peak velocity has been estimated at around 186 m.p.h. The disaster wasn't totally regretted. Pre-1974 Darwin was no showpiece of urban planning; rebuilding has been carried out along more orderly lines, with the provision of a satellite town, Palmerston, 12 miles to the southeast.

▶ Darwin Botanic Gardens 180C2
Gardens Road
Plants grow rapidly in Darwin's climate, and the damage done to these fine gardens in 1974 has been made good. The opportunity was taken to add new features, including collections of orchids, figs, ferns, and an exceptional array of around 400 tropical palms. As much a park as a scientific institution, the gardens are the city's favorite cool retreat.

▶ East Point Military Museum 180D2
East Point Road, Fannie Bay
Concrete bunkers and military hardware lie scattered around East Point headland. The 9-inch guns installed here to repel an invader who never came were, ironically, finally removed by a Japanese scrap metal dealer.

▶ Fannie Bay Gaol Museum 180D2
East Point Road, Fannie Bay
With no history of convict settlement, Darwin nevertheless stresses the importance of its prison, built in 1883 and in use until 1979. The museum features a gallows, used for the Territory's last execution in 1952.

▶▶▶ Museum and Art Gallery
of the Northern Territory 180C2
Conacher Street, Bullocky Point
This modern complex on Fannie Bay emphasizes the unique geographical position of the territory and its capital. In addition to an excellent collection of traditional and contemporary Aboriginal art and artifacts, there is a wealth of fascinating objects from Southeast Asia and the Southwest Pacific, and the Cyclone Tracy gallery. A huge shed houses the Maritime Museum with its original seagoing vessels, among them sinister war canoes, dugouts, fantastic outriggers, a lipa-lipa, proas, and the last of Darwin's pearling luggers, the *Vivienne*. There is also a powerful Cyclone Tracy exhibit, but pride of place goes to Sweetheart, a monster crocodile, which is now stuffed and harmless.

Crocodiles are compelling because many of us can't resist our morbid fascination with the havoc they can wreak. The crocodiles of the Northern Territory, Western Australia, and Queensland have loomed large in the public mind not only because of the movie Crocodile Dundee *but also because of their increasing numbers (a result of effective conservation measures), the opening-up of their habitat to wilderness tourism, and the readiness of the media to dramatize any crocodile attack.*

Two kinds of crocodile live in Australia. Harmless to humans, the relatively small freshwater crocodile frequents rivers and billabongs between the Gulf of Carpentaria and Broome in Western Australia. Double its size (20-foot specimens are not uncommon), and distinguished by a broader snout, the saltwater or estuarine crocodile prefers the brackish waters of tidal rivers though it is quite capable of penetrating far inland as well as out into the ocean. It occurs from India to the western Pacific, and in Australia from the central Queensland coast around Rockhampton to the Broome area.

Salties prey on fish and animals of all sizes, including human beings. Many victims are taken unawares at the water's edge; the crocodile makes its approach underwater, then uses the massive muscle of its tail to propel itself from the deep like a Polaris missile. The prey is dragged underwater and drowned rather than immediately torn apart; the croc can stay below the surface for up to an hour. Male crocodiles lord it over a territory they defend from other males. Much of its time is spent lying log-like in the shallows, conserving energy that is expended in sudden, violent maneuvers to secure dinner.

Look before you dive Darwin's swimming pools and ornamental waters have to be checked before they are opened to the public. Swimming or paddling in areas frequented by crocodiles could well be fatal. Remember, too, that crocodiles are amphibians, capable of reaching high speeds on land. Always obey the signs forbidding swimming (though people sometimes take them for souvenirs!) and seek local advice if in doubt. The best way to see these intimidating creatures is to take a conducted tour in a steel-bottomed boat (one legendary beast—long since dealt with—developed a taste for the more chewy kind of outboard motor, so don't trail your hand in the water!). Craft of this kind ply Yellow Water in Kakadu and, nearer Darwin, the Adelaide River.

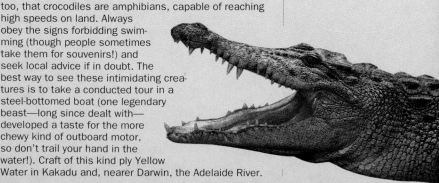

DARWIN CROCODILE FARM
This establishment 25 miles south of Darwin is home to thousands of crocodiles reared for their skins. Feeding time is always spectacular.

183

WARNING
Crocodiles respect neither man nor beast, so take no chances. Just because you can't see them, it doesn't mean they're not there.

ALBERT NAMATJIRA

Born at Hermannsburg Mission in 1902, this member of the Aranda tribe became a talented watercolorist in the European tradition, his subject the stunning landscapes of his native MacDonnell Ranges. He and his work were acclaimed; he was presented to the Queen during a royal visit, and in 1957 he was given the extraordinary privilege (for the time) of full citizenship. But Namatjira was destroyed by the tension between white and Aboriginal society and by alcohol; imprisoned for supplying drink to a fellow Aborigine, his morale collapsed and he died in 1959 at the age of 57. His wonderfully fresh paintings can be seen in many Australian galleries. His representational, European style of painting has since been generally abandoned by contemporary Aborginal artists in favour of a more abstract, traditional form of expression, typified by so-called "dot" paintings.

Alice Springs has a number of memorials to...

▶▶▶ Alice Springs　　　　　176B2

Smack in the middle of the continent, The Alice (as it is widely known) has transformed itself from a dusty outpost to an indispensable stop on the tourist itinerary. Equipped with all modern amenities, this pleasant town makes an excellent base for exploring the Red Centre.

The township began in 1871 as a convenient place for a repeater station on the Overland Telegraph between Adelaide and Darwin—it was named for local waterholes, and after the wife (Alice) of Sir Charles Todd, the Post-master General of South Australia. Development was slow until the arrival of the railroad from Adelaide in 1929, the famous but rickety "Ghan." In World War II, the railhead acquired strategic value, particularly after the Stuart Highway leading on up to Darwin had been given its first coat of asphalt. But it was the advent of mass tourism from the 1970s onward that persuaded the town to provide comfortable hotels, sophisticated restaurants, and even a tastefully landscaped shopping mall. All this came as something of a surprise to the old-timers, who not so long ago would ride in for an evening's drinking and hitch their horse to the rail in the main street.

The best place to get an overall impression of the Alice in its desert setting is to climb (or drive up) **Anzac Hill▶** with its obelisk memorial. The town center stretches out on the west bank of the bed of the Todd River. The fact that it rarely contains any water has not stopped the hilarious Henley-on-Todd Regatta becoming a major annual event, with legs rather than oars supplying the motive power for the bottomless craft. For much of the rest of the year the dry river bed serves as a camping ground for some of the Alice's substantial Aboriginal population. To the south are the long ridges of the MacDonnell Ranges, pierced by the Heavitree Gap, through which run road and railroad. Beyond is the airport, and then the top-secret U.S./Australian Pine Gap communications base.

Although visitors come to Alice Springs more because of where it is than for what it is, there are a fair number of

attractions in the town and its immediate vicinity. A few older buildings recall its beginnings; the **Old Stuart Town Gaol** is the most venerable of these, a jail dating all the way back to 1907. **Adelaide House** was built in 1920–1926 to serve as a hospital; it now houses memorabilia related to the early days of the Royal Flying Doctor Service—with settlements and homesteads hundreds of miles apart, doctors need aircraft to make house calls. For a short time in the 1920s the administration of the N.T. was split between Darwin and Alice Springs. The **Residency►** dates from this period, and now houses a small but well-presented museum of local history. The town's main museum is the **Museum of Central Australia►** at the Araluen Precinct; it has extensive exhibits on the art and natural history of central Australia.

Transportation and communications are one theme of Alice Springs, if not *the* theme. The place's *raison d'être* was the **Old Telegraph Station►►**, and its plain but evocative stone buildings still stand just north of the town. Both the **School of the Air** and the **Royal Flying Doctor Service** have bases in town that are open to the public. To the west is the **Museum of Technology, Transport and Communications**, which celebrates early flight in the Outback as well as the history of automobile transportation, while off the Stuart Highway beyond the Heavitree Gap is the National Transport Hall of Fame and **Ghan Preservation Society**, dedicated to rehabilitating the rolling stock of the original, narrow-gauge railway line. In pioneering days, the arid interior relied on camel trains for supplies; at the **Frontier Camel Farm** you can ride one and find out about them and their Afghan masters.

Alice Springs is one of the places where the overseas visitor can become better acquainted with the Aboriginal presence. Part of the town's living comes from money spent by Aborigines, even more from the merchandising of Aboriginal souvenirs, though you are unlikely to be able to buy a painting by Albert Namatjira (see panel opposite). A particularly poignant story about the European/Aboriginal relationship is told in the modern **Strehlow Research Centre**, which celebrates the culture of the Aranda people and the German missionary's son who lived and worked among them.

...and reminders of the Royal Flying Doctor Service

They both feed and entertain you in The Alice

THE STUART HIGHWAY

This 1,678-mile road unrolls its thin band of bitumen through the vast and deserted spaces of central Australia between Port Augusta and Darwin. Known to all as "The Track," it follows the route first traced in 1862 by the tough Scotsman John McDouall Stuart. For many years it was a notorious axle-breaker, but nothing was done until Australia's war situation became desperate in 1942 when, with U.S. Forces' help, the road was speedily asphalted from the railhead at Alice Springs to Darwin. Several decades passed before the southern half of the highway was completely paved, and the adventure of gravel, rock, and bull-dust replaced by the predictabllity of bitumen.

One of the huge road trains that travel across the continent's north and Outback

How to travel

By air Darwin's international airport acquired a bright new terminal in 1991. From here there are connections to many overseas destinations, including direct flights to Japan, Singapore, Indonesia, and Malaysia, and to all major Australian cities. Alice Springs also has a modern airport, again linked to a variety of Australian destinations. Connellan Airport, serving Ayers Rock and its resort, has a more limited range of connections. If you are in a hurry, light aircraft will take you virtually anywhere you want to go in the territory; day tours are also available. The desert looks at its most dramatic from the air; try the hot-air balloon operation at Alice Springs.

By bus Long-distance buses link Darwin, Alice Springs, Ayers Rock, and other points in the territory with major Australian cities. Tour operators offer any number of trips, particularly in the Red Centre. Some day trips, like Darwin–Kakadu–Darwin, are not recommended for the faint-hearted—it is often better to arrange an overnight stop. Only Darwin has any local bus service.

By train The rebuilt line north from Tarcoola in South Australia carries the revived "**Ghan**" (also see page 189), a luxury train connecting Sydney, Melbourne, Adelaide, and Alice Springs; this is the only railway within the Northern Territory. There are bus and air connections from various towns to the railhead at Mount Isa, terminus for the "Inlander" train from Townsville, almost 620 miles away on the Queensland coast.

By car From Darwin, the **Stuart Highway** runs south through Alice Springs to Port Augusta and Adelaide (1,678 miles); at Three Ways the **Barkly Highway** leaves the Stuart for Mount Isa and on to Townsville (1,588 miles); at Katherine, the **Victoria Highway** branches off towards the Kimberley and thence to Perth (2,536 miles). Paved roads reach Ayers Rock and Jabiru in Kakadu National Park, and all-weather roads will take you to most major tourist destinations.

▶ Arnhem Land   176E2

East of Kakadu a rugged sandstone escarpment seems to
bar the way to this mysterious and inaccessible area.
Given the name of the Dutch ship whose crew were the
first Europeans to sight it, Arnhem Land stretches spectacularly eastward to form the western coastline of the
Gulf of Carpentaria. Now in the hands of its Aboriginal
owners, most of it can only be entered by permit, though
a limited number of guided tours do take place from
Darwin and Kakadu, and you can also fly into the remote
resort of Seven Spirit Bay on the Cobourg Peninsula.

▶▶▶ Ayers Rock (Uluru) and
The Olgas (Kata Tjuta)   176A1

Reproduced a million times on film, tape, and glossy
brochures, the great red monolith of Ayers Rock has
become one of the world's greatest tourist clichés, yet it still
retains the power to stir the spirits of all those who visit it.
Not surprisingly, Uluru, the Aboriginal name for Ayers
Rock, has a unique spiritual significance for the Aboriginal
people of the area, whose ancestors may have frequented
the area for at least 20,000 years. A number of sacred sites
around the base are protected, and they must not be
entered or photographed.

The first European to sight the rock was the explorer
Ernest Giles in 1872. In 1985 the land, which includes the
World Heritage listed Uluru–Kata Tjuta National Park,
was ceremonially handed back to an Aboriginal trust on
behalf of the traditional owners, then immediately leased
for 99 years to the Northern Territory's parks service.
Hotels and other visitor facilities are located at **Ayers
Rock Resort▶**, a respectful distance away at 11 miles
from the Rock itself.

The sediments that make up Ayers Rock and the neighboring Olgas were laid down some 500–600 million years
ago and they were then tilted almost vertically by earth
movements. Ayers Rock rises 1,142 feet above the plain
and Mount Olga rises 1,791 feet, but their foundations go
far deeper.

Continued on page 190.

*The domes of The Olgas,
or Kata Tjuta, just wait-
ing to be explored*

187

**ABORIGINAL
PLACE-NAMES**
While many Australian
place-names were
borrowed from the "old
country," the early settlers
also used Aboriginal
names. Parramatta was
the first town to be
designated in this way,
and others can be seen
all over the map, often
sounding more appropri-
ate than names recalling
the villages, suburbs or
shire towns of faraway
England. Who could resist
Woolloomooloo?
Nowadays, many of these
foreign names are being
replaced with Aboriginal
ones; The Olgas (named
after a 19th-century queen
of Spain) are now officially
called Kata Tjuta ("many
heads") and Ayers Rock is
called Uluru.

In such a vast country, the battle to overcome "the tyranny of distance" was a long and difficult one, and the role of the railroad in shaping the country, helping it both to grow economically and to grow together politically was of outstanding importance.

188

A LONG SHORT CUT

Once the Transcontinental Railway had linked west to east, travelers from Europe who were in a hurry to get to Melbourne or Sydney would leave their ship at Fremantle and continue their journey by rail. In spite of having to change trains each time there was a break of gauge (at Kalgoorlie, Port Augusta, and again at Albury), the advantage was that a day or two would be saved. The fare, just as on the ocean liner, included all meals—as it still does—but today you no longer need to change trains as the standard gauge stretches right across the continent from Perth to Sydney.

There is plenty of time to study the route

Gauging success The first iron road in Australia was a short line in Adelaide for horse-drawn traffic. The earliest steam railroads were those linking Melbourne to its port (September 1854) and Sydney to Parramatta (a year later). But already there was trouble. What track gauge should be adopted?

The colonies initially agreed among themselves that the gauge should be George Stephenson's standard of 4 feet 8½ inches, but then a broader gap between the rails of 5 feet 3 inches, as used in Ireland, was introduced. In the end each colony went its own way, Victoria and South Australia adopting the broad gauge and New South Wales adopting the standard gauge. Queensland and Western Australia came up with a different idea altogether, that of systems built entirely on the narrow gauge of 3 feet 6 inches. Tasmania began with standard gauge, then converted to narrow gauge.

This was fine as long as each system remained self-contained, but eventually the tracks reached out to connect (or rather not connect) with those of the neighboring network. Through-passengers had to disembark, goods had to be unloaded and re-loaded, and the most hated three words in all Australia at the time were supposed to have been "All change! Albury!." the name of the station on the border between New South Wales and Victoria. In 1897, Mark Twain was more than vexed to have to change trains here, because it involved a tedious walk along a lengthy track.

Natural hazards Railroads were often difficult and expensive to build in Australia, because of the distances that had to be covered, the variety of natural obstacles that had to be overcome, and the high cost of importing rails and other materials. The capricious nature of the landscape didn't help, and flooding often occurred in places where no rain had fallen for years, washing the track away. To keep costs down, many countryside lines were built to a low standard, resulting in irksome speed restrictions. Bridges remained unbuilt; the train ferry that for years carried the coaches and wagons of Sydney–Brisbane trains over the Clarence River was replaced by a bridge only in 1932. Secondary lines were built not only to the 3 feet 6 inches gauge but to an even narrower 2 feet 6 inches standard, virtually a miniature railroad of the kind that still chuffs between Ferntree Gully and Belgrave in the Victorian Dandenongs today (the famous Puffing Billy). Narrower still—a mere 2 feet—are the sugarcane railroads that wander through the plantations of Queensland.

From time to time some parts of Australia have toyed with the idea of going their own way. Such a stance was taken up by Western Australia at the end of the 19th century, when it only joined the Federation on condition that it was physically linked to the rest of the country by a transcontinental railroad (paid for by the Federation). It took years to lay the rails across the 298 miles of the waterless Nullarbor Plain, but the line was ready for traffic in 1917 and is now traversed by the world-famous *Indian Pacific*.

The Ghan A still incomplete but nevertheless fascinating railroad project was the South Australia–Northern Territory link, Shakily built narrow-gauge tracks snaked out from Port Augusta in the south and from Darwin in the north. The southern section was called the Ghan because it replaced the Afghan camel trains that had hitherto been the most effective means of transportation along the route, Reaching Oodnadatta in 1890, it took another 39 years to get as far as Alice Springs, and the top section only went as far as Birdum, 311 miles south of Darwin.

Both lines were ripped up in the 1970s, the northern section disappearing altogether and the southern section being rebuilt along a less flood-prone alignment that now carries a luxury train. Also called the Ghan, this train provides one of the world's classic train journeys, in standards of comfort that would have been quite alien to Wilfred Thomas's travelling companions (see panel).

AFGHAN NIGHTS
An early traveler on the Ghan, Wilfred Thomas, settled down to try to get some sleep, but was amazed when his fellow-travelers—a tough-looking bunch of miners and stockmen—cleared the seats away brusquely, brought out the drink and some bagpipes, and then danced the night away together.

The luxury Ghan connects Sydney and Melbourne with Adelaide and The Alice

*The spectacular view
from Ayers Rock.
Visitors are discouraged
from climbing as the rock
is a sacred site and quite
dangerous to walk on*

AN OUTBACK DRAGON
The fearsome-looking
thorny devil is one of the
most astonishing
denizens of the desert,
well deserving its zoological name *Moloch horridus*.
In spite of its bulbous
spine-covered body and
multi-colored blotches, it
is an inoffensive creature,
relying on its unappetizing
appearance to deter
any predator.

Continued from page 187.

Much is made of the mysterious responsiveness of both
Ayers Rock and The Olgas to lighting conditions, and few
visitors will want to miss the uncanny changes produced
by dawn and sunset; the basic red color is due to the presence of iron.

Most visitors rush to climb the Rock, but the expedition
should not be undertaken lightly, least of all by the
elderly or by those with a medical condition. Take the
advice of rangers and tour guides concerning timing,
water supplies and the route (the only one) that must be
followed. You might even bow to the Aborigines'
expressed preference that the Rock should not be
climbed, but experienced in a more respectful way by a
circular walk or Aboriginal ranger-led tour around its
6-mile base. This is worth doing in any case—revealing as
it does a wealth of fascinating detail, such as the strange,
almost cookie-like texture of the stone, and the way in
which the almost vertical lower slopes have been eroded
into deep furrows. If you are really lucky, you could experience a storm and the subsequent extraordinary
spectacle of myriad waterfalls standing out against a
sinister black background.

Of geologically related origin, the 36 domes of **The
Olgas** offer a quite different but no less fascinating experience, not least because of the rich vegetation and wildlife
that flourish in the sheltered gorges between the individual summits. All those able to undertake one of the
somewhat stony walks through the area should certainly
do so, though perhaps the most spectacular way to view
these sleeping dinosaurs (as they have been called) is
aboard a light plane on one of the short flights that also
takes in the Rock. As well as the isolated table mountain
known as Mount Conner, which is perfectly aligned with
the Rock and Olgas, this aerial perspective reveals the layout of the Ayers Rock Resort (see panel). Designed in

1981, its architecture and landscaping represent a remarkably sensitive response to its desert environment.

The visitor to Ayers Rock will find an array of tours available, ranging from bus trips to a personalized commentary given while riding pillion on a Harley-Davidson. The **Uluru Experience▶** aims to bring small groups of participants into more intimate contact with the plants and animals of the desert, as well as with Aboriginal life and lore.

▶ Bathurst and Melville Islands   *176E1*

Lying off the coast to the north of Darwin and separated from each other by the narrow Apsley Strait, these two large islands are the home of the Tiwi people. Lacking contact with the Aborigines of the mainland, they developed their own distinct culture, including the making of the extraordinary and highly decorated Pukamani burial poles. The British settlement at Fort Dundas, the first on the north Australian coast (1824–1829), was a failure. A Catholic mission was set up in the early 1900s, but the islands have now been returned to their traditional owners and can only be visited on an organized tour.

▶ Chambers Pillar   *176A2*

This 164-foot-high red and yellow sandstone monolith rises abruptly from its spreading foundation to make one of the desert's most striking landmarks. Located on the fringes of the bleak Simpson Desert, the pillar, now protected in a historical reserve, was long used as a navigational aid by intrepid explorers, some of whom left their inscriptions in the soft rock.

▶ Cutta Cutta Caves Nature Park   *176D2*

South of Katherine on the Stuart Highway, these ancient limestone chambers linked by narrow passages are the home of the orange horseshoe bat, once believed to be extinct. Nearby are the recently opened Tindal Caves, which feature unusual sponge formations.

191

BARRAMUNDI
This fine tropical fish is Australia's favorite catch, making an excellent meal as well as providing good sport. Barramundi can grow to huge sizes; specimens 6 feet long weighing up to 22½ pounds are not uncommon. They live in most northern aquatic environments, traveling to river estuaries to breed. The barramundi also has a feisty reputation as a fighting fish. Barramundi are still plentiful but catches are restricted.

The rare orange horseshoe bat, in the Cutta Cutta Caves

The rounded granite forms of the Devils Marbles, 64 miles south of Tennant Creek

CASTLES OF CLAY
In a land of minimal moisture, there are no earthworms to turn the soil. This role is taken over in the Northern Territory and other arid lands by termites, which pattern whole landscapes with their extraordinary mounds (see below). Sometimes rising to a height of 10 feet, these insect fortresses are built from a mixture of soil, spit, and dung. However hostile conditions outside may be, behind the rock-hard walls the interior of the mound is a climate-controlled environment of 100 percent humidity and a constant temperature of 122°F.

▶▶ Devils Marbles 176C2

Hundreds of granite boulders lie scattered across the plain beside the Stuart Highway just north of the village of Wauchope—some huge, some tiny, and some perched in impossible positions. To the geologist they are all that remains of the ancient mountains that once rose here, but to the Aborigines they are the eggs of the Rainbow Serpent, Wanambi. They are best seen in the early morning.

▶▶ Finke Gorge National Park 176A2

Access to the famous gorge in the Western MacDonnell Ranges known as Palm Valley is along the rocky bed of the Finke River, normally dry but impassable after rain. In utter contrast to the desert is the lush vegetation thriving in the protected environment of the gorge. The 113,666-acre national park's 3,000 or so cabbage palms are unique to the area, the descendants of prehistoric trees that grew on the shore of what was then a tropical sea. A climb up **Initiation Rock**, where youths of the Aranda people were once introduced to the mysteries of manhood, affords a great view of the rugged sandstone gorge.

▶▶ Gurig National Park 176F2

Now returned to its traditional Aboriginal owners, this national park covers the whole of the remote Cobourg Peninsula protruding westward from Arnhem Land. There is splendid sailing and fishing, as well as the experience of utter isolation, since the number of visitor permits issued is strictly limited (permits are obtainable from the Parks and Wildlife Commission of the Northern Territory). The superb natural harbor of **Port Essington** was the site of Victoria, one of the early British settlements.

▶ Henbury Meteorite Craters Conservation Reserve 176A2

At the end of a dirt road off the Stuart Highway south of Alice Springs is a genuine curiosity: a swarm of craters formed about 5,000 years ago when a big meteorite split into pieces on entering the earth's atmosphere. The largest crater is 590 feet across and 49 feet deep.

▶▶▶ Kakadu National Park 176E2

Some 155 miles east of Darwin, Australia's largest national park joined Unesco's World Heritage Area list in 1987 on account of the Aboriginal art sites it contains and its almost unbelievably rich and varied wildlife.

Kakadu extends over a number of distinct landscapes. The tidal zone along the shore of Van Diemen's Gulf is pierced by the estuaries of four great rivers, the East, West and South Alligator Rivers, and the Wildman River. Here the gray of tidal mudflats contrasts with the bright green of mangrove swamps, breeding grounds for the well-known barramundi (see panel on page 191). The floodplains of the rivers become a vast freshwater sea in the Wet, teeming with migratory birds and other waterfowl, including egrets, brolgas, pelicans, and jabiru. Salt and freshwater crocodiles lurk in creek and billabong. As the land rises southwards, eucalyptus woodland develops, interspersed with termite mounds or dramatically interrupted by massive rock outcrops, isolated fragments of the formidable sandstone escarpment marking the western edge of Arnhem Land. This rugged north–south barrier runs for 310 miles, broken by gorges cut by the streams draining the vast interior, the scene of spectacular waterfalls in the wet season. Two of the best known of these are **Jim Jim Falls▶** and **Twin Falls▶**, in the south of the park, both with abundant tropical wildlife.

Natural galleries in the escarpment sandstone contain some of the country's choicest examples of early Aboriginal art. The most visited are those at **Ubirr▶▶**, where there are "X-ray" paintings as well as other styles, and at **Nourlangie Rock▶**. The Bowali Visitor Center for the park is near the main town of Jabiru, but there is also an excellent complex, the Warradjan Aboriginal Cultural Centre, which provides more insight into the area's indigenous history and culture. It is just possible to get some idea of Kakadu in the course of a day visit by air from Darwin (there are bus trips too, in spite of the distance).

ART OF THE OUTBACK
Aboriginal art is traditionally connected to ritual and ceremony rather than self-expression, and is ephemeral or renewable. Much of the art of central Australia is abstract and symbolic. The artist's canvas could be a rock wall or the ground itself, with sand paintings executed in colored earths, pebbles, feathers, and so on. The wall paintings at Kakadu National Park are representational. Some of them, depicting hunting scenes, are incredibly old, dating from the pre-estuarine period up to 23,000 years ago. The X-ray style, showing the internal organs and bone structure of fish and animals, dates from the estuarine period, which followed a rise in sea level some 7,000–9,000 years ago. More recent depictions of Europeans and their accoutrements belong to the so-called contact period.

193

Dawn over Kakadu—a sight to remember

In the early part of the 20th century, it seemed as if the Aborigines of Australia were doomed as a race. Their numbers had diminished drastically—from an estimated population of half a million at the onset of European colonization to perhaps 60,000 in the 1920s; and many of these were of mixed blood.

GOOD GRUB
While Aboriginal men hunted game with boomerang and fire, women and children foraged for smaller animals, lizards, insects, seeds, and fruit. A particular delicacy is the witchetty grub, which is usually seared briefly in hot ashes before being eaten. Initiation into the delights of "bush tucker" can be a fascinating experience.

194

These children live near a school; for those too far away there is always the radio-transmitted School of the Air

Christian missions established in the Outback destroyed the Aborigines' ancient spiritual links with the land, government "Protectors" moved them around at will, and Aboriginal children were removed from their parents and brought up in homes or by foster parents. Devastated by alcoholism, exploited by cattle and sheep ranchers as cheap labor, and consistently denied the rights and privileges available to other Australians, it seemed to some as if it would only be a matter of time before mainland Aborigines suffered the fate of the Tasmanians.

A genius not extinguished At the end of the century the situation is more hopeful. A voice has been found, one moreover that is listened to and sometimes acted on by those in positions of power. The Aboriginal plight has been noticed by the white majority, thanks to protests like the "tent embassy" established for years in front of the Canberra Parliament, or the march of 30,000 people through the streets of Sydney, part of a boycott of the 1988 Bicentennial (or "Invasion") celebrations. On a small scale, Aboriginal voices are heard over the air on Aboriginal-owned radio and television stations.

In the realm of politics, reforms have been carried out. The incredible situation in which Aborigines were not classed as citizens or even counted in the official census

of population was rectified by the 1967 referendum that gave the Federal Government overall responsibility for Aboriginal affairs. One outcome was the drafting and passing of the Aboriginal Land Rights Act of 1976 that enabled Crown lands to be handed back to the "traditional owners." A dramatic illustration of the effect of this took place in 1985, when **Ayers Rock** and the **Uluru National Park** formally became the property of the Uluru–Kata Tjuta Land Trust on behalf of the traditional owners. Entry to such lands is now only possible by means of a permit. In the case of a world-famous national park, this is obtained both instantly and easily; in the case of less well-known places it is by no means automatic, a fact resented by many white Australians.

As seen by others White attitudes have undergone change, even transformation. In an age of environmental devastation and loss of spiritual direction, the way in which Aborigines lived for thousands of years in material and religious harmony with their surroundings has earned respect. Aboriginal art, both traditional and contemporary, is widely admired. There is a widespread wish, expressed by politicians as well as by ordinary people, to make restitution for the injustices perpetrated over 200 years. But problems remain, even if they no longer seem quite so insurmountable.

While some younger people of Aboriginal descent try to combine old ways of living with some of the benefits of European civilization, others fail to find a place anywhere and continue to live on the margins of society. Aborigines are far more likely to face a court for minor offences than other Australians; a shameful number of young blacks have died while in police custody. Rejection and contempt live on in many white hearts.

It may be that Aborigines need to stand back from white values and return as far as possible to their traditional customs before the races can come together again in harmony, and the right of refusal of entry to Aboriginal lands should be seen in this light, rather than denounced as incipient apartheid. In any case, many Aborigines wish to share their heritage with their fellow Australians and with visitors. Contemporary Aboriginal art is widely available, while traditional rock paintings are best experienced in the company of an Aboriginal ranger. Music, dance and ritual are performed in many places, but the high point of many people's experience of Australia is a visit to an Aboriginal community (arranged through the Australian Tourist Commission—see page 266).

A RIGHT TO LAND
Since 1976, Northern Territory Aborigines have owned the land in what were formerly reserves and have been able to lay claim to vacant Crown Land. Many claims have been opposed, and even when successful do not necessarily inhibit mining and quarrying. But royalties have to be paid to the owners, and quite a few communities in areas like Arnhem Land now derive some income from this exploitation of resources.

195

Some communities are willing to share and explain their traditions

The total number of sheep in Australia today amounts to over 160 million, over three-quarters of them the resilient merino with a fleece of up to 4½ pounds in weight. Australia accounts for about a quarter of the world's wool and is the biggest exporter of lamb and mutton. In some places the sheep/people ratio begs belief: one million sheep roam South Australia's Kangaroo Island, for example, compared with only 4,000 humans.

RECORD SHEARING

Traditionally working in teams that moved from station to station during the shearing season, shearers honed their skills to an almost incredible pitch; in 1892 a Queensland man, Jackie Howe, set the record for hand-shearing, having shorn 321 sheep in 7 hours 40 minutes. Even with electric clippers, today's shearers find this difficult to match.

Will this be a new sheep-shearing record?

A tough breed One of the animals most closely identified with Australia, sheep were among the passengers of the first fleet, though 59 of Governor Phillip's 90 beasts soon perished. A certain Captain John Macarthur had better luck; he cannily bred Bengal ewes with English rams, then crossed them with Spanish merinos. This mixed breed flourished in the new environment, yielding a fleece of fine quality and good weight—making Macarthur a rich man and providing the foundation of Australia's wool industry, a mainstay of the national economy even today. In the 19th century, it was sheep as much as people that colonized the vast spaces of the new country; by 1900 there were nearly 100 million of them.

Sheep shearers Watching sheep shearers at their highly skilled work is quite a spectacle. The sheep are driven into the shearing shed, thrown to the ground by the shearer, and held fast between their legs. The electric clippers, which long ago replaced the more laborious hand shears, are run swiftly through the fleece, which is removed in one piece if possible. The heaps of wool are sorted according to quality and are then dispatched in huge bales.

▶ Katherine   176E2

This township is the center of the vast and remote territory described by Jeannie Gunn in her classic 1908 novel of the Outback *We of the Never Never*. The area derives its name from the saying that those who live there can "never never" leave. You can visit the Northern Territory's oldest surviving homestead, Springvale, but most of the town's 250,000 annual visitors come for the spectacular Katherine Gorge at **Nitmiluk National Park▶▶**, about 18 miles to the east. Rising in Arnhem Land, the Katherine River has cut a series of stunning gorges through the sandstone plateau, providing a refuge for a surprising variety of flora and fauna. The first two gorges can be seen aboard tourist boats, the defiles farther upstream in your own canoe. There are a number of walks from the information center to points along the gorge.

▶▶ Kings Canyon   176A1

One of the most spectacular natural landscapes of Central Australia, this deep canyon (within Watarrka National Park and located some 220 miles southwest from Alice), with its rugged sandstone cliffs rising 650 feet above the dry river bed, is becoming increasingly popular with visitors. A short walk leads up the floor of the canyon to a lookout point, but anyone with proper walking shoes who is reasonably fit should not miss the more challenging (3¾ miles) walk up onto the plateau and around the rim of the canyon. Steep to start with, it gives panoramic views over the canyon and a distant glimpse of Ayers Rock.

▶▶ Litchfield National Park   176E1

This 250-square-mile tract of sandstone plateau and lush rain forest, until relatively recently part of a private farming property, is becoming increasingly popular with both tourists and local people from the Darwin area, not least because of the excellent swimming in the clear pools at the foot of its numerous waterfalls. The park also features many tall termite mounds and the free-standing sandstone pillars of the "Lost City." Access is via the pleasant tree-shaded township of Batchelor.

Kings Canyon, rugged, but good walking country

197

A LIVING TRADITION
As a result of both increasing interest in indigenous Australian history and culture, and the initiative of Aboriginal people, several cultural centers have sprung up in the Territory. There is an excellent establishment in Kakadu (see page 193), as well as the Uluru-Kata Tjuta Cultural Centre, near the base of Ayers Rock and featuring traditional dance, art, and craft demonstrations.

SPINIFEX
Early explorers cursed the spiky tussocks of spinifex as its spear-like blades impeded their progress through the desert. Spinifex grasses are often the only plants able to withstand the extreme heat and aridity of the center, thanks to a deep tap root that manages to extract moisture from far below the surface. Growing outward into hollow clumps, the plants provide a habitat for other forms of desert life, such as insects, lizards, skinks, and even a species of pigeon.

SUNBEAMS
AUSTRALIA'S OWN
SULTANAS
40 g
NET

THE LARAPINTA TRAIL
This long-distance trail leads from the old Alice Springs Telegraph Station right into the West MacDonnells. Hikers can either walk its entire 137-mile length or undertake shorter sections with an overnight camp. Full details can be obtained from the N.T.'s Parks and Wildlife Commission.

The blue lagoon of the Glen Helen Gorge

▶▶▶ MacDonnell Ranges　　　　176A2

These parallel ridges of red quartzite and sandstone extend their corrugations hundreds of miles across Central Australia, an almost frightening panorama of total desolation when seen from the air. But this was home to the Aranda people until well after the arrival of the white man, and in the gorges cut long ago by the now infrequently flowing rivers there flourishes a lush vegetation of palms and ferns, descendants of the flora that grew on the shore of an ancient tropical sea.

Some of the most spectacular landscapes of the **West MacDonnell National Park** are easily accessible from Alice Springs via Namatjira Drive. Overlooking the Alice itself from a height of 3,084 feet is the distinctive peak of Mount Gillen. Only a little farther out at 11 miles from Alice Springs is **Simpsons Gap▶▶**, where the steep-sided gorge, pale sands and fine specimens of river red gums and ghost gums make an excellent introduction to the landscape of the ranges. The reserve is accessible by vehicle but, as always, the best way to explore is on foot, using one of several marked hiking tracks—there is also a special bicycle path. Among the wildlife of the gorge is a colony of black-footed rock wallabies.

In dramatic contrast to the impressively wide gorge at Simpsons Gap is **Standley Chasm▶▶**, an incredibly narrow cleft between 330-foot quartzite cliffs. For a short period around midday the sun fills the red walls of the gorge with vibrant light, a popular spectacle for visitors who have walked the half-mile or so along the bed of the creek. At **Ellery Creek Big Hole▶▶**, high red cliffs frame the water-filled gorge, which is a favorite spot for swimming and fishing. **Serpentine Gorge▶** consists of a narrow winding defile with semi-permanent waterholes and ghost gums, and has been left deliberately undeveloped. **Ormiston Gorge and Pound▶▶** is the largest of the reserves in West MacDonnell National Park, and has

A noble face, first imported but now native

permanent waterholes and magical ghost gums, while **Glen Helen Gorge►►** has rugged rust-colored cliffs contrasting with the blue of the water that forms a deep lagoon in the bed of the Finke River. Farther west is **Redbank Gorge►** with its chilly rockpools. Further on still, Tylers Pass leads to Gosse Bluff, then back towards Alice Springs via the old Hermannsburg Mission; a possible detour is to spectacular **Palm Valley►**, see page 192.

In the MacDonnells east of Alice Springs, **Emily and Jessie Gaps Nature Park►** has semi-permanent waterholes and Aboriginal paintings, while in **Trephina Gorge Nature Park►►** the pale stems of splendid ghost gums stand out starkly against the rugged cliffs. High above **John Hayes Rookhole►** is a vista of spectacular scenery and Aboriginal rock art. **Ross River**, where there is a resort, makes a good base for further exploration, to **Arltunga Historical Reserve** for example.

► Mataranka   176D2

Just off the Stuart Highway, 60 miles southeast of Katherine, is the Mataranka Homestead and the nearby thermal pool, a popular stop-off. Every minute, 4,500 gallons of water at a constant temperature of 93°F gush into a crystal-clear waterhole fringed by palm trees.

►►► The Olgas/Kata Tjuta   176A1

See pages 187 and 190.

► Pine Creek   176E1

Ah Toy's store in this tiny Stuart Highway township is a reminder of the gold-rush days of the 1870s, when the Chinese population outnumbered Europeans 15 to 1. The old times are recalled in the **Pine Creek Miners' Park**.

► Tennant Creek   176C2

Legend has it that Tennant Creek came into existence in the 1930s when the axle broke on a wagon carting beer and building materials for a new hotel farther north. Moving on seemed too much bother, so once the beer had been drunk the building was put up here. Then gold was found and Tennant Creek became one of the roughest places along the track. Relatively calm now, the town has plenty of amenities for the passer-by. The **Gold Stamp Battery** still crushes the region's gold and has an interesting Mining Museum, and the 1874 **Overland Telegraph Station** is open to the public.

NOT A MIRAGE
Right up to the 1930s, camels played an indispensable part in opening up the center of the continent. Explorers, surveyors, miners and pastoralists all used camel trains to transport food, equipment, building materials, barbed wire, and metal ores. Their equally tough attendants all acquired the epithet "Afghan," though many of them were from India. Turned loose when trucks, jeeps and planes took over their work, the camels adapted easily to the wild and today are numbered in the thousands. In captivity, they are successfully bred for export to Arabia, as well as giving many visitors the thrill of a humpback ride. The Frontier Camel Farm 3¾ miles south of Alice Springs is one of the best known of such establishments.

199

Idyllic Green Island

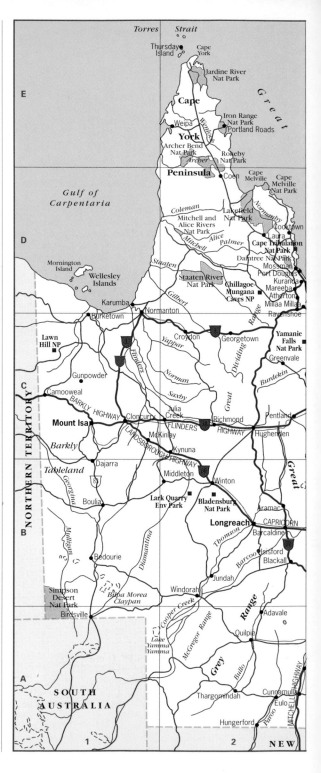

Torres Strait

Thursday Island
Cape York
Jardine River Nat Park

Cape

Weipa
Iron Range Nat Park
Portland Roads

York
Archer Bend Nat Park
Rokeby Nat Park
Coen
Cape Melville
Cape Melville Nat Park

Gulf of Carpentaria

Peninsula

Coleman
Mitchell and Alice Rivers Nat Park
Lakefield Nat Park
Cooktown
Laura
Cape Tribulation Nat Park

Mornington Island
Wellesley Islands
Staaten
Mitchell
Alice
Palmer
Daintree Nat Park
Mossman
Port Douglas

Staaten River Nat Park
Chillagoe Mungana Caves NP
Kuranda
Mareeba
Atherton
Milaa Millaa
Ravenshoe

Karumba
Normanton
Gilbert

Burketown
Croydon
Yappar
Georgetown
Yamanie Falls Nat Park
Greenvale

Lawn Hill NP
Norman
Burdekin

Gunpowder
Saxby

Camooweal
BARKLY HIGHWAY
Cloncurry
Julia Creek
FLINDERS
Richmond
Pentland

Mount Isa
McKinlay
HIGHWAY
Hughenden

Barkly
Kynuna
Tableland
Dajarra
Middleton
Winton

Georgina
Boulia
Lark Quarry Env Park
Bladensburg Nat Park
Aramac
CAPRICORN

Mulligan
Bedourie
Diamantina
Longreach
Thomson
Barcaldine

Barkly
Jundah
Barcoo
Isisford
Blackall

Simpson Desert Nat Park
Birdsville
Bilpa Morea Claypan
Windorah
Cooper Creek
McGregor Range
Range
Adavale

Lake Yamma Yamma
Quilpie

Grey
Bulloo
SOUTH AUSTRALIA
Thargomindah
Cunnamulla
Eulo
MITCHELL HIGHWAY

Hungerford
Paroo

NEW

E

D

C

B

A

1

2

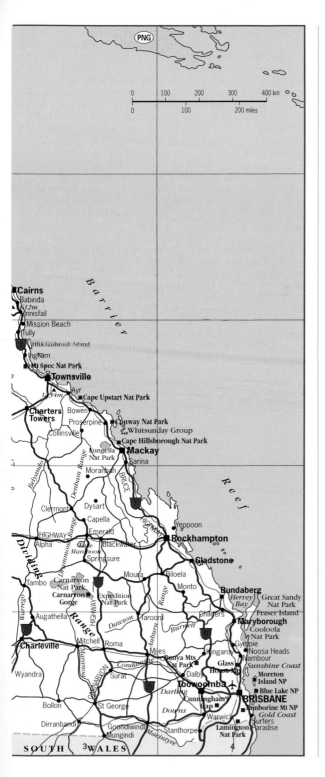

Queensland

▶▶▶ REGION HIGHLIGHTS

SUGAR CANE
One of the spectacles of Queensland is the fires that rage through the cane plantations in winter near towns such as Mossman (43 miles from Cairns), when the dry stalks are burned off to get rid of debris, snakes, and insects. At other times the tall green crop presents a peaceful sight, often combined on the coastal plain with tropical fruits like pineapples, mangoes, paw-paws, and guavas. Sugar production goes back to the mid-19th century, when South Sea Islanders were brought in in large numbers as indentured laborers (called "Kanakas"). Many of Queensland's sugar mills can now be visited.

QUEENSLAND Second only to Western Australia in area, the Sunshine State straddles the Tropic of Capricorn between the New South Wales border and the Torres Strait separating Australia from Papua New Guinea. The immensely long and fertile coastline, with its beaches and island paradises, is mostly within sight of the hills and mountains of the **Great Dividing Range**. To the east, across the transparent waters of a broad lagoon, is the **Great Barrier Reef**, the largest structure in the world to have been built by living creatures. To the west, the subtropical rain forest covering the seaward slopes of the mountains gives way to plateau farmlands of gradually diminishing quality; here, where cattle stations sometimes provide the only names on the map, is some of the country's most authentic Outback, merging in the end with the sands, stones, and spinifex of true desert. In the far north, the **Cape York Peninsula** remains one of the continent's strangest and most remote places.

Almost overendowed with natural beauty and a benign climate, Queensland has become a favorite destination with visitors from abroad as well as with Australians on vacation or in retirement. Together with a super-abundance of mineral wealth, mined in such areas as **Mount Isa** (the world's largest city in terms of area), the growth of tourism has helped Queensland prosper when the economy of other states has languished. Agriculture maintains its importance; along the coastal plain it has created richly textured landscapes of tropical crops including sugar cane, which is delivered to mills by a network of narrow-gauge agricultural railroads.

CONVICT ROOTS Queensland's recent history began with the establishment of a convict settlement at Moreton Bay in 1824. This dumping ground for particularly recalcitrant offenders was soon transferred to an upriver site nearby, which was named Brisbane after the Governor of New South Wales at the time. In 1859 independence from New South Wales was granted, and the new colony was given its name in honor of Queen Victoria.

The population increased and settlement spread; timber workers took the best trees from the rain forest, leaving farmers to clear the resulting scrub. Gold and other mineral finds helped open up the country; Queensland's richest goldfield was the remote and disease-ridden Palmer River, scene of a rush in the 1870s. Immigrant labor has played a minor role in Queensland's history, but at one point the gold-digging Chinese on the Palmer outnumbered the rest of the Far North's population. Another immigrant group were the Kanakas—many thousands were abducted from their islands in the South Pacific and New Guinea to work in the canefields (see panel).

A high proportion of Australia's Aborigines lived in Queensland, perhaps more than 200,000 at the time of white settlement. Of a fiercer and more warlike disposition than their fellows elsewhere, they put up a spirited resistance to their dispossession. To little avail, however; by the turn of the century the white settlers had reduced the number of these Aboriginals to no more than 15,000.

POLITICS AND PEOPLE For a generation, Queensland was governed by the ultra-conservative National Party, who were formerly known as the Country Party and represented rural interests.

This organization was led from 1968 by the robust peanut farmer Sir Joh Bjelke-Petersen, a sworn opponent of moral permissiveness, conservation, or anything that stood in the way of "development." Under his authoritarian rule, demonstrations were banned, books were censored, homosexuals harrassed and protected buildings demolished.

Building speculators prospered and foreign capital was encouraged to share in the state's wealth, with few strings attached or questions asked. Sir Joh's demise was accompanied by numerous revelations of police misconduct and corruption.

The typical Queenslander is popularly supposed to be the most Australian of Australians. A macho frontier mentality lasted longer here than in the southern states, with the result that the metropolitan refinements of Sydney and Melbourne were looked down on, as was anything that smacked of "culture."

Until fairly recently, Brisbane took a positive pride in its decidedly provincial character. Much of this attitude has now changed, but enough still remains to make the state quite distinct.

View from the world-famous Cairns–Kuranda train

203

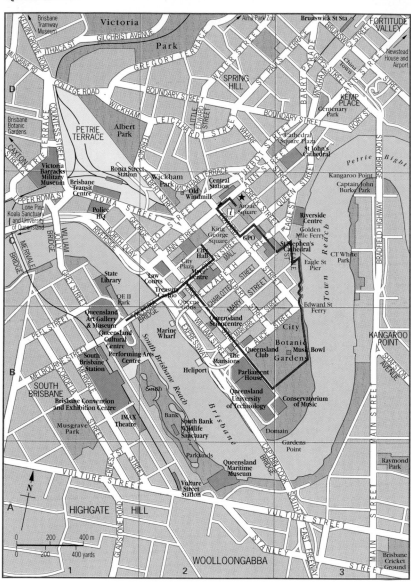

Brisbane

Australia's third largest city stands on the banks of the winding Brisbane River just inland from Moreton Bay. For long it was regarded as a provincial backwater, a kind of agricultural town that as recently as 1961 had hundreds of miles of unpaved streets. Perhaps in order to combat this image, since the mid-1980s Brisbane has embraced the idea of progress with an enthusiasm that some people find altogether regrettable.

OLD-TOWN SIGHTS Not all traces of an older charm have been erased in a misguided pursuit of modernity, and enough of the town's older buildings remain to tantalize the visitor with thoughts of the stylish tropical metropolis that Brisbane perhaps never was, but might well have become. One such example is at the corner of George and Alice Streets, where the **City Botanic Gardens** help to frame the white stuccoed fronts of the **Queensland Club** and **Old Parliament House**.

A more positive face of modernization than the new high-rise parliamentary annex is on the south bank at South Bank Parklands. **Expo 88** was held here, leaving behind a legacy of parkland as well as a number of cultural and recreational buildings of the very highest standard.

SUBURBAN SPLENDOR The suburbs are among the best places in which to savor the city's special quality. Spread over a vast and largely hilly area, they consist almost entirely of single-family houses, and in areas like Red Hill, Paddington, and Bardon, the Queensland stilt house can be studied in all its variety.

CITY CENTER ORIENTATION Brisbane's city center is surprisingly small and easily explored on foot, although a nice idea is to take the City Sights Trambus that wanders around most of the sights, allowing you to jump on and off whenever you wish for a flat fare. A boat cruise to historic **Newstead House** makes a pleasant excursion, too, while ferries link a number of destinations along the river bank.

The handsome 1868 Parliament House has been carefully restored

205

Walk

Brisbane's buildings and City Botanic Gardens

See map opposite.

Allow a half-day for this exploration of the peninsula on which the city of Brisbane is built.

Extending almost an entire block, the **Central Railway Station** of 1901 faces **Anzac Square** with its **Shrine of Remembrance**. At the corner of Ann and Edward Streets stands the extraordinary **People's Palace** with its verandas and cast-iron balustrades. The **General Post Office** is an imposing building; its arcade leads to Elizabeth Street, to **Old St. Stephen's Church**, and to **St. Stephen's Cathedral** near the waterfront.

The riverside walk extends beyond the Edward Street gates of the **City Botanic Gardens**, and the **University of Technology** flanks the gardens. An intimation of the tropical paradise Brisbane might once have been is given by the lovely **1880s Queensland Club** in its garden setting. Opposite are **The Mansions**, striking row houses, now home to stores and restaurants. Just off Queens Gardens in William Street are the 1829 **Commissariat Stores**, one of only two convict-era buildings remaining intact in the city. On George Street, the Lands Building and old Treasury have been restored to become the Conrad International Hotel and Treasury Casino respectively and the nearby **Sciencecentre** (see page 206).

On the far side of Victoria Bridge are the **Queensland Cultural Centre** and the **South Bank Parklands**. A visit here could easily last a whole day; a quicker tour can be made using the Brisbane Transport ferry to return to the city center. **Queen Street Mall** is more commercial, though there are some fine late 19th-century and interwar buildings. The walk ends in **King George Square**, which is dominated by the tall tower of **City Hall**.

Home of the Queensland State Parliament

SOUTH OF THE RIVER

South Brisbane's Parklands have a man-made beach and the Butterfly and Insect House (see opposite page), while the neighboring Queensland Maritime Museum is also worth visiting. Also in this area is the vast new Convention and Exhibition Centre.

PARKS AND GARDENS

Brisbane has numerous green spaces in its center and immediate environs. The **Brisbane Forest Park** comprises 102 square miles of forests, hills, and reservoirs, while the **City Botanic Gardens** occupy the tip of the peninsula formed by the great bend in the Brisbane River. There is a riverside walk, and the gardens form an ideal setting for the buildings of the Queensland University of Technology, among them the Old Government House of 1860. At the foot of **Mount Coot-tha** (751 feet), about 4 miles from the city are the splendid Brisbane Botanic Gardens, with stunning tropical greenhouses and a planetarium.

▶ City Hall   *204C2*
King George Square
In the late 1920s, a determined attempt was made to overcome Brisbane's provincial image by the erection of this colossal edifice, whose 299-foot tower shoots up behind the array of columns facing King George Square. The gallery at the top offers a view of the city center. Inside, there is an art gallery and museum, with plenty of exhibits celebrating the city's importance. Starting from City Hall, Brisbane's Heritage Trail takes in the city's most important historic sites and buildings.

▶ Newstead House   *204D3*
Breakfast Creek Road, Newstead
Built in 1846, this white mansion (2½ miles north of the center) with its elegant verandas is the oldest surviving house in Brisbane. Now a museum of colonial days, it was once owned by Captain John Wickham, commander of the *Beagle* during its survey of Australia's coastline, who made Newstead the center of the city's social life.

▶ Old Windmill   *204C2*
Wickham Terrace
This is Brisbane's oldest structure, convict-built in 1829 and overlooking the city from the pleasant heights of Wickham Terrace. What if its sails failed to work? Put in a treadmill! Plenty of convict feet to keep it turning, and more reliable, too! It was later used as an observatory.

▶ Parliament House   *204B2*
Corner of George and Alice Streets
Opened in 1868, this fine French Renaissance-style building is still the home of the Queensland State Parliament. Tours are available when Parliament is not sitting.

▶▶ Queensland Cultural Centre   *204B1*
Melbourne Street, South Brisbane
"Culture" seems to have been something that Brisbane was, for many years, content to leave to the fancy folk

down in Sydney. But times change and, having decided that it was a good thing after all, Brisbane set about accommodating culture in a lavish way. Completed in 1985, this complex includes the Queensland Art Gallery, Queensland Museum, State Library, and Performing Arts Complex, the latter with a 2,000-seat theater and an equally large concert hall.

The **Queensland Art Gallery**▶▶ has a good selection of Australian and Aboriginal art, and a beginner's collection of European painting, some of it interestingly arranged by theme rather than by artist or country. But the pictures have little chance of competing with the architecture, which is on a huge scale and very concrete.

The exhibits in the **Queensland Museum**▶▶, particularly the dinosaurs and the aircraft, are more of a match for their surroundings and there is a major display on the history, art and culture of the Aborigines.

▶ Queensland Sciencentre

110 George Street
Housed in a beautifully restored old building, this interactive science and technology center is one of Brisbane's most entertaining attractions. There are around 170 fun, hands-on exhibits here, and even the most non-scientific visitor will be captivated.

▶▶ South Bank Parklands 204B2

South Brisbane
Once the international crowds have gone, Expo sites often become forlorn places, but many of the pavilions and facilities erected for Brisbane's 1988 bonanza are still here, bringing life to this area of parkland stretching along the river across from the city center. The attractions include a state-of-the-art **IMAX Theatre**, the **Butterfly and Insect House**, with around 850 butterfly varieties and a good range of Australian insects, stores, restaurants, a Nepalese pagoda and much more (see panel on page 206).

KOALA CAPITAL
Brisbane styles itself the "koala capital," and the Alma Park Zoo and Lone Pine Koala Sanctuary are both good places to see these friendly marsupials.

207

Modern Brisbane is Australia's third largest city

Glass House Mountains scenery

Drive

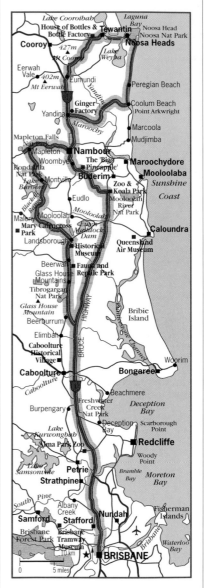

The Sunshine Coast and hinterland

This full day's drive along Queensland's Sunshine Coast goes into the hinterland of farming and hill country along the Bruce Highway.

About 37 miles north of Brisbane, the **Glass House Mountains** interrupt the monotony of the coastal plain. These old volcanic hills are best viewed from the old main road north of Caboolture as well as from the Mary Cairncross Park near Maleny. The **Blackall Range** panoramic drive gives access to this superb upland country of undulating hills and verdant valleys, tea rooms and craft studios. Just north of the little highland resort of Montville is the **Kondalilla National Park**, where splendid 295-foot waterfalls crash down through the rain forest. Equally spectacular falls can be experienced at **Mapleton Falls National Park**.

In **Nambour**, a center of tropical fruit production, a narrow-gauge sugar-cane train trundles through the streets. A sequence of splendid beaches unravels along the Sunshine Coast north of Coolum to the multicentered and highly fashionable community of **Noosa Heads**, while **Tewantin** boasts a couple of curiosities—a house built of bottles and the Big Shell. Back inland, the charming village of **Eumundi** makes a good stopping place, though it is packed on market day (Saturday). The Bruce Highway is the best route for a swift return to Brisbane.

National parks

As may be expected in a state of its vast size, Queensland has an extraordinary variety of landscapes, many protected by designation as national or environmental parks.

Tropical coastline to desert heartlands Most visitors will become familiar with the reef and rain forest parks of the tropical and subtropical coastline, but the spectacular and often unique parks of the interior demand attention too. More than 745 miles to the west of the coast are the monotonous sandhills of the **Simpson Desert**, "stretching interminably like waves of the sea" according to the explorer Charles Sturt, who gave up his attempt to conquer them. First crossed on foot in 1973, they still offer a challenge to anyone venturing into them today.

Farther east, the sparse vegetation of the desert gives way to grasslands, wattle scrub, eucalyptus woodland, or scattered individuals of the strange Queensland bottle tree. Among the spinifex and rugged hills of the **Lark Quarry Environmental Park**, the footprints of dinosaurs that perished in a stampede 100 million years ago are preserved in mud that has long since turned to rock.

Farther east still, a broad belt of sandstone gives rise to spectacular scenery. This is where many of Queensland's major rivers have their origin; their erosive action has formed deep gorges in which a rich flora thrives, including the cabbage palms of **Carnarvon National Park**, also well known for its strange rock formations. As the land rises and rainfall increases, the blue-green of eucalypts gives way to the dark green of tropical rain forest, with its incredible wealth of species including ferns, climbers, and other epiphytes. In parts of far north Queensland the rain forest descends to the beaches fringing the Great Barrier Reef, whose cays and islands are now preserved as part of the **Great Barrier Reef Marine Park**.

Wild north to friendly south Cape York has some of the finest but least accessible of Queensland's national parks, where nature displays herself in all her savage unpredictability. In the wet season, rivers fill with fierce-flowing, silt-rich water, closing fords and cutting off communications for weeks on end, only to dry up into a series of isolated pools when the rain has finally stopped. Strange termite mounds stud the inland landscape, while mangrove swamps grow from the mud of the coastal plain. Brisbane must be one of the world's best endowed capital cities when one thinks in terms of grand scenery that is within easy reach of the center. A crescent of gloriously wooded highlands extends from close to the city boundary south to **Lamington National Park** on the border that lies between Queensland and New South Wales.

Brisbane's Lone Pine Koala Sanctuary is the state's best-known animal park, where kangaroos, Tasmanian devils, and other creatures can be seen

209

IN THE SOUTH
Near the market center of Warwick, at Cunningham's Gap in the Main Range National Park, there are fine views and a number of trails through rain forest and eucalyptus woodland.

Keep an eye out for the beautiful crimson rosella

The Pacific Highway to the south of Brisbane runs through eucalyptus country

A QUEENSLAND HIGHLAND LINE

Although there is now an alternative form of transportation (see page 220), half a million people travel the Cairns–Kuranda railroad line every year. Few are disappointed by the spectacular 21-mile ride from coast to mountain rain forest. The line climbs from sea level to a summit at 1,076 feet via a series of tunnels and sharp bends, stopping for a breather at the spectacularly tall Barron Falls. The railroad was built in 1886–1891 to link the agricultural Atherton Tableland with the port at Cairns; it immediately put an end to Port Douglas as a harbor of any significance. The terminus at Kuranda, planted with palms and shady with ferns, would win any international award for the best-kept station.

How to travel

By air Queensland is unique among Australian states, because it has three international airports—Brisbane, Townsville, and Cairns—all with regular connections to many overseas airports. A variety of airlines links cities elsewhere in Australia with many places in Queensland, for example with the airports serving the Gold Coast (Coolangatta) and Sunshine Coast (Maroochydore). Given the large size of the state, internal travel by air is well developed, and may sometimes be the only way of reaching remote northern destinations during the wet season. Smaller aircraft, including helicopters and sea-planes, spin a web of services spanning mainland and islands; some islands can only be reached in this way.

By water Visitors are bound to find themselves afloat at some point in their Queensland holiday, even if it is only for a day trip to part of the Great Barrier Reef aboard a high-speed wave piercer or a more humble craft hired locally. Most, but not all, of the islands are accessible by ferry or launch, which also carry vehicles to Fraser Island and a few of the Brisbane region isles. The best way of getting the feel of reef and islands might be to cruise; there are any number of operators competing for your business, some with sleek modern vessels calling at luxury resorts, others offering a more adventurous experience involving camping on uninhabited islands. Do not forget to take a cruise or ferry trip up the Brisbane River.

By bus Bus services link Brisbane with other Australian cities as well as with major destinations within Queensland. Local services are variable, though quite well developed in Brisbane and on the Gold Coast.

By train Queensland has the longest rail network in the country, with several well promoted tourist services. These rail lines include: the luxury **Queenslander** (weekly Brisbane–Cairns); the **Sunlander** (more frequently Brisbane–Cairns); the **Inlander** (Townsville–Mount Isa); the **Spirit of the Outback** (Brisbane–Longreach via Rockhampton); the **Westlander** (Brisbane–Charleville), and the **Spirit of Capricorn** (Brisbane–Rockhampton). Australia's most popular tourist train labors up from Cairns to Kuranda (see panel), and there are two rail curiosities to attract the adventurous: the weekly run from Cairns to Forsayth in the deep interior on the **Savannahlander**, and the strange **Gulflander** running on an isolated section of line near the Gulf of Carpentaria. The only interstate rail link is with Sydney.

By car The road system in the densely populated coastal strip is well developed, and reaches east–west across Queensland and into the Northern Territory via Mount Isa. Many places in the state are only accessible on unpaved roads. Cape York and other far northern places may be cut off in the wet season when fords become impassable and roads are swept away. Your own car or 4WD will be an almost indispensable asset if you want to visit many national parks, though if you persevere some sort of guided tour can be found for almost any destination.

► Atherton Tableland 200D2

From Cairns south for over 90 miles to near Innisfail, high tablelands rise steeply from the coastal plain. There are remnants of the once dense rain forest, but the area's rich volcanic soils now mostly support sugar and banana plantations and a range of exotic fruits. Southeast of Atherton on the Gillies Highway is **Yungaburra**►►, with extinct volcanoes and crater lakes.

►►► Cairns 201D3

Cairns is closer to Papua New Guinea than to most of Australia. The city, the key to far north Queensland, breathes in the balmy air of Trinity Bay. It helped open up the goldfields and tin mines of the interior, then became a major outlet for the booming agriculture of the area, particularly sugar cane. But tomorrow seems to promise even more expansive times; because of the proximity of the Barrier Reef, superb beaches, and the rivers and forests of the Daintree and the Atherton Tableland, tourism flourishes. Cairns International Airport, only opened in the mid-1980s, is already fifth among Australian ports of entry in the amount of traffic it handles.

The town's founders laid out a generous grid of streets, whose width and relative absence of traffic contribute to the relaxed atmosphere. The waterfront complex housing boutiques, stores, the Reef Casino, opened in 1996, cruise boat wharves, and a luxury hotel adds a sophisticated note, as do the ocean-going vessels of the super-rich in the adjacent marina.

Cairns Museum and the nearby **Art Gallery**► give an insight into a past populated by Aborigines, railroad workers, goldminers, and Chinese laborers. For a different experience, journey just outside town to the **Flecker Botanic Gardens**►, with more than 200 varieties of palm trees and the tranquil Centenary Lakes. Also on the edge of town is the excellent **Tjapukai Aboriginal Cultural Park**, which offers a re-created Aboriginal camp, traditional dance performances, and much more.

RUM BUNDABERG
The name of this substantial town about 230 miles north of Brisbane at the end of Hervey Bay is synonymous with its principal product—rum, distilled from the canefields of the coastal plain. Bundaberg is also the main gateway to the southern Barrier Reef. Mon Repos Environmental Park, a beach to the north, is a spot favored by turtles during their egg-laying season (November–February).

BIRDS AND BEACHES
The wildfowl enjoying the muddy flats of Trinity Bay in Cairns have won their battle against proposals to turn the flats into an artificial beach, but swimmers and sun-worshipers are more than well provided for in the string of beaches stretching along the 16-mile "Marlin Coast" to the north, each of them more paradisical than the last. From October to May, there is no swimming because of the presence of box jellyfish (see page 212).

The Esplanade and pier at sunny tropical Cairns

Drive

The Daintree and Cape Tribulation

If you can resist the temptation of the glorious beaches along the way, this full day's drive from Cairns will take you over the Daintree River to tropical rain forest and coral reef.

The **Captain Cook Highway** is without doubt one of the world's finest coastal roads. Rarely overburdened with traffic, it runs inland at first from Cairns, rejoining the shore north of the exclusive resort of Palm Cove. **Port Douglas**, the coastline's northernmost resort of any consequence, is home to the **Rainforest Habitat Wildlife Sanctuary**, an ambitious re-creation of the tropical rain forest environment.

The canefields around **Mossman** feed the town's sugar mill via miles of narrow-gauge railroad. A short detour leads to the rain forest of the Mossman Gorge in **Daintree National Park**, with its graded walking track, rapids, and delightful swimming holes. At the turn leading to the ferry over the Daintree River the pavement comes to a (temporary) end; non-4WD vehicles should proceed with caution or not at

The goanna, or monitor lizard

all in the wet season. The wide river is lined with mangrove swamp and is home to crocodiles.

Beyond the ferry begins the ecological wonderland **Cape Tribulation National Park**, a remnant of the forests in which flowering plants first appeared on earth. The road lurches through the forest and across dry river beds, pale dust from passing vehicles coating the luxuriant vegetation with a thin film.

The **Heights of Alexandra Lookout** gives a superb view over the forest tumbling down to the sea. The best initiation into the complex ecology and sheer beauty of the World Heritage Area is at the **Daintree Rainforest Environment Centre** with its boardwalk leading deep into this mysterious realm.

Even if highly toxic box jellyfish inhibit swimming, you should at least walk along one of the incomparable beaches of **Cape Tribulation**, several of which are easily accessible from the road. Beyond the cape itself, the 20-mile Bloomfield Track begins; it is only negotiable by 4WD.

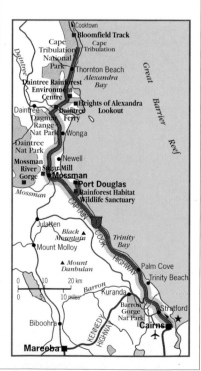

213

▶▶ Cape York Peninsula   200E2

Often described as one of the world's last wildernesses, this great peninsula tapers northward for hundreds of miles to its tip at Cape York itself, overlooking the island-studded Torres Straits separating Australia from Papua New Guinea. A total of perhaps 10,000 people are thinly distributed over this vast area, most of them Aborigines whose ancestors left a legacy of remarkable rock painting, best seen around **Laura**. This little township straddles the lower end of the Peninsula Developmental Road, a less developed highway than its name implies, especially in the Wet when river crossings become impassable even for the most rugged of 4WDs.

In the Dry, the Cape becomes a fascinating destination for the more adventurous tourist. The rain forest along the Pacific coast gives way to savannah-like country farther inland, punctuated by the surreal turrets of termite mounds, some of them reaching an extraordinary 10 feet. The peninsula possesses some remarkable national parks—including Lakefield, coastal Cape Melville, and the remote crocodile habitat of Archer Bend N.P. The future of the peninsula probably lies in wilderness tourism; civilization's other activities, apart from bauxite mining at Weipa, have left little mark on the land.

▶▶ Carnarvon National Park   201B3

Much of this spectacular park is difficult to get to, but the extraordinary gorges cut by the Carnarvon Creek and its tributaries into the soft sandstone of the plateau can be reached from the Carnarvon Developmental Road between Roma and Rolleston. Here 650-foot-high cliffs tower over cabbage palms, ferns, mosses, and orchids, a shady world quite different from the exposed plateau far above it with its open eucalyptus woodland. A number of caves shelter evocative Aboriginal rock paintings. A 6¼-mile footpath leads up the gorge from the ranger station, with side tracks giving access to all the park's delights.

▶ Charters Towers   201C3

In contrast to the sweltering heat at Townsville, 84 miles away, this modest-sized upland town enjoys an invigorating climate. It has some of the best early Australian architecture to be seen anywhere (see panel).

IF DOCTORS COULD FLY
Set up in 1927–1928 by the Reverend John Flynn, the Royal Flying Doctor Service (R.F.D.S.) began operations in Cloncurry with a plane supplied by the Queensland and Northern Territory Aerial Service (QANTAS). The event is recalled in a memorial to Flynn, its missionary founder, and in the John Flynn Place Museum in Cloncurry.

SAVING THE WILDERNESS
Destruction of the Daintree by volcanic explosions and lava flows may have been avoided in the remote geological past; more recent threats have involved the dividing of the rain forest into handy packages for "development" and the construction of the controversial Bloomfield Track. World Heritage designation has now rescued this irreplaceable tract of wild nature.

▶ **Chillagoe–Mungana Caves National Park**   *200D2*

Around the old mining village of Chillagoe are extensive and spectacular caves eroded in the local limestone by the headwaters of the Mitchell River. Not all are accessible, but the Donna and Trezkinn caves are artificially lit to enhance the drama and strangeness of the limestone formations. On the surface, the same rock has been weathered into equally peculiar shapes—turrets, pinnacles and forms resembling animals.

▶ **Cloncurry**   *200C1*

Once a bustling gold and copper town, Cloncurry sits astride the main road and railroad line from Mount Isa to the coast, earning its living nowadays from sheep and cattle grazing. It was here in 1928 that the Royal Flying Doctor Service began operating (see panel).

▶ **Cooktown**   *200D2*

A late 19th-century boomtown in the rip-roaring days of gold strikes on the Palmer River, Cooktown was named for Captain James Cook. The great navigator beached the *Endeavour* here after she had been badly holed on the Barrier Reef. Though the peak population of 30,000 or more has shrunk to less than 1,000, enough traces of the past remain to make Cooktown an attractive tourist destination. The Captain's enforced stay is recalled in the Victorian villa housing the **James Cook Museum**, as well as by his statue and by the annual reenactment in June of his landing. Cooktown is easily reached from Cairns by the inland road or, more picturesquely, by the mostly unpaved Cape Tribulation coast road. The town is also a useful base for expeditions into the Cape York interior.

▶▶▶ **Daintree National Park**   *200D2*

The outstanding international significance of the Queensland rain forest has been recognized by the designation of the Daintree and Cape Tribulation region as a World Heritage Area. A relic of Cretaceous times over 100 million years ago, the jungle of far north Queensland escaped the volcanic eruptions that destroyed other primitive forests in the region, and consequently has a unique ecological value.

The tiny settlement of Daintree is located on the banks of the Daintree River, famous for its mangroves and crocodiles. The rain forest is penetrable only by the most experienced of bushwalkers; the best place for novices to appreciate its wonders is at the **Daintree Rainforest Environment Centre▶▶**.

▶▶ **Fraser Island**   *201B4*

This is the largest sand island in the world, stretching 75 miles along the south Queensland coast and partly enclosing Hervey Bay. With wonderful beaches, dunes rising to an extraordinary 790 feet, heathland, rain forest, mangroves, and dozens of freshwater lakes, this World Heritage island attracts many visitors, though formal facilities are few and access is only by 4WD (there are no roads). A drive along the east coast takes you past the wreck of the *Maheno* and cliffs of colored sandstone to the resort villages of Eurong Beach and Happy Valley.

Fraser Island is easily reached by ferry from the mainland (Inskip Point, Urangan and River Heads), or by air.

▶ Glass House Mountains 201A4

Inland from the Bruce Highway north of Brisbane rises a group of steep and strangely shaped peaks, the cores of old volcanoes. Given their enigmatic name by Captain Cook, they are a favorite with climbers; the inexperienced can best view them from the Old Gympie Road or from Mary Cairncross Park near Maleny.

▶▶▶ Gold Coast 201A4

Between Tweed Heads on the New South Wales border and Paradise Point in the north stretches a 44-mile chain of 35 glorious sandy beaches blessed by regular rolling surf and basking in regular sunshine. Everyone is catered to here. Swimming, surfing, and sunbathing all have their place, but so do many other activities—golf and adventure sports like parasailing, for example. There are any number of theme parks and similar establishments, among them the incredibly successful **Sea World** at Main Beach, smoothly entertaining its tidal wave of visitors, and the popular Warner Bros. Movie World theme park.

Surfers Paradise, with its lavish malls, excellent restaurants and good nightlife, and Jupiters Casino at nearby Broadbeach, is where the full flavor of this seaside Arcadia can be relished. A somewhat quieter (and cheaper) ambience can be enjoyed to the south, around Currumbin or at wooded Burleigh Heads, where a discreet national park visitor center introduces what is left of the coast's natural environment.

High-rise buildings loom over the beautiful beach of Surfers Paradise

UNPLANNED UTOPIA
The sprawling Gold Coast is a textbook example of how not to plan an urban environment. The approach from Brisbane, an hour away, is reminiscent of the outskirts of Moscow, save that the high-rise buildings are more varied in shape and decorated in tasteful pastel shades. They jostle each other for a glimpse of the beach, which, because it is to the east and they are too close, is plunged into shade in the course of the afternoon. Through the wire fencing festooning the main highway an array of signs, each more lurid than the last, calls for your business; Charcoal Chicken competes with Korean Cooking, Cocktail Academy with Coastal Chiropracters, and Jesus is The Answer with the Drive-Thru Bottle Shop.

215

The reef is Australia's greatest tourist attraction. It stretches for more than 1,240 miles along the east coast from the Gulf of Papua to a point near Gladstone.

REEF FISH
The Reef is home to thousands of species of fish, from the greedy potato cod (see picture below), to colorful parrot fish, graceful rays, and poisonous lion fish. It also harbors many types of shark—attacks are rare, however, and the sharks will probably be more scared of you than you are of them!

216

Giant potato cod expect to be fed and stroked at Cod Hole, 12 miles off Lizard Island and one of the world's best diving sites

The coral of the reef's outer rim forms a steep submarine escarpment, dropping abruptly into the abyss of the Pacific; only some 19 miles out from Cairns, this Outer Reef gradually extends farther away from the mainland until, opposite Mackay, it is some 160 miles off shore. To landward is warm and shallow water forming a kind of lagoon broken up by more reefs and hundreds of islands, some of them true coral cays, most of them detached fragments of the mainland, separated from it when sea levels rose. They vary enormously in character, from exposed and sparsely vegetated cays of sand and coral barely rising out of the water at low tide, to reef-fringed mountain ranges covered in splendid rain forest.

Creatures of the deep Hardly another ecosystem on earth can surpass the reef for sheer beauty or variety. Responsible for its formation are humble polyps, tiny organisms with limestone outer skeletons that form a coral reef's basic building blocks. With wildly differing shapes recalling trees, plates, fungi and even brains, the still living polyps paint the underwater scene with vivid color, to which is added a kaleidoscope of other living creatures. These include not only tropical fish of brilliant hue and intriguing personality, but also sponges, starfish, crabs, sharks, turtles, giant clams, and an occasional dugong, a large and harmless creature also known as the sea-cow.

Another creature that is drawn to this watery paradise in large numbers is *Homo sapiens*, tourist variety. This medium-sized, sometimes amphibious mammal can be

observed gazing at the wonders of the reef from aircraft, wave piercers, and vessels of all kinds, including flat-bottomed boats and semi-submersibles, or socializing with its other inhabitants while wearing a snorkel or diving mask. Large numbers of visitors stay on the mainland, venturing out to the Reef on day trips from the main tourist centers such as Port Douglas, Cairns, Townsville, and the Whitsunday region; others stay on the islands themselves, in exclusive resorts, and crowded hotels and apartments, or the more adventurous camp on tranquil uninhabited isles with no resources whatsoever.

The Reef is a great place to learn how to snorkel

Problems of conservation The reef is a World Heritage Area, controlled and managed since 1976 by the Great Barrier Reef Marine Park Authority. Conservation problems arise not only through the influx of tourists and pressure from developers (who by 1989 had applied for permission to build 250 new resorts along the Queensland coast), but also because of agricultural and other pollutants washed into the sea from the rivers draining the interior. Exploratory drilling in the ocean may have been halted, but the petrochemical industry continues to keep a watchful eye on the reef's potential as an offshore oilfield.

A more immediate threat comes from a natural phenomenon. The crown-of-thorns starfish has a voracious appetite for the coral polyp, which it easily sucks out of its protective skeleton, and in recent years has devastated huge areas of coral. It is thought by some that over-fishing of the starfish's natural predators may have caused its population to explode; scientists are at a loss for a solution.

Butterfly fish: one of the natives of the world's largest living organism

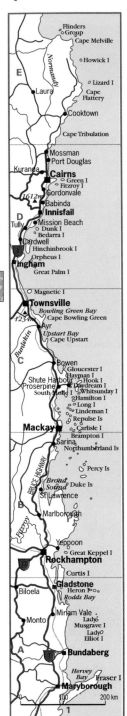

Queensland's islands

►►► Great Barrier Reef Islands *201C3*

The following information does not cover all the islands of the reef, but gives details of those that are more popular or more easily accessible, dealing with them from south to north.

Southern Reef At the southernmost end of the reef, **Lady Elliot Island►►** and uninhabited **Lady Musgrave Island►►** are small coral cays right on the reef and both of them offer excellent diving and snorkeling. The former is accessible by air or boat from Bundaberg (50 miles) or Hervey Bay, while the latter, which is a national park island with the most basic facilities and no resort, is reached on a day trip by launch or seaplane from Bundaberg (also 50 miles distant).

Heron Island►► is part resort and part national park, famed for its teeming wildlife, with optimal diving and snorkeling, semi-submersibles, and reef-walking. Access is by helicopter or launch from Gladstone (45 miles).

Large, wooded **Great Keppel Island►►** is popular with young singles and has glass-bottomed boats, a coral submarine, an underwater observatory, jet-skis and water-skiing, plus bush-walking and nightlife. It has some secluded beaches and is accessible by air from Rockhampton (35 miles) or by ferry from Rosslyn Bay.

Finally, **Brampton Island►►** (a national park and part of the Cumberland group) is a favorite with honeymooners and other couples for its romantic setting. It has good facilities, including golf and walking tracks, and is accessible by air and launch from Mackay (20 miles).

Whitsunday Islands These hilly, wooded islands, usually fringed with reefs, once formed the tips of ancient mountains and lie scattered to either side of the Whitsunday Passage. Only seven of the 70-plus islands have been developed for tourism, the rest remaining uninhabited.

Numerous high-rise hotels and apartments characterize popular, medium-sized **Hamilton Island►►**. It has an international airport with flights from some southern Australian cities and Cairns; alternatively, access is by aircraft from Proserpine or Mackay, and by boat from Shute Harbour (10 miles).

Of the six other developed Whitsunday Islands, **Hayman Island** is luxurious and expensive, **Lindeman Island**, although a national park, is now a popular Club Med resort, while **South Molle** and **Daydream Island** cater particularly to families. **Hook Island** (with a splendid underwater observatory) and **Long Island** are casual and their less expensive resorts are popular with the young. All offer day trips to the Outer Reef.

North Islands Large **Magnetic Island▶▶** (just off Townsville) has 1,640-foot granite hills, superb sandy beaches, an abundance of koalas, and a large national park. Access is by helicopter or ferry from Townsville (5½ miles) and the island has a bus service. Farther north, **Orpheus Island▶▶** is of volcanic origin and is densely wooded. It has fine beaches, exceptional coral and a biological research station. Access is by air from Townsville or Cairns, or launch from Townsville (50 miles).

Largest and perhaps wildest of the Queensland islands, national park **Hinchinbrook Island▶▶** has peaks rising through rain forest to 3,746 feet. The Coastal Walk along the east coast takes experienced hikers several days to complete; access to the island is by launch from Cardwell or seaplane from Townsville (93 miles).

Medium-sized **Dunk Island▶▶** and smaller **Fitzroy Island▶▶** both have rain forest-clad hills. The former has wonderful beaches and rich wildlife, and is accessible by air from Townsville (100 miles) and Cairns (75 miles), and by launch from Clump Point. Fitzroy Island has excellent diving and snorkeling as well as good views from its lighthouse, and is accessible by launch from Cairns (11 miles).

Green Island▶ can easily be reached from Cairns (17 miles) by boat and is therefore popular for a day trip, although the coral cay now has a luxury resort. It has the reef's longest-established underwater observatory.

Lizard Island▶▶ is sometimes called "the jewel of the Barrier Reef." Accessible by air from Cairns (150 miles), it has wonderful bays and fringing coral, and a superb view from Cook's Lookout.

ISLAND ACCOMMODATIONS
Basic and budget Lady Elliot Island (safari cabins and tents), Lady Musgrave Island (self-sufficient camping with permit from the National Parks and Wildlife Service), Great Keppel Island (youth resort and camping), Magnetic Island (backpackers' accommodation), Hinchinbrook Island (camping), Dunk Island (camping with permit) and Fitzroy Island (hostel).
Mid-range and moderate Great Keppel Island (resort and cabins), Brampton Island (resort), Hamilton Island (resorts), Magnetic Island (resorts), Hinchinbrook Island (resort), Dunk Island (resort) and Fitzroy Island (villas).
Exclusive and expensive Luxury resorts are located on Heron, Hayman, Orpheus, Bedarra, Green, and Lizard islands.

Opposite, above; Blue semicircle angel fish seen around Heron Island

Heron Island becomes a breeding ground for green and loggerhead turtles in October and November

Queensland

THROUGH THE TROPICS BY DUCK
Equally happy climbing a steep jungle track or crossing a turtle-thronged pool, the Kuranda ducks are really "D.U.K.W.s," the code name for a rugged amphibious vehicle developed for army use in World War II.

ABOVE THE RAIN FOREST
Although the Cairns–Kuranda Railway is still the most delightful way to reach this charming village, the Skyrail Rainforest Cableway offers a spectacular new option. Opened in late 1995, the cars of this cableway provide a stunning view of the scenery on their 5-mile route up the escarpment.

Lamington National Park, a paradise for hikers and bird-watchers

► **Innisfail**   201D3
A useful gateway to far north Queensland with good access to the Barrier Reef and the Atherton Tableland, the high rainfall area of Innisfail is also well known as a sugar town. Cane was first planted in the 1880s, and the industry was boosted by a wave of Italian immigrants after World War II. Innisfail's Chinese community is of much longer standing; their joss-house (temple) is one of only two still in use in Australia. Another, very different, attraction is the Johnstone River Crocodile Farm.

►► **Kuranda**   200D2
High up in the Atherton Tableland, this "village in the rain forest" is very popular with visitors, most of whom have taken the spectacular train ride up from Cairns (see panel). Kuranda is a full-blooded tourist paradise, with rides in amphibious ex-army "ducks" through the rain forest, a butterfly sanctuary, a wildlife noctarium, a huge open-air market, and arts and crafts stores—everything has been accommodated without damaging the town's character too much. Other attractions are a rain forest interpretation center, walking tours, Aboriginal dance presentations, and a wildlife park. Kuranda is also the ideal base for exploring other areas of the Atherton Tableland.

►► **Lamington National Park**   201A4
In utter contrast to the glitz and concrete of the Gold Coast is its lush hinterland of upland farms and forests. Rising to 3,950 feet on the New South Wales border, the green mountains of Lamington National Park are remarkable for their superb stands of Antarctic beech trees, some of them thousands of years old. The forest, of which they form a part, is best experienced by braving the spectacular treetop walk near O'Reilly's Guesthouse. Between here and Binna Burra Lodge, the other main focal point of the park, runs another famous walk, this one of 14 miles and with stupendous views out over the New South Wales border country.

▶ Longreach 200B

Far inland on the Capricorn Highway and railroad from Rockhampton, Longreach is the center for a vast pastoral area of the Outback. It was here that QANTAS made its base in the 1920s and here that Australia's first aircraft factory was established. Tourists come here now mostly to visit the splendid **Australian Stockman's Hall of Fame▶▶**; opened for the Bicentenary in 1988, this large and lavish modern building houses every conceivable kind of display on Outback life.

▶ Mackay 201C3

This city of over 40,000 people prides itself on its important sugar industry, shipping a third of Australia's total production from its deep-water harbor. But tourism is of growing significance, with good access to the adjacent Barrier Reef, mainland beaches, and the wonderful **Eungella National Park▶▶** to the northwest. This tract of rain forest-covered upland ("land of the clouds" to the Aborigines) offers a cool contrast to the torrid coast, and has unusual—and often unique—plants, animals, and birds like the Eungella honeyeater. You may also catch sight of the normally elusive platypus.

▶ Maryborough 201A4

Near the mouth of the Mary River, Maryborough serves a rich agricultural hinterland. Founded in 1842, it has a good number of surviving 19th-century buildings as well as parks and gardens of subtropical splendor.

▶ Millaa Millaa 200D2

This tiny dairying village is famous for the **Millaa Millaa Falls**, one of several picturesque waterfalls along the unpaved scenic route known as the Waterfall Circuit. To the west of the township is situated the **Millaa Millaa Lookout**, 3,608 feet up, with fantastic views over the Atherton Tableland, one of the most densely vegetated areas in Australia.

Quite an experience— inside the "Big Pineapple"

FLAMBOYANT FRUIT
One of Australia's most emphatic examples of kitsch is the "Big Pineapple." Almost 50 feet high, this fiberglass fruit cannot fail to catch your attention as you drive up the Bruce Highway inland from the Sunshine Coast. Advertising the attractions of an extensive pineapple plantation, it has become something of an unofficial emblem of the tropical fruit country centered on the town of Nambour.

Having been logged for its wood, cleared to make way for cane plantations, and threatened by roads, airports, reservoirs, and tourist developments, Australia's rain forest has finally been recognized as a unique habitat, not only worthy of conservation for its own sake but also for its immense appeal to visitors.

Although it is both shy and rare, the cassowary, Australia's second largest bird, is very powerful

222

ANIMAL LIFE
Rain forest is as abundant in animals as it is in plants. Some of the animals, like varieties of tree kangaroos and ringtail possums, or the tiny musky rat kangaroo, are unique to this habitat. One endangered species is the cassowary, a flightless bird related to the emu, whose thuggish habits include a grunting cry, kicking to kill with its sharp toe, and an ability to head-butt its way through the densest undergrowth.

Subtropical rain forest in Bunya Mountains National Park

Remnants from the past Scattered along the east coast from Cape York to Tasmania, today's rain forest is a mere fragment of the ancient mosaic of vegetation that covered the whole of the continent millions of years ago. Rain forest flourishes in sheltered, moist conditions, and gradually perished as ancient Australia's climate became drier and drier. But splendid remnants still grace the surface of the land where the complex equation of rainfall, evaporation, soil, and temperature balances out. The eastward-facing slopes of north Queensland's coastal mountains, for example, are sheltered by the high ridges of the Great Dividing Range from the parching winds of the interior and enjoy the benefit of moisture-rich onshore breezes. Here are the country's most luxuriant, and perhaps most spectacular rain forests.

Variety A variant, littoral rain forest occurs in unexpected locations close to the sea where sand dunes offer shelter from the scorching effects of salt spray, as on a number of Barrier Reef islands. Farther south, into New South Wales and Victoria, the composition of the rain forest changes; its structure becomes simpler and there are fewer species. Nevertheless, the appearance is still one of great luxuriance, and a number of the New South Wales temperate and subtropical rain forests stretching from the Queensland border to the Newcastle area have been grouped together to form one of the country's World Heritage Areas. This type of forest merges imperceptibly with cool-temperate rain forest, characterized by the trees known as southern beech and Antarctic beech. These trees flourish in the cooler climate of Tasmania, although they can also be seen at high altitude in Queensland's **Lamington National Park**.

► Mission Beach   201C3

The fine beaches between Tully and Innisfail, known collectively as the Mission Beach area, stretch over 8 miles along the coast within sight of Dunk Island. Cassowaries frequent the nearby forest, and there is spectacular white-water rafting on the upper reaches of the Tully River.

►► Noosa Heads   201A4

The many-centered Noosa Heads area (Noosaville, Noosa, Tewantin, and Sunshine Beach) at the northern tip of the Sunshine Coast 93 miles from Brisbane (see also page 225) is the place to come if the brazen style of the Gold Coast is not your scene. Stylish Noosa offers low-rise hotels and resorts, some excellent restaurants, and beautiful sandy beaches. It is the starting point for boat trips up the Noosa River and its lagoons or across the river into **Cooloola National Park►►**, where there is a 40-mile beach and the largest sand dune system in the world. Inland, in the Blackall Range area, is the charming village of **Eumundi►** whose Saturday market is justly famous.

► Port Douglas   200D2

This little harbor town and resort 43 miles north of Cairns exudes a charm all its own, especially on a tropical evening when only the occasional car disturbs the calm of the broad streets, still lined with old colonial buildings. You can ride through the cane fields on the little Bally Hooley train or visit the fascinating **Rainforest Habitat Wildlife Sanctuary**, and nearby is a Shipwreck Museum and a quaint seaside chapel with a view of the Pacific from behind the altar.

► Rockhampton   201B4

Australia's "Beef Capital" lies inland up the Fitzroy River astride the Tropic of Capricorn. A note of distinction is struck by the elegant late 19th-century buildings and tropical trees and shrubs; the Botanical Gardens are among the finest in the country. Nearby is the **Dreamtime Cultural Centre►**, with displays on the life of Torres Strait Islanders as well as mainland Aborigines.

COAL FROM THE TROPICS
Queensland makes an important contribution to Australia's coal production. In the Bowen Basin and adjoining country inland from Rockhampton, the coal is extracted on the opencast system from huge pits and exported worldwide through Gladstone and special coal ports like Hay Point. Several of the mines (Blackwater, Blair Athol, Goonyella and Peak Downs) welcome visitors.

223

Cruising home to Port Douglas harbor

Today, steak-happy Australians bite into about half the 1½ million tons of the beef their country produces. The rest is exported, mostly to Canada, the U.S.A., and Japan.

The convicts and soldiers landed from the First Fleet seem to have subsisted on Bengal beef, meat from cattle brought out from India. Later, English breeds were introduced, and the colony became first self-sufficient, then embarrassed by the production of a surplus of beef that could not be consumed locally. Canning and refrigeration eventually solved this problem, enabling Australia to become a major exporter of beef; until the advent of the European Community, a good proportion of the roast beef of Olde England started life in the Outback.

Together with sheep, beef cattle were the companions of the white settlers in their conquest of the continent's vast interior. Some treks were epic: in 1870 cattle thief Harry Redford drove 1,000 stolen animals from Longreach in Queensland to Outback South Australia, and in 1883–1885 the Durack family overlanded 10,000 head of stock 3,100 miles from Queensland to the Ord River in the Kimberley, a journey lasting more than two years.

Farming on a grand scale Most of Australia's beef cattle are Herefords or Shorthorns, though there has been cross-breeding with Brahmans in an attempt to increase resistance to extreme heat and pests. Numbers peaked in the 1970s at some 33½ million, but they have declined and today's total is about 18 million.

The majority of animals graze the arid lands of the center and north of the country, their thirst slaked by the water pumped up from artesian wells. Because of the poverty of the pasture, stocking rates are incredibly low and cattle stations are huge, some of them the size of European states. There are few fences to stop the beasts roaming freely until the time comes for round-up. From the stockyard they are taken by mammoth cattle trucks for the rest cure, which puts flesh on their often meager bones before they are finally slaughtered.

THE ROUND-UP
At muster time the cattle are rounded up by a handful of cattlemen on horseback or, more likely these days, by men on motorbikes or in 4WD vehicles. On the vast stations of the far north helicopters are often used to locate the more wily creatures and drive them from their hiding places.

There is some prime beef cattle country in New South Wales

▶▶ Sunshine Coast   201A4

This fabled strip of fine beaches stretches some 40 miles north of Brisbane from Caloundra to Noosa Head and is much favored by those who enjoy a quieter alternative to the Gold Coast. Should you tire of sun and sand there is the garden-like hinterland to explore, including the green world of the Blackall Range.

The Sunshine Coast encompasses dozens of sandy beaches and clear blue waters, like these at the popular resort town of Caloundra

▶ Toowoomba   201A4

High up among the grainfields and pastures of the fertile Darling Downs, Toowoomba is Queensland's largest inland city, distinguished by wide, tree-shaded streets and attractive parks and gardens. Nearby is the **Ravensbourne National Park▶**, rich in birdlife, and **Crows Nest Falls▶**, whose waters crash into a deep granite gorge.

▶ Townsville   201C3

Overlooked by its Castle Hill, Australia's largest tropical city is the outlet for an awesomely vast region stretching inland to Mount Isa and to the distant Gulf of Carpentaria. As well as a university city and a defense center, it is an important stop-off for tourists heading north or embarking for the Barrier Reef. Townsville has botanic gardens dating from the late 19th century and a number of buildings from the same period, but visitors are likely to be drawn first and foremost to the complex known as the **Great Barrier Reef Wonderland▶▶**. Here, the glass tunnel of the world's largest coral reef aquarium enables you to marvel at the wonders of the reef without donning wetsuit or snorkel, an experience not to be missed. Almost equally vivid are the films shown on the 360° screen of the **Omnimax Theatre▶**, while a branch of the **Queensland Museum▶** has displays on natural history, history and technology. As if this weren't enough, there is also the **Visitor Centre** of the **Marine Park Authority**, the body responsible for the management of the Reef.

CANE TOADS
Not far behind the rabbit in nuisance value, these unlovely creatures are an example of an introduced animal that has become more of a menace than the pest it was supposed to control. The toad was originally imported from Hawaii in 1935 in the hope that it would eliminate the beetles attacking the cane fields. Unfortunately it has proved highly successful in reducing the numbers of many kinds of native animals, exuding toxins poisonous enough to kill most of its predators, apart from road vehicles; squashed toads are a common sight along Queensland highways. Unfortunately, cane toads are now spreading south into New South Wales.

▶ Warwick   201A4

A thriving market center for the southern Darling Downs, picturesque Warwick is Queensland's second oldest town (after Brisbane), dating back to 1840.

Tasmania

King Island

- Cape Wickham
- Egg Lagoon
- **Lavinia Nature Reserve**
- Naracoopa
- Currie
- Grassy
- Stokes Point

E

D

- Curtis Group
- Hunter Island
- Three Hummock Island
- Robbins Island
- Cape Grim
- Stanley
- Rocky Cape Nat Park
- Montagu
- Smithton
- Boat Harbour Beach
- Marrawah
- Irishtown
- **Wynyard**
- Somerset
- **Burnie**
- Penguin
- Asbestos Range Nat Park
- *Arthur*
- Calder
- **Ulverstone**
- Yolla
- Ridgley
- **Devonport**
- Port Sorell

B a s s   S t r a i t

C

- Temma
- Sandy Cape
- Arthur Pieman Protected Area
- *Savage River*
- Waratah
- Savage River
- *Pieman*
- Gunns Plains
- Sprent
- Latrobe
- Railton
- △ *1339m Black Bluff*
- **Leven Canyon**
- Sheffield
- Mole Creek
- **Marakoopa Cave**
- **Lake Dove**
- ▲ *1545m Cradle Mt*
- **Walls of Jerusalem Nat Park**
- Tullah
- Rosebery
- Cradle Mt -
- **Lake St Clair Nat Park**
- ▲ *1617m Mt Ossa*
- *Lake Augusta*
- Zeehan
- *West Coast Range*
- **Mt Lyell Mine**
- Queenstown
- *1447m Mt Olympus*
- *Lake St Clair*
- Derwent Bridge

B

- Strahan
- Cape Sorell
- *Lake Burbury*
- **Franklin-Gordon**
- *L King William*
- Tarraleah
- *Lake Echo*
- *Lake Binney*
- Wayatinah
- *1443m Frenchmans Cap*
- **Wild Rivers Nat Park**
- Macquarie Harbour
- **Sarah Island**
- *Franklin*
- Point Hibbs
- **Mt Field Nat Park**
- *Lake Gordon*
- *Gordon*
- Strathgordon
- Maydena
- *Lake Pedder*
- Low Rocky Point
- *Frankland Range*
- **Southwest**
- *Arthur Range*

A

See Drive page 246

- Port Davey
- **National**
- **Park**
- South West Cape
- Maatsuyker Group

| 0 | 20 | 40 | 60 | 80 | 100 km. |
| 0 | 20 | 40 | 60 miles |

1   **2**   **3**

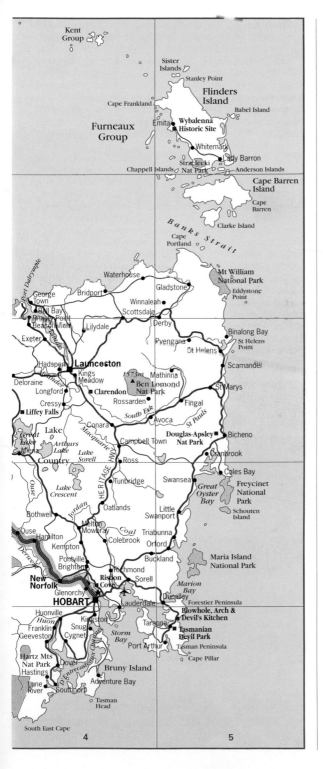

Map Labels

Kent Group

Sister Islands
Stanley Point

Cape Frankland

Flinders Island

Babel Island

Furneaux Group

Emita
Wybalenna Historic Site

Whitemark

Strzlecki Nat Park
Lady Barron

Chappell Islands
Anderson Islands

Cape Barren Island

Cape Barren

Clarke Island

Banks Strait

Cape Portland

Waterhouse
Mt William National Park
Eddystone Point

George Town
Bridport
Gladstone

Bell Bay
Winnaleah
Scottsdale

Granite Point
Beaconsfield
Lilydale
Derby

Exeter
Pyengana
Binalong Bay
St Helens Point

St Helens

Hadspen
Launceston
Scamander

Deloraine
Kings Meadow
1573m
Mathinna

Longford
Clarendon
Ben Lomond Nat Park
St Marys

Cressy
Rossarden
Fingal

Liffey Falls
South Esk
Avoca
St Pauls

Conara
Douglas-Apsley Nat Park
Bicheno

Great Lake
Lake
Arthurs Lake
Campbell Town
Cranbrook

Miena
Lake Sorell
Coles Bay

Country
Ross

Lake Crescent
Tunbridge
Swansea
Great Oyster Bay
Freycinet National Park

Bothwell
Oatlands
Little Swanport
Schouten Island

Ouse
Melton Mowbray
Triabunna

Hamilton
Colebrook
Orford

Kempton

Pontville
Brighton
Buckland
Maria Island National Park

New Norfolk
Risdon Cove
Sorell

Glenorchy
Marion Bay

HOBART
Dunalley
Forestier Peninsula

Lauderdale
Blowhole, Arch & Devil's Kitchen

Huonville
Kingston
Taranna
Tasmanian Devil Park

Huon
Snug
Port Arthur
Tasman Peninsula

Franklin
Cygnet
Storm Bay
Cape Pillar

Geeveston

Hartz Mts Nat Park
Dover

Hastings
Bruny Island

Lune River
Southport
Adventure Bay

Tasman Head

South East Cape

4   5

TASMANIA Early explorers assumed Van Diemen's Land (Tasmania's name until 1856) to be part of the mainland, but this error was rectified by George Bass and Matthew Flinders in 1798, and by 1804 Hobart had become the capital of the second British colony to be founded in Australia. This green and mountainous island's intimate links with mainland Australia are celebrated each summer by one of the world's great spectacles of sail, the Sydney to Hobart race, an exciting sprint down the coast of New South Wales and across the often turbulent waters of Bass Strait.

SMALL IS BEAUTIFUL "Tassie" certainly is different. It's a fully functioning state of the Australian Commonwealth, but everything else about it conspires to distinguish it from the rest of the country. Australia's smallest state, about the size of Ireland, Bavaria or West Virginia, it revels in a temperate climate that nourishes its forests with an abundant rainfall while providing blue skies often enough for all but the most fanatical of sun-worshippers. In the interior, stone-built bridges, villages, townships and Georgian mansions are set among neat farmlands where hedgerows and deciduous trees recall the early settlers' British origin. Beyond the pastures and orchards rise rugged uplands, with clear lakes, rushing rivers and the continent's most magnificent mountain scenery, some of it still hardly explored. The three great national parks of Tasmania's southwest have been declared a World Heritage Area, a wilderness of high peaks, deep gorges, and dense rain forest of unequaled grandeur.

VISITORS WELCOME Tasmania's relatively long history has left an exceptional wealth of old settlements and historic buildings, including what for many people is one of the most compellingly poignant of all Australia's

CONFLICT
In recent decades bitter conflict has arisen between narrowly conceived economic interests and the environment. Unique Lake Pedder was destroyed by the construction of a dam, but public opinion saved the Franklin and Gordon Rivers from going the same way. The environment seems to be winning at the moment.

228

monuments to convict days, the Port Arthur complex in its evocative setting of sea inlet and parkland. Although small, Hobart, Tasmania's capital, is a city of European style and dignity, its deep-water harbor opening onto the broad River Derwent against a backdrop of splendid green hills and mountains.

Perhaps it is the island's small size and relative isolation that have made it a welcoming place, even by the exceptional standards of Australian friendliness. The pace of life is slow, the locals are usually happy to pass the time of day with a stranger; "no worries" is even more applicable here than in the rest of the country. (This openness has not stopped Tassie's 470,000 or so inhabitants becoming the butt of jokes for other Australians.)

All this, together with generally lower prices, has made tourism an important bastion of the local economy, though surprisingly few foreigners make the short journey (150 miles) from the mainland. Visitors' dollars are particularly welcome; the island faces the perennial problems of an economy based mostly on primary products, and its unemployment rate has remained consistently higher than that of the mainland. Agriculture thrives in the Midlands, the southeast and along river valleys, though orcharding was dealt a devastating blow when the European Common Market, seeking to trade primarliy with other E.C. member countries, began to exclude Australian products. Mining of metal ores continues in the thinly populated west, and around Queenstown has left a severely denuded landscape. Forestry is a major industry, though its scope is increasingly restricted by awareness that trees have an ecological and scenic value as well as a short-term financial one. Much wild nature survives to attract the visitor, however—around a third of the state is protected and there are 17 national parks.

It is easy to find historic corners in Launceston

229

Lovely Freycinet National Park, on the east coast

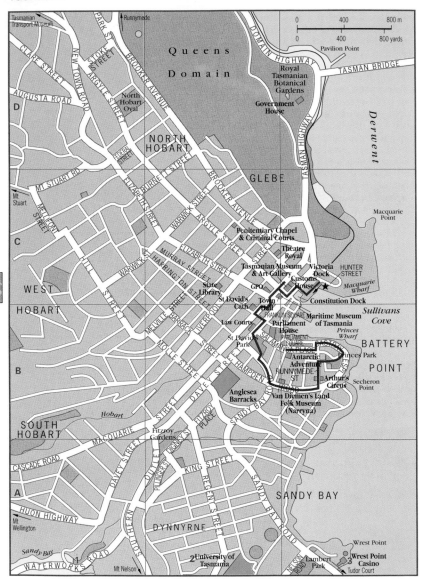

Hobart

The second oldest city in Australia (after Sydney), Hobart is the country's smallest state capital. It stretches out along both shores of the broad estuary of the River Derwent, one of the deepest harbors in the world, linked by the 336-foot span of the Tasman Bridge.

The old city center, with its wealth of colonial buildings, clusters compactly around **Sullivans Cove** on the west bank, backed by wooded slopes rising to the often snow-capped peak of 4,167-foot high Mount Wellington. Its rich architectural heritage and incomparable setting make Hobart a delight to explore.

HISTORY The city was founded in 1804 by Lieutenant-Governor David Collins, after the first attempt at settlement the previous year at Risdon Cove just upstream, had failed. For many years the population consisted mostly of convicts and their overseers, though the harbor soon became a base for the whalers and sealers pursuing their prey in the Antarctic and South Pacific.

The city spread inland along the grid of streets leading uphill from the wharves and warehouses of Sullivans Cove, leaving a legacy of fine building; individual monuments abound, but it is the almost European quality of the townscape as a whole that makes Hobart virtually unique in Australia. Streets dominated by imposing Victorian structures like the town hall or the Theatre Royal of 1837 contrast with the delightful informality of the village suburb of **Battery Point**.

LAID-BACK LIFESTYLE Life in Hobart proceeds at an easy pace, leavened by the good temper of its inhabitants, who seem perfectly content to live in this least metropolitan of capital cities. This is not to say that amenities are lacking; today's Hobart has a full range of facilities to keep both locals and visitors stimulated and entertained. Its hotels and eating places equal those found elsewhere, while the casino complex at Wrest Point (Australia's first) has introduced a note of sophistication previously lacking. Every Saturday the dignified sandstone warehouses of **Salamanca Place** look down on what is one of the country's liveliest and most colorful open-air markets, while December 31 and the first week in January are enlivened by the excitement of the Sydney–Hobart yacht race, when thousands of spectators line the shore. This is also the time of the lively Hobart Summer Festival, a month-long event which features Tasmania's gourmet foods.

231

TASMANIA DISCOVERED
Dutch mariner Abel Tasman caught sight of an uncharted shore on November 24, 1642 and named it Van Diemen's Land after Anthony van Diemen, Governor-General of the East Indies. Mounts Heemskerk and Zeehan in the west of the island recall the name of his expedition's two ships. Unaware that his discovery was not part of the mainland, much less that it would eventually bear his name, he sailed off, leaving George Bass and Matthew Flinders to circumnavigate the island more than a century and a half later, in 1798. Evidence of French interest was provided by the scientific voyage of Nicolas Baudin in 1800, and it was partly in order to forestall any French designs on the island that Lieutenant John Bowen was sent to plant the British flag on the shores of Risdon Cove in 1803.

Hobart's spectacular harbor

CHURCH LANDMARKS
Hobart's churches were mostly built on prominent sites to act as city landmarks. With its commanding octagonal tower, St. George's Church at Battery Point is no exception, although its Egyptian-style stonework, fashionable during the early 19th-century when the church was built, is most unusual.

Hobart's Botanical Gardens feature a wide range of native and exotic plants, including ferns and the native Huon pine

▶ Antarctic Adventure   230B3

1 Salamanca Square

The headquarters of the Australian Antarctic Division is located in Hobart. This educational science centre, opened in 1998, gives visitors an insight into the geography, natural history and exploration of the frozen continent through interactive displays, a planetarium, and a thrilling simulator ride.

▶▶ Battery Point   230B3

This is the name given to the promontory separating Sullivans Cove on the north from Sandy Bay to the south. Its commanding position made it a natural site for the battery of guns placed here in 1818 to protect the approach to the harbor. Battery Point's interest today is in its delightfully domesticated 19th-century townscape. There are cottages and villas, and little row houses looking (apart from their tin roofs) as if they have just been transplanted from late-Georgian England. Grander altogether is "Narryna," a solid, pilastered stone-fronted home of 1836, protected from the street by fine iron railings. Housing the **Van Diemen's Land Folk Museum**, the interior has been refurnished to evoke the more elegant side of life in 19th-century Hobart, and the gardens and outbuildings are being restored in the same spirit. Battery Point also has excellent restaurants, and many art and craft stores.

▶▶ Harbor area   230B3

The true spirit of Hobart can still be sensed along the wharves and quaysides of the harbor fronting Sullivans Cove, although the whalers have long since sailed away.

Fishing boats and pleasure craft tie up in the twin basins known as Victoria Dock and Constitution Dock, the name of the latter a reminder of the great day in 1853 when the granting of a constitution marked the end of convictism in Tasmania. A venerable Sydney ferry contrasts with trim trawlers and with the spick-and-span survey ship of the Commonwealth Scientific and Industrial Research Organisation (C.S.I.R.O.) tied up at Battery Point to the west. The buildings around the harbor are some of the best in Hobart; they include the **Customs House**, now part of the museum, and the restored warehouses along Hunter Street. You will have to make your own mind up about the controversial Hotel Grand Chancellor.

▶ Maritime Museum of Tasmania   230B3
The Carnegie Building, 16 Argyle Street
This delightfully old-fashioned museum is housed in "Secheron," a fine Battery Point residence dating back to the 1830s, and has a comprehensive collection of maritime memorabilia showing how intimately Tasmania's history has been linked with the sea.

▶ Royal Tasmanian Botanical Gardens   230D3
Sloping steeply down to the Derwent near the Tasman Bridge, these superlative gardens are studded with fine specimen trees and structures like the wooden Fernery or the Conservatory with its changing floral displays, each more dazzling than the last. It's not just botanists who will be fascinated by the carefully maintained array of specifically Tasmanian plants, some still awaiting classification and some under threat of extinction.

▶▶ Salamanca Place   230B3
In the 1830s the stony slopes of Battery Point were quarried away to build the wharf to the south of Sullivans Cove, and warehouses of magnificently solid appearance were erected to serve the ships docked there. Long since vacated, these superb sandstone structures have happily found new users: boutiques, craft studios, galleries, restaurants, antiques dealers and bookstores. Every Saturday morning the place is transformed by the arrival of an army of stallholders offering wares of incredible variety, a must for every visitor.

▶▶ Tasmanian Museum and Art Gallery   230C3
40 Macquarie Street
Tasmania's principal museum is housed in a complex of buildings of various dates, including 40 Macquarie Street, erected in 1808 and supposedly the oldest continuously occupied building in Australia. The Natural History section has displays on Tasmanian creatures (and their ancestors, the megafauna of Pleistocene times that included 10-foot kangaroos and giant wombats); the Tasmanian Aboriginal Gallery tells the sad story of the island's Aborigines; and the Colonial Gallery's exhibits, guarded by a redcoat, bring to life the decades dominated by convictism. The gallery features colonial art; of more than passing interest are John Glover's depictions of Tasmania as a paradise populated by Aborigines, and the famous *Conciliation* by Benjamin Duterrau, marking the fateful meeting that led to their exile and death.

The 1837 Theatre Royal has been carefully restored

233

HOBART'S MOUNTAINS
In clear weather both Mount Nelson and Mount Wellington give sensational views of Hobart in its incomparable setting. Mount Nelson (1,115 feet), the residences of the privileged dotting its slopes, rises over Sandy Bay; a little signal station still stands at the summit, though the signalman's house has become a tearoom. Mount Wellington (4,167 feet) is reached via the panoramic road built in 1937 to enable the lazy to enjoy the views that were previously only accessible to determined hikers. At the summit is a boardwalk as well as a shelter with notices explaining what you are looking at, though most visitors will probably be quite content to gaze in wonder at the glorious prospect before them.

Constitution Dock, mooring point for sailboats in the Sydney–Hobart race

Walk

Sullivans Cove to Battery Point

This walk from Sullivans Cove begins at the north end of the harbor by the memorial commemorating the city's foundation in 1804 and links Hobart's waterfront to the charming old quarter of Battery Point.

The handsome old warehouses flanking Hunter Street contrast with the modern hotel overlooking Victoria Dock. Take time to enjoy the activity around the **harbor**. Inland from the harbor are the old buildings of the **Tasmanian Museum and Art Gallery** whose entrance is around the corner in Macquarie Street, where you will also find the 1864 Town Hall and the tall-towered **General Post Office** of 1905. Now planted with fine trees and with a fountain at its center, **Franklin Square** was once a parade ground fronting the first Government House. The intersection formed by Murray Street and Macquarie Street is unique in Australia in having retained all its early buildings: **St. David's Cathedral**, the old **Law Courts**, and a number of mid-19th-century row houses.

Opposite St. David's Park is a real curiosity, a royal-tennis court, still in use by players of what has become a very exclusive indoor game. The park itself, with its sweeping lawns and fine native and exotic trees, was once the city's cemetery. A memorial recalls John Woodcock Graves, author of the song "Do ye ken John Peel?", who visited Tasmania in 1886.

Beyond Harrington Street is **Hampden Road**, the artery of Battery Point, with a pleasingly variegated collection of 19th- and early 20th-century buildings. To the left, **Arthurs Circus** is a delightful enclave of quaint 1840s and 1850s cottages, then Runnymede Street leads you to Princes Park, that descends abruptly to the 1818 **Signal Station**. Beyond Castray Esplanade, the modern C.S.I.R.O. laboratories occupy the headland, but it is still possible to find a way through and enjoy views across the Derwent. The Esplanade leads back toward the city center. Inland from Princes Wharf is the magnificent set of 19th-century warehouses fronting **Salamanca Place**, a fine conclusion to your walk.

How to travel

By air Tasmania is linked to the mainland by a large variety of air services from airports such as Hobart, Launceston, Burnie/Wynyard and Devonport. There are also more limited services to airfields at Queenstown, Smithton and Strahan, as well as to Flinders and King Islands in Bass Strait. Regular internal flights between all these airfields are supplemented by local firms operating tourist flights; of these, the seaplane trip that takes off from Strahan to fly over Macquarie Harbour and Frenchman's Cap to land in the gorge of the Lower Gordon River cannot be recommended too highly.

By sea Bringing passengers and their vehicles from Australia to Tasmania: the *Spirit of Tasmania* takes about 15 hours on alternate days between Melbourne (departs Monday, Wednesday, and Friday) and Devonport (departs Saturday, Tuesday, Thursday). This modern, luxurious ship can carry almost 1,300 passengers and up to 490 vehicles.

By car Most visitors bring their own vehicle with them or rent a car once here. Distances are relatively short and roads mostly good, though logging trucks in a hurry to deliver their load can on occasion slow traffic down. The freedom you get from your own car is particularly useful in Tasmania where there is really only the skeleton of a public transportation system.

By train Although a narrow-gauge network still exists, passenger trains (except for enthusiasts' specials) stopped running many years ago.

By bus Every settlement of any size has its bus service, though its frequency may be strictly limited. There are two main operators—**Tasmanian Redline Coaches**, who issue "Tassie Passes" that are valid for varying periods, and **TassieLink**, which provides regular bus services and a vital link to the wilderness. Buses operate to and from the major national parks and bushwalking start and finish points.

235

TRAVELING ON FOOT
Anyone who comes to Tasmania should be prepared to walk, even if it is only for a short distance along the numerous marked boardwalks and nature trails. The adventurous can climb the more accessible peaks like Cradle Mountain, walk the five- to ten-day Overland Track, or enjoy a guided adventure rafting down the Franklin River.

Prime bushwalking country

The Franklin River is the ideal location for exciting whitewater rafting

The lush rain forest of the Wild Rivers National Park

National parks

Around a third of Tasmania is designated as national parks, state reserves or marine reserves.

World Heritage Area The largest tract of protected land (about 540 square miles) was declared a World Heritage Area in the 1980s, and stretches from Cradle Mountain to South West Cape, taking in several parks and reserves. One of the world's last great temperate wildernesses, its pristine rivers, rain forest, and rugged mountain ranges can be appreciated from the Lyell Highway or by flights and cruises from Strahan, but its deepest secrets will only be revealed to the dedicated bushwalker or whitewater rafter. Cradle Mountain-Lake St. Clair, the Franklin-Gordon Wild Rivers and the Southwest national parks are all described separately below, but the wild heart of the island also includes the great natural amphitheater of the **Walls of Jerusalem** as well as the "land of a thousand lakes," as the Central Plateau area is sometimes known. Through it passes the Lake Highway linking Deloraine with Melton Mowbray, a fascinating and unhurried alternative to the usual Heritage Highway for north–south journeys.

Beautiful and protected National park or reserve designation applies to many of Tasmania's outstanding natural landscapes: beaches, caves, lakes, and forests. The granite hills of the Freycinet Peninsula, the alpine moorlands, tree ferns, and waterfalls of Mount Field were the first to be listed as a national park. In the northeast of Tasmania rise the bare ridges of Ben Lomond, its ski slopes reached by a twisting mountain road. The eucalypts of the island's last major tract of dry sclerophyll forest are protected in the **Douglas-Apsley National Park**. Most of the smaller islands have important conservation areas: King Island's **Lavinia Nature Reserve** is home to endangered orange-bellied parrots, while Wybalenna Historic Site on Flinders Island preserves what is left of the ill-fated attempt to re-settle the last of Tasmania's Aborigines between 1833 and 1847.

▶ Bicheno   227C5

Pronounced Bee-sheno, this east coast town was once a base for sealers and whalers as well as a port for exporting coal from the nearby mines. Nowadays its boats bring in crayfish and abalone, and it is popular with fishermen, artists and beach-lovers, attracted by the mild climate, beautiful beaches and superb scenery. The nearby Douglas-Apsley National Park is excellent for walking.

▶ Bothwell   227B4

Pleasantly set in the beautiful Clyde Valley, Bothwell is of considerable historic interest, containing numerous colonial buildings, as well as acting as the southern gateway to Tasmania's mountainous Central Highlands.

▶ Burnie   226D3

Most visitors hurry through Tasmania's fourth largest town, but workaday Burnie makes an interesting contrast to the rather self-conscious rusticity of much of the island. There are industrial plants, the Pioneer Village Museum, and a cheese factory, and great trainloads of ore.

▶▶▶ Cradle Mountain–Lake St. Clair National Park   226C3

Part of Tasmania's World Heritage Area, this national park of rugged mountain peaks and high moorlands is one of the great landscapes of Australia. The gateways to the park are **Cradle Valley**▶▶▶ to the north and Lake St. Clair near the Lyell Highway in the south. At Cradle Valley the spacious visitor center introduces the national park to its public with displays, talks and events; a boardwalk penetrates the depths of the rain forest and gives a fine view of the Pencil Pine Creek waterfall. A number of shorter or longer walks radiate from the center, but most visitors will want to press on up the gravel road to the north shore of **Lake Dove**▶▶▶. Bearing in mind that the park generally receives no less than 103 inches of rain each year and that most days will bring at least some, let us hope that you will see the unforgettable outline of Cradle Mountain reflected in the clear waters of the lake.

Source of the River Derwent, **Lake St. Clair**▶▶▶ is the deepest (656 feet) body of freshwater in Australia and certainly one of the clearest. It is easy to escape into wild nature, even if it is only as far as Watersmeet, confluence of the Cuvier and Hugel Rivers.

WEINDORFER'S "HOME IN THE WOODS"
In 1912, deep in the primeval woodland, an Austrian called Gustav Weindorfer built himself a chalet of King Billy pine and named it "Waldheim" (Forest Home). It was Weindorfer's enthusiasm that was largely responsible for the area's designation, first in 1922 as a scenic reserve, then later as a national park. Waldheim still stands, albeit rebuilt, but it has been joined by other forms of accommodation ranging from the comfort of Cradle Mountain Lodge to the more basic amenities of a campsite, all designed to harmonize with their incomparable surroundings.

237

THE OVERLAND TRACK
The route from Cradle Valley to Cynthia Bay on Lake St. Clair is 53 miles long. Walking it is perhaps the best way to savor to the utmost the varied landscapes of the national park—wild open heaths, forested valleys, deep gorges, lakes and tarns, and rocky peaks, among them Mount Ossa (5,305 feet), Tasmania's highest point. The trek takes a minimum of five days, but it is better to allow longer to avoid rushing and to be able to explore a little at will. There are huts along the way, but their capacity is limited and you should be prepared to camp. Always check with a ranger before setting off into the wilderness.

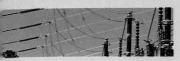

With its abundant rainfall and mountainous terrain, Tasmania's potential for the generation of hydroelectricity is easily the greatest of all the Australian states.

GORDON DAM

238

One of the many Tasmanian dams

WATER POWER
Tasmania developed its hydroelectric power supplies partly so that it could expand its aluminum processing industry. It takes huge quantities of electricity to turn aluminum ore (bauxite) into the metal. Hydroelectric power is economical, so it must have seemed the ideal solution. Bell Bay in northern Tasmania was selected as a suitable site for an aluminum plant in the 1950s, lying as it does between the cheap power produced in Tasmania's interior and Queensland's large deposits of bauxite.

Early developments The first projects were built before World War I, but it was in the interwar period that grandiose visions were expounded of Tasmania becoming Australia's Ruhr, whose new industries would feed off cut-price electricity and solve the island's economic problems forever. Founded in 1930, the **Hydro-Electric Commission** (H.E.C.) became a kind of state-within-a-state, Tasmania's biggest employer, capable of overcoming whatever technical challenges might be involved in wresting power from the trackless wilderness.

By the late 1960s the H.E.C. had its eye on glacial **Lake Pedder**, and was able to flood this unique ecosystem in the face of gathering protests from a growing minority of people concerned about the impact of hydro-power on the environment. The destruction of Lake Pedder was described by UNESCO as "the greatest ecological tragedy since European settlement in Tasmania."

Power or greenery The H.E.C.'s next major proposal was the transformation of the Franklin and Lower Gordon Rivers and the surrounding temperate rain forest.

Tasmanian society was bitterly divided, but opposition was better organized this time in the shape of the **Tasmanian Wilderness Society**. A referendum showed the extent of concern, the construction site was block-aded, 1,500 arrests were made, and the project was finally halted in 1983 by a newly elected Federal Labor government anxious to cultivate the "Green vote." The wild rivers of the southwest, once described by Premier Gray as "brown and leech-ridden," were saved; in the end it may well be that Tasmania will gain more from tourists drawn to one of the world's great wildernesses than from any extra wattage that might have been generated.

▶ Deloraine 227C4

Now bypassed, but well worth the detour, this attractive old township lies in fertile country on the Meander River halfway between Launceston and Devonport. In and around the town are any number of interesting colonial buildings, including Bonney's Inn (1831).

▶ Devonport 226D3

Devonport is one of the principal gateways into Tasmania. It is here that the overnight *Spirit of Tasmania* vehicle ferry ties up after crossing Bass Strait from Melbourne; and there is an airfield, too. Just inland from the 1889 lighthouse, on the rocky promontory of Mersey Bluff, is the **Tiagarra Aboriginal Culture and Art Centre▶**, with excellent displays on the life led by the first Tasmanians as well as a guided walk around the collection of over 250 enigmatic carvings that are a feature of the area. Other places to visit include the Maritime Museum and excellent Devonport Gallery and Arts Centre, as well as National Trust-listed 1916 **Home Hill▶**, the white house that belonged to Joseph Lyons, the only Australian to have been both State Premier and Prime Minister. Outside the town to the west is the terminus of the **Don River Railway▶** where you will find Tasmania's largest collection of veteran locomotives and rolling stock. Vintage trains run regularly, and the museum is quite fascinating.

▶▶ Flinders Island 227E5

Guarding the eastern end of Bass Strait, Flinders is the largest island of the Furneaux Group, Once the abode of sealers, then the site of G. A. Robinson's ill-fated Aboriginal refuge (see page 241), it is a lonely place, with an agricultural and fishing population of just over 1,000. But there is an abundance of wildlife (including the famed muttonbirds—see panel), as well as splendid white beaches contrasting with the rugged granite outcrops of the **Strzelecki National Park▶▶**.

MUTTONBIRDS
The islands of Bass Strait are the breeding ground of the short-tailed shearwater, a rather nondescript brown bird that migrates in a clockwise direction around the Pacific. The nestlings, chubby creatures rich in fat and oil, are bred in yard-long burrows, then left to their own devices by their parents. This made them easy prey for the Aborigines, who harvested them in huge numbers.

239

The beautiful Liffey Falls to the south of Deloraine are well worth a visit

The beautiful beaches of the unspoiled Freycinet Peninsula

HUON PINES
Easily identified because of its feathery foliage and trailing branches, this is a uniquely Tasmanian conifer, occurring mainly in the wetter areas of the far southwest. Extraordinarily slow-growing, it is also extraordinarily long-lived—some specimens still alive may go back to the pre-Christian era. Respect for age meant little in colonial days, when the "piners" prized the Huon for its exceptionally resilient timber. Today it is valued more for its beauty when converted into ornamental objects such as fruitbowls, and has become a mainstay of the Tasmanian souvenir industry.

▶▶▶ **Franklin–Gordon Wild Rivers National Park**   *226B3*

This glorious tract of rain forest, wild rivers and rugged uplands extends from the sheltered waters of Macquarie Harbour to the Lyell Highway, forming the central portion of Tasmania's World Heritage Area. Its highest point (4,734 feet) is the spectacular quartzite monolith known as **Frenchmans Cap▶▶▶**, whose sheer eastern face drops an alarming 985 feet. Experienced bushwalkers can make the round trip to Frenchmans Cap in four days; others must content themselves with views from the highway. The adventurous can go whitewater rafting on the Franklin River, an immensely rewarding trip through gorges and over rapids that takes more than a week to reach the little jetty near the mouth of the Gordon. This point is also accessible by launch from Strahan or, more excitingly, by a seaplane that drifts down the gorge to land gracefully on the limpid, tea-colored stream. A boardwalk leads deep into the damp and mossy forest where, among the tree ferns, Huon pines and Antarctic beeches, a waterfall crashes into its pool.

▶▶ **Freycinet National Park**   *227B5*

Approached via the fishing township of Coles Bay, the Freycinet Peninsula extends southward into the azure waters of the Tasman Sea towards little Schouten Island. With its backbone of red granite peaks, immaculate beaches of white sand, forests of eucalyptus, and wealth of wildflowers, this was one of Tasmania's first national parks and has long been popular with locals.

▶ **Geeveston**   *227A4*

At the old timber town of Geeveston, dating from 1842 and 38 miles southwest of Hobart, is the **Geeveston Forest and Heritage Centre▶**, a starting point for explorations of the woodland area. The **Arve Road▶▶** has picnic areas and lookouts, and a little further inland is **Hartz Mountains National Park▶▶**, a rugged alpine region that is part of the state's World Heritage area.

In December 1642, the crew of Captain Abel Tasman's Heemskerk *heard voices calling in the forest fringing their landing place near Cape Sorell on the west coast. The owners of the voices failed to show themselves—perhaps they had premonitions about the fate of their descendants at the hands of later colonists.*

Early conflict Tasmanian Aborigines were quite distinct in character from their mainland counterparts. Thinly spread around the island, they totaled an estimated 4,000–5,000 at the start of white settlement in 1803. The usual complicated relationships arose between the two races. There was plenty of cooperation; Aboriginal women in particular gave freely of their skills in the seal hunts that formed such a staple of Tasmania's early economy. But conflict inevitably grew, in spite of earnest professions of concern on the part of white officialdom; the natives' living patterns were disrupted as their hunting grounds were turned into fenced-off farmland. In the face of the destruction of their way of life, some resisted violently, to be met with more effective violence by the settlers. Within 20 years Aboriginal numbers had been halved.

The end of a race The most fateful episode was reconciliation. The undoubtedly well-meaning George Augustus Robinson traveled the island, making contact with all remaining Aborigines, winning their trust and persuading them to settle in a kind of Christian protectorate on Flinders Island. Here, religion, drink, disease and the loss of their land and culture gradually destroyed those who had survived thus far. The last full-blooded Tasmanian Aborigine, a woman called Truganini, died in 1876.

Above: Aboriginal rock carving in Devonport

LOST BUT NOT FORGOTTEN
The disappearance of Tasmania's full-blooded Aborigines is often characterized as genocide, though the processes involved were essentially the same as those at work on the mainland. Many people of mixed blood remain, however.

241

John Glover's 1836 painting, The Last Muster

Hazards aplenty presented themselves to early mariners negotiating the uncharted coastal waters of the great southern continent: vicious storms, unexpected islands, hidden reefs, and no hope of succor from land. Even the skilful navigator Captain Cook ran aground on the coral of the Barrier Reef, though his disciplined crew was able to refloat the stranded Endeavour *on the next high tide.*

CAPTAIN BLIGH

Often called "Bligh of the Bounty," the naval officer William Bligh (1754–1817) was also known to his contemporaries as "Breadfruit Bligh," since one of his tasks had been to introduce that fruit to the West Indies. Strict to the point of harshness and beyond, he had the misfortune to suffer not one, but two mutinies. The first, aboard the *Bounty*, is part of popular history. The second rebellion against his rule, in 1808, was led by the officers of the "Rum Corps," as the New South Wales Corps was disparagingly known. Bligh, as Governor of the colony, had attempted to curb what he saw as the Corps' excessive influence over the colony's commercial life (including a monopoly on the sale of spirits). A *coup d'état* was staged, and Bligh was arrested by his own guards. Undaunted, he refused to return to London as a prisoner, and was later completely cleared by the British government of any misconduct.

A Dutch disaster The first to experience the inhospitable aspect of Australia were the Dutch, who favored an indirect but rapid route to their possessions in the East Indies. This led them around the Cape of Good Hope, then swiftly eastward with the winds of the Roaring Forties filling their sails, turning north before reaching the coast of Western Australia (which they named Nova Hollandia—New Holland).

However, not every captain made the turn in time, among them Commander Pelsaert; his vessel the *Batavia* was named after the chief town of a Dutch colony (now Jakarta) and her cargo included the carefully chiseled stones for the town's main gate. On a fateful morning of 1629, the *Batavia* ran aground on one of the low coral atolls of the Houtman Abrolhos Islands, some 33 miles off Geraldton. Crew and passengers struggled ashore, rescuing what provisions they could.

Once a degree of organization had been established, Pelsaert set sail for distant Java in a small boat to fetch help. His departure gave the signal for the mutiny that had long been brewing aboard the *Batavia*. Disaffected sailors and marines set up a reign of terror; rape and casual murder became the order of the day, though some managed to flee to neighboring islands and hold out against the mutineers. By a miracle, Pelsaert's frail craft managed to survive the ocean voyage. He returned to the Houtman Abrolhos Islands and arrested the rebels, executing the ringleaders on the spot.

This improbable tale is told in full detail in the **Western Australian Maritime Museum** at Fremantle. Many of the *Batavia's* timbers have been recovered, and enough of them put together again to make up her stern, a most impressive and evocative sight. Here, too, the ready-cut masonry from her hold has been erected to form the classical gateway once intended to adorn the approach to the city of Batavia.

The Shipwreck Coast The *Batavia* was not alone in coming to grief off Western Australia, but it is probably Bass Strait between Victoria and Tasmania that has been responsible for the greatest number of Australian shipwrecks. In the last century, the stormy waters of the Strait formed the principal approach for vessels making for eastern Australia; King Island was only provided with a lighthouse in 1861, and until then ships would hug the

coast of the mainland, and they frequently ran aground on hidden rocks.

The most famous wreck occurred in 1878, when the iron clipper *Loch Ard* foundered on rocks near Port Campbell in Victoria. Of the 50 or so souls aboard, only two survived. Apprentice-boy Tom Pearce clung to a lifeboat and was swept into a narrow cliff-bound gorge. Badly knocked about, he was nevertheless able to rescue young Eva Carmichael, whom the current had also brought into the gorge. Leaving the semi-conscious Eva on the beach, Tom somehow managed to climb the cliff and stagger for help. Only four bodies were recovered from the *Loch Ard*; their graves are in the nearby cemetery, one of several containing the remains of victims of this treacherous shore, which bears the name of the Shipwreck Coast.

Between Princetown in the east and Port Fairy in the west, the Historic Shipwreck Trail has markers and information boards indicating the locations of 25 wrecks of coasters, cargo boats, and ships full of hopeful immigrants. At Warrnambool the re-created port called **Flagstaff Hill Maritime Museum** has many objects recovered from these wrecks, and there are other maritime displays at the **Old Cable Station Museum** at Apollo Bay **Portcampbell Information Centre**.

Above: The rugged cliffs of Cape Raoul on the Tasman Peninsula

Below left: The waters around Flinders Island are treacherous

243

Above and below: Precious objects have been salvaged from the 17th-century Batavia

An old windmill attracts visitors in Launceston

► George Town   227D4

A center for historic sites, unspoiled beaches, and gentle scenery, George Town stands near the mouth of the beautiful Tamar River, the 35-mile-long combined estuary of the North Esk, South Esk and Macquarie rivers. One of the oldest towns in Australia, it has several early colonial buildings, including the elegant Georgian house known as **The Grove**, built in the early 1830s for port officer and magistrate Mathew Curling Friend.

► Hamilton   227B4

A useful stopping point on the way to the west from Hobart, this charming little place of sandstone cottages and a few larger buildings never realized the ambitions of those early colonists who predicted a great future for it as a minor metropolis. Even Jackson's Emporium has been reduced from two stories to one.

►► King Island   226E1

Far out in the stormy waters of Bass Strait, northwest of Tasmania, verdant King Island has an enviable reputation for dairy products, though much of the 36-mile-long island consists of unpopulated bushland teeming with wildlife. In the early 19th century it was one of the great battlefields in what has been called "Man's War on Animals," when the rough and ready "Straitsmen" butchered vast numbers of seals for their oil and skins.

►► Launceston   227C4

Located at the point where the North and South Esk Rivers combine to form the beautiful Tamar, Tasmania's second city is the unofficial capital of the northern part of the island. It has retained much of its Georgian and Victorian heritage and offers continuous pleasures to the urban stroller, even though few buildings are outstanding in themselves.

The city was laid out on the usual grid pattern of streets, some of which, like the Mall and Civic Square, have been given over to pedestrian use. In Civic Square is an intriguing sculpture of Tasmanian wildlife, including tail-biting thylacines (tigers—see panel opposite), as well as **Macquarie House►**, now housing the local history museum. Nearby are other reminders of the past—the red-brick Queen Anne-style post office and the Italianate town hall, while the Old Umbrella Shop in George Street, now the National Trust store and information center, has retained its authentic 1860s frontage.

Launceston's other major attractions lie to the east of the city center. In a prettily landscaped setting, the **Queen Victoria Museum and Art Gallery►** rivals Hobart's Tasmanian Museum for the interest of its collections and innovative displays. Close to King's Bridge over the South Esk is **Penny Royal World►**, with an array of re-erected and reproduced 19th-century buildings including water mills and windmills, as well as a fully operational gunpowder mill, reached by vintage tramway. Upstream is the most dramatic of Launceston's many parklands, **Cataract Gorge Reserve►►**, a wild and rocky canyon in miniature, crossed by a chairlift and suspension bridge.

There is a great deal to see and do around Launceston. Scenic cruises operate on the Tamar; and there are many excellent wineries, such as the acclaimed Heemskerk Wines, to visit on both banks of the river. And a collection of fine country houses graces the hinterland.

Finely proportioned **Franklin House▶** near Kings Meadow would not have been out of place in the countryside of Georgian England, while single-storied **Entally House▶** at Hadspen, with its veranda, seems much more rooted, and more "Tasmanian."

Clarendon▶, behind its restored Ionic portico, is on a grander scale altogether, one of the great rural residences of Australia, overlooking its grounds and the South Esk River with a haughty eye.

▶ Maria Island National Park   227B5

Reached by ferry from Triabunna, this east coast island will appeal to those seeking undisturbed nature. Though pre-dating Port Arthur as a penal settlement—convicts were first sent to Maria Island in 1825—and once exploited for various commercial purposes, the island is now an oasis of tranquility, with an abundant wildlife enjoying total freedom from motor vehicles. Visitors will need to take their own staples, as there are no stores or electricity on the island.

▶ Mole Creek   226C3

The limestone rock around this tiny township is riddled with caves, most of them inaccessible. But two of the more spectacular can be reached: **King Solomon Cave▶**, where a limestone formation recalls the biblical monarch, and the longer **Marakoopa Cave▶**, watered by two streams and lit by glow-worms.

...AND TIGERS
Devils are not an endangered species, but the thylacine or Tasmanian tiger is officially extinct. What is generally thought to have been the last of the race died in Hobart Zoo in 1936, ironically within three months of tigers being declared a protected species. Thylacines were wolf-like marsupials, with stripy backs and wide-opening jaws; their liking for sheep and lambs didn't endear them to farmers. The question of whether the tiger lives on in seclusion somewhere has divided Tasmanians into believers and skeptics; there have been plenty of supposed sightings, but no definite proof.

245

The delights of Cataract Gorge, Launceston's favorite recreation area

Drive

Through the wilderness on the Lyell Highway

See map on pages 226–227

Allow a day for this trip from Hobart across the mountain core of Tasmania on the Lyell Highway to the remote fishing port and resort of Strahan.

The first section of the drive runs up the valley of the Derwent, through well-tamed countryside of fields and farms

The attractively wooded Derwent Valley and its villages lie just a short drive from Hobart

and pleasant towns like English-looking New Norfolk and historic Hamilton. More rugged country follows, with increasing evidence of Tasmania's highly developed hydro-electricity industry—signs point down side-roads to dams, there is a surprise of a canal, and huge pipelines snake up and down the slopes. After Tarraleah, a residential village for Hydro-Electric Commission workers, and Lake Binney, the forest thins and gives way to featureless button-grass plains.

Shortly before Derwent Bridge, **Mount Olympus** comes into view; this grand mountain overlooks the clear waters of **Lake St. Clair**, which is reached via a short side-road from Derwent Bridge. The ranger station at Cynthia Bay marks one end of the famous Overland Track between here and Cradle Mountain. The recommended time to complete this famous trek is at least five days, but there are plenty of shorter hikes available in the area—anything from a nature stroll on the level to relatively easy day walks.

One of the world's great mountain roads, the Lyell Highway was only completed in 1932. There are several, mostly well-marked stopping points along the way between Derwent Bridge and Queenstown: King William Saddle marks the watershed between the Derwent and Franklin–Gordon river systems, while Surprise Valley Lookout has a view of the imposing 4,734-foot peak **Frenchmans Cap**. A number of short walks can be made from the Franklin River Bridge along part of the Frenchmans Cap Walking Track to the Donaghy's Hill Wilderness Lookout, to the Alma River Crossing or to Nelson Falls.

The road then skirts round the flooded valley bottom of the H.E.C.'s **Lake Burbury**, a mountain scene of incomparable grandeur. Equally extraordinary, albeit in an utterly different way, are the denuded and devastated uplands around the mining center of **Queenstown**. The final leg of the journey is along the twisting but otherwise uneventful road through the forest and down into the little port of **Strahan**, one of the best starting points for further exploration of the wild western coast or the rain forest, rivers and mountains of the interior.

▶ New Norfolk   227B4

Upstream from Hobart, the Derwent Valley recalls the landscapes of southern England, with rolling hills as a background to a countryside of big deciduous trees and, around historic New Norfolk, hops fields and their attendant oast houses, one of which is now a museum.

▶ Oatlands   227B4

Extension of British power into the interior of Tasmania was marked by the construction of highways; one of the most important was the road now known as the Heritage Highway, linking Hobart with Launceston. A small number of strategic settlements were planned along the route, of which Oatlands was one. First surveyed in 1832, the township is no bigger than a modest village, but nevertheless boasts an outstanding number of fine colonial buildings.

▶▶▶ Port Arthur   227A5

Port Arthur is the most evocative of all the places recalling the days of the convict system, offering an experience that no visitor should miss. (See also panel on page 248.)

The Tasman Peninsula is virtually an island, linked to the rest of Tasmania only by a slender isthmus. The first prisoners were brought here in 1830 to fell and saw the wood that formed the basis of the first of Port Arthur's thriving industries. As more convicts and those sent to guard them arrived, a vast range of activities began to flourish. In time the place became virtually self-sufficient, supporting a population of more than 2,000, housed, working and worshiping in an array of handsome brick and stone structures. To make officials feel more at home, touches of Old England were contrived; oaks and elms were planted and blackbirds released to sing from their branches.

Both extreme cruelty and weird forms of enlightenment were features of life at Port Arthur. Floggings were given for the slightest offense, but it was also here, at Point Puer, that juvenile delinquents received the first compulsory education in the world. By the mid-19th century, the desire to reform rather than punish led to the building of the Model Prison, whose inmates spent their time in total "solitary." However, madness rather than rehabilitation was the frequent outcome. With the end of the convict era, Port Arthur was closed down as a penal colony, and in the late 19th century became a tourist attraction. Many of its more substantial structures remain. They include the 1844 building used as a penitentiary from 1857; guard towers; the sinister Model Prison and, looking down on the site from landward, the fine church with tower and pinnacles.

The Tasman Peninsula has other attractions, including high cliffs, strange coastal rock formations and the **Bush Mill**, a re-created logging settlement and steam railway.

NEW NORFOLK FIRSTS
The town boasts a number of "firsts:" St. Matthew's, the island's oldest surviving church; the Bush Inn, Australia's oldest continuously licensed inn (you are likely to come across several of these); and the nearby salmon ponds, where a batch of ice-packed eggs survived the long trip from England to hatch into the first trout and salmon to swim the streams of the southern hemisphere.

THE GENTLEMAN BUSHRANGER
Filled with "a deep and concentrated hatred of that power which was undeservedly persecuting me," the Irish convict Martin Cash and two companions braved the sharks in about 1840 by swimming to freedom from the Tasman Peninsula. Recognized in the course of an overconfident visit to a lady friend in Hobart in 1843, Cash shot a police constable while being re-arrested, but avoided execution and eventually settled down to the life of a farmer.

Port Arthur, a legacy of the convict era

Eroded hills behind Queenstown

TRAGEDY AT PORT ARTHUR
A tragic postscript to Port Arthur's strange and often brutal history was added in April 1996, when Hobart resident 28-year-old Martin Bryant went on a so far unexplained rampage. In just a few hours, Bryant shot and killed 35 people and injured many more, leaving Tasmania, and indeed the whole of Australia, in shock. Bryant is now serving a life sentance, and Port Arthur is recovering its status as one of the nation's premier tourist attractions.

LEATHERWOOD HONEY
One of Tasmania's most distinctive trees is *Eucryphia lucida*, or leatherwood, a characteristic species of the temperate rain forest. For many years, local beekeepers have hung hives in the vicinity of leatherwoods in order to take advantage of the bees' liking for the nectar-rich flowers that bloom in spring and early summer. The nectar is converted into a particularly delicious honey.

►► Queenstown 226B2

Few scenes of industrial devastation are quite as spectacular as the bare highlands surrounding this mining town in western Tasmania. For visitors approaching from the east, the contrast between the vast tracts of luxuriant rain forest to either side of the Lyell Highway and the denuded slopes around Queenstown could not come as more of a surprise.

The miners who came here from the early 1880s onward were prospecting for gold, but it was not long before copper extraction took precedence. The copper smelters' insatiable demand for fuel was responsible for the wholesale clearance of the rain forest all around, while their emissions poisoned any regrowth that might have occurred. With no vegetative cover to bind it together, the soil was quickly washed away by the abundant rainfall (up to 118 inches each year), leaving deep gullies and bare rock faces which are now being slowly revegetated.

Queenstown is not without a certain quiet pride in this horror story, which undoubtedly gave it a distinctive identity, commemorated by the rather odd collection of sculptures at the **Miners Siding**, together with a sturdy little rack-and-pinion locomotive. Copper is still processed at the **Mount Lyell Mine** and the company's museum can be visited. The entire venture is under constant threat of closure, however, and it is likely that the mine will eventually become a "living" museum of the area's rich mining history.

►► Richmond 227B4

For Tasmanians, tiny Richmond embodies all that is "historical" about their island. Along the township's main street are a number of fine old buildings from colonial days, some of them dating from the 1820s. Two attractions in particular capture the imaginations: the 1825 jail, erected to house convicts engaged in public works, and the convict-built bridge, Australia's oldest road bridge, which was constructed from local sandstone in 1823–1825. The bridge carried the highway that for many years linked Hobart with Port Arthur, and now benefits from its pretty setting of riverside lawns, trees and ducks.

►► Ross   227C4

Driving the Heritage (Midland) Highway is an almost continuous pleasure; the well-engineered road speeds you past a background of blue hills through a countryside that was remade by the early settlers into a facsimile of the England they had left behind.

Ross is one of a number of strategic settlements established along the route in the 1820s to act as staging posts for travelers. Church Street, with its attractive old stone buildings, is nicely shaded by the ubiquitous elms, but it is Ross's famous stone bridge that is quite exceptional. An elegant structure dating from 1836, it is decorated with carvings of such virtuosity that they earned their convict stonemason his freedom.

► St. Helens   227C5

The most populous place on Tasmania's east coast, the fishing port of St. Helens is also the most popular, with vacationers outnumbering locals five to one in the height of summer. As well as attracting game fishermen, the port makes an excellent base from which to explore the magnificent northeastern coast of the island, where there are splendid sand dunes, white sandy beaches and bands of Forester kangaroos.

►►► Southwest National Park   226A3

Forming the southern part of Tasmania's World Heritage Area, this is a vast wilderness of mountain ranges rising from virgin forest of southern beech and Huon pine, with great sweeps of buttongrass, glacial lakes and wild rivers, and a wonderful coastline of deserted sandy beaches.

Until quite recently only the more hardy type of bushwalker, mountaineer or canoeist ventured into this remote and unspoiled world. But in the late 1960s, Tasmania's Hydroelectric Commission drove a road deep into the heart of the area, a harbinger of its plan to drown Lake Pedder beneath an artificial water body 20 times its size. The outrage this provoked, not only among conservationists but also in a wider public, turned out to be in vain; Lake Pedder, with its unique fauna and beach of brilliant white sand, was duly submerged in the interest of generating marginally cheaper electricity.

However, the advantage for the visitor is that it is now possible to taste, if not fully experience, something of one of the world's last temperate wildernesses by driving up the Strathgordon and Scotts Peak Roads. Both highways give spectacular views of the new Lake Pedder in its rugged setting.

For those wishing to penetrate even farther into the wilderness, the track from Scotts Peak Dam via the coastal inlet of Port Davey to South East Cape will take up to two weeks' strenuous trekking; there are several specialist tour operators in the area.

► Stanley   226D2

On its peninsula protruding into Bass Strait, this historic port and vacation center nestles beneath its famous landmark,The Nut; properly known as **Circular Head**, this 490-foot basalt outcrop is the core of an ancient volcano. Walk or take the chairlift to the breezy summit for terrific views along the northwest coastline.

FISHING IN TASMANIA

Fishing is one of Tasmania's main industries and fresh seafood is one of the delights of eating out on the island. There are plenty of opportunities for visiting enthusiasts to go sea fishing, particularly for tuna and marlin from the little ports of the east coast. But it is probably the lure of the trout that will most entice the angler from abroad. Ever since trout spawn from England was successfully hatched in 1864 in the famous Salmon Ponds hatchery near New Norfolk, the island's unpolluted streams and lakes have proved an excellent habitat for both brown and rainbow trout.

249

Catching tuna the "kind" way off the Tasman Peninsula

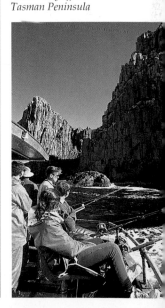

▶▶ Strahan   226B2

A small settlement on the inland sea of Macquarie Harbour, Strahan (pronounced "Strawn") grew to export the wood and minerals of the western interior. Its main functions today are fishing, forestry, and tourism. The Strahan Visitor Centre on the waterside has deliberately tendentious displays on the history of the area.

Hell's Gates, as the narrow and dangerous entrance to Macquarie Harbour is known, were so named because they guarded Sarah Island, from 1822 to 1834 one of Britain's most brutally administered penal colonies. Strahan is also the base for exploring the Gordon River—by cruise boat or seaplane.

▶ Swansea   227B5

From the beach there is a wonderful prospect across Great Oyster Bay toward the Freycinet Peninsula. One of the best places to stay along the "Sun Coast", Swansea has such visitor attractions as the imposing three-story brick General Store constructed around 1838 and the 1885 Bark Mill.

▶ Wynyard   226D3

Linked to the mainland by flights from its own airport, this fishing port at the mouth of the Inglis River is a useful gateway to Tasmania's scenic northwest coast. To the east are the wonderful white sands of **Boat Harbour** and **Sisters Beach**, as well as the rugged coastline of the **Rocky Cape National Park▶▶**. The headland at Table Cape has a lighthouse and offers splendid views.

▶ Zeehan   226C2

Named after one of Abel Tasman's ships, this isolated mining town in Tasmania's far west saw both boom and bust before beginning a modest recovery, brought about by the reopening of a tin mine in recent years. Legacies of turn-of-the-century prosperity based on silver-lead extraction include the **Gaiety Theatre** and the **West Coast Pioneers Memorial Museum▶** (see panel).

RAILROAD DELIGHTS
The West Coast Pioneers Memorial Museum in Zeehan is home to a comprehensive array of local exhibits as well as locomotives built long ago in Glasgow, Manchester and Germany. These were shipped across the seas to work the ore trains of one of the most mineralized areas on earth.

Georges Bay at St. Helens is still a bustling fishing port despite an influx of summer visitors

Travel Facts

Arriving and departing

All visitors to Australia must have a valid passport and, with the exception of New Zealanders, a visa. Visas must be obtained in advance from an Australian High Commission, Embassy, or Consulate; a fee is charged only if you intend to stay more than three months or if you require a multiple-entry visa.

A Working Holiday Maker visa (which is valid for 12 months) allows you to take employment of a casual nature during your stay, and also carries a charge.

By air All Australian state capitals (but Canberra) are served by international airlines, and there are also international flights from Darwin, Cairns, and Townsville. There are many opportunities for combining a visit to Australia with stopovers at intermediate destinations or by buying a "round-the-world" flight. Many visitors will want to take advantage of the option of arriving at one point in Australia and departing from a different one.

Fares vary considerably among the 40 or so international airlines serving Australia and also fluctuate according to the time of year; the cheapest fare may turn out to be a false economy if it involves an exhaustingly long flight with several stops. Check prices and availability well in advance through a travel agent or reputable media outlets; there are some real bargains, particularly in charter flights.

By sea Those with time to spare can travel to Australia on board the cruise ships of operators like C.T.C., Cunard, P & O, and Royal Viking, albeit at a price. Some freighters carry a small number of passengers too, but this is by no means a cheap alternative.

Camping

Despite the insect nuisance, Australia is wonderful for camping not just because of its climate but also because of its exception-

ally generous and varied campsites, both on the edge of towns and in the bush. Site equipment is good, and might include electricity hook-up, hot and cold water, showers, lavatories and laundromats. Some sites offer pre-erected tents, and many more have trailers and cabins for rent. Operators range from town councils to commercial chains or national park authorities. Some of the national park sites are "basic." Camping on your own in the wild is also possible, but discretion is always advisable; check that your presence is not going to annoy a landowner.

Camper-vans and motorhomes are increasingly popular among Australians exploring their own country in a leisurely way. Consider renting such a vehicle if you intend to spend most or part of your time touring rather than visiting city sights.

Car breakdown

When renting a car, check with the rental company about emergency road service; they will normally arrange help for you. Membership in a motoring association in your own country will in many cases give you access to the facilities of the various state motoring clubs (contact the

The Overland Train runs between Adelaide and Melbourne

National Roads and Motorists Association for details).

Breaking down in the Outback is potentially fatal and should be avoided by making sensible preparations for your journey (see Driving tips on pages 257–258).

● **National Roads and Motorists Association**, 388 George Street, Sydney, NSW 2000 (tel: 13 2132).

Car rental

Vehicles are available from a range of agencies (both international and local) at most airports as well as from town and city centers. To rent a car you will need a valid driving license and, normally, be over 21. One-way rentals between major cities are possible, but will not offer the cheapest deal.

The total cost of the rental will consist of the basic daily or weekly rate plus various additions like a collision damage waiver and possibly a mileage charge. Choice of vehicle is very much an individual matter; 4WDs and camper-vans are available, and you might find a six-cylinder home-grown model more restful for

long trips than a hatchback. There may be restrictions on driving vehicles on unsealed roads.

Climate

As befits a country that is also a continent, Australia has a wide variety of climates. Visitors from the northern hemisphere will need to get used to the seasons being reversed (summer is from December through February, and winter is from June through August).

In general terms, the best time to visit the south is between September and April, while the north and center can be seen at their best between May and October.

The southwest and the southeast (which includes southwest Western Australia, much of South Australia, Victoria, much of New South Wales, Australian Capital Territory and Tasmania) are at their best in spring and summer, although mid-summer temperatures can get very high.

Winters here can be dull and rainy, though frost is rare except at high altitudes where snow can be expected—as in the Snowy Mountains.

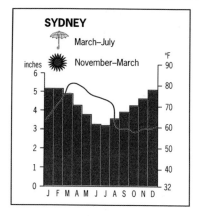

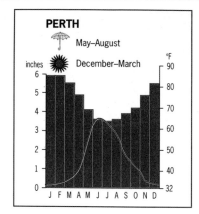

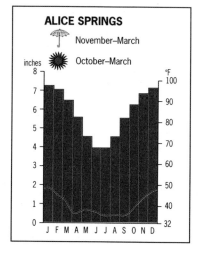

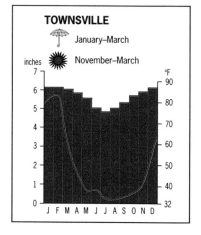

Many Australians enjoy a winter vacation in the Red Centre or northwestern Western Australia, where they are likely to find sunny days with temperatures of around 68–77°F, although nights will be cold—in the low 40°F—in the Centre. Summer in these areas can be unbearably hot, with temperatures of 113°F not uncommon.

The subtropical and tropical parts of the country (much of Queensland, Western Australia and the Northern Territory) are at their least comfortable in the Wet season (usually November through April), when heavy rainfall and high humidity prevail. This is also the season when box jellyfish make the sea unsafe for swimmers, and when roads may be washed away. In the Dry season (May through October) conditions are much more pleasant, with warm (but not too hot: average temperatures hover around the upper 70°F mark) and sunny days.

Crime

Political and business scandals of sometimes spectacular dimensions, and the activities of a well-organized criminal underworld dominate the headlines in Australia more than casual offenses against the person. Thieves and muggers do exist, but Australian cities are still among the safest in the world, and no more than the normal precautions against pickpockets, muggers and car thieves are necessary— don't flash expensive jewelry or wads of cash, keep all valuables in a safe place, always keep your car locked.

CONVERSION CHARTS

FROM	TO	MULTIPLY BY
Inches	Centimeters	2.54
Centimeters	Inches	0.3937
Feet	Meters	0.3048
Meters	Feet	3.2810
Yards	Meters	0.9144
Meters	Yards	1.0940
Miles	Kilometers	1.6090
Kilometers	Miles	0.6214
Acres	Hectares	0.4047
Hectares	Acres	2.4710
Gallons	Liters	4.5460
Liters	Gallons	0.2200
Ounces	Grams	28.35
Grams	Ounces	0.0353
Pounds	Grams	453.6
Grams	Pounds	0.0022
Pounds	Kilograms	0.4536
Kilograms	Pounds	2.205
Tons	Tonnes	1.0160
Tonnes	Tons	0.9842

MEN'S SUITS

UK	36	38	40	42	44	46	48
Rest of Europe	46	48	50	52	54	56	58
US	36	38	40	42	44	46	48
Australia	92	97	102	107	112	117	122

DRESS SIZES

UK	8	10	12	14	16	18
France	36	38	40	42	44	46
Italy	38	40	42	44	46	48
Rest of Europe	34	36	38	40	42	44
US	6	8	10	12	14	16
Australia	8	10	12	14	16	18

MEN'S SHIRTS

UK	14	14.5	15	15.5	16	16.5	17
Rest of Europe	36	37	38	39/40	41	42	43
US	14	14.5	15	15.5	16	16.5	17
Australia	36	37	38	39	41	42	43

MEN'S SHOES

UK	7	7.5	8.5	9.5	10.5	11
Rest of Europe	41	42	43	44	45	46
US	8	8.5	9.5	10.5	11.5	12
Australia	7	7.5	8.5	9.5	10.5	11

WOMEN'S SHOES

UK	4.5	5	5.5	6	6.5	7
Rest of Europe	38	38	39	39	40	41
US	6	6.5	7	7.5	8	8.5
Australia	6.5	7	7.5	8	8.5	9

Customs regulations

Personal effects can be brought in without payment of duty, as can 250 cigarettes or 250 grams of tobacco and 1,125 mls (about one U.S. quart) of liquor (beer, wine, or spirits), and gifts up to a value of A$400. There are tough penalties for importing weapons, drugs, protected wildlife, and associated products, and for attempting to bring in quarantinable articles, particularly plants that may be disease carriers.

Visitors with disabilities

Public bodies and the tourist industry try to make life easier for people with disabilities. Modern buildings and facilities are designed to high standards of accessibility for wheelchairs, pedestrian crossings have audible signals when the way is clear, and many national parks have special trails for people with disabilities. The **Australian Council for Rehabilitation of the Disabled**, (P.O. Box 60, Curtin, A.C.T. 2605 (tel: 02 6282 4333) provides information about facilities and services throughout Australia.

Renting a 4WD is sensible if you wish to journey into the Outback

Domestic travel

By air As you would expect in such a huge country, air travel is very popular, with more than three-quarters of all long-distance journeys made by plane. There are few places that cannot be reached by aircraft, usually in the comfortable cabin of a large modern jet or riding the thermals next to the pilot during an outback joyride or remote-area flight.

Internal airlines are now deregulated, with benefits to passengers in terms of good prices and availability of services. In addition to a number of regional airlines, the main carriers are **Ansett Australia** and **Qantas Airways**, both of which offer visitors from abroad discounts on ordinary fares. Travelers using Qantas to get to Australia can usually make discounted internal flights with that company. Check on what offers are available when planning your journey and bear in mind that flights fill up quickly during the main holiday periods. Student discounts are available, as are standby fares.

Smoking is not permitted on any internal flights, or in any of Australia's domestic or international air terminals

● **Ansett Australia** 501 Swanston Street, Melbourne, Victoria (tel: 03 9623 3333 or 13 1300).
● **Qantas Airways** 203 Coward Street, Mascot, N.S.W. 2020 (tel: 02 9691 3636 or 13 1313).

By car Australia's roads are of variable quality. In the metropolitan areas around the great cities they compare well with those anywhere in the developed world, while in remote areas they may consist of dirt tracks liable to disappear altogether in the Wet. Expressways are confined to relatively short sections leading out of the major cities. Most main roads have two lanes, although some still consist of a single strip of bitumen with gravel shoulders and others are made entirely of gravel. The asphalting of main roads in Western Australia and the Northern Territory has made it possible to drive all around the country "on the bitumen."

Having your own vehicle offers the usual flexibility and independence, but you should never forget the great distances likely to be involved in any extensive traveling around Australia. The great majority of the popular tourist areas can be reached in an

Ansett Australia flights are frequently offered at discount rates

Australia is great for backpackers

ordinary car; a 4WD vehicle will be necessary only if you are contemplating extensive traveling on dirt roads in the Outback—for example, on one of the South Australian "tracks" (see page 143). A camper-van or similar vehicle offers even more flexibility.

An alternative to renting a vehicle (see Car rental on page 253) is to buy one, especially if your stay is going to be a long one. Secondhand vehicles can be obtained in the usual ways (dealers, auctions and so on), or from your fellow travelers. Noticeboards in backpackers' lodges may be a useful source of information here, and in some places dusty camper-vans displaying hopeful prices are lined up on the street. The stress of disposing of your vehicle at the end of your stay can be alleviated by purchasing it from a dealer who offers a guaranteed buy-back, although obviously this will not be the cheapest way.

By train A railroad map of Australia seems incomplete, with huge areas empty of any trace of tracks. However, the big cities are accessible by train, and some Australian rail journeys count among the great railroad experiences of the world. Among them are the three-night transcontinental trip aboard the *Indian Pacific* between Sydney (or Adelaide) and Perth across the Nullarbor Plain, or the famous *Ghan*, a 20-hour foray from Adelaide (with new services connecting here from Sydney and Melbourne) to Alice Springs. These, together with trains like the *Sunlander* (Brisbane–Cairns), are a relaxing way of appreciating the vastness and diversity of Australia in great comfort (ingeniously luxurious sleeping cars, fine meals, attentive service and showers).

Other railroad services are best developed in the east and southeast of the country, with extensive metropolitan networks around Sydney, Melbourne, Brisbane and Adelaide. Europeans, used to frequent services, may be surprised to find that long distance trains may run only once a day. Speeds are less impressive than standards of comfort.

Visitors from abroad can buy an **Austrailpass**, giving unlimited travel for various periods over the whole network (available only outside the country). An **Austrail Flexipass** is a better option for those who want to make more frequent stopovers.

Driving tips

The Australian smile sometimes becomes a snarl behind the wheel of a vehicle. However, road safety is improving and Australia has a fairly low road fatality rate in view of the number of vehicles and the vast distances traveled.

Drinking and driving were once very much part of ordinary life, and may still be so in Outback areas, but crackdowns (in which police use "booze buses" to conduct random tests) seem to be having an effect in major cities. The legal permitted limit for alcohol is 0.05 per cent blood alcohol level in all states and territories.

In principle, Australians drive on the left and pass on the right. However, this may not immediately be obvious on a multiple-lane highway where many drivers prefer to stay in the right-hand lane, impervious to the traffic passing them on the left. Driving down the central strip of bitumen on a partly paved highway is acceptable, but it can turn into a test of nerves as oncoming traffic approaches. The monstrous "road trains" to be encountered in Western Australia, Queensland, and the Northern Territory expect you to give way to them at all times and have no strategy for coping if you don't. Passing a road train that may be 165 feet or more long and throwing up clouds of dust can be very tricky; if you can't see a long way ahead, it's better to give up altogether.

Driving on unpaved roads requires special skills that take time to acquire. It's best to avoid these roads or take them carefully. At dawn, dusk and at night many animals stray onto the highway; "roo bars" are not fitted to vehicles just for macho reasons but to minimize the damage that a collision with a large kangaroo can cause. Don't drive in the country at night if you can avoid it.

Road signs in Australia differ from those in other countries, but their meaning is clear!

Speed limits are 50 or 60 k.p.h. (31 or 37 m.p.h.) in urban areas and 100/110 k.p.h. (62/68 m.p.h.) elsewhere unless indicated. Some road signs are peculiar to Australia, but most of these will be immediately understandable to visitors; seatbelts must be worn in both front and back seats. On some stretches of winding road, long passing places are provided that should be used by slow traffic to enable other drivers to pass, but remember that the passing traffic has the right of way.

Visitors from abroad must have a valid driver's license with a translation if the license is not in English or, better still, an international driving license. Gas is sold (by the liter) in leaded and unleaded varieties. Gas stations are fairly numerous but tend to have restricted opening hours; there may be problems in some areas with filling up on Saturday afternoons and on Sundays.

Adequate preparations must be made for driving in the Outback. The vehicle must be in good condition and it is sensible to carry a selection of spare parts, including an emergency plastic windshield. Enough fuel and water (5 quarts of drinking water a day) to see you through is essential. On some routes you may be required to complete a police form, giving your itinerary and arrival time.

In case of breakdown it is vital that you stay in or near your vehicle, for it will offer shade and protection, and will also be much more visible than you are on your own.

Electricity
Current emerges at 240/250 volts A.C. from Australian sockets, these being of a three-pin type unlike those used in most countries. You will need to bring an adapter for your appliances or fit them with an Australian plug on arrival. Most shaver points are of the universal type.

Embassies and consulates
● **British High Commission**
Commonwealth Avenue, Yarralumla, Canberra (tel: 02 6270 6666).
● **Canadian High Commission**
Commonwealth Avenue, Yarralumla, Canberra (tel: 02 6273 3844).

259

The best way to explore Simpsons Gap is on foot, but go prepared

● **New Zealand High Commission**
Commonwealth Avenue, Yarralumla,
Canberra (tel: 02 6270 4211).
● **United States Embassy** 21 Moonah
Place, Yarralumla, Canberra
(tel: 0 6270 5000).
There are U.S. consulates in Sydney
and Melbourne, and British
consulate-generals in Sydney,
Melbourne, Perth and Brisbane.

Emergency telephone numbers
For police, ambulance or fire brigade
services, dial 000.

Health
No special health precautions are
required before visiting Australia.
Standards of hygiene are high, and
food and drinking water are safe.
Sunburn is a common hazard; wear a
broad-brimmed hat, a shirt with a
collar, and apply plenty of sunscreen.
Free hospital medical treatment
under the Australian **Medicare** plan
is available to visitors from the
United Kingdom and New Zealand,
although ambulance charges and the
cost of medicines must be paid.
Medicare also covers the bulk of the
cost of a visit to a doctor. Visitors

from most other countries will need
full medical insurance. Dental
treatment has to be paid for in full.

Language
The peculiarities and delights of
Australian English are widely known
all over the English-speaking world,
not least through the efforts of the
humorist Australian Barry
Humphries, creator of Dame Edna
Everage, Sir Leslie Patterson
("Australian Cultural Attaché"), and
Barry "Bazza" McKenzie.
Having some affinities with the
English "Cockney" accent, the rather
nasal Australian accent is, however,
quite distinctive and is spoken without any real regional variation—
except for the differences between city
(which is fast) and country (which is
slow and drawn out)—throughout the
whole country. Differences in speech
are much more likely, however, to be
a matter of occasion or class; the
people you might meet in the bar on
Friday night would probably pour
scorn on what is often considered the
"posh" Australian Broadcasting
Corporation voice. In turn, their
speech would probably present difficulties to a non-native English
speaker who has conscientiously
learned the "standard" language.

*Enjoying a beaut barbie down under
with a few mates*

The Australian vocabulary contains a number of words of Aboriginal origin (mallee, didgeridoo and kangaroo), as well as plenty of invented terms to describe characteristic Australian phenomena (Outback, bottlebrush and bloodwood), and not a few English words whose original meaning has changed (creek means river, mountain ash is a kind of eucalyptus and mob is a group of people or animals). But the real joy of "Strine" (Australian) is its slang. Anything that can be reduced to a more or less affectionate diminutive, is: "barbie" means barbecue, "cossie" is a swimming suit (costume), and "garbo" is a garbage collector; and there are any number of quirky inventions (dunny is an outside toilet, while bludger is a scrounger) that may be the remnants of the slang of Georgian England. A lot of slang is sexual, scatological, or connected with heavy drinking. Terms evocative of throwing up after a binge are plentiful ("to chunder," "have a liquid laugh," "speak into the big white telephone"). Insults are common, sometimes delivered with

affectionate intent ("you old bastard"); a recently devised university course instructs "New Aussies" (new residents from abroad) on how to swear like dyed-in-the-wool Aussies.

Although Strine is based on British English, the biggest influence on it today is American English—in terms of pronunciation ("quarder" instead of quarter), of vocabulary ("take on board" and "yuppie"), and in spelling ("program"), although the A.L.P. has been the "Labor" Party since its foundation in the late 19th century.

The following is a short and a very highly selective list of words, phrases and abbreviations that a visitor might well encounter:

A.B.C.	Australian Broadcasting Corporation
A.C.T.	Australian Capital Territory (Canberra area)
The Alice	Alice Springs
A.L.P.	Australian Labor Party
A.N.Z.A.C.	Australian and New Zealand Army Corps
arvo	afternoon
barbie	barbecue

beaut	wonderful
billabong	cut-off river bend
billy	tin used for brewing tea
bloke	man
bludger	scrounger
blue	a fight, a redhead
bottle shop	liquor store
bush	countryside
bushranger	outlaw
B.Y.O.	bring your own (drink to a restaurant)
cask	wine-box
chook	chicken
chunder	to vomit
crook	ill, no good
dag, daggy	tangled dirty wool at rear end of a sheep, used abusively (or affectionately) of persons or things
daks	trousers
dinkum	genuine
drongo	a slow-witted person
Dry	the dry season
dunny	outside lavatory
fossicking	hunting, as in for precious stones
galah	a kind of parrot, an idiot
garbo	garbage collector
g'day	good morning, good afternoon, hello
greenie	conservationist
hoon	hooligan
international	foreign (as in "international visitors")
interstate	anything to do with the other Australian states ("he's interstate" means the person referred to is away from his home state)
journo	journalist
larrikin	rogue, hoodlum
mate	universal greeting
mob	group of persons or animals, for example sheep
mozzie	mosquito
Never-Never	the far-off Outback
new Australian	recent immigrant
ocker	Australian male of crude manners
pokie	poker machine, fruit machine
Pom, Pommie	English person
property	farm
rort	rowdy party or scam
R.S.L.	Returned Servicemen's League
salties	saltwater crocodiles
semi-trailer	articulated truck
Sheila	female
she'll be right	it'll all be O.K.
shout	a treat, as in buying a round of drinks
slab	24-pack of beer
smoko	work break
station	extensive farm
stingers	jellyfish
strides	pants
swag	gear or personal belongings
ta	thank you
tea	evening meal
thongs	flip-flops
tucker	food
uni	university
ute	pickup truck
Wet	rainy season
wowser	puritan, killjoy
yakka	work

261

The best food in town next to the river!

Media

Newspapers and periodicals A glance inside a newsagent's (news seller's) will be enough to convince you that Australians are great readers. The array of publications includes national and regional daily broadsheets, lurid tabloids with screaming headlines, local newspapers, and countless magazines dealing with every conceivable interest.

The Australian was founded in 1964 by media tycoon Rupert Murdoch to perform the role of a national general interest daily paper, supplementing the more specialized Australian Financial Review. Regionally produced papers like the Melbourne Age and Sydney Morning Herald are considered superior by many readers, although visitors from abroad may find coverage of non-Australian news rather selective (check how well your favorite home paper covers Australian affairs before judging them too harshly). Australian tabloids, like most such newspapers, are not of the highest standard. Most ethnic groups have dailies or weeklies in their own languages.

Television and radio Radio recalls newspapers in its divisions. The A.B.C. (Australian Broadcasting Corporation) has countrywide coverage and offers by far the best mix of broadcasting, with excellent news coverage and magazine programs. In contrast are the numerous commercial stations, many of which run on a shoestring, broadcasting pop music, phone-in shows, traffic reports and similar time-fillers. In addition, there are a number of special interest and community radio stations.

Commercial television, as elsewhere in the world, relies on advertising and imported programs (though this may enable foreign visitors to catch up on their favorite soap). A.B.C. T.V. maintains high standards generally and S.B.S. (Special Broadcasting Service, not available over the whole country) is largely devoted to programs for ethnic minorities that are broadcast in their own languages.

Money matters

The Australian currency was decimalized in 1966, when sterling (pounds, shillings and pence) was replaced by dollars and cents (100¢ = $1). Coins come in 5¢, 10¢, 20¢, 50¢, $1 and $2 denominations, and there are $5, $10, $20, $50 and $100 bills, made of durable polymer. You can take as much money as you want into and out of the country, although for amounts over A$10,000 you must complete a report form.

Changing money is rarely a problem, with plenty of exchange bureaus at places where tourists congregate, as well as at banks. Bank hours are usually 9:30–4 Mon to Thu, and 9:30–5 on Fri. Traveler's checks made out in Australian dollars are likely to be dealt with more speedily. Credit cards are widely in use, but may not be particularly welcome in remote areas or in small stores.

The Abbey Church at New Norcia, Western Australia

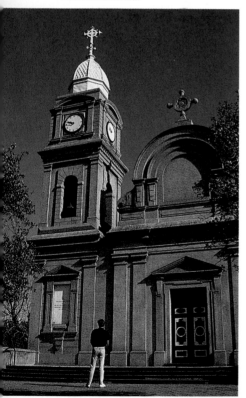

Australia Day celebrations, Sydney

National holidays
- **New Year's Day**
January 1
- **Australia Day**
Fourth Monday in January
(commemorates the landing of the
First Fleet on January 26, 1788)
- **Labor Day**
Varies from state to state—first
Monday in March, Western Australia
and Tasmania; second Monday in
March, Victoria; first Monday in May,
Northern Territory and Queensland;
first Monday in October, New South
Wales, Australian Capital Territory
and South Australia (commemorates
achievement of the eight-hour
working day)
- **Good Friday**
- **Easter Monday**
- **Anzac Day**
April 25 (commemorates Gallipoli
landings on April 25, 1915)
- **Queen's Birthday**
Second Monday in June except WA
- **Christmas Day**
December 25
- **Boxing Day**
December 26 (December 28 in South
Australia)

Opening hours
Museums and galleries Usually
closed on Christmas Day and Good
Friday, with some also closed on
Anzac Day. Major institutions are
usually open 10 AM–5 PM daily,
although they may be closed on one
day of the week. Many of the smaller
museums open only on weekends or
during school or public holidays, so
the best advice is to check opening
times before you set out.

Offices *Open* Mon–Fri, 9 AM–5 PM.

Stores These are generally open
9 AM–5 PM (or 5:30 PM) Monday to
Friday and 9 AM–4 PM on Saturday,
with late-night shopping on
Thursday or Friday until 8 PM or
9 PM. Corner stores keep longer hours
and also open on Sundays.

Pharmacies
Called both pharmacies and
"chemists," these dispense a range of
medicines and products that will
probably be familiar to you. Many
are open long hours, and you will
find a 24-hour service in big cities.
Prescriptions must be written by an
Australian-registered doctor. Prices
of pharmaceuticals are fairly high.

Places of worship
Most religions are represented in
Australia, although outside the big
cities only the major Christian deno-
minations have places of worship.
The Roman Catholic Church and the
Anglican Church have roughly the
same number of adherents; their
cathedrals were once among the
dominant buildings of city centers.
The Uniting Church was formed in

Fly fishing on London Lakes in Tasmania

1977 as a union of Methodists and Congregationalists. Islam was introduced by the Afghan camel drivers in the 19th century and there are now some two dozen mosques throughout the country. Synagogues are concentrated in the state capitals.

Police
Australia has both state and federal police, the latter (the A.F.P.) being responsible for the investigation of major crimes, intelligence work and antiterrorist activities, as well as for policing the Canberra area (A.C.T.).

The men and women in blue are usually extremely helpful to visitors from abroad, but don't expect any special privileges if you break the law (see Driving tips on pages 257–258). In the unlikely event that you are arrested, you must give your name and address, but are then entitled to say nothing until you have contacted a friend or legal representative. In this situation, the best thing to do is to ask to be put in touch with your consul (see Embassies and consulates on pages 258–259).

Post offices
The offices of Australia Post are to be found in city centers, suburban areas and all over the country, often combined with a general store in smaller places. Larger offices have a wide range of services like fax and electronic post.

Services are reasonably efficient. Airmail letters can arrive in Great Britain or the U.S. after a few days, provided the correct rate has been paid and the letter or postcard is clearly addressed. A package sent by surface mail to Europe will undergo an interminable sea voyage. An alternative to paying the full airmail charge in this case is to send it Economy Air, which should ensure its arrival in the U.K. or U.S. after two to four weeks. Post offices usually have a good range of stationery and packaging material for sale, and poste restante and telegram facilities are also available. Australia's rectangular mail boxes are painted red with a white stripe or yellow for the special express post service.

Public transportation
The sprawl of low-density suburbs surrounding major cities is not conducive to the operation of an effective public transportation system, and Australians have become very dependent on cars for work, shopping, and recreational trips. However, city public transportation services based on bus, rail, tram (Melbourne), and ferry (Sydney and Brisbane), are surprisingly extensive, frequent and efficient, albeit a heavy drain on the

public purse. Most systems offer special deals that are likely to be of interest to a tourist (day tickets covering the whole network, reduced fares for travel outside the rush hour and so on). Further details are given in the travel sections within each chapter. For long-distance transportation, see Domestic travel on pages 256–257.

Student and youth travel

There are relatively few official concessions in Australia for young visitors from abroad, but given the relative cheapness of the country this is not a problem. Accommodation is provided by the countless hostels and backpackers' lodges. Membership in your national Youth Hostels Association may get you the occasional discount and also entitles you to use Australian youth hostels. Long-distance travel by bus is not expensive, and hitchhiking is easier than in many countries, although not entirely without danger. The noticeboards in lodges and hostels are a good source of information on carsharing and on what is available in terms of meals, excursions and entertainment. Working vacations, once very popular, have become less feasible in harder economic times. **S.T.A. Travel**, a specialist in youth travel, may be able to help here, as well as with other travel arrangements; they have offices in the U.S. at 5900 Wilshire Boulevard, Suite 2110, Los Angeles, CA 90036 (tel: 800/825 3001, 1800/925 4777) as well as in Australia.

Telephones

The public telephones of Telstra are easy to find in most places. Long-distance, or STD (Subscriber Trunk Dialling) calls can be made from most telephone booths; international calls can be made from booths designated I.S.D. (International Subscriber Dialling). Many machines take phone or credit cards. Local calls have no time limit, while interstate calls are relatively inexpensive given the distances involved. Inexpensive rates apply between 7 PM and 7 AM on weekdays and all weekend. Be warned that hotels frequently double the cost of a call made from your room.

To call an Australian number from overseas, dial the international access code, the country code for Australia (61), the local code (minus the initial 0), then finally the subscriber's number. To call an overseas number from Australia, dial the international access code (0011), the country code (U.S.: 1; U.K.: 44), the local code (minus its initial 0), then finally the subscriber's number. It is also worth working out the time disparity between home and Australia (see Time below).

Time

The enormous width of Australia has resulted in the creation of three time zones. Eastern Standard Time (E.S.T.) applies to New South Wales, A.C.T., Victoria, Tasmania and Queensland; Central Standard Time (C.S.T.) to South Australia and the Northern Territory; and Western Standard Time (W.S.T.) to Western Australia. C.S.T. is half an hour behind E.S.T., while W.S.T. is two hours behind. Daylight Saving time is practiced in all states except Queensland, the N.T. and Western Australia, from October or November through March, when clocks are advanced one hour.

Wading on Bondi Beach

Eastern Standard Time (Australia) is 10 hours ahead of Greenwich Mean Time, and 15 hours ahead of U.S. Eastern Standard Time.

Tipping
Tipping is not common in Australia —for example, tips are not expected by taxi drivers, airport porters and hairdressers. Railway porters have set charges and hotel porters can be tipped at your discretion. Service charges are not normally added to restaurant bills; given good service you might leave a tip of 10 percent.

Tourist information
The Australian Tourist Commission provides information on individual states and the country as a whole from its offices abroad (see below), while each state has its own Tourism Board with headquarters in the state capital, and offices in some other state capitals. Places of any size in Australia have one or more information centers, with plenty of material on local attractions and reservation facilities for accommodations and excursions. The advice given may not always be impartial, however, since the center may have links with the

services it recommends. Other useful sources of information are motoring organizations, which give out free maps for members of allied organizations abroad, and the visitor centers or offices of the National Parks and Wildlife Service.

Australian Tourist Commission:
● **New Zealand**: Level 13, 44–48 Emily Place, Auckland 1 (tel: 09 379 9594).
● **U.K.**: 1st Floor, Gemini House, 10–18 Putney Hill, London SW15 6AA (tel: 0181-780 2229).
● **U.S.A.**: 2049 Century Park East, Suite 1920, Los Angeles, CA 90067 (tel: 310/229 4870).

Washrooms
Australian cities are exceptionally well provided with public lavatories, that are usually very clean. City maps often make a point of identifying their location.

Women
Australia is reasonably safe for women, and female travelers should encounter no special problems, although the more extreme manifestations of "ockerism" (see Language on page 259–61) may be irritating.

The Northern Territory Tourist Commission will provide information on sights of interest such as the Devils Marbles

Accommodations & Restaurants

ACCOMMODATIONS

The wide variety of accommodations available in Australia ranges from some of the world's finest and most luxurious hotels through motels, "units" (equipped apartments), "hotels" (which may be the most basic of inns), to backpackers' hostels. You are rarely likely to have difficulty in finding somewhere to stay, although it's advisable to reserve in advance during the peak seasons (July through September and December through February). Prices compare very favorably with those in other developed parts of the world, and discounts can often be obtained for longer stays or if you use hotels in a particular chain.

The following recommended hotels have been divided into three price categories:

($) = budget
($$) = moderate
($$$) = expensive

SYDNEY

Aarons Hotel ($–$$)
37 Ultimo Road, Haymarket
tel: 02 9281 5555
Better than average budget accommodations near Darling Harbour and Chinatown.

ANA Hotel Sydney ($$$)
176 Cumberland Street, The Rocks
tel: 02 9250 6000
This large Japanese-owned high-rise hotel offers superb service and facilities. Located close to The Rocks and with fantastic views.

Chateau Sydney ($$)
14 Macleay Street, Potts Point
tel: 02 9358 2500
In the Kings Cross area, with a pool, good facilities and views of the harbor.

Citistay Westend Hotel ($–$$)
412 Pitt Street tel: 02 9211 4822
Very reasonably priced city center hotel, with easy access to the stores, the George Street entertainment district, and Darling Harbour.

Cremorne Point Manor ($–$$)
6 Cremorne Road, Cremorne Point
tel: 02 9953 7899
A charming old mansion just a short ferry ride from the city center. Good value.

Harbour Rocks Hotel ($$)
34 Harrington Street, The Rocks
tel: 02 9251 8944
This medium-sized hotel is situated in an excellent location in the heart of The Rocks.

Hotel Ibis Darling Harbour ($$)
70 Murray Street, Pyrmont
tel: 02 9563 0888
Good value accommodation on the western side of Darling Harbour. The hotel has good views, as well as its own restaurant and bar.

Hotel Inter-Continental Sydney ($$$)
117 Macquarie Street tel: 02 9230 0200
Partly housed in the restored Treasury Building dating from 1851, the hotel occupies a landmark site on historic Macquarie Street, close to Circular Quay and the Opera House.

Hotel Nikko Darling Harbour ($$$)
Corner Sussex and King streets
tel: 02 9299 1231
A glossy modern five-star hotel overlooking Darling Harbour and close to the city center.

Manhattan Park Inn International ($$)
8 Greenknowe Avenue, Elizabeth Bay
tel: 02 9358 1288
The rooms in this reasonably priced art deco hotel feature a T.V., fridge, and coffee-making facilities. The Manhattan is located close to the heart of lively Kings Cross.

Manly Beach Resort ($)
6 Carlton Street, Manly tel: 02 9977 4188
This budget hotel is a short distance from all the attractions of Manly and its popular beach.

Manly Pacific Parkroyal ($$$)
55 North Steyne, Manly tel: 02 9977 7666
This Pacific Parkroyal hotel has a beachfront location in Sydney's seaside resort of Manly, only a short ferry trip from the city center.

Millenium Hotel Sydney ($$$)
Top of William Street, Kings Cross
tel: 02 9356 1234
In the heart of the Kings Cross nightlife precinct, the Millenium has good facilities, two restaurants and city and harbor views.

Oakford Apartments ($$)
10 Wylde Street, Potts Point
tel: 02 9358 4544
Comfortable self-contained apartments with water views in the Kings Cross area.

The Observatory Hotel ($$$)
89–113 Kent Street tel: 02 9256 2222
Situated close to The Rocks area, this is one of Sydney's most luxurious boutique hotels.

Oxford Koala Hotel & Apartments ($$)
Corner of Oxford and Pelican Streets,
Darlinghurst tel: 02 9269 0645
Close to the city center in trendy Darlinghurst, this large complex offers both standard hotel rooms and apartments with kitchens.

Park Hyatt Sydney ($$$)
7 Hickson Road, The Rocks
tel: 02 9241 1234
Sydney's most expensive hotel in a superb location around the edge of the harbor.

Ravesi's on Bondi Beach ($$)
Corner of Campbell Parade and Hall Street,
Bondi Beach tel: 02 9365 4422
Small and interesting boutique-style hotel overlooking world-famous Bondi Beach. The restaurant is excellent.

The Regent Hotel Sydney ($$$)
199 George Street tel: 02 9238 0000
Situated near The Rocks, The Regent has terrific views of the harbor and city.

The Russell Hotel ($$)
143a George Street, The Rocks
tel: 02 9241 3543
In a charming 19th-century Rocks building, this small guesthouse-style hotel is known for its good service and beautifully decorated rooms.

Sebel of Sydney ($$–$$$)
23 Elizabeth Bay Road, Elizabeth Bay
tel: 02 9358 3244
Not far from Kings Cross, this intimate hotel is where the visiting rich and famous stay.

Sir Stamford Double Bay ($$$)
22 Knox Street, Double Bay
tel: 02 9363 0100
This upscale boutique-style hotel is located in one of the city's most exclusive inner suburbs.
Star City ($$$)
80 Pyrmont Street, Pyrmont
tel: 02 9777 9000
Part of Sydney's vast casino complex near Darling Harbour. The first-class facilities include a health club, pool and restaurants.
Sydney Central YHA ($)
corner of Pitt Street and Rawson Place
tel: 02 9281 9111
Close to Central Station, this is the world's biggest youth hostel (530 beds). It offers a licensed café and rooftop pool/barbecue area.
Victoria Court Hotel ($$)
122 Victoria Street, Potts Point
tel: 02 9357 3200
This delightful Victorian-style guesthouse is located in a leafy street near Kings Cross.
Wynyard Vista Hotel ($$)
7–9 York Street tel: 02 9274 1222
Situated close to Circular Quay, Wynyard bus station and the city's business area.

CANBERRA (A.C.T.)

Brassey Hotel ($$)
Belmore Gardens, Braddon tel: 02 6273 3766
Established in 1927, and set in attractive gardens, this elegant hotel is close to Parliament House and the attractions south of the lake.
Hyatt Hotel Canberra ($$$)
Commonwealth Avenue, Yarralumla
tel: 02 6270 1234
Canberra's best hotel. Excellent service and full facilities in this restored art deco building.
Macquarie Hotel ($)
18 National Circuit, Barton tel: 02 6273 2325
Situated in a peaceful suburb within walking distance of Parliament House.
Olims Canberra Hotel ($$)
Corner Ainslie and Limestone avenues,
Braddon tel: 02 6248 5511
Good quality accommodations at a reasonable price, and located close to the city center.
Rydges Canberra ($$–$$$)
London Circuit, Canberra City
tel: 02 6247 6244
Close to the center and with great views.
Tall Trees Motel ($$)
21 Stephen Street, Ainslie
tel: 02 6247 9200
A short distance from the city center in a quiet and attractively landscaped setting.

NEW SOUTH WALES

Blue Mountains

Balmoral Guest House ($$)
196 Bathurst Road, Katoomba
tel: 02 4782 2264
Dating from 1876, this is the region's oldest guesthouse. Beautifully restored, it offers Victorian-style splendor complete with log fires.

Fairmont Resort ($$$)
1 Sublime Point Road, Leura
tel: 02 4782 5222
Excellent accommodations as well as good recreation facilities in this modern resort. There are also some wonderful clifftop views.
Jemby Rinjah Lodge ($$)
336 Evans Lookout Road, Blackheath
tel: 02 4787 7622
The accommodations are in timber cabins, some of which are self-catering, and the lodge, located right next to the Blue Mountains National Park, includes an excellent restaurant.
Jenolan Caves House ($$$)
Jenolan Caves tel: 02 6359 3322
A rambling and very comfortable 19th-century survivor in Tudor style dating from the days of mountain lodge vacations.
Lilianfels Blue Mountains ($$$)
Lilianfels Avenue, Echo Point, Katoomba
tel: 02 4780 1200
The most exclusive place to stay in the Blue Mountains. The original 1890s home now houses an award-winning restaurant.
Mountain Heritage Country House Retreat ($$)
Corner of Apex and Lovel streets, Katoomba
tel: 02 4782 2155
A charming old-style hotel, with log fires, comfortable rooms, and some excellent views.

Hunter Valley

Peppers Guest House Hunter Valley ($$–$$$)
Ekerts Road, Pokolbin tel: 02 4998 7596
The colonial-style Peppers consistently receives awards for its comfort, facilities, hospitality and the excellent food in its restaurant.
Vineyard Hill Country Motel ($$)
Lovedale Road, Pokolbin tel: 02 4990 4166
With great views of the valley, this good-value motel provides comfortable one- and two-bedroom units, each with its own private deck.

Southern Highlands

Links House Small Hotel ($$)
17 Links Road, Bowral tel: 02 4861 1977
In a quiet position opposite the local golf course, this friendly hotel provides a garden and tennis court, pleasant rooms, two lounge areas with log fires, and a popular restaurant.
Mercure Grand Bowral Heritage Park ($$)
9 Kangaloon Road, Bowral
tel: 02 4861 4833
This award-winning hotel offers a full range of resort facilities, including large gardens, tennis, croquet, golf and billiards.
Milton Park Country House Hotel ($$$)
Hordern's Road, Bowral tel: 02 4861 1522
This prestigious country hotel is set in splendid grounds and has good facilities and fine dining.
Peppers Mount Broughton ($$$)
Kater Road, Sutton Forest
tel: 02 4868 2355
A delightful boutique hotel with spacious rooms and suites and a fine restaurant. The property, surrounded by gardens, is next to a golf course.

VICTORIA

Melbourne

Albany Motel ($)
Corner Toorak Road and Millswyn Street,
South Yarra tel: 03 9866 4485
Budget-priced accommodations in the normally
more expensive South Yarra area of the city.

All Seasons Crossley ($$–$$$)
51 Little Bourke Street tel: 03 9639 1639
Modern "boutique" hotel with good facilities.

Batmans Hill Hotel ($$)
66–70 Spencer Street tel: 03 9614 6344
Located opposite Spencer Street Station
behind a fully restored historic façade.

Centra St. Kilda Road ($$)
Corner St. Kilda Road and Park Street
tel: 03 9209 9888
Opposite the Botanic Gardens and close to
the Arts Centre: good value in a prime location.

City Limits Motel ($)
20–22 Little Bourke Street
tel: 03 9662 2544
In the heart of the city center, this is a budget-
priced hotel that provides no-frills comforts.

City Park Hotel ($–$$)
308–10 Kingsway, South Melbourne
tel: 03 9686 0000
Reasonably priced accommodations, close to
the city's Botanic Gardens.

Georgian Court Guest House ($)
21–25 George Street, East Melbourne
tel: 03 9419 6353
This guesthouse is located in the exclusive and
attractive area of East Melbourne, and is within
easy walking distance of the city center.

Grand Hyatt Melbourne ($$$)
123 Collins Street tel: 03 9657 1234
Probably the most luxurious hotel in the city
center, the Hyatt offers a full range of facilities.

Hotel Grand Chancellor Melbourne ($$)
131 Lonsdale Street tel: 03 9663 3161
A centrally located hotel that offers good
service and facilities at reasonable rates.

The Hotel Y ($–$$)
489 Elizabeth Street tel: 03 9329 5188
One of Melbourne's best budget accommodations, located opposite Queen Victoria Market.

Le Meridien at Rialto Melbourne ($$$)
495 Collins Street tel: 03 9620 9111
Splendidly Gothic late 19th-century hotel with
all the usual comforts you would expect.

Lygon Lodge Carlton ($$)
220 Lygon Street, Carlton tel: 03 9663 6633
This high standard motel in the inner suburb of
Carlton (a short distance north of the city) represents good value accommodation.

Magnolia Court Boutique Hotel ($$)
101 Powlett Street, East Melbourne
tel: 03 9419 4222
An elegant small hotel is just east of the city
center, close to the Melbourne Cricket Ground.

Marco Polo Inn ($$)
Corner Harker Street and Flemington Road,
North Melbourne tel: 03 9329 1788
A mile or so north of the city, this good-quality
hotel also offers a pool and restaurant.

Novotel Bayside Melbourne ($$)
16 The Esplanade, St Kilda
tel: 03 9525 5522
Overlooking Port Phillip Bay in the cosmopoli-
tan suburb of St Kilda, this 200-room hotel
features a heated pool, spa and gymnasium.

Oakford Gordon Place ($$–$$$)
24 Little Bourke Street tel: 03 9663 2888
Oakford's luxuriously appointed apartments
open onto a vine-clad interior courtyard with a
huge palm tree. The historic building also
offers a deli, a bar and a Places Restaurant.

Parkroyal on St. Kilda Road ($$–$$$)
562 St. Kilda Road, St. Kilda
tel: 03 9529 8888
A boutique-style hotel with large rooms and
excellent service. Located a short tram ride
from the center, this Parkroyal is in one of
Melbourne's most interesting inner suburbs.

Punt Hill Serviced Apartments ($$)
115 Flemington Road, North Melbourne
tel: 03 9820 9911
These fully-equipped one-, two- or three-
bedroom apartments or studios are located
just to the north of the city center.

Rockman's Regency Hotel ($$$)
Corner Exhibition and Lonsdale streets
tel: 03 9662 3900
Melbourne's most luxurious boutique hotel is
close to the center. Excellent facilities and, in
addition, upmarket bars and restaurants.

Sheraton Towers Southgate ($$$)
1 Southgate Avenue, Southbank
tel: 03 9696 3100
Part of the lively Southgate complex, this excellent hotel provides a high standard of rooms,
facilities and service.

South Yarra Hill Suites ($$–$$$)
14 Murphy Street, South Yarra
tel: 03 9868 8222
These serviced one- to three-bedroom apartment come complete with fully equipped
kitchens and spacious living rooms.

Victoria Hotel ($$)
215 Little Collins Street tel: 03 9653 0441
This comfortable turn-of-the-century hotel is
located in the city center and has become a
Melbourne institution.

The Windsor ($$$)
103 Spring Street tel: 03 9633 6000
This grand old hotel, opposite Parliament
House, has been splendidly restored. It has
been classified by the National Trust.

Great Ocean Road

Caledonian Inn ($)
Corner Bank and James streets, Port Fairy
tel: 03 5568 1044
With its bar and seafood lounge, the
Caledonian Inn claims to be the oldest
continuously licensed hotel in Victoria. No such
claim is made for the motel section.

Cumberland Lorne Resort ($$$)
150 Mountjoy Parade, Lorne
tel: 03 5289 2400
An award-winning luxury apartment resort in the
center of this well-established seaside resort.

Erskine House ($$)
136 Mountjoy Parade, Lorne
tel: 03 5289 1209
Rudyard Kipling stayed in this hotel, situated among immaculately maintained gardens.
Seacombe House Motor Inn ($$)
22 Sackville Street, Port Fairy
tel: 03 5568 1082
An old building in a delightful harbor town, Seacombe House is National Trust classified, but the Inn consists of modern motel units.

Northeast Victoria

Eucalpyt Ridge ($$$)
564 Skyline Road, Eildon tel: 03 5774 2033
An upscale mountain lodge with views of Lake Eildon. Elegant suites and fine dining, with 250 acres of bushland and a national park nearby.
Mount Buffalo Chalet ($$)
Mount Buffalo National Park
tel: 03 5755 1500
A splendidly old-fashioned Alpine-style establishment situated in the exhilarating surroundings of this mountain national park.
Mount Buller Chalet Hotel ($$$)
Summit Road, Mount Buller
tel: 03 5777 6566
Open all year and the ideal base for winter skiing or summer alpine walking, this 65-room hotel offers many top facilities, including a sports center, a restaurant and a cocktail bar.
Rose Cottage ($$)
42 Camp Street, Beechworth
tel: 03 5728 1069
Bed and breakfast style accommodations in a charming, atmospheric old cottage.
Tanswells Commercial Hotel ($)
50 Ford Street, Beechworth
tel: 03 5728 1480
This 19th-century hotel has fine iron-work and is authentically furnished. The building has been National Trust-classified.
Trackers Mountain Lodge ($$–$$$)
88 Schuss Street, Falls Creek
tel: 03 5758 3346
Luxurious accommodations in one of the country's most popular ski resorts. Also perfect for walking, horse-riding, or fishing in summer

SOUTH AUSTRALIA

Adelaide

Apartments on the Park ($$)
274 South Terrace tel: 08 8223 0599
Self-contained units at the south of town. The apartments are ideal for families or groups.
Adelaide Barron Townhouse Motel ($$)
Corner of Hindley and Morphett streets
tel: 08 8211 8255
This hotel provides apartments in a very convenient and central location.
Centra Adelaide ($$)
208–223 South Terrace tel: 08 8223 2744
Overlooking the southern parklands, this reasonably priced hotel features a pool, restaurant and good facilities and service.

Festival Lodge Motel ($)
140 North Terrace tel: 08 8212 7877
Reasonably priced motel-style accommodations in Adelaide's most famous street.
Hilton Adelaide ($$$)
233 Victoria Square tel: 08 8217 2000
The usual good standards of the Hilton group, this time right in the very heart of the city.
Hindley Parkroyal ($$–$$$)
65 Hindley Street tel: 08 8231 5552
A good-quality hotel with a pool, spa and restaurant, situated on one of Adelaide's main restaurant and nightlife streets.
Hotel Adelaide International ($$)
62 Brougham Place, North Adelaide
tel: 08 8267 3444
A short walk from the city center and the O'Connell Street café and shopping strip, this good value hotel also has excellent city views.
Hyatt Regency Adelaide ($$$)
North Terrace tel: 08 8231 1234
Decorated with stunning works of art, the Hyatt is the city's most sumptuous hotel, centrally located near major attractions.
The Mansions Quest Inn ($$)
21 Pulteney Street tel: 08 8232 0033
A well-located hotel with self-contained apartments in an interesting old building.
North Adelaide Heritage Apartments ($$–$$$)
tel: 08 8272 1355
A superb collection of self-contained heritage apartments in the refined suburb of North Adelaide. The choices include everything from cosy cottages to an old chapel and even an imaginatively renovated fire station.
Stamford Grand Adelaide ($$$)
Moseley Square, Glenelg tel: 08 8376 1222
The best hotel in Adelaide's most famous beach suburb—a short and pleasant tram ride from the city center.
Stamford Plaza Adelaide ($$$)
150 North Terrace tel: 08 8461 1111
Adelaide's most elegant hotel offers superb views, excellent service and tastefully decorated rooms and suites.

Adelaide Hills

Grand Mercure Hotel Mount Lofty House ($$$)
74 Summit Road, Crafers tel: 08 8339 6777
Luxury country house living, South Australian style. The hotel is located just below the summit of Mount Lofty only a short drive from the city. There is also a gourmet restaurant.
Hahndorf Resort & Convention Centre ($–$$)
145a Main Street, Hahndorf
tel: 08 8388 7921
With both motel-style units and spacious chalets, plus large grounds that include a pool and canoeing lake, this is a good choice for a Hahndorf stay.
Panmure Estate ($$–$$$)
32 Sturt Valley Road, Stirling
tel: 08 8339 6655
One of the area's finest bed and breakfast establishments, Panmure offers luxurious suites, gourmet meals and a delightful garden.

Accommodations and Restaurants

Barossa Valley

All Seasons Premier Barossa Valley Resort ($$–$$$)
Golf Links Road, Rowland Flat
tel: 08 8524 0000
A good alternative to motel or bed and break-fast accommodation. Facilities include two restaurants, a pool, tennis courts, and easy access to an 18-hole golf course.
Collingrove Homestead ($$–$$$)
Eden Valley Road, Angaston
tel: 08 8564 2061
A fine National Trust property on the edge of the Barossa, once the home of one of Australia's greatest landowning families. Dinner is available by arrangement.
Lawley Farm ($$)
Krondorf Road, Tanunda tel: 08 8563 2141
This rustic bed and breakfast establishment has six self-contained suites, some of which have their own private spa.
Tanunda Hotel ($)
51 Murray Street, Tanunda tel: 08 8563 2030
Budget accommodations in a historic pub in the often expensive Barossa Valley area.

WESTERN AUSTRALIA

Perth

Baileys Parkside Motel ($)
150 Bennett Street tel: 08 9325 3788
These budget-priced self-contained units are centrally located—family units and suites.
Burswood International Resort Hotel and Casino ($$$)
Great Eastern Highway, Rivervale
tel: 08 9362 7777
On the far bank of the Swan River from the city center, this is a luxury resort with its own golf course. The casino is one of the largest in the southern hemisphere.
Chateau Commodore Hotel ($$)
417 Hay Street tel: 08 9325 0461
Good quality accommodations at a reasonable price close to the city's business district. The hotel has a swimming pool and restaurant.
City Waters Lodge ($–$$)
118 Terrace Road tel: 08 9325 1566
Self-contained apartments by the Swan River.
Cottesloe Beach Hotel ($–$$)
104 Marine Parade, Cottesloe
tel: 08 9383 1100
Just 15 minutes drive from the city, this beach-side pub provides good-value accomodations, as well as bars and a café.
Hyatt Regency Perth ($$$)
99 Adelaide Terrace, East Perth
tel: 08 9225 1234
One of the city's best hotels, the Hyatt Regency is located just to the east of the city center and overlooks the Swan River.
Metro Inn Apartments ($)
22 Nile Street, East Perth
tel: 08 9325 1866
Budget self-contained apartments and hotel rooms, close to the city center and the river.

Miss Maud Swedish Hotel ($$)
97 Murray Street tel: 08 9325 3900
Scandinavian chic in a handy city center loca-tion. Miss Maud also provides good and reasonably priced eating.
Parkroyal Perth ($$$)
54 Terrace Road tel: 08 9325 3811
Luxury accommodations in the heart of the city, yet with good views of the Swan River.
Parmelia Hilton ($$$)
14 Mill Street tel: 08 9322 3622
One of the most individual of all the hotels in the Hilton chain, located right in the city center.
Rendezvous Observation City Hotel ($$$)
The Esplanade, Scarborough
tel: 08 9245 1000
A luxurious five-star resort on the boardwalk at Scarborough beach, just a 15-minute drive from the city center.
Riverview on Mount Street ($)
42 Mount Street tel: 08 9321 8963
Self-contained studio apartments, complete with cooking facilities. Situated close to both the city center and Kings Park.
The Royal Hotel ($)
Corner Wellington and William streets
tel: 08 9324 1510
A pub-style hotel in the city center with both self-contained and shared facility rooms.
Sheraton Perth Hotel ($$$)
207 Adelaide Terrace tel: 08 9224 7777
Sheraton comforts and conveniences on one of Perth's main arteries.
Sullivans Hotel ($$)
166 Mounts Bay Road tel: 08 9321 8022
A small, friendly hotel that is at the edge of Kings Park. Some rooms have river views.
Terrace Hotel ($$)
195 Adelaide Terrace tel: 08 9492 7777
An affordable option to the nearby Sheraton.

Fremantle

Esplanade Hotel Fremantle ($$$)
Corner of Marine Terrace and Essex Street
tel: 08 9432 4000
This international standard hotel is situated in the heart of historic Fremantle. Rooms, studios and suites are available, and the hotel also has excellent recreation and dining facilities.
Tradewinds Hotel ($$)
59 Canning Highway, East Fremantle
tel: 08 9339 8188
Overlooking the Swan River, a short walk from central Fremantle, this hotel provides self-contained apartments that are serviced daily.

Kalgoorlie–Boulder

Hannan's View Motel ($$)
430 Hannan Street, Kalgoorlie
tel: 08 9091 3333
Recommended central motel.
Mercure Hotel Plaza Kalgoorlie ($$)
45 Egan Street, Kalgoorlie
tel: 08 9021 4544
Claimed to be the finest hotel in town. Good comforts and facilities. Reasonably central.

York Hotel ($–$$)
259 Hannan Street, Kalgoorlie
tel: 08 9021 2337
This is a splendid hotel from the early 1900s, with an authentic feel of the gold-rush days including darkly furnished rooms and balcony bathrooms. The restaurant will even serve you chops and steak for breakfast.

Other historic hotels in Kalgoorlie/Boulder include the **Exchange** on Hannan Street (tel: 08 9021 2833) and the **Palace**, also on Hannan Street (tel: 08 9021 2788).

NORTHERN TERRITORY

Darwin

Carlton Hotel Darwin ($$$)
The Esplanade tel: 08 8980 0800
Housed in a pink and blue post-modern complex on Darwin's Esplanade, the luxury Carlton is one of the more striking additions to the city's post-Tracy skyline. Comfortable rooms, excellent service and good restaurants here, including the sophisticated Siggi's.
Capricornia Motel ($)
44 East Point Road, Fannie Bay
tel: 08 8981 4055
Comfortable and well priced units, situated just out of the town center. The motel has a restaurant and a swimming pool.
Centra Darwin ($$–$$$)
122 The Esplanade tel: 08 8981 5388
A good quality modern hotel on the waterfront.
Cherry Blossom Motel ($)
108 The Esplanade tel: 08 8981 6734
This motel provides acceptable accommodations in an excellent Esplanade location that is convenient for the city center.
City Gardens Apartments ($$)
93 Woods Street tel: 08 8941 2888
Centrally located complex that offers apartments and family units, as well as a swimming pool and barbecue area.
MGM Grand Darwin ($$$)
Gilruth Avenue, The Gardens
tel: 08 8943 8888
This deluxe hotel that is part of Darwin's casino complex has a good location on the beach, just out of the city center.
Novotel Atrium Hotel Darwin ($$–$$$)
Corner Peel Street and The Esplanade
tel: 08 8941 0755
This medium-sized modern hotel has good facilities and service. The rooms vary from standard to deluxe suites. A great position.
Poinciana Inn ($$)
Corner Mitchell and McLachlan streets
tel: 08 8981 8111
Good-value single to family rooms, just a five-minute walk from the city center.
Rydges Plaza Darwin ($$$)
32 Mitchell Street tel: 08 8982 0000
The tallest building in Darwin, the Plaza has a cool and spacious atrium that provides some welcome relief when Darwin's heat and humidity start to become too much for weary visitors.

Alice Springs

Alice Springs Resort ($$–$$$)
34 Stott Terrace tel: 08 8952 6699
This attractive resort-style accommodation has both family, standard, and deluxe categories.
Alice Tourist Apartments ($)
Corner Gap Road and Gnoilya Street
tel: 08 8952 2788
Good value one and two-bedroom apartments. The small complex is just out of town and provides a pool and full cooking facilities.
All Seasons Frontier Oasis Alice Springs ($$)
10 Gap Road tel: 08 8952 1444
Well located motel-style accommodations with good facilities, including pool and gardens.
Fortland Diplomat Hotel ($–$$)
Corner Gregory Terrace and Hartley Street
tel: 08 8952 8977
Decorated in tasteful two-tone pink, this central hotel offers superior motel-style accommodations laid out on two levels. Executive suites with spa baths are also available.
Lasseters Hotel Casino ($$–$$$)
93 Barrett Drive tel: 08 8950 7777
This is one of the town's most up-scale hotels, and is part of the Alice Springs casino development. The hotel offers both rooms and suites.
Melanka Lodge Motel ($)
94 Todd Street tel: 08 8952 2233
Possibly the best range of inexpensive accommodations in central Australia, from basic rooms to motel-style accommodations with own bathroom. Centrally located with a licensed restaurant and two pools.
Rydges Plaza Alice Springs ($$$)
Barrett Drive tel: 08 8950 8000
Provides resort-type luxury at the foot of the stark MacDonnell Ranges, just a short distance to the south of town.

Ayers Rock

All accommodations and most other facilities at Ayers Rock are provided and managed outside the National Park at Ayers Rock Resort. You can stay in luxury at the superbly landscaped **Sails in the Desert Hotel**, in comfort at both the **Desert Gardens Hotel**, and the somewhat plainer but very affordable **Outback Pioneer Hotel**. All three can be contacted on the central resort telephone number of 08 9360 9099 Backpackers and campers are also welcome. There are restaurants in each of the hotels, all of approximately the same quality and in the same price range.

QUEENSLAND

Brisbane

Albert Park Hotel ($$)
551 Wickham Terrace, Spring Hill
tel: 07 3831 3111
A comfortable hotel located near Albert Park, a short walk from the city center. The pool and terrace overlook the park and the hotel dining room has full à la carte dining.

Accommodations and Restaurants

Camelot Motor Inn ($)
40 Astor Terrace tel: 07 3832 5115
With 70 large studio apartments that come complete with kitchenettes, this hotel represents great value close to the city center.

Centra Brisbane ($$)
Roma Street tel: 07 3238 2222
In a convenient city location, the Centra features extra-large rooms, two restaurants, four bars and spa, sauna and gym.

Conrad Treasury Brisbane ($$$)
Corner of William and George streets
tel: 07 3306 8888
Brisbane's most luxurious hotel is connected with the nearby casino—both are housed in historic sandstone buildings that have been renovated with no expense spared.

Gazebo Hotel Brisbane ($$)
345 Wickham Terrace tel: 07 3831 6177
The most prominent among the cluster of hotels on the leafy heights overlooking the city.

The Heritage ($$$)
Corner Margaret and Edward streets
tel: 07 3221 1999
A luxurious city center hotel that makes the best of its location near the waterside and the famous Botanic Gardens.

Mercure Hotel Brisbane ($$)
85–7 North Quay tel: 07 3236 3300
Overlooking the river and South Bank Parklands, this central hotel has excellent facilities, including bars, restaurants, and pool.

Metro Inn Tower Mill ($$)
239 Wickham Terrace tel: 07 3832 1421
With views over the city from high on Wickham Terrace, this comfortable hotel has balconies, a cocktail bar and 24-hour room service.

Powerhouse Boutique Hotel ($$–$$$)
Corner Kingsford Smith Drive and Hunt Street, Hamilton tel: 07 3862 1800
This elegant boutique-style hotel is conveniently close to the airport, yet only a short drive from the city. It has good facilities, including an excellent restaurant and bar.

Sheraton Brisbane Hotel and Towers ($$$)
249 Turbot Street tel: 07 3835 3535
All the luxury of a Sheraton hotel located in the heart of the city.

Story Bridge Motor Inn ($$)
321 Main Street, Kangaroo Point
tel: 07 3393 1433
Across the river from the city center, this well-priced hotel consists of modern self-contained units and two-bedroom apartments.

Sunshine Coast

Hyatt Regency Coolum ($$$)
Warran Road, Coolum Beach
tel: 07 5446 1234
A self-contained and luxurious resort with a variety of different types of accommodations, as well as a wide range of sports and recreational facilities. Located between Mount Coolum National Park and the glorious sands of the Sunshine Coast. Among the places to eat, FishTales offers fine seafood cuisine. Enquire about bargains and special offers.

Netanya Noosa Resort ($$)
75 Hastings Street, Noosa Heads
tel: 07 5447 4722
A delightful resort right on the boardwalk. All suites have a balcony and kitchenette, and the hotel is close to a selection of restaurants.

Novotel Twin Waters Resort ($$$)
Ocean Drive, Mudjimba Beach
tel: 07 5448 8000
An exclusive resort on the Sunshine Coast, Twin Waters has a range of facilities and is located near the mouth of the Maroochy River.

Sheraton Noosa Resort ($$$)
Hastings Street, Noosa Heads
tel: 07 5449 4888
Upscale accommodations in a well designed, low-rise, resort complex. Rooms are spacious and provide spas and kitchenettes.

Sun Lagoon ($$)
Quamby Place, Noosa Sound
tel: 07 5447 4833
This waterfront resort is on the Noosa River and provides fully equipped self-contained apartments that can accommodate up to six people. Good value in an excellent location.

Noosa has a variety of accommodations, mostly in pleasing modern buildings. Details can be obtained from: **Accom Noosa**, Hastings Street, Noosa Heads, P.O. Box 694, Noosa, Qld 4567 (tel: 07 5447 3444).

Gold Coast and Hinterland

ANA Hotel Gold Coast ($$$)
22 View Avenue, Surfers Paradise
tel: 07 5579 1000
In the heart of Surfers Paradise, near the beach, this 22-story 400-room hotel offers bars, restaurants, two pools and tennis courts.

Conrad Jupiters ($$$)
Broadbeach Island tel: 07 5592 1133
With its 600-plus rooms and a 24-hour casino, this is a prime place to see and be seen.

Diamonds Resort ($$)
19 Orchid Avenue, Surfers Paradise
tel: 07 5570 1011
Diamonds is situated in the heart of Surfers Paradise, a block back from the beach. Affordable rooms, apartments, and suites.

Paros on the Beach ($$)
26 Old Burleigh Road, Surfers Paradise
tel: 07 5592 0780
Mediterranean-style apartments on the beach. There are 35 one- to three-bedroom units.

Sheraton Mirage ($$$)
Sea World Drive, Main Beach
tel: 07 5591 1488
The Sheraton is a tasteful and luxurious low-rise complex of buildings. The famous eat at the prestigious Horizons Restaurant.

In the green hills beyond the coast

Binna Burra Mountain Lodge ($$)
Beechmont, via Nerang tel: 07 5533 3622
A good alternative to O'Reilly's (see below).

O'Reilly's Rainforest Guesthouse ($$)
Lamington National Park, via Canungra
tel: 07 5544 0644
Still run by a pioneer family, O'Reilly's
Guesthouse has been welcoming people into
the mountains for over 80 years. Prices include
accommodations, meals, and activities.

Cairns and the Far North

Coconut Beach Rainforest Resort ($$$)
Cape Tribulation tel: 07 4098 0033
A unique resort in wonderful rain forest and
tropical beach surroundings.
Country Comfort Outrigger ($$)
Corner Florence and Abbott streets, Cairns
tel: 07 4051 6188
This modern interpretation of traditional north
Queensland architecture can be found just
back from the waterfront in central Cairns.
Daintree Cape Tribulation Heritage Lodge ($$)
Turpentine Road, Cooper Creek, via Mossman
tel: 07 4098 9138
A range of stylish modern units designed to fit
into their rain forest surroundings.
Garrick House ($$)
11–13 Garrick Street, Port Douglas
tel: 07 4099 5322
High-standard apartment units with all ameni-
ties in a quiet street in delightful Port Douglas.
Mercure Hotel Harbourside ($$)
209 The Esplanade, Cairns
tel: 07 4051 8999
This impeccable but rather anonymous modern
hotel is located along The Esplanade, and is an
easy walk from the center of Cairns.
Radisson Plaza at the Pier ($$$)
Pierpoint Road, Cairns tel: 07 4031 1411
The Radisson offers luxury living atop the lively
Pier Marketplace on the Cairns waterfront.
The Reef Hotel Casino ($$$)
35–41 Wharf Street tel: 07 4030 8888
This sophisticated hotel is part of the Cairns
casino development, completed in 1996. The
Reef offers butler service, fine restaurants,
tasteful décor and the ultimate in comfort.
Rihga Colonial Club Resort ($$)
18–26 Cannon Street, Manunda, Cairns
tel: 07 4053 5111
A resort-style complex a short drive from the
town center. Features include tennis courts,
pools, two restaurants, and extensive gardens.
Rydges Club Tropical Resort ($$$)
Corner Wharf and Macrossan streets,
Port Douglas tel: 07 4099 5885
Club Tropical offers total luxury—expensive,
but one of the most exotic resorts in the area.
Sebel Reef House ($$$)
99 Williams Esplanade, Palm Cove
tel: 07 4055 3633
Situated on one of the beaches north of
Cairns, this is a tropical-style resort with the
best facilities and a high reputation.
Tradewinds Esplanade Hotel ($$)
137 The Esplanade, Cairns
tel: 07 4052 1111
An attractive and central hotel with views of
Trinity Bay, gardens or the swimming pool.

TASMANIA

Hobart

Balmoral Motor Inn ($)
511 Brooker Highway, Glenorchy
tel: 03 6272 5833
Budget-priced motel units: a few minutes out of
town, but good value.
Battery Point Guest House ($$)
"Mandalay," 7 McGregor Street, Battery Point
tel: 03 6224 2111
Near Salamanca Place are the attractively con-
verted coach house and stables of "Mandalay."
Country Comfort Hadley's Hotel ($$)
34 Murray Street tel: 03 6223 4355
Good value central accommodations. The hotel
has two bars and a licensed restaurant.
Crabtree House ($$)
Crabtree Road, Crabtree, about 4 miles north
of Huonville tel: 03 6266 4227
An easy drive from Hobart down the Huon
Highway is this colonial residence, which is
beautifully furnished and provides bed and
breakfast and a sumptuous dinner.
Islington ($$)
321 Davey Street tel: 03 6223 3900
Located just outside the city center, this elegant private hotel (with just eight rooms) dates
from 1845 and features well-tended gardens
and a swimming pool.
Lenna of Hobart ($$$)
20 Runnymede Street, Battery Point
tel: 03 6232 3900
This is a Victorian villa with a modern extension
and overlooks the Derwent River.
The Lodge on Elizabeth ($$)
249 Elizabeth Street tel: 03 6231 3830
At the top end of town is the oldest residential
building in Hobart, tastefully converted.
Marquis of Hastings Hotel ($)
209 Brisbane Street, West Hobart
tel: 03 6234 3541
A somewhat forbidding 1960s red-brick building, but the accommodations are good value.
Pacific Vista Hotel ($$)
Kirby Court, West Hobart tel: 03 6234 6733
Comfortable, reasonably priced rooms in a
stunning location—just a few minutes from the
center with great views over the city.
Regent Park Apartments ($$)
17–22 Regent Street, Sandy Bay
tel: 03 6223 3200
Located near the casino, these well-appointed
self-catering apartments are ideal for small
groups and for families.
Salamanca Inn ($$$)
10 Gladstone Street tel: 03 6223 3300
Integrated with unusual sensitivity among the
old warehouses of Salamanca Place, the
Salamanca is a luxury apartment hotel.
Wrest Point Hotel Casino ($$$)
410 Sandy Bay Road, Sandy Bay
tel: 03 6225 0112
The casino's hotel provides some of the best
accommodations in Hobart, in a riverside setting. There are good dining and entertainment
facilities, and top-class service.

Cradle Mountain

Accommodations for visitors to the national park range from the chic cabins (log fires) of **Cradle Mountain Lodge** ($$) *(P.O. Box 153 Sheffield, tel: 03 6492 1303)* to a campground and bunkhouses. Farther into the park are the **Waldheim Huts** ($) which offer wilderness living with some home comforts. The wooden lodge has bars and an excellent restaurant. Possums and maybe a Tasmanian devil or two are likely to keep you company after dinner.

Launceston

Adina Place Motel Apartments ($$)
50 York Street tel: 03 6331 6866
Fully serviced self-contained apartments just a few minutes from the city center.
Ashton Gate Guest House ($)
32 High Street tel: 03 6331 6180
This elegantly restored Victorian home is a short walk from the city center and overlooks St. George's Square Park. Good value.
Colonial Motor Inn ($$)
Corner George and Elizabeth streets tel: 03 6331 6588
Once an old school, this building has been modernized and accommodations added, to say nothing of the Quill and Cane restaurant.
Country Club Casino ($$$)
Country Club Avenue, Prospect Vale tel: 03 6344 8855
Although situated some distance from the city, this pricey international standard resort and casino is a great place to stay. A golf course, horseback-riding, and fishing are on offer.
Kilmarnock House ($$)
66 Elphin Road tel: 03 6334 1514
With National Trust classification, this splendid large villa has been carefully refurbished to evoke the atmosphere of the night in 1904 when it was patronized by the Prince of Wales.
Novotel Launceston ($$)
29 Cameron Street tel: 03 6334 3434
All the services and comforts of a modern luxury hotel. Call to check for special offers.
The Old Bakery Inn ($$)
270 York Street tel: 03 6331 7900
This well-restored old inn is a member of Historic Hotels of Australia and offers accommodations along traditional lines.
Tamar River Villas ($$)
23 Elouera Street, Riverside tel: 03 6327 1022
This standard but well-priced motel offers comfortable accommodations with river views.

RESTAURANTS

Eating out is relatively inexpensive in Australia, with a wide choice of ethnic cuisines and generally excellent ingredients. Costs can be farther trimmed if you B.Y.O.—bring your own (wine or other liquor), which is allowed by many establishments. The "counter meals" served in many pubs are usually excellent value, and most places where tourists congregate have a reasonable variety of take-out outlets.

The following recommended restaurants have been divided into three price categories:

($) = budget
($$) = moderate
($$$) = expensive

SYDNEY

Arun Thai ($$)
13/39 Elizabeth Bay Road, Elizabeth Bay tel: 02 9357 7414
One of Sydney's most reliable Thai restaurants with a pleasant outdoor dining area. Convenient for the hotels of the Kings Cross area.
Balkan Continental ($$)
209 Oxford Street, Darlinghurst tel: 02 9360 4970
This meat eater's paradise specializes in grills—huge steaks of all varieties and delicious Eastern European sausages and kebabs.
Bayswater Brasserie ($$–$$$)
32 Bayswater Road, Kings Cross tel: 02 9357 2177
The best and most stylish brasserie in town. A three-course meal tends toward the expensive, but there are cheaper alternatives.
Bennelong ($$$)
Sydney Opera House, Bennelong Point tel: 02 9250 7578
The best of the Opera House's food and drink outlets, with excellent Modern Australian food served with 180° views over the harbor.
Bills ($–$$)
433 Liverpool Street, Darlinghurst tel: 02 9360 9631
A popular café in the Kings Cross area; open only during the day and serving everything from breakfasts to Modern Australian style lunches.
Borobodur ($)
123–125 Glebe Point Road, Glebe tel: 02 9660 5611
Good value and friendly service are provided in this B.Y.O. Indonesian restaurant.
Chinta Ria Temple of Love ($$)
Roof Terrace, Cockle Bay Wharf, Darling Harbour tel: 02 9264 3211
With its dramatic Asian decor and good value Malaysian food, Chinta Ria is one of the stars of the smart new Cockle Bay Wharf complex.
Doyle's On the Beach ($$$)
11 Marine Parade, Watsons Bay tel: 02 9337 2007
Classic "fish and chips" served to up to 700 diners at this, one of the world's most famous fish restaurants, with great views of the harbor. There is another branch of Doyle's at Circular Quay West (tel: 02 9252 3400).
Flavour of India ($$)
120 New South Head Road, Edgecliff tel: 02 9326 2659
Sydney is not renowned for its Indian restaurants, but this is one of the best. There are traditional and South Indian dishes, and some inventive Aussie-Indian concoctions.

Hyde Park Barracks Café ($–$$)
Queens Square, Macquarie Street
tel: 02 9223 1155
Set in the grounds of the historic Hyde Park Barracks, this long-running café is excellent for lunch or daytime snacks (closed evenings).

Jordons Seafood Restaurant ($$)
197 Harbourside, Darling Harbour
tel: 02 9281 3711
One of the best places to eat at Darling Harbour. Good seafood and an excellent atmosphere with views of the water.

Kam Fook ($$)
Market City, 9 Hay Street, Haymarket
tel: 02 9211 8988
One of Sydney's newer restaurants, the 800-seater Kam Fook specializes in seafood, and also offers some unusual options for yum cha.

Kamogawa ($$$)
Corn Exchange Building, corner Sussex and Market streets, Darling Harbour
tel: 02 9299 5533
Specializing in banquet-style cuisine, this is Sydney's most traditional Japanese restaurant.

Malaya ($$)
761 George Street tel: 02 9211 0946
This attractively decorated old-established restaurant offers good Malaysian food such as satay and sambal at reasonable prices.

Marigold Citymark ($$)
683–689 George Street, Haymarket
tel: 02 9281 3308
This large restaurant in the Chinatown area offers a wide range of predominantly Cantonese dishes. A great spot for weekend yum cha.

MCA Fish Cafe ($$)
140 George Street, The Rocks
tel: 02 9241 4253
Reasonably priced seafood, with a terrace and a view of Circular Quay and the Opera House. Located in the Museum of Contemporary Art.

Nelson Bistro ($$)
The Nelson Hotel, 232 Oxford Street, Bondi Junction tel: 02 9389 1442
Some of Sydney's best-value Modern Australian cuisine in the back of an Aussie pub.

Pier ($$$)
594 New South Head Road, Rose Bay
tel: 02 9327 6561
One of Sydney's most acclaimed seafood restaurants, right on the harbor in the Eastern Suburbs. Expensive, but perfect for a night out.

Ravesi's ($$–$$$)
Corner Campbell Parade and Hall Street, Bondi Beach tel: 02 9365 4422
Another great brasserie, this restaurant can be found in the boutique-style Ravesi's Hotel overlooking Bondi Beach.

Rockpool ($$$)
107 George Street, The Rocks
tel: 02 9252 1888
Owned by Sydney's most famous chef and restaurateur, Neil Perry, restaurant is renowned for its Modern Australian cuisine.

Rossini's Rosticceria ($)
Shop W5, Circular Quay tel: 02 9247 8026
There are harbor views to accompany Rossini's swiftly served and tasty Italian food and drink.

Sailors Thai ($–$$$)
106 George Street, The Rocks
tel: 02 9251 2466
There are two superb options at this restaurant—a noodle bar with communal cafeteria-style seating, or a much more exclusive downstairs restaurant.

The Sports Bard ($$)
32 Campbell Parade, Bondi Beach
tel: 02 9130 4582
With an excellent view of Bondi Beach, this bistro serves innovative Modern Australian food and some particularly good breakfasts.

The Summit Restaurant ($$)
Level 47, Australia Square, George Street
tel: 02 9247 9777
This revamped 1960s revolving restaurant in the city center now offers a menu that is good enough to match the magnificent views.

Suntory ($$$)
529 Kent Street tel: 02 9267 2900
Something of a Sydney institution, Suntory offers Japanese food in elegant surroundings.

Tetsuya's ($$$)
759 Darling Street, Rozelle tel: 02 9555 1017
One of Sydney's very best restaurants, Tetsuya's blends Australian, French and Japanese cuisines in stunning combinations.

277

CANBERRA (A.C.T.)

Canberra Fringe Benefits ($$)
54 Marcus Clarke Street, City
tel: 02 6247 4042
Fringe Benefits has been described by Sydneysiders as the nearest thing the capital has to a trendy Sydney brasserie.

Cavalier Carousel Restaurant ($–$$)
Red Hill Lookout, Red Hill tel: 02 6273 1808
Modern international cuisine is on offer here. In the downstairs café, there is the bonus of spectacular lake and city views.

The Chairman and Yip ($$$)
108 Bunda Street, Canberra City
tel: 02 6248 7109
A popular modern Asian restaurant that manages to blend flavors from East and West.

The Oak Room ($$$)
Hyatt Hotel Canberra, Commonwealth Avenue, Yarralumla tel: 02 6270 8977
The Oak Room provides an elegant setting for equally refined food.

Tosolini's Civic ($$)
Corner of London Circuit and East Row, Canberra City tel: 02 6247 4317
This Italian eatery serves wonderful homemade pastas and other traditional dishes.

NEW SOUTH WALES

Blue Mountains

Café Bon Ton ($$)
192 The Mall, Leura tel: 02 4782 4377
At this pleasant café you can dine on anything from snacks to a hearty breakfast or a three-course dinner. There is a fire in winter, and a garden for dining al fresco.

Cleopatra ($$$)
118 Cleopatra Street, Blackheath
tel: 02 4787 8456
Some of the best French cooking in N.S.W.
Paragon Café ($$)
65 Katoomba Street, Katoomba
tel: 02 4782 2928
A National Trust-classified building, dating from 1916, the Paragon Café is worth visiting.
Silks Brasserie ($$–$$$)
128 The Mall, Leura tel: 02 4784 2534
This brasserie has a deservedly high reputation for its Modern Australian menu.

VICTORIA

Melbourne

Arriverderci ($$)
191 Nicholson Street, Carlton
tel: 03 9347 8252
Authentic provincial Italian fare is served in this popular restaurant, just north of the city center.
Blakes ($$$)
2 Southgate, Southbank tel: 03 9699 49100
Enjoy innovative world cuisine at this stylish eatery, across the river from the city center.
Blue Train Cafe ($–$$)
Mid West Level, Southgate, Southbank
tel: 03 9696 0111
Well-priced snacks and main meals that include delicious wood-fired pizzas.
Caffe Grossi ($$)
199 Toorak Road, South Yarra
tel: 03 9827 6076
A popular Italian restaurant with great food.
Colonial Tramcar Restaurant ($$$)
tel: 03 9696 4000
Dine on Australian fare while traveling through the city in a beautifully renovated old tram car.
Dogs Bar ($–$$)
54 Acland Street, St Kilda tel: 03 9525 3599
Great for coffee and cake or a good-value meal.
Donovans ($$$)
40 Jacka Boulevard, St. Kilda
tel: 03 9534 8221
Great seafood served in a splendidly restored bathing pavilion overlooking the bay.
Est Est Est ($$$)
440 Clarendon Street, South Melbourne
tel: 03 9682 5688
Fine dining with an extensive wine list, French-style food and elegant surroundings.
Fanny's ($$$)
243 Lonsdale Street tel: 03 9663 3017
This Melbourne institution serves award-winning French food in elegant surroundings.
Flower Drum ($$$)
17 Market Lane tel: 03 9662 3655
An exceptionally good Cantonese restaurant.
Geppetto ($)
78a Wellington Parade, East Melbourne
tel: 03 9417 4691
A quiet café and inexpensive Italian restaurant.
Langtons Wine Bar ($$–$$$)
61 Flinders Lane tel: 03 9663 0222
This trendy central wine bar and restaurant serves fine food in ultra-modern surroundings.

Madame Joe Joe ($$)
9 Fitzroy Street, St. Kilda tel: 03 9534 0000
This popular, fun place serves Modern Australian meals with a Mediterranean emphasis.
Nudel Bar ($)
76 Bourke Street tel: 03 9662 9100
A city center café that offers a range of noodles—from pastas to fried Thai varieties—with a choice of sauces. Great value.
Stella ($$–$$$)
159 Spring Street tel: 03 9639 1555
One of Melbourne's favorite Modern Australian restaurants: the food is excellent, the décor stylish, and the service very professional.
Sukhothai ($)
234 Johnston Street, Fitzroy
tel: 03 9419 4040
Good, reasonably priced Thai cooking. Salads and curries are a specialty and there is a large vegetarian selection. B.Y.O. is available.
Suntory ($$–$$$)
74 Queens Road tel: 03 9525 1231
Fine Japanese food and service in traditional oriental garden surroundings.
Thy Thy ($)
First floor, 142 Victoria Street, Richmond
tel: 03 9429 1104
Excellent and very inexpensive Vietnamese food. It is also worth trying the other branch of **Thy Thy** just down the street (116 Victoria Street, Richmond tel: 03 9428 5914).

SOUTH AUSTRALIA

Adelaide

Bangkok ($–$$)
217 Rundle Street tel: 08 8223 5406
Adelaide's longest established Thai restaurant offers good value authentic cooking. It is conveniently located in the city center.
Blake's ($$$)
Hyatt Regency Adelaide, North Terrace
tel: 08 8238 2381
This elegant hotel restaurant serves innovative Modern Australian food, with an emphasis on South Australian produce and wines. The ideal location for a really special night out.
Botanic Dining Room ($$)
309 North Terrace tel: 08 8232 3266
Located in a historic old pub in the city center, this excellent restaurant has a growing reputation for its fine modern-style food.
Charlick's Feed Store ($$$)
Ebenezer Place tel: 08 8223 7566
This is the latest venture by South Australian food legend Maggie Beer. Expect superb local produce and wines.
Chloe's ($$–$$$)
36 College Road, Kent Town
tel: 08 8362 2574
In a splendidly restored Victorian villa, elegant but friendly gourmet French food is served.
Cibo ($–$$)
10 O'Connell Street, North Adelaide
tel: 08 8267 2444
A popular café, with an outdoor terrace, serving wood-fired pizzas, pastas and great coffee.

Jolleys Boathouse ($$)
Jolleys Lane tel: 08 8223 2891
This refurbished boathouse on the River
Torrens serves mainly Modern Australian food.
Lemongrass ($–$$)
289 Rundle Street tel: 08 8223 6627
A popular city center bistro with excellent Thai
cuisine and an outdoor dining area.
The Oxford North Adelaide ($$)
101 O'Connell Street, North Adelaide
tel: 08 8267 2652
Located in trendy North Adelaide, this award-
winning restaurant has an excellent wine list.
Red Rock Noodle Bar & Restaurant ($)
187 Rundle Street tel: 08 8223 6855
Great-value noodles and other Asian dishes at
this popular East End eatery.
The Stag ($–$$)
299 Rundle Street tel: 08 8223 2934
A beautifully renovated old pub serving Modern
Australian fare, bistro meals and coffee.
Stanley's Fish Caf ($$)
76 Gouger Street tel: 08 8410 2457
This award-winning centrally located restaurant
serves local seafood and other dishes
Universal Wine Bar ($$–$$$)
285 Rundle Street tel: 08 8232 5000
A trendy East End wine bar and bistro, famous
for its extensive wine list and modern menu.

Adelaide Hills

The Summit ($–$$)
Summit Road, Mount Lofty tel: 08 8339 2600
This modern restaurant serves everything from
snacks and coffee to lunches and wine.

Barossa Valley

1918 Bistro & Grill ($$)
94 Murray Street, Tanunda tel: 08 8563 0405
Imaginative modern regional cuisine is the spe-
cialty of this fine Barossa restaurant.

WESTERN AUSTRALIA

Perth

Chez Uchino ($$–$$$)
120 Wellington Street, Mosman Park
tel: 08 9385 2202
An innovative restaurant offering an unusual
blend of French and Japanese cuisines.
Dusit Thai ($$)
249 James Street, Northbridge
tel: 08 9328 7647
This very popular Northbridge establishment
serves excellent, authentic Thai cuisine.
Fraser's ($$)
Fraser Avenue, Kings Park tel: 08 9481 7100
Fine Western Australian produce provides the
flavor at this Kings Park eatery. Great views.
Gershwin's ($$$)
99 Adelaide Terrace, East Perth
tel: 08 9225 1274
You'll find good international cuisine in this
upscale restaurant located in the city's Hyatt
Regency hotel.

The Loose Box Restaurant ($$$)
6825 Great Eastern Highway, Mundaring
tel: 08 9295 1787
This restaurant has one of the best reputations
in eastern Australia, and is worth the half-hour
drive out of Perth into the Darling Range.
Indiana Tea House ($$$)
99 Marine Parade, Cottesloe
tel: 08 9385 5005
This award-winning establishment serves
Asian-style Modern Australian food in casually
elegant surroundings. Excellent service, and
there are great ocean views.
Mamma Maria's ($)
Corner Aberdeen and Lake streets, Northbridge
tel: 08 9328 4532
Both cheap and highly cheerful, Mamma
Maria's is a Perth institution *all'Italiana.*
Matilda Bay Restaurant ($$$)
3 Hackett Drive, Crawley tel: 08 9386 5425
Excellent seafood specialties are served in a
relaxed setting by the Swan River.
Mead's Fish Gallery ($$–$$$)
15 Johnson Parade, Mosman Park
tel: 08 9383 3388
Regarded as Perth's best seafood restaurant,
Mead's is famous for its fine food, excellent
service, and wonderful Swan River setting.
Orlel Cafe Brasserie ($$)
483 Hay Street, Subiaco tel: 08 9382 1886
An extremely popular brasserie, where you'll
find everything from hearty breakfasts to stylish
Modern Australian meals.
Origins Restaurant ($$$)
Sheraton Perth Hotel, 207 Adelaide Terrace
tel: 08 9224 7777
This upmarket hotel restaurant is the perfect
venue for intimate à la carte dining—on highly
original "East meets West" cuisine.
Perugino ($$)
77 Outram Street, West Perth
tel: 08 9321 5420
A fully licensed restaurant serving Italian fare.

Fremantle

Café Panache ($$–$$$)
*Esplanade Hotel, corner Marine Terrace and
Essex Street tel: 08 9432 4000*
Excellent seafood, but not just seafood, imagi-
natively prepared. At the same address is the
more affordable **Atrium Garden Restaurant**.
Chunagon ($$$)
46 Mews Road tel: 08 9336 1000
A large Japanese restaurant with views of
Fremantle's harbor and the ocean.
Pricklers Café ($$)
*Corner Douro Road and South Terrace,
Fremantle tel: 08 9336 2194*
A "bush tucker" restaurant. Sample buffalo,
prawns, emu, and kangaroo.

Kalgoorlie–Boulder

Basil's on Hannan ($$)
168 Hannan Street tel: 08 9021 7832
A pleasant all-day café, serving snacks, cof-
fees, cake, lunches and dinner (some nights).

Top End Thai ($$)
71 Hannan Street tel; 08 8021 4286
Excellent Thai restaurant.

NORTHERN TERRITORY

Darwin

Christos on the Wharf ($$)
Stokes Hill Wharf tel: 08 8981 8658
In Darwin's wharfside precinct, this restaurant is deservedly popular for its seafood.
Corellas Restaurant ($)
The Novotel Atrium Hotel, corner The Esplanade and Peel Street tel: 08 8941 0755
Inexpensive soups, salads, and buffet meals are dished up in a tropical garden setting.
The Darwin Sailing Club ($–$$)
Aitkins Drive, Vesteys Beach tel: 08 8981 1700
Darwin's sailing club's Waterfront Bistro, has a good Australian, Asian and seafood menu.
The Hanuman ($$–$$$)
28 Mitchell Street tel: 08 8941 3500
Arguably Darwin's finest restaurant—the food consists of Thai and Malaysian Nonya dishes.
The Magic Wok ($$)
48 Cavenagh Street tel: 08 8981 3332
Wok meals using buffalo, crocodile, deer and camel as well as seafood and vegetables.
Pee Wee's at the Point ($$$)
Alec Fong Lim Drive, East Point tel: 08 8981 6868
In a beachfront location, this tropical-style restaurant offers some of Darwin's best à la carte dining—great views of the city.
Raymond's ($$)
21 Cavanagh Street tel: 08 8981 2909
Locals come here for fine international cuisine. Good ingredients and well-presented dishes.
Rock Oyster ($$)
110 Mitchell Street tel: 08 8981 3472
This long-running establishment has a reputation of being Darwin's best seafood restaurant.

Alice Springs

Al Fresco's Café and Pasta House ($$)
Todd Mall tel: 08 8953 4944
An ideal spot for anything from coffee to dinner. Good pasta, salads and Italian dishes.
Bojangle's Saloon & Restaurant ($$)
80 Todd Street tel: 08 8952 2873
Buffalo and camel feature on the menu of this cheerful establishment. Live entertainment.
Kings Restaurant ($$$)
Lasseters Hotel Casino, 93 Barrett Drive tel: 08 8950 7777
Kings offers a carvery buffet, salad bar, and à la carte menu. Seafood buffet on Wednesday.
Oriental Gourmet ($$)
80 Hartley Street tel: 08 8953 0888
The menu of this Outback restaurant is traditional Chinese, the food fresh and good.
Overlander Steakhouse ($$)
72 Hartley Street tel: 08 8952 2159
Popular steakhouse in an Outback setting.

Ristorante Puccini ($$–$$$)
Ansett Building, Todd Mall tel: 08 8953 0935
Considered by many to be the best restaurant in The Alice, this family-owned establishment has an unusually good Italian menu. The service is efficient and friendly, and there is a cheaper bistro section ($–$$).

Ayers Rock
See hotel listings on page 273.

QUEENSLAND

Brisbane

ARC Bistro ($$)
561 Brunswick Street, New Farm tel: 07 3358 3600
Acclaimed Modern Australian dishes are the specialty of this stylish bistro.
City Gardens Café ($–$$)
Brisbane Botanic Gardens tel: 07 3229 1554
In the city's botanical gardens, this café serves delicious snacks and full meals at lunchtime.
Emperor's Palace ($$)
31B Duncan Street, Fortitude Valley tel: 07 3252 3368
One of the more upmarket of the many eateries that characterize Brisbane's Chinatown.
Green Papaya North Vietnamese Restaurant ($$)
898 Stanley Street East, East Brisbane tel: 07 3217 3599
Innovative Vietnamese dishes in one of Brisbane's best Asian restaurants.
Himalayan Café ($)
640–642 Brunswick Street, New Farm tel: 07 3358 4015
Good value Tibetan and Nepalese dishes.
Il Centro ($$$)
Eagle Street Pier tel: 07 3221 6090
Modern Italian food is served in this popular, elegant riverside restaurant.
Kookaburra Queen ($$)
Departs from Eagle Street Pier, Eagle Street tel: 07 3221 1300
The food isn't sensational, but this dinner cruise (with live entertainment) along the Brisbane River is worth the price.
Marco Polo East West Cuisine ($$$)
Conrad Treasury Casino, George Street tel: 07 3306 8744
An elegant Oriental and Western restaurant in the beautiful old Treasury building.
Michael's Restaurant ($$$)
Riverside Centre, 123 Eagle Street tel: 07 3832 5522
Seafood and international cuisine in two dining rooms, both of which have views over the river.
Sirocco ($$)
South Bank Parklands tel: 07 3846 1803
A good, casual waterfront dining option in the South Bank region. Mediterranean-style food.
Summit Restaurant ($$–$$$)
Sir Samuel Griffith Drive, Mount Coot-tha tel: 07 3369 9922
Good food and stunning views out to Moreton Bay from this mountaintop restaurant.

Pier Nine ($$–$$$)
Eagle Street Pier tel: 07 3229 2194
Here, riverside views and menus reflect the
availability of delicious seafood.
Romeo's Italian Restaurant ($$)
216 Petrie Terrace tel: 07 3367 0955
Italian restaurant specializing in northern fare.
Siggi's at The Heritage ($$$)
*Corner Edward and Margaret streets
tel: 07 3221 4555*
The place to meet and celebrate in Brisbane.

Sunshine Coast

Artis Restaurant ($$)
*8 Noosa Drive, Noosa Heads
tel: 07 5447 2300*
Delicious European-Australian-Asian style food.
Chilli Jam Café ($–$$)
*195 Weyba Road, Noosaville
tel: 07 5449 9755*
This is a popular, innovative Thai restaurant.
Lindoni's ($$)
*Hastings Street, Noosa Heads
tel: 07 5447 5111*
Delicious Italian food and excellent service.

Gold Coast and Hinterland

Hard Rock Café Surfers ($–$$)
*Corner Cavill Avenue and Gold Coast Highway,
Surfers Paradise tel: 07 5539 9277*
A lively, budget eatery in Surfers Paradise.
RPR's Restaurant ($$$)
*Royal Pines Resort, Ross Street, Ashmore
tel: 07 5597 1111*
RPR's is famous for fine food and great views.

Cairns and the Far North

Barnacle Bills Seafood Inn ($$)
65 The Esplanade tel: 07 4051 2241
A popular seafront seafood-eating emporium:
an essential experience for any visitor.
Fishlips Bar and Grill ($$)
*228 Sheridan Street, Cairns
tel: 07 4041 1700*
Affordable seafood in a lively setting with an
outdoor dining area and local specialties.
Macrossans ($$$)
*Sheraton Mirage, Davidson Street,
Port Douglas tel: 07 4099 5888*
Macrossans presents elegant fine food.
Marina Connection ($)
*Marina Mirage, Port Douglas
tel: 07 4099 5258*
Food is served both indoors and outside near
the jetty for the Barrier Reef wave piercers.

TASMANIA

Hobart

Alexander's ($$$)
*20 Runnymede Street, Battery Point
tel: 03 6232 3900*
International fare in the elegant surroundings
of the Victorian Lenna of Hobart hotel.

The Asian Restaurant ($$$)
*Wrest Point Hotel Casino, 410 Sandy Bay
Road, Sandy Bay tel: 03 6225 0112*
Serves dishes that are far above the usual
standard, presided over by a very genial host.
Ball & Chain Grill ($$)
87 Salamanca Place tel: 03 6223 2655
Charcoal-grilled steaks, poultry and seafood
are dished out at affordable prices.
Blue Skies Dining ($–$$)
Murray Street Pier tel: 03 6224 3747
In a superb location right on the Hobart water-
front, this lively brasserie offers a good Modern
Australian menu.
Drunken Admiral Restaurant ($$)
17–19 Hunter Street tel: 03 6234 1903
Established in one of Victoria Dock's old ware-
houses, this restaurant specializes in seafood.
Lebrina Restaurant ($$)
*155 New Town Road, New Town
tel: 03 6228 7775*
Located in a cottage in one of Hobart's inner
suburbs, this establishment offers fine tradi-
tional food, and a comprehensive wine list.
Mit Zitrone ($$)
*333 Elizabeth Street, North Hobart
tel: 03 6234 8113*
This eatery specializes in innovative Modern
Australian cuisine using local ingredients.
Mures Lower Deck ($)
Victoria Dock tel: 03 6231 2121
Long lines form next to the fishmonger's
counter for top value seafood to eat here or
take out.
Mures Upper Deck ($$)
Victoria Dock tel: 03 6231 2121
From its glazed second floor pavilion, Mures
serves seafood with great flair. Reserve.
Sisco's on the Pier ($$)
Murray Street Pier tel: 03 6223 2059
Sisco's is famous for its innovative Spanish/
Mediterranean-style cuisine and fine service.

Cradle Mountain
See hotel listing on page 275.

Launceston

Fee and Mee ($$–$$$)
190 Charles Street tel: 03 6331 3195
One of the best restaurants in Tasmania, spe-
cializing in fine Modern Australian cuisine.
The Gorge Restaurant ($$)
Cliff Grounds tel: 03 6331 3330
Fine Tasmanian produce and wines in a superb
location, overlooking Launceston's gorge.
Pepper Berry Café ($–$$)
91 George Street tel: 03 6334 4589
A popular café, where you'll find hearty meat
and game dishes, risottos, home-baked cakes
and scones.
Shrimps ($$)
72 George Street tel: 03 6334 0584
A National Trust-classified building in the town
center, with an excellent seafood menu.
Star Bar Café ($–$$)
113 Charles Street tel: 03 6331 9659
Very reasonably priced casual city center café.

281

Index

Index

283

Index

Index

Index

287

Acknowledgments

The Automobile Association would like to thank the following photographers, libraries, and associations for their assistance in the preparation of this book.
ACT TOURISM 82 Skiing Snowy Mountains. **ALLSPORT UK LTD** 166 Melbourne Cup. **ARDEA LONDON** 88a Feather Star (V Taylor), 88c Taipan (C J Mason), 228–9 Freycinet Nat Park (Jon P Ferrero), 236b The Lower Gordon (Jon P Ferrero), 238b Gordon Dam (Jon P Ferrero), 242–3 Tasman Peninsula (Jon P Ferrero). **BRIDGEMAN ART LIBRARY** 19 Dog & Duck Hotel by Sidney Nolan (1917–92), Roy Miles Gallery, 29 Bruton Street, London W1/Bridgeman Art Library, London. **DEPARTMENT OF MARITIME ARCHAEOLOGY, WA MARITIME MUSEUM** 243a Silver dish with decorations, 243c Astrolabe. **MARY EVANS PICTURE LIBRARY** 26a Convicts Sydney, 26b Dampier attacked by natives, 27 Governor Phillip Sydney Cove, 28–9 Burke & Wills, 30b Prospectors, 76 Captain Cook, 77 Cook at Botany Bay, 161b Pearl diving. **CHRIS FAIRCLOUGH COLOUR LIBRARY** 116a Aborigines, 166–7 Diamond mine, 194 Aborigine children at school, 195 Aborigines in the bush. **CORBIS** 17 Lifeguard, 45 Circular Quay (Nick Rains). **FFOTOGRAFF** 24a Cave paintings Nourlangie Rock, 174 Dolphins, Monkey Mia, 241 Aboriginal rock engraving. **FOOTPRINTS** 216–17 Coral Reef (A Dalton), 216 Feeding potato cod (N Hanna), 217b Butterfly fish (Carlos Lima), 218 Angel fish (A Dalton), 219 Heron Island (N Hanna). **RONALD GRANT ARCHIVES** 18c Paul Hogan, Crocodile Dundee. **INTERNATIONAL PHOTOBANK** 12a Acacia, 13 Kangaroo, 14a Boat to Great Barrier Reef, 24b Aborigine, 29 Alice Springs, 31 Sovereign Hill, 32 Eucalyptus gum, 34 Caravan park Sydney, 82–3 Lake Blowering, 90 Native plant, 97 Trams, 114 Olinda Rhododendron Garden, 114b Grampians, 118 Great Ocean Road, Twelve Apostles, 127 Bethany Church, 134 Commuter bus, 135 Cleland Wildlife Park, 137 Flinders Ranges, 138 Goolwa P S Mundoo, 140–1 Barossa Valley grapes, 140 Penfolds winery, 142 Victor Harbor, 175b York sign, 177 Ghost gum tree, 178 Alice Springs sign, 184 Memorial to Rev John Flynn, 185b Restaurant sign Alice Springs, 200 Green Island, 208 Glass House Mountains, 209b Crimson rosella, 210 Pacific Highway, 211 Cairns, 213 Bottle brush plant, 217a Snorkeling instruction, 252 Australian, 253 Overland train, 257 Backpackers, 267a Standley Chasm. **MICHAEL** IVORY 8b, 25 Ranger Kakadu National Park. **NATURE PHOTOGRAPHERS LTD** 121 Southern right whale (R Tidman), 222b Cassowary (S C Bisserot). **NORTHERN TERRITORY TOURIST COMMISSION** 181 Government House Darwin, 182 Nat Mus of Arts & Sciences Darwin, 189 The Ghan, 191 Cutta Cutta Caves, 198 Glen Helen Gorge, 255 Jeep, 259 Simpsons Gap. **CHRISTINE OSBORNE PICTURES** 53 Sydney Casino, 224b Cowboy. **PHOTO INDEX** 159 Albany. **ANDY PRICE** 18a Tjapukai Aboriginal dance, 21a Aboriginal art, 178–9 Katherine Gorge, 192b Termite mounds, 193 Kakadu National Park, 194–5 Aboriginal art. **QUEEN VICTORIA MUSEUM & ART GALLERY** 241b J Glover Last Muster of Aborigines Brighton, **ROYAL GEOGRAPHICAL SOCIETY** 23 map. **SPECTRUM COLOUR LIBRARY** 99 Melbourne Cricket Ground, 103 Melbourne Zoo, 120 Gum tree 203b Kuranda train, 215 Surfers Paradise, 220 Lamington National Park, 222a Rainforest, 222c Rainforest Bunya Mountains, 223 Yacht Port Douglas, 225 Sunshine Coast, 235 L Dove, 237 Cradle Mountain National Park, 247 Port Arthur Convict Museum, 250 Fishing boats St. Helens. **TOURISM SOUTH AUSTRALIA** 130 Port Adelaide, 131 Ayers House, 132 Tandanya Aboriginal Culture Centre, 133 Remarkable Rocks, Kangaroo Island, 139 R Murray. **TOURISM TASMANIA** 236a Rafting, 240 Boat Freycinet Peninsula, 243 Shipwreck, 246 Derwent Valley, 248 Queenstown, 249 Tuna fishing, 264 Trout fishing. **WESTERN AUSTRALIAN TOURISM COMMISSION** 148 Warren National Park, 151 Kings Park, Perth, 157b Bungle Bungle National Park, 160 Bunbury, 167 Iron ore mine Pilbara, 168 Mandurah , 170 Ningaloo Reef, 173a Gibb River road truck, 173b Argyle Diamond Mine, 175a Wave Rock, 262 New Norcia Abbey Church.

All remaining pictures are held in the Association's own picture library (AA PHOTO LIBRARY) with contributions from:
ADRIAN BAKER 2, 5b, 5c, 6a, 7a, 7b, 8a, 10–11, 10, 11, 15, 20, 21b, 22–3, 22, 23, 28, 30a, 33a, 35, 47, 48, 49, 52a, 54, 55b, 60, 64–5, 66, 67a, 69, 70, 71, 72, 73, 75, 76–7, 78, 79, 83, 85, 87, 88b, 89, 92a, 92–3b, 98, 100a,100b,102b, 106, 107, 109, 111, 112–13, 112, 113, 115, 117, 119, 120b, 122, 123, 126–7, 136, 143a, 143b, 145, 146, 149, 152, 153, 154, 156, 157a, 158, 161a, 162, 163, 164, 165, 169a, 169b, 169c, 171, 172, 185a, 186, 187, 188–9, 190a, 190b, 192a, 196a, 196b, 197, 199, 202, 203a, 205, 207, 209a, 212, 221, 228, 229, 231, 232, 233, 234, 238a, 239, 244, 245, 256, 258, 260, 261, 263. **PAUL KENWARD** Spine, back cover a, b, 3, 4, 5a, 9b, 12b, 14b, 16a, 33b, 39, 40, 40–1, 42, 43, 46a, 46b, 50, 51, 52b, 55a, 58, 59, 61, 62, 67b, 68, 74, 80–1, 84, 86, 183b, 188, 251a,b, 265, 266, 267b. **CHRISTINE OSBORNE** 96a, 96b, 101, 102a, 104, 105, 108, 110, 166. **KEN PATERSON** 183a.

Contributors

Revision copy editor: Grapevine Publishing Services Ltd, London
Original copy editor: Sally Knowles
Revision verifier: Anne Matthews